Package on the Market!

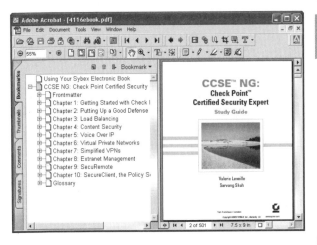

Search through the complete book in PDF!

- Access the entire *CCSE Study Guide*, complete with figures and tables, in electronic format.

- Search the *CCSE Study Guide* chapters to find information on any topic in seconds.

- Use Adobe Acrobat Reader (included on the CD-ROM) to view the electronic book.

Use the Electronic Flashcards for PCs or Palm devices to jog your memory and prep last minute for the exam!

- Reinforce your understanding of key concepts with these hardcore flashcard-style questions.

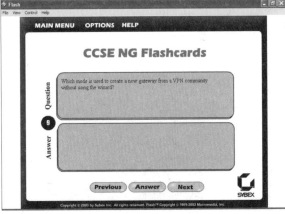

Prepare for the CCSE exam on the go with your handheld device!

- Download the Flashcards to your Palm device and go on the road. Now you can study for the CCSE exam anytime, anywhere.

CCSE NG:
Check Point
Certified Security Expert

Study Guide

CCSE™ NG:
Check Point™
Certified Security Expert
Study Guide

Valerie Leveille

Sarvang Shah

San Francisco • London

Associate Publisher: Neil Edde
Acquisitions Editor: Maureen Adams
Developmental Editor: Heather O'Connor
Production Editor: Liz Burke
Technical Editors: Alan Bailey, Gareth Bromley
Copyeditor: Tiffany Taylor
Electronic Publishing Specialist: Jill Niles
Graphic Illustrator: Tony Jonick
CD Coordinator: Dan Mummert
CD Technician: Kevin Ly
Proofreaders: Nancy Riddiough, Emily Hsuan, Sarah Tannehill, Monique van den Berg, Amey Garber, Dave Nash
Indexer: Ted Laux
Book Designer: Bill Gibson
Cover Design: Archer Design
Cover Photograph: Bruce Heinemann, PhotoDisc

Library of Congress Card Number: 2002113839

ISBN: 0-7821-4116-1

SYBEX

To Our Valued Readers:

The Check Point certification program well deserves its position as the leading vendor-specific security certification in the IT arena. And with the recent release of the Check Point NG exams, current and aspiring security professionals are seeking accurate, thorough, and accessible study material to help them prepare for the new CCSA and CCSE exams.

Sybex is excited about the opportunity to provide individuals with the knowledge and skills they'll need to succeed in the highly competitive IT security field. It has always been Sybex's mission to teach exam candidates how new technologies work in the real world, not to simply feed them answers to test questions. Sybex was founded on the premise of providing technical skills to IT professionals, and we have continued to build on that foundation. Over the years, we have made significant improvements to our study guides based on feedback from readers, suggestions from instructors, and comments from industry leaders.

Check Point's certification exams are indeed challenging. The Sybex team of authors, editors, and technical reviewers have worked hard to ensure that this Study Guide is comprehensive, in-depth, and pedagogically sound. We're confident that this book, along with the collection of cutting-edge software study tools included on the CD, will meet and exceed the demanding standards of the certification marketplace and help you, the Check Point certification exam candidate, succeed in your endeavors.

Good luck in pursuit of your Check Point certification!

Neil Edde
Associate Publisher—Certification
Sybex, Inc.

To the one who helped me through this whole ordeal...Jesus Christ.
—Valerie Leveille

This book is dedicated to the angel in my life, my wonderful wife, Nisha Shah.
—Sarvang Shah

Acknowledgments

This book would not be possible without the hard work and patience of the team at Sybex (Liz Burke, Heather O'Connor, Maureen Adams, and Tiffany Taylor) as we worked through not one, not two, but three different versions of Check Points NG product. I think this book was almost done at least twice!

Thanks also to my understanding coworkers at Intelligent Connections. I appreciate the patience it took while I toiled on this project for 6 months. Thanks to my co-author and friend Sarvang Shah who toiled right along with me. We're going out for sushi after this book is published! Thanks to our tech editors, Alan Bailey and Gareth Bromley, their "nit-picking" really helped make this a better book.

Thanks to all of my friends especially Patti, Diane, Byron, Don, and Amber who stood patiently by me while I *refused* to spend time with them to finish this project. I've really missed you all! I can't wait to go out for lunch after church next week!

Last but certainly not least…thank you, God, for giving me the patience and the determination to sit down and get this project done when all I really wanted to do was kick back and relax this summer. I truly could not have completed this without You!

—Valerie Leveille

There were many people involved in the planning and development of this book. I'd like to thank the entire Sybex team: Liz Burke, Heather O'Connor, Maureen Adams, and Tiffany Taylor who worked very hard and displayed great patience as we worked through chapter after chapter of this book and then upgraded it and did it all over again for FP3.

I'd also like to express my gratitude to my friend and co-author Valerie Leveille who balanced an intense work and school schedule while working on this book. Thank you to our tech editors Alan Bailey and Gareth Bromley, who kept our book on the right track.

I would like to thank those that directly or indirectly had something to do with me writing my portion of this book. In general, I'd like to thank my friends and family who constantly invited me to do stuff this summer, I am sorry that I consistently declined the invitation. We'll make up for it next summer! I'd like to thank my parents and in-laws who kept trying to plan family events around my writing schedule; my sister, Angana Shah, who has inspired me in many ways throughout my life; and my brother-in-law, Dr. Falgun Patel, who is always there when we need him.

Most importantly, I would not be where I am today without my beautiful and beloved wife, Nisha Shah. I would especially like to thank Nisha for her continual support, patience and guidance.

—Sarvang Shah

Contents at a Glance

Contents

Introduction

Welcome to the exciting world of Check Point certification! You have picked up this book because you want something better: namely, a better job with more satisfaction. Rest assured that you have made a good decision.

Check Point certification can improve your understanding of how network security works in areas that extend beyond Check Point products. For instance, currently more than 300 products integrate VPN-1/FireWall-1 through protocols such as Voice over IP (VoIP) and Lightweight Directory Access Protocol (LDAP) as well as technologies such as Network Address Translation (NAT) and content filtering. Check Point's Open Platform for Security (OPSEC), located at www.opsec.com, is the foundation responsible for creating the standards used to incorporate products from third-party vendors with Check Point products.

It certainly can't hurt to have Check Point certifications, considering that Check Point is the worldwide market leader in firewalls and VPNs and has been since 1995. According to Check Point's website, Check Point's solutions are "sold, integrated and serviced by a network of 2,500 certified partners in 149 countries." To ensure that organizations can measure the skill level of Check Point administrators and engineers, Check Point provides various levels of certification that quantify network security knowledge and an administrator's ability to implement network security using Check Point products. Obtaining any Check Point certification makes you a CCP (Check Point Certified Professional), which in turn makes you eligible to use the Certified Professional password-protected website. There you'll find tools, features, transcripts, and other information not available to the general public. Other benefits of being a CCP include access to the SecureKnowledge database, notification of product updates, use of logos and credentials, and invitations to seminars and other Check Point events. For more information about the CCP program, visit www.checkpoint.com/services/education/certification/index.html.

While pursuing Check Point certifications, you will develop a complete understanding of networking security. This knowledge is beneficial to every network security job and is the reason Check Point certification has become popular recently.

How to Use This Book

If you want a solid foundation for the Check Point Certified Security Expert (CCSE) exam, then look no further. We have spent hundreds of hours putting together this book with the sole intention of helping you to pass the VPN-1/FireWall-1 Management II-NG (156-310) exam.

This book is loaded with valuable information, and you will get the most out of your study time if you understand how the book is structured.

To best benefit from this book, we recommend the following study method:

1. Take the assessment test immediately following this introduction. (The answers are at the end of the test.) It's okay if you don't know any of the answers; that is why you bought this book! Carefully read the explanations for any question you get wrong and note which chapters the material comes from. This information should help you plan your study strategy.

2. Study each chapter thoroughly, making sure that you fully understand the information and the test objectives listed at the beginning of each chapter. Pay extra-close attention to any chapter where you missed questions in the assessment test.

3. If you do not have Check Point VPN-1/FireWall-1 equipment and software available, be sure to study the examples carefully.

4. Answer all the review questions related to each chapter. (The answers appear at the end of each chapter.) Note questions that confuse you and study those sections of the book again. Do not just skim these questions! Make sure you completely understand the reason for each answer.

5. Try your hand at the practice exams that are included on the companion CD. The questions in these exams appear only on the CD. These exams will give you a complete overview of what you can expect to see on the real VPN-1/FireWall-1 Management II-NG exam.

6. Test yourself using all the flashcards on the CD. The new and updated flashcard programs on the CD will help you prepare for the VPN-1/FireWall-1 Management II-NG exam. They are great study tools!

The electronic flashcards can be used on your Windows computer, Pocket PC, or Palm device.

7. Make sure you read the Key Terms and Exam Essentials lists at the end of the chapters. These study aids will help you finish each chapter with the main points fresh in your mind; they're also helpful as a quick refresher before you head into the testing center.

To learn every bit of the material covered in this book, you'll have to apply yourself regularly, and with discipline. Try to set aside the same time every day to study, and select a comfortable and quiet place to do so. If you work hard, you will be surprised how quickly you learn this material.

If you follow the steps we've listed, and really study and practice the review questions, CD exams, and electronic flashcards, it will be hard for you to fail the VPN-1/FireWall-1 Management II-NG exam.

What Does This Book Cover?

This book covers everything you need to know to pass the VPN-1/FireWall-1 Management II-NG exam:

- Chapter 1 deals with the preparation for installation, the installation, and the post-installation tasks required for VPN-1/FireWall-1.

- Chapter 2 discusses two defensive options. UserDefined tracking allows the use of custom logging options, and the SYNDefender options let you protect yourself against SYN floods.

- Chapter 3 covers load balancing. This Check Point option allows the firewall administrator to use a logical server defined on the firewall to determine which servers in a group of mirrored servers will get the next connection based on the algorithm chosen.

- Chapter 4 discusses Content Security features that incorporate intelligent filtering of HTTP, SMTP, FTP, and TCP traffic with or without the use of an external CVP or UFP server.

- Chapter 5 provides an overview of the two VoIP protocols supported by Check Point: H323 and SIP.

- Chapter 6 provides in-depth discussion of encryption and VPNs and how to deploy traditional VPNs with VPN-1/Firewall-1.

- Chapter 7 deals with a new NG feature called Simplified VPNs (VPN communities), which automates most of the VPN configuration within a corporation.

- Chapter 8 discusses the configuration of extranet management, which is a semi-automated way to configure VPNs between your company and another company.

- Chapter 9 covers SecuRemote, a software client used to configure a client-to-firewall VPN. Software client configuration and firewall configuration are both covered.

- Chapter 10 provides an in-depth view of configuring and deploying SecureClient, Policy Servers, and VPN-1/FireWall-1 in a client-to-site VPN. SecureClient acts as a personal firewall for each computer on which it is loaded, whether within the corporate network on outside the corporate firewall.

- The Glossary is a handy resource for Check Point and other security terms. It is a great tool for understanding some of the more obscure terms used in this book.

Each chapter begins with a list of objectives covered by the VPN-1/FireWall-1 Management II-NG test. Make sure you read them before working through the chapter. In addition, each chapter ends with review questions specifically designed to help you retain the information presented. To really nail down your skills, read each question carefully and, if possible, work through the chapters' hands-on exercises.

The Check Point NG software is updated periodically. In the past, Check Point released service packs to improve the current product with patches and code enhancements. With NG, Check Point releases Feature Packs (FPs) that not only include patches, but also offer significant feature and code improvements. The most current version of FireWall-1 at the time of this writing is Check Point NG Feature Pack 3. Due to its broad enhancement of features, this version should be your minimum choice for deployment and is the deployment on which this book is based.

You may notice we've used Check Point NG Feature Pack 3 on both a Windows 2000 machine and a Windows XP machine. Some FP3 screens may look different to you, depending on which Windows OS you are using.

What's on the CD?

We worked hard to provide some great tools to help you with your certification process. You should load all of the following tools on your workstation and use them when studying for the test.

All-New Sybex Test Preparation Software

The test preparation software, made by experts at Sybex, prepares you to pass the VPN-1/FireWall-1 Management II-NG exam. In this test engine, you will find all the review and assessment questions from the book, plus two additional bonus exams that appear exclusively on the CD. You can take the assessment test, test yourself by chapter or by topic, take the practice exams, or take a randomly generated exam comprising all the questions.

Electronic Flashcards for PC, Pocket PC, and Palm Devices

To prepare for the exam, you can read this book, try the hands-on exercises, study the review questions at the end of each chapter, and work through the practice exams included in the book and on the companion CD. But wait, there's more! You can also test yourself with the flashcards included on the CD. If you can get through these difficult questions and understand the answers, you'll know you're ready for the VPN-1/FireWall-1 Management II-NG exam.

The flashcards include 150 questions specifically written to hit you hard and make sure you are ready for the exam. Between the review questions, practice exams, and flashcards, you'll be more than prepared for the exam.

CCSE Study Guide in PDF

Sybex offers the *CCSE Study Guide* in PDF format on the CD so you can read the book on your PC or laptop. This electronic version will be helpful to readers who travel and don't want to carry a book, as well as to readers who prefer to read from their computer. (Acrobat Reader 5 is also included on the CD.)

Check Point—A Brief History

Founded in 1993 by Gil Shwed, Marius Nacht, and Shlomo Kramer, Check Point Software Technologies quickly rose to the top as an industry and worldwide leader in Internet and network security and in the VPN and firewall markets. What started out as a small software company has grown into an international leader in the security marketplace with more than 1,000 employees and revenue in excess of $500 million dollars in 2001. The company's international headquarters is in Ramat-Gan, Israel; its U.S. base of operations is in Redwood City, California.

With products such as Check Point VPN-1/FireWall-1, Provider-1, and FloodGate-1 (which are based on the Secure Virtual Network (SVN) architecture), Check Point is constantly updating its security offerings and providing valuable solutions to Internet and network security. OPSEC partner alliances expand Check Point's capabilities through integration and interoperability with more than 325 leading companies.

Check Point has been honored with awards every year since 1997. In October 2000, it was named in the top 10 list of the "Most Important Products of the Decade" by Network Computing.

Check Point VPN-1/FireWall-1 has received countless certifications, both in the United States and internationally, by meeting the strict security standards required by government and commercial bodies worldwide. Check Point NG has achieved the following certifications:

- The Common Criteria for Information Technology Security Evaluation (CCITSE or "Common Criteria"). This is a set of evaluation criteria agreed to by the U.S. National Security Agency/National Institute of Standards and Technologies and equivalent bodies in 13 other countries. CCITSE is a multinational effort to write a successor to the previous Trusted Computer System Evaluation Criteria (TCSEC or "Orange Book"). The CCITSE is available on the Internet at www.radium.ncsc.mil/tpep/library/ccitse/.

- The Federal Information Processing Standard (FIPS) 140-1 level 2 certification, administered by the U.S. National Institute of Standards and Technology's (NIST) and the Communications Security Establishment (CSE) of the Government of Canada, specifies security requirements designed to protect against potential threats such as hacking and other cybercrimes. FIPS information can be found at www.itl.nist.gov/fipspubs/index.htm.

- IT Security Evaluation Criteria (ITSEC E3), awarded by the Communications Electronics Security Group (CESG) of the United Kingdom, is equivalent to the Common Criteria EAL 4 standard. For more information visit `www.cesg.gov.uk/assurance/iacs/itsec/index.htm`.

Check Point VPN-1/FireWall-1 Security Certifications

Check Point sponsors a number of different certifications for its products. The first certifications to tackle include the Check Point Certified Security Administrator (CCSA), Check Point Certified Security Expert (CCSE), and CCSE Plus, based on the VPN-1/FireWall-1 product. From there, candidates can advance to Check Point Certified Quality of Service Expert (CCQE) for the FloodGate-1 product and Check Point Certified Addressing Expert (CCAE) for the Meta IP product. Finally, for those implementing VPN-1/FireWall-1 and Provider-1 Internet security solutions, Check Point offers the advanced Check Point Certified Managed Security Expert (CCMSE), which requires passing the CCSA, CCSE, and Managing Multiple Sites with Provider-1 exams. Certifications are valid for a minimum of 18 months and are considered current if they are for the current major product release or the product release immediately prior to the current release.

Check Point Certified Security Administrator (CCSA)

Check Point Certified Security Administrator (CCSA) is the base certification that validates a candidate's ability to configure and manage fundamental implementations of FireWall-1. Before pursuing this certification, you should possess the skills to define and configure security policies that enable secure access in and out of your networks. You should also be able to monitor network security activity and implement measures to block intruder access to networks.

The first step in obtaining the CCSA certification is to attend hands-on training at a Check Point Authorized Training Center. Many times attending training is not physically or financially possible, so this study guide is the next best thing to being there. Even after you attend training or study this text, Check Point recommends six months of experience with VPN-1/FireWall-1. Check Point's products have so many nuances that no one can learn it all in one sitting. You must work with the firewall on a regular basis to become familiar with the inner workings of the product. After that, candidates may take Exam 156-210: VPN-1/FireWall-1 Management I-NG. CCSA candidates will be tested on the following:

- Administering and troubleshooting a security policy

- Testing and improving VPN-1/FireWall-1 performance

- Creating network objects and groups

- Logging management operations

- Configuring anti-spoofing on the firewall to prevent intruders from accessing the network

- Creating users and groups to be implemented for user, client, and session authentication

- Configuring Network Address Translation (static NAT and hide NAT)

- Backing up VPN-1/FireWall-1

- Uninstalling VPN-1/FireWall-1

Candidates who successfully pass the VPN-1/FireWall-1 Management I-NG exam are awarded their CCSA and can go on to gain other worthwhile Check Point certifications.

Sybex offers the *CCSA™ NG: Check Point™ Certified Security Administrator Study Guide* (ISBN 0-7821-4115-3) as a preparation solution to the CCSA exam (Exam 156-210). Check out www.sybex.com for more information.

Check Point Certified Security Expert (CCSE)

Before taking the Check Point Certified Security Expert (CCSE) exam (Exam 156-310), you should possess the knowledge and expertise to configure VPN-1/ FireWall-1 as an Internet security solution as well as the ability to configure virtual private networks (VPNs). CCSE certification builds on the CCSA certification; therefore, you must pass the CCSA exam before taking the CCSE exam. You will be tested on your ability to configure content security, set up user-defined tracking, and protect against SYN floods, among other things.

Check Point demands a certain level of proficiency for its CCSE certification. In addition to mastering the skills required for the CCSA, you should be able to do the following:

- Use scanning and network assessment tools to look for weaknesses and then modify your Security Policy to close any holes.

- Be able to define a secure network architecture with components such as VPNs and DMZs as well as use Content Security to filter HTTP, SMTP, FTP, and TCP traffic.

- Install VPN-1/FireWall-1 and perform the pre- and post-installation tasks that go along with it, such as loading and hardening the operating system.

- Be able to edit system files such as `smtp.conf` and `objects_5_0.C` as well as import and export users from your database.

- Configure Secure Internal Communications (SIC) in a distributed environment as well as between VPN-1/FireWall-1 and OPSEC products.

- Perform basic troubleshooting using the logs and basic network tools such as TCPDUMP.

- Be familiar with OPSEC partners and their ability to integrate with VPN-1/FireWall-1.

Other Check Point Certifications

Once you have obtained your CCSE, you may feel compelled to advance to the Check Point Certified Security Expert Plus: Enterprise Integration and Troubleshooting (CCSE Plus) certification. This is the highest level of certification for VPN-1/FireWall-1; it builds on the CCSA and CCSE certifications. The CCSE Plus certification validates your in-depth technical expertise with Check Point's VPN-1/FireWall-1. This certification requires extensive knowledge of troubleshooting, network planning, and implementing complex VPN-1/FireWall-1 configurations. To obtain the CCSE Plus, a candidate must pass the VPN-1/FireWall-1 Management I-NG (Exam 156-210), VPN-1/FireWall-1 Management II-NG (Exam 156-310), and a third exam: VPN-1/FireWall-1 Management III-NG (Exam 156-510). Check Point offers two other certification tracks beyond the VPN/Security Track: Performance/Availability and Management.

Check Point's Performance/Availability certification is the Check Point Certified Quality of Service Expert (CCQE), which focuses on network bandwidth management. CCQEs are expected to configure, implement, and manage bandwidth policies using Check Point's FloodGate-1 software as well as the VPN-1/FireWall-1 software. To become a CCQE, candidates must pass Exam 156-605: Quality of Service Using FloodGate-1.

In the Management track, Check Point offers two certifications: Check Point Certified Addressing Expert (CCAE) and Check Point Certified Managed Security Expert (CCMSE). The CCAE certification requires the ability to implement and configure Check Point's Meta IP software in a corporate network and the ability to streamline IP address management. CCAEs must also be able to configure and manage DNS and Dynamic DNS. CCAE status is earned by passing Exam 156-705: Introduction to Meta IP / Deploying and Troubleshooting Meta IP.

CCMSE candidates acquire certification by becoming CCSAs as well as CCSEs. After earning a CCSE, candidates must be able to implement VPN-1/FireWall-1 as an enterprise security solution and deploy Provider-1 software in a Network Operating Center environment as a centralized policy management solution. CCMSEs are held in the highest regard. They are the premier experts for managed security services based on Check Point solutions.

To earn the CCMSE certification, candidates must pass VPN-1/FireWall-1 Management I-NG (Exam 156-210), VPN-1/FireWall-1 Management II-NG (Exam 156-310), and Managing Multiple Sites with Provider-1 NG (Exam 156-810).

For more information about Check Point's certification offerings, updates, and certification news, visit `http://www.checkpoint.com/services/education/certification/index.html`.

Remember that test topics and tests can change at any time without notice. Always visit the Check Point website for the most up-to-date information (www.checkpoint.com/services/education/certification/index.html).

Where Do You Take the Exams?

You may take the exams at any of the more than 3,300 authorized VUE testing centers in over 120 countries (www.vue.com). Calling is not the way to register for an exam, because you'll be instructed to register on the Web. Go to www.vue.com, click IT Certification, select Check Point Software from the list of certifications, and click Go. On the resulting page (www.vue.com/checkpoint/) you can register with VUE and set up your exam for a testing center near you.

To register for the Check Point Certified Security Expert exam:

1. Create your VUE username and password and then sign in. Determine the number of the exam you want to take.

2. Register with the nearest VUE testing center. You will be asked to pay in advance for the exam. At the time of this writing, the exam costs $150.

3. When you schedule the exam, you'll receive instructions regarding all appointment and cancellation procedures, ID requirements, and information about the testing-center location. Briefly, you can schedule the exam in advance, but if you want to schedule the exam for the same day, you must call the VUE testing center directly. If you fail the exam, you must wait until the next day before you will be allowed to retake it. If something comes up and you need to cancel or reschedule your exam appointment, contact VUE one business day prior to your exam appointment. Canceling or rescheduling an exam less than 24 hours in advance is subject to a same-day forfeiture of the exam fee. Exam fees are due for no-shows.

Tips for Taking Your CCSE Exam

The CCSE exam contains approximately 75 questions to be completed in 90 minutes if the exam candidate is from Australia, Bermuda, Canada, Japan, New Zealand, Ireland, South Africa, the United Kingdom, or the United States. All other candidates are allotted 120 minutes. You must get a score of 69% to pass this exam. As stated earlier, check the Check Point website for more information about the specifics before you take your exam.

There are no upgrade exams if you are certified on a previous version of VPN-1/FireWall-1. The exam is not adaptive and consists of multiple-choice and true/false questions. Remember to read each question carefully. Also, never forget that the right answer is the Check Point answer. In many cases, more than one appropriate answer is presented, but the *correct* answer is the one that Check Point recommends. Don't let common sense and experience cloud your answers.

Check Point does not subtract points for incorrect answers, so even if you don't know the answer, give it your best shot. Each subject area (which correspond to the chapters in this book) pulls from a pool of questions. Not every objective is represented on the exam, and therefore each exam is unique. The exam also contains a series of questions pulled from common events and questions encountered in Check Point's Technical Assistance Centers.

Here are some general tips for exam success:

- Arrive early at the exam center, so you can relax and review your study materials.

- Read the questions *carefully*. Don't jump to conclusions. Make sure you're clear about *exactly* what each question asks.

- When answering multiple-choice questions that you're not sure about, use the process of elimination to get rid of the obviously incorrect answers first. Doing this greatly improves your odds if you need to make an educated guess.

- You can move forward or backward during the exam. You can also mark questions for review if you're not immediately sure of your answer. We find this most helpful because something later in the exam may trigger a memory that will enable you to answer the question you marked for review.

After you complete an exam, you'll get immediate, online notification of your pass or fail status, a printed Examination Score Report that indicates your pass or fail status, and your exam results by section. (The test administrator will give you the printed score report.) If you pass the exam, you'll receive confirmation from Check Point within four to six weeks, in the form of a letter that outlines the benefits of your certification as well as your username for the SecureKnowledge website and your Professional ID. Your password will be distributed via e-mail.

About the Authors

Valerie Leveille is a certified Check Point, Nokia, and RSA instructor. She provides consulting services to a wide variety of clients in her employment with Intelligent Connections L.L.C. in Oak Park, Michigan. To contact Valerie, e-mail her at levelhead@wideopenwest.com.

Sarvang Shah is a CISSP and a certified Check Point and Nokia instructor. Sarvang provides freelance security consulting and training to a wide variety of clients throughout Michigan through Elite-1 Security, Inc. (www.elite1security.com), his IT security consulting firm. To contact Sarvang, e-mail him at sarvang@elite1security.com.

Assessment Test

1. What types of traffic can the Content Security feature filter?

   1. HTTP
   2. FTP
   3. AOL
   4. SMTP

   A. 1, 2
   B. 2, 3
   C. 3, 4
   D. 1, 2, 4
   E. All of them

2. Which command provides a menu for configuring the Check Point firewall?

   A. fwconfig
   B. fwstart
   C. cpconfig
   D. fw putkey
   E. fw putlic

3. Two rules are needed to implement HTTP load balancing.

   A. True
   B. False

4. What does Secure Internal Communications (SIC) provide?

   A. A way for administrators to communicate with each other
   B. A way for firewalls to perform health checks on each other
   C. A point-to-point VPN between firewalls using IPSec
   D. Secure communication between Check Point modules
   E. A digital certificate authority

5. Where do you define alert scripts?

    A. In the Alert Commands tab of the Global Properties

    B. In the Track element of the rule base

    C. In the object properties

    D. In the Visual Policy Editor

    E. None of the above

6. To enhance security in a server-based VoIP solution, the server that the product is running on should have which of the following?

    A. Modem

    B. Hard drive

    C. Operating system

    D. Hardened operating system

    E. IP address

7. Persistent Server Mode should always be turned on.

    A. True

    B. False

8. IPSec encrypts the payload and leaves the headers alone.

    A. True

    B. False

9. Which command is used to install a license in Check Point VPN-1/ FireWall-1?

    A. `fw printlic`

    B. `cplic put`

    C. `fw putlic`

    D. `fw putkey`

    E. `cp putlic`

10. How many load balancing algorithms does Check Point support?

    A. 1

    B. 2

    C. 3

    D. 4

    E. 5

11. What process drives Check Point's Content Security features?

    A. Content Security daemon

    B. fwauthd.conf

    C. Security Servers

    D. fwssd

    E. CVP

12. What names are used for the Check Point component that must be installed prior to installing the firewall? (Choose all that apply.)

    A. CPOS

    B. SVN Foundation

    C. SecureOS

    D. CPShared

    E. IPSO

13. SMTP, FTP, and HTTP traffic can be filtered with Content Security without using an OPSEC server.

    A. True

    B. False

14. What is the name of the Policy Server process?

    A. Policy.ps

    B. dtps

    C. psdt

    D. cpd

    E. None of the above

15. An SIP proxy is required to communicate via the SIP protocol.

    A. True

    B. False

16. Which VoIP protocols are supported by Check Point NG? (Choose all that apply.)

    A. V.325

    B. H.323

    C. SIP

    D. Real Media

    E. Multi Media

17. SYN Relay completes the TCP/IP handshake with the server while waiting for the completed handshake from the client.

    A. True

    B. False

18. Which Check Point product offers encryption but limited firewall functionality?

    A. FireWall-1

    B. FireWall-1/VPN-1

    C. VPN-1 Net

    D. VPN-1 Pro

    E. FloodGate

19. The information behind a firewall in a VPN is encrypted (see the following picture).

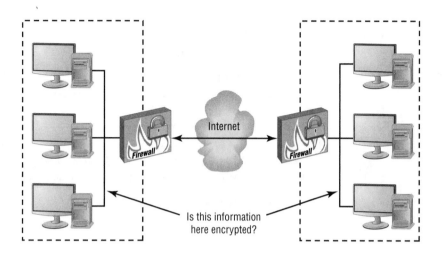

A. True

B. False

20. ConnectControl is the same as load balancing.

A. True

B. False

21. VPNs can be set up between satellites in a star topology.

A. True

B. False

22. A Simplified VPN policy requires that all participating gateways be under the control of a single SmartCenter Server.

A. True

B. False

23. Which of the following Internet-enabled components would be capable of using Clientless VPNs without additional software? (Choose all that apply.)

   A. Palm Pilot

   B. Cellular Phone

   C. Laptop

   D. Pocket PC

   E. All of the above

24. In the Extranet Management Interface, what type of network objects can you not define for export? (Choose all that apply.)

   A. Networks.

   B. Clusters.

   C. Address ranges.

   D. Workstations.

   E. All of the above can be defined.

25. What kind of product needs to be on the other end of an Extranet Management Interface extranet VPN?

   A. Check Point Firewall

   B. Any firewall

   C. Any encrypting device

   D. Check Point NG Firewall with EMI license

   E. Encrypting device that supports IKE

26. Where is SecuRemote configured in the Global Properties?

   A. Desktop Security

   B. VPN-1 Net

   C. SecuRemote

   D. Remote Access

   E. VPN-1 Pro

27. Which encryption schemes are supported by SecuRemote? (Choose all that apply.)

  A. FWZ

  B. IKE

  C. SKIP

  D. Manual IPSec

  E. Blowfish

28. Which file holds topology information for SecuRemote users?

  A. `objects.c`

  B. `manage.lock`

  C. `userc.C`

  D. `rulebases.fws`

  E. `standard.W`

29. What needs to be enabled on a firewall or a cluster to run the Extranet Management Interface?

  A. The Extranet-Enabled Gateway option

  B. VPN-1/Firewall-1

  C. VPN Net

  D. Encryption

  E. Extranets

30. What is the name of the file that carries the Desktop policy on the SecureClient machine?

  A. `Userc.C`

  B. `Objects.C`

  C. `Local.dt`

  D. `Policy.ps`

  E. None of the above

31. Which Voice over IP methodology requires creating both gateway and gatekeeper VoIP Domain objects?

    A. POTS

    B. SIP

    C. ATM

    D. H.323

    E. PBX

32. Where is the Desktop policy installed on the SecureClient machine?

    A. In the protocol

    B. In the NIC

    C. In the memory

    D. In the kernel

    E. In the Policy

33. Access rules defined in the Security Policy affect VPN communities.

    A. True

    B. False

Answers to Assessment Test

1. **E.** With NG, Content Security can filter all these types of traffic. FTP, HTTP, and SMTP are carryovers from 4.1. You can filter protocols like AOL with the new TCP resource option. See Chapter 4 for more information.

2. **C.** The `cpconfig` command provides you with a menu to configure the different components of either the Management Module or the enforcement point, depending on the machine from which you issue the command. See Chapter 1 for more information.

3. **A.** HTTP load balancing requires one rule to access the logical server followed by another rule to allow the redirect to occur. See Chapter 3 for more information.

4. **D.** SIC is the new method for Check Point modules to communicate in NG. SIC has replaced the old `fw putkey` command and has enhanced internal communications. All communication using SIC is encrypted. See Chapter 1 for more information.

5. **A.** The alert is defined in the Track element of the rule base. The actual alert scripts are configured in the Alert Commands tab of the Global Properties. See Chapter 2 for more information.

6. **D.** If you are deploying a server-based VoIP solution, the server will be running on an operating system which, will have inherent vulnerabilities. The best way to prevent exploitation of these vulnerabilities is to harden the operating system. See Chapter 5 for more information.

7. **A.** In the real world, you will always want the connection to stay with a specific server once it's directed there, especially if you're using HTTPS or some other secure protocol. See Chapter 3 for more information.

8. **B.** FWZ encrypts the payload and leaves the headers alone. IPSec encrypts the entire original package and adds new headers. See Chapter 6 for more information.

9. B. In earlier versions, you could use `fw putlic`. In NG, the command is `cplic put`. All the other license commands follow this trend, so the `fw printlic` command used in earlier versions is now a `cplic print` command. See Chapter 1 for more information.

10. E. The algorithms supported are server load, round robin, round trip, domain, and random. See Chapter 3 for more information.

11. D. All processes are run through the fwssd process. Specific Security Servers are tied to this process through the `fwauthd.conf` definitions file located in `$FWDIR/conf`. See Chapter 4 for more information.

12. B, D. CPShared and SVN Foundation are the two names used for the Check Point OS that is new to NG. See Chapter 1 for more information.

13. A. You can strip MIME types, filter URLs, and control FTP GETs and PUTs without the use of a third-party server. See Chapter 4 for more information.

14. B. The dtps process is the Policy Server process. In Windows, it runs as `dtps.exe`. This file has three threads that facilitate the Policy Server's functions. See Chapter 10 for more information.

15. B. An SIP proxy is not required but can be used along with an SIP redirect server to implement SIP. See Chapter 5 for more information.

16. B, C. H.323 and SIP are the two communication protocols supported by Check Point NG. These two protocols are the most widely used on the existing VoIP products. See Chapter 5 for more information.

17. B. SYN Gateway completes the handshake from the firewall to the server while waiting for the completed handshake from the client. SYN Gateway is no longer an option after NG FCS. See Chapter 2 for more information.

18. C. Only VPN-1 Net offers only encryption and very limited firewall functionality. See Chapter 6 for more information.

19. B.   Only the information between the firewalls is encrypted. Everything behind the firewalls is in cleartext. See Chapter 6 for more information.

20. A.   Essentially, these are the same things. This feature performs load balancing. It's also sometime referred to as ConnectControl (it's listed that way in the Global Properties) because that's the name of the feature in the license string that activates the functionality. See Chapter 3 for more information.

21. B.   With a single star topology, VPNs cannot be set up between satellites. The only way to accomplish this task is to create another star topology with one VPN being the center and the other being a satellite, or to pull the two satellites into their own meshed topology. See Chapter 7 for more information.

22. A.   By definition, a Simplified Policy works only if all the participating gateways are under the control of a single SmartCenter server. See Chapter 7 for more information.

23. E.   All components that have Internet access and have a web browser that supports HTTPS can use Clientless VPNs. The concept behind the technology is that it can be used by any SSL-enabled browser from anywhere. See Chapter 10 for more information.

24. B.   Clusters cannot be defined as export network objects. The others are the only types of objects that can be defined. Groups can also be defined, as long as they consist of only networks, address ranges, and workstations. See Chapter 8 for more information.

25. D.   The EMI only works with other Check Point NG firewalls running EMI. The product must be licensed on both sides for the extranet VPN to work. See Chapter 8 for more information.

26. D.   SecuRemote is configured in the Remote Access tab of the Global Properties. Under the Remote Access tab, the VPN tab also has some settings for SecuRemote. See Chapter 9 for more information.

27. B.   IKE is the only encryption scheme supported by SecuRemote after NG FP1. FWZ was supported in earlier versions. See Chapter 9 for more information.

28. C.   The `userc.C` file holds the topology information for SecuRemote clients and can be pre-configured to ease the deployment of SecuRemote software. See Chapter 9 for more information.

29. A.   The Extranet-Enabled Gateway check box on the firewall or cluster object must be checked. This check box is found on the Extranet tab of the firewall object. If you're running a cluster, the option appears on the Extranet tab of the cluster object. See Chapter 8 for more information.

30. C.   The `local.dt` file carries the Desktop policy and is stored on the SecureClient machine. Some of the other files that are listed serve their own purpose. See Chapter 10 for more information.

31. D.   Out of the two supported protocols, H.323 is configured with a Gateway and a Gatekeeper. SIP is configured differently. See Chapter 5 for more information.

32. D.   The Desktop policy resides in the kernel of the operating system on the SecureClient machine. The policy is downloaded and updated every time the SecureClient machine logs on to the Policy Server. See Chapter 10 for more information.

33. B.   Access rules are totally independent of the VPN communities. See Chapter 7 for more information.

Chapter
1

Getting Started with Check Point NG

THE CCSE EXAM TOPICS COVERED IN THIS CHAPTER INCLUDE:

- ✓ The system requirements for and components involved in VPN-1/FireWall-1 NG.

- ✓ The necessary steps for Windows NT and Solaris VPN-1/FireWall-1 NG installation.

- ✓ Installing and setting up VPN-1/FireWall-1 NG Gateway/Server Module.

- ✓ Installing and setting up VPN-1/FireWall-1 NG SmartCenter Server and GUI Client.

- ✓ Upgrading Check Point 4.1 FireWall to VPN-1/FireWall NG.

- ✓ Uninstalling VPN-1/FireWall-1 NG.

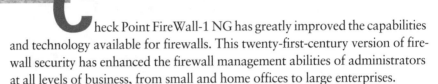

heck Point FireWall-1 NG has greatly improved the capabilities and technology available for firewalls. This twenty-first-century version of firewall security has enhanced the firewall management abilities of administrators at all levels of business, from small and home offices to large enterprises.

The Internet's growing demands for security require companies to protect their networks in a variety of ways. In the past, a company could deploy a single firewall as a gateway between itself and the Internet, and consider itself somewhat secure. However, the number of hacks and attacks over the past five years have proven that much more security is needed over the Internet.

Today, companies have expanded the ways they do business over the Internet. Business has become dependent on the Internet for communication with customers, coworkers, suppliers, and partners. Company demands have grown to included multiple firewalls, increased performance, VPNs, extranet VPNs, remote access, and other security capabilities. Check Point's Secure Virtual Network (SVN) architecture has grown with the needs of companies and provides enterprises throughout the world with the best in network security technology, coupled with a comprehensive, one-stop network security management solution.

This first chapter covers the planning of your security architecture, preparation for installation, licensing, installation on both Windows and Solaris, and the NG upgrade procedure.

Check Point NG includes periodic updates to the software. In the past, Check Point released Service Packs to improve the current product with patches and code enhancements. With NG, Check Point releases *Feature Packs (FPs)* that not only include patches, but also offer significant feature and code improvements. The most current version of FireWall-1 at the time of this writing is Check Point NG Feature Pack 3. Due to its broad enhancement of features, this version should be your minimum choice for deployment.

Planning Your Security Architecture

You should approach the installation of firewalls with long-term goals in mind. Your firewalls will act as your perimeter protection from the Internet and your gateway to the subnets throughout your network. Because of the changing security environment and the gradual enhancements in technology, your security architecture today may be insufficient in the years to come. On the other hand, because of budgetary constraints, most companies' firewalls will be in place for two to five years, so proper long-term planning is needed.

Choosing an Operating System

The first step in building your security architecture is to choose an operating system. VPN-1/FireWall-1 will run on a variety of platforms, including Windows NT/2000, Solaris, Linux, Nokia IPSO, and AIX. The CCSE exam focuses on two major platforms: Sun Solaris and Microsoft Windows NT/2000.

Solaris is a popular OS for enterprise-wide FireWall-1 deployments because of its security and stability. Check Point support on Solaris is readily available. The major drawbacks of deploying FireWall-1 on Solaris are the cost of the hardware and the skill needed to manage the OS. Although the OS does not need much tweaking after its initial install and configuration, you need some understanding of Unix to administer a Unix firewall.

Windows NT/2000 is a more economical choice for a firewall OS, and Check Point support is readily available. Installation and administration on the Windows platform are more GUI based; and, if you don't have in-house staff with Unix skills, a Windows firewall is easier to configure and maintain. Keep in mind that you'll still find yourself using the command line—rather than issuing commands in Unix, you'll be issuing almost the same commands from a DOS prompt. You'll edit files in Notepad or another text editor rather than Unix's vi editor.

Many companies are looking at Linux as an efficient and economical way to deploy a firewall. VPN-1/FireWall-1 on Red Hat Linux can deliver better performance on less expensive hardware than Solaris or Windows.

An alternative to choosing a vendor-based operating system is Check Point *SecurePlatform* NG FP3, which comes on a bootable CD-ROM that provides Check Point NG on a hardened Linux platform. Configuring SecurePlatform is easy: The install program hardens the Intel platform as it installs. SecurePlatform will install on any Intel-based PC or server and can significantly simplify the Check Point NG installation.

VPN-1/FireWall-1 Components

When deciding on architecture, you need to understand the three components of VPN-1/FireWall-1: the *Management Server*, the FireWall Module, and the *Management Clients (GUI)*. The components in this architecture have been renamed in Check Point NG FP3 to better describe the functionality and enhanced features that have been added to the product. Feature Pack 3 introduces Check Point's Security Management Architecture (SMART), which enables you to manage all elements of a security policy from a single console. In FP3, the Management Server is now called the *SmartCenter Server,* and the Management GUI Clients are now called *SMART Clients.*

The SmartCenter Server stores all the configuration files and configuration information, including the rule bases, objects database, user database, logs, and so forth. The *FireWall Module*, also referred to as an *enforcement point* or enforcement module, acts as a gateway that enforces the rule base with the objects and users configured by an administrator and sends logs to the SmartCenter Server. The SMART Client's *SmartDashboard* GUI is the front-end configuration tool to the SmartCenter Server, where firewall administrators create objects, rules, users, and so on to customize the firewall(s) they manage. Figure 1.1 illustrates the three components of the Check Point architecture working together; each of the components can run on separate machines with different operating systems. Each of the three firewalls in Figure 1.1 is managed remotely by the SmartCenter Server, which is configured by the SmartDashboard. The communication between the components will still be encrypted and secure.

FIGURE 1.1 Distributed modules

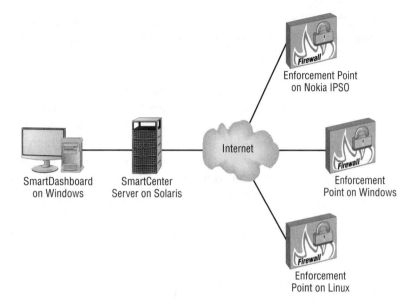

Selecting Hardware
==================

When selecting the hardware necessary for your firewall deployment, always plan for growth: Decide on the architecture necessary to accomplish your long-term goals. Your enforcement point will be acting as a router, so you will need a minimum of two network interfaces: one internal (LAN) and one external (Internet). Each interface will represent a network routed through your firewall. If you plan to have a *demilitarized zone (DMZ)*, then you need a minimum of three interfaces: internal, external, and DMZ.

You may not need a fourth interface right now, but you may want to install it for future additions. You also may need more disk space available for logs on your SmartCenter Server.

Perhaps you need only one firewall right now; but down the road you may need to add a second firewall as a high-availability solution, so you have to plan for additional interfaces.

If you are deploying one firewall, you must also decide whether to install it in a distributed configuration to accommodate additional firewalls down the road, or whether to deploy it as a stand-alone firewall so the *SmartCenter Server* and enforcement point are running on the same machine. You may also want a secondary SmartCenter Server to achieve full redundancy.

Now that you understand your architecture options, let's move on to preparing for installation. The next section will discuss pre-installation preparation for successfully deploying Check Point NG VPN-1/FireWall-1 and help you make the final decisions about how to design your security architecture.

Preparing for Installation

At this point, you've thought about your security architecture. Now it's time to prepare for installation by considering system requirements, reviewing operating system security, and understanding licensing to ensure the success of your firewall deployment. Understanding system requirements will help you determine what hardware and what operating system version to deploy. After you choose these components, securing the operating system will ensure that your firewall is running on a secure platform. From there, we'll discuss how to license the Check Point product and the options available.

System Requirements

When you refer to the minimum system requirements listed in Table 1.1, keep in mind that these requirements are absolute minimums. The software will run on this minimal hardware but probably will not achieve your performance expectations. These minimums are good to know for test purposes.

TABLE 1.1 Minimum System Requirements

Module	Operating Systems	Disk Space	Memory	Supported NICs
SmartDashboard Management GUI	Windows 98, Me, NT SP4, NT SP5, NT SP6, 2000, XP; Sun Solaris SPARC	40MB	128MB recommended	Ethernet, Fast Ethernet, Gigabit Ethernet, ATM, FDDI, Token Ring
SmartCenter Management Server and enforcement point	Windows NT Server SP6a; Windows 2000 Server and Advanced Server; Sun Solaris 2.7 with patch 106327-08 (2.7 supports 32-bit mode only); Solaris 2.8 with patches 108434-01 and 108435-01 (2.8 supports 32- and 64-bit mode); Red Hat Linux 6.2, 7.0, 7.1, 7.2	40MB	128MB recommended	Ethernet, Fast Ethernet, Gigabit Ethernet, ATM, FDDI, Token Ring

It's important to install your firewalls on the proper hardware with the right amount of network interface cards (NICs), hard drive space, RAM, and processing power to last you at least a couple of years, because upgrading is difficult once firewalls are in production. A good approach is to deploy firewalls with the most powerful hardware your budget will allow, to accomplish the throughput and performance you will need for the next three to five years. Although there is a good chance you will upgrade your firewalls within two years, by deploying with enough hardware and throughput to last longer, you will not find that it's critically urgent to upgrade or deploy new firewalls sooner.

Hardware is getting faster and less expensive every month, so there is no reason to deploy a firewall using the minimum requirements: The amount of RAM and the processor speed will directly affect the performance of your Check Point firewall.

If you're implementing multiple firewalls, be sure not to sacrifice performance in order to achieve high availability. For example, it would not be beneficial to use only 128MB of RAM in each of two firewalls because your budget could only afford a total of 256MB.

Now that you've chosen your operating system and your hardware, it's time to prep the boxes to be firewalls.

Operating System Security

If you are installing the Check Point software on your chosen machines, the OS must be secured and optimized to be a firewall. Because these machines will act as a gateway between the untrusted (external) and trusted (internal) sides of your WAN, you must be sure the OS contains no insecure vulnerabilities that can be compromised. In addition, because these machines are gateways, they must be optimized to route packets. For this reason, it's important to perform a fresh installation of the OS with only the minimal installation requirements. In Unix, you can be selective about which components you want to install. In Windows, many of the components are installed by default, and you must go back and remove them afterward.

Hardening the operating system is a process of removing vulnerabilities and unnecessary services. This process locks down and limits the functions of the OS so it will better serve as a firewall. As you harden a Unix machine, for example, you add all the necessary patches and hotfixes to bring the OS to a current secure state. Then, you remove insecure services like rlogin, rsh, rexec, Telnet, and so forth. Hardening a Windows machine requires several steps, including going into Control Panel and disabling a list of unneeded services like Server, Workstation, Computer Browser, Net Logon, Network DDE, and so on. A firewall running on a vulnerable OS defeats the purpose of its existence.

A variety of hardening documents are available for every OS; you can find them by doing a simple Internet search. Some good sources for hardening documents are `support.checkpoint.com`, `www.enteract.com/~lspitz/`, `www.cert.org`, `www.sans.org`, `www.securityfocus.com`, and `www.phoneboy.com`.

There are also tools and scripts that will automatically harden an OS for you. However, it is better not to use an automatic approach to harden your

OS, because you don't know what the script is doing. Although it will take longer, it is better to manually remove and disable services on the OS. Then, if something goes wrong or does not work, you know the procedure followed during the hardening process and can back out and fix the issue.

Be sure not to harden the OS to a point where the NG software does not run properly due to restrictive permissions or removed services. To avoid this, Check Point actually recommends performing some hardening and performance tuning after the firewall software is installed so the hardening procedure does not interfere with the Check Point software installation. The courseware recommends to first install the operating system, then the OS service packs, patches, and hotfixes. After the OS is installed and up-to-date, configure the routing and make sure all networking works. Then, install the Check Point NG software with the appropriate feature packs and hotfixes, and then harden the OS.

Appliance firewalls have gained great popularity over the last few years. There are many firewall appliances that ease the OS installation and hardening process. Appliances come in all shapes and sizes to meet the needs of everyone from the home office user with 1 small firewall to the enterprise customer with 500 large firewalls. Appliances add much more convenience in their initial configuration and, in many cases, provide better performance than a traditional server because they are pre-hardened, purpose-built boxes that are optimized to run Check Point FireWall-1.

 Check Point SecurePlatform offers a secure hardened operating system and Check Point NG in one install. After the five-minute SecurePlatform install, you just need to configure IP addresses, routes, and so on.

 Real World Scenario

Evaluating an Appliance

The most popular Check Point firewall appliances are the Nokia Secure Network Solutions product line. Nokia runs its own hardened OS called IPSO. IPSO is a stripped-down Free BSD Unix that is optimized for running Check Point FireWall-1. Many new Linux-based appliances have come out recently; you can find a list at www.opsec.com.

The most-compared appliance features are performance, ease of configuration, support, and price. The Open Platform for Security (OPSEC) is a framework of best-of-breed security products that integrate well with Check Point software. The OPSEC website provides insight and information about the many integration products that complement the Check Point architecture.

When considering an appliance, evaluate the vendor by the number of years it has been in business, the number of happy customers it has, and the amount of support it offers. Unfortunately, many companies with good products and sharp engineers are struggling to keep their doors open. You can buy the best firewall appliance on the market today, and it will probably still require support some time in the next three years. Be sure the vendor that built your appliance will still be in business with a strong support team two to five years from now.

Once the OS has been installed and properly hardened, the next step is to configure your network to be sure the machines properly route packets between each network interface. Be sure that IP routing/forwarding is enabled in your OS and that the routing tables are correct. Connect each NIC to the switch or hub it will be connected to in production, and ping machines residing on each subnet. For example, if there are three interfaces on the firewall—internal, external, and demilitarized zone (DMZ)—make sure machines behind the internal interface properly route packets through the other interfaces. Check that DMZ packets are properly routing from DMZ servers out through the external and internal interfaces. In addition, be sure the machine that will act as the SmartCenter Server can ping all the machines that will act as firewalls or *enforcement points*.

Licensing

Once all routing is configured properly, you are ready to license your firewall software. You do this after configuring your network because accurate IP address information is needed to generate a valid license.

One of the major components of the Check Point installation is the *license key*. The license key controls the components that are installed on your firewall. The architecture and features of your Check Point product depend on your license. To generate a license, you must enter registration information on the Check Point User Center website at `usercenter.checkpoint.com`, as shown in Figure 1.2.

FIGURE 1.2   Check Point User Center website

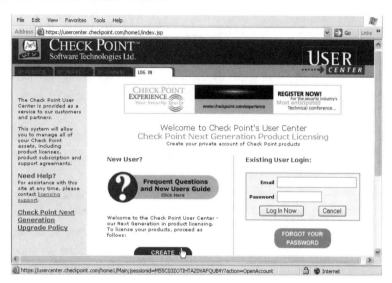

 Starting with Check Point NG FP3, all purchased Check Point products have a 15-day trial period. During this 15-day period, all features of the product are fully functional and available without a license. In versions prior to FP3, you could not use the software until a license was installed.

The Check Point licensing process has been a bit confusing for customers over the years. Check Point NG has made it easier to manage licenses by greatly improving the registration website and by centralizing the license management process with the SmartUpdate product component. This licensing process makes FireWall-1 one of the most legally licensed software packages in the world. The steps to license Check Point products are as follows:

1. In the Check Point User Center, click the Create New Account button to begin the registration process. You are first prompted for an e-mail address and password. You're also asked to confirm both, to ensure that you haven't made an error in typing.

2. If you do not have a login ID, you must create one by clicking Create. Enter your contact information to create a user profile; this information will be stored in a database for future reference. If you register

another Check Point product, this user profile will be accessed, and you won't have to retype your contact information.

3. Click Update. An e-mail message with the subject "Check Point User Center [*confirmation code*]" will be sent to the e-mail address you specified. This e-mail will say something like this:

```
This is an email generated by the Check Point
User Center

Thank you for visiting the Check Point User Center.

Your custom confirmation code is: EA247ED1

Please enter this at the UserCenter where requested,
or if your session has already ended, login again
at: https://usercenter.checkpoint.com/

Thank you,

Check Point Software Technologies
```

4. Take the confirmation code from the e-mail message, plug it in as shown in Figure 1.3, and click Continue.

FIGURE 1.3 Entering the confirmation code

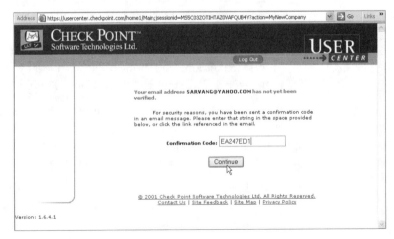

5. Once you've confirmed your e-mail address, you can log in to the usercenter.checkpoint.com website and view your user, company, and product information. The My Products tab, shown in Figure 1.4, provides a pull-down menu with a list of options for your licensed products.

FIGURE 1.4 Licensing menu

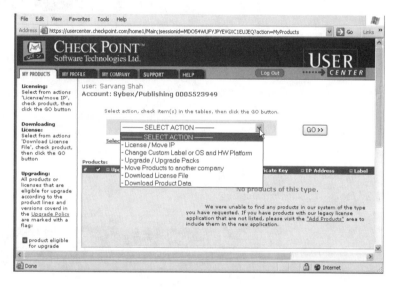

6. Before modifying any licenses, you need to add one. Scroll to the right to locate the Add Products button. By clicking this button, you'll be able to register your license by adding your *Certificate Key*. As shown in Figure 1.5, your Certificate Key is a 12-character alphanumeric code that identifies your product to the Check Point User Center website. Your license will be generated based on this information.

7. Once you've entered the Certificate Key, the User Center website will determine the type of product for which you are generating a license. As you can see in Figure 1.6, our Certificate Key came from an educational CD.

FIGURE 1.5 Adding a Certificate Key

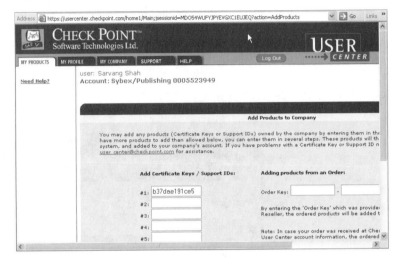

FIGURE 1.6 Product details

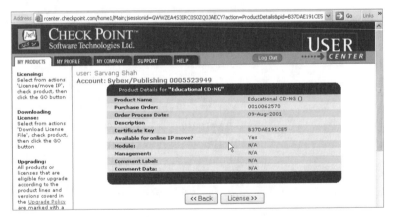

8. You can now generate a license or go back. Click License. You can choose whether to generate a local or central license. Choosing a central license will allow you to manage all your licensing from the Smart-Center Server. This feature is new to NG with a product component called SecureUpdate. In past versions, Check Point ran a separate license on every module. Central licensing is very handy when you

have more than a few firewalls to manage or are managing firewalls in multiple or distant locations. For the purposes of this book, you will use a local license.

9. Once you've chosen your license type, you are asked for IP address and platform information. Because in our case we installed the Smart-Center Server and the Firewall Module on the same machine, we input our information with the same IP address. Notice in Figure 1.7 that we've chosen different operating systems and hardware platforms, to show you the flexibility of Check Point NG. You can manage multiple firewalls running on multiple platforms.

FIGURE 1.7   Details of modules

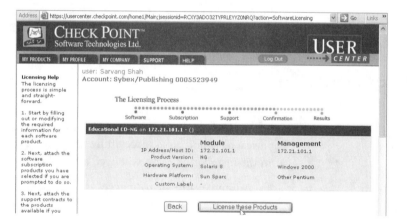

10. Confirm the information you've entered by clicking the License These Products button shown in Figure 1.7. Figure 1.8 shows you the generated license. An e-mail message will automatically be sent to you with the license information and an attached `CPLicenseFile.lic` file that you can use to enter the license into the software. You can also copy the license to the Clipboard from your browser. (When you print the license from the browser, be sure to print it in a landscape layout so the characters aren't cut off.)

11. Notice in Figure 1.8 that you're given an option to download a license. This downloaded license is the same file that is e-mailed to you as an attachment. This option comes in handy if you accidentally delete your e-mailed license.

FIGURE 1.8 The generated license

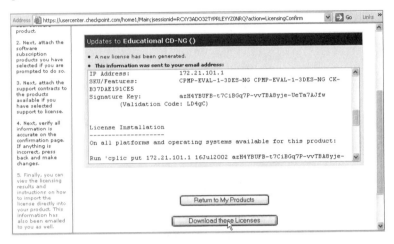

Installation

Now that you have reviewed the planning and preparation for installing FireWall-1 and have successfully generated a license, you are ready to perform the installation. You will need a few things for a smooth installation:

- Administrator or root access to the machine(s) so you will have permission to install software

- The Check Point license you generated

- FireWall administrator names and passwords

- IP addresses of GUI clients (administrators' machines)

This section will cover both the Windows and Solaris installations. The steps in the two installations are similar; however, the Windows installation is graphical, whereas the Solaris installation is text based.

If you are installing your firewalls in a *distributed environment*, where the SmartCenter Server is on a separate machine from the Firewall Module(s), it's a good idea to install the SmartCenter Server first and then the FireWall Module(s). In this section we'll present the installation in a stand-alone architecture, which is how it's done in the CCSE courseware. In a stand-alone installation, the steps that are unique to the Management Module installation and enforcement point installation are combined.

The Installation Procedure

This section explains the installation procedure and highlights some important things that you need to know. Later, as you move through the steps of the installation in the exercises, you will be presented with some unusual or unexplained options. Understanding the components involved in the installation will not only help you on your CCSE exam, but will also help you better understand how the firewall works. The following sections explain the various nuances of the installation steps and identify which module the installation step is part of.

The following items are explained with the assumption that you are installing from a Check Point CD. If you are installing from a downloaded copy and not a CD, install the bundled wrapper. The Secure Virtual Network (SVN) Foundation should always be installed before the VPN-1/FireWall-1 software. This same process applies to a Nokia IPSO package install.

Product Menu

Once you've agreed to the End User License Agreement, the Product Menu will appear. The Product Menu, displayed in Figure 1.9, allows you to choose the Check Point products you want to install. Notice that in Figure 1.9, only the VPN-1 & Firewall-1 product is selected.

After you choose the product(s) to install, the next screen (Figure 1.10) lets you choose whether to install a Server/Gateway component or a Mobile/Desktop component. The Server/Gateway components include the Enforcement Module, SmartCenter Server, SMART Clients, Policy Server, and more. The Mobile/Desktop Components are Secure Remote, Secure Client, or the Session Authentication Agent, mainly for client machines. Most of the time you will choose Server/Gateway components.

FIGURE 1.9 Product Menu

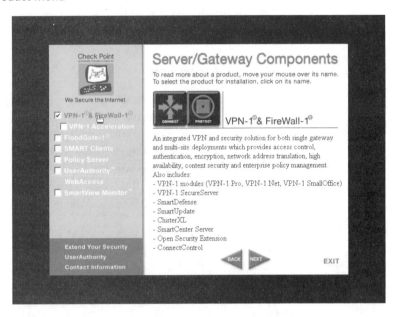

FIGURE 1.10 Server/Gateway or Mobile/Desktop

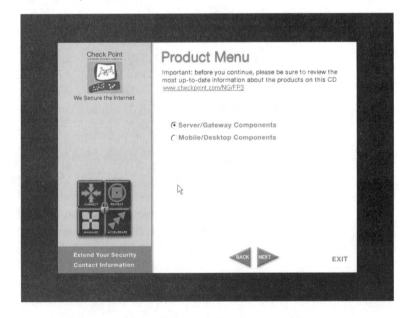

Product Type

Now that you've chosen which product to install, you must identify how you will install it. As mentioned earlier, you will be installing a stand-alone firewall in the exercises. Choose the Enforcement Module and Management Server options, as shown in Figure 1.11. The SmartCenter Server and enforcement point will be installed on one machine.

FIGURE 1.11 SmartCenter Server and enforcement point

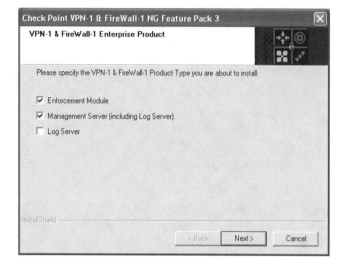

The next selection asks which type of Management Server you want to install: Primary or Secondary. Because this is our only firewall machine and we are installing both components on the same machine, we will choose Enterprise Primary Management. You would select Enterprise Secondary Management if you were building a backup SmartCenter Server to achieve redundancy in a distributed environment.

Backward Compatibility

Backward compatibility is a choice that is dependent on the rest of the architecture. Many companies cannot upgrade all their firewalls at one time, so they must accommodate backward compatibility. The NG SmartCenter Server can manage 4.1 VPN-1/FireWall-1 Modules if the Backward Compatibility option is selected, but some NG features will not work for the older versions. Check Point NG Feature Pack 1 (FP1) backward compatibility will work for versions 4.0 and 4.1. Feature Packs beyond FP1 will not support FireWall-1 version 4.0 or earlier. If there are no other Check Point products in your network architecture, then you don't need backward compatibility.

Installing Files

Now the installation script will begin copying files to the hard drive. The Windows installation lets you choose the directory where you want the Check Point product installed. Check Point recommends installing the files in the default directory unless you have a good reason not to.

The *Secure Virtual Network (SVN) Foundation* is always installed before VPN-1/FireWall-1. The SVN Foundation, also called *CPShared*, is a Check Point operating system that facilitates ease of integration and management between Check Point products installed on the same machine. Because it's an OS, it's installed before any Check Point components are installed and removed last during an uninstall.

Once the files are copied, you will go through the configuration procedure.

Running *cpconfig*

Because this is an initial installation, you are prompted to configure important firewall settings such as licenses, administrators, GUI clients, and a certificate authority. Running the cpconfig command from the command line produces a configuration menu that you can use to reconfigure the same components. For that reason, it's recommended that you go through all the initial configuration steps without canceling—any settings you configure can be changed later in the cpconfig menu.

License Configuration

In this step, you enter the license generated on the User Center website. If you were installing in a distributed environment, you would need a license for the SmartCenter Server and each Enforcement Module (local or centralized).

In Windows, you can add the license in a graphical way by either importing the .lic file that was e-mailed to you or copying the whole license command to the Clipboard and pasting it into the form. In Unix, it's easiest to skip the license question until the install is finished and then add the license from a command line by copying and pasting. In the installation you will perform during the exercise, you'll add the license from the command line.

Configuring Administrators

When you're configuring administrators on the SmartCenter Server, you must add at least one Read/Write administrator; otherwise, you will not be able to access the SmartCenter Server through the SmartDashboard GUI. You can come back later to add other administrators with their appropriate levels of permissions.

Check Point recommends choosing unusual administrator names and unique passwords. As shown in Figure 1.12, you can set permissions and different levels of access control for each administrator. In addition to Read/Write, you can be selective about what components each administrator is allowed to access and give them either Read/Write or Read Only permission per component.

FIGURE 1.12 Adding administrators

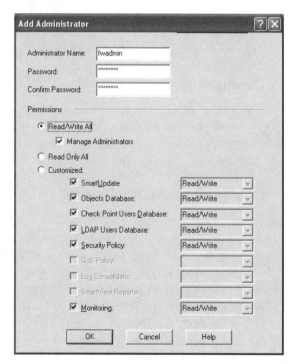

Configuring GUI Clients

Adding *GUI clients* to the SmartCenter Server allows you to create an Access Control List (ACL) to limit GUI access to the SmartCenter Server by hostname or IP address. Only the hostname or IP addresses you specify will be allowed access to the SmartCenter Server through the specific GUI, based on that administrator's permissions. This list is written to a gui-clients file and can be edited later. Although it is possible to add wildcards and ranges to this list, doing so is not recommended; it is a better security measure to add IP addresses individually for easier manageability. You do not want to add unnecessary access to this ACL, and while adding ranges and wildcards, you may be allowing unknown or unwanted access to the SmartCenter Server.

Configuring SNMP Extension

Unless Simple Network Management Protocol (SNMP) is needed, it is suggested that you keep the SNMP Extension daemon turned off to limit potential vulnerabilities on the Firewall Module. Some companies use SNMP monitoring products, so they run the SNMP daemon. If you plan to use SNMP Traps with a network management device or for Check Point's SNMP Trap alerts, then turn on the daemon. The SNMP vulnerabilities published in February 2002 at www.cert.org clarify the security risks in turning on the SNMP daemon.

Configuring Groups

In the Unix installation, you can configure groups to allow access and execution permissions to the Firewall Module. Generally, the root account is all that's needed; so, we usually choose not to specify any groups. This option does not appear in the Windows installation.

Configuring a Random Pool

The Key Hit Session screen is shown in Figure 1.13. It allows you to create a random seed that is used to generate cryptographic keys. You generate the random seed by typing random characters at a random pace until the software replies, "Thank you!"

This random seed is used in the next step to generate a certificate that facilitates secure communication between the SmartCenter Server and all enforcement points. In a distributed environment, this random seed would be generated on both the enforcement point and the SmartCenter Server. This random key generator process is also the seed for the keys needed for certificate-based encryption, such as Internet Key Exchange (IKE) or secure sockets layer (SSL).

FIGURE 1.13 Creating a random seed in the Key Hit Session dialog box

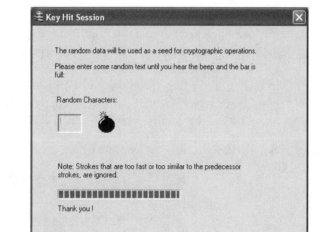

Configuring a Certificate Authority

The SmartCenter Server is a certificate authority for the firewalls it manages. The SmartCenter Server issues the certificates for *Secure Internal Communications (SIC)*. SIC is a certificate-based SSL encryption method used to provide secure communication between Check Point modules. Communication between the SmartCenter Server and FireWall Module, or the GUI and SmartCenter Server, in any order, is encrypted and authenticated using SIC to ensure confidentiality and data integrity. SIC must be established for every Check Point module that is created in the SmartDashboard and managed by that specific SmartCenter Server.

Previous versions of VPN-1/FireWall-1 used an fw putkey command to establish communication between modules. The SIC architecture is new with NG and is considered a major improvement over the old putkey process.

Configuring the Certificate Fingerprint

The *fingerprint* is a unique set of words used in conjunction with SIC. An example of a fingerprint during the Windows installation is shown in Figure 1.14. It is recommended that you save this fingerprint for verification later. When you successfully connect with your GUI the first time, you will see this fingerprint again. If the fingerprint on your GUI is identical to the one on your Smart-Center Server, then SIC worked properly and all communication between the GUI and the SmartCenter Server is encrypted and secure.

FIGURE 1.14 The SmartCenter Server fingerprint

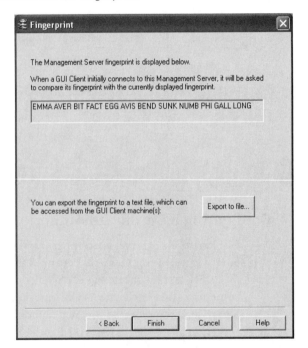

The Final Step

The final step before rebooting is to add the license. You can do so by issuing a `cplic put` command from the command line. The easiest way is to copy the command from the e-mail you received when you generated the license. Simply copy the command and then paste it at the prompt:

```
cplic put 172.21.101.1 16May2003 azH4YBUFB-t7CiBGq7P-
vvTBA8yje-UeTa7AJfw CPMP-EVAL-1-3DES-NG CPMP-EVAL-
1-3DES-NG CK-B37DAE191CE5
```

After installing the license, you are ready to run *cpconfig* if you want to go back and reconfigure the firewall install settings. Otherwise, reboot, and you'll be ready to run VPN-1/FireWall-1 NG.

If installing in a distributed installation, the *default filter* turns off IP forwarding so it blocks all IP connectivity to the firewall as a security mechanism; this filter must be altered to allow for connectivity. Otherwise, after the installation, you will not be able to connect to the machine.

Windows Installation

Now that you understand the steps involved, it's time to try your hand at the installation. We designed Exercise 1.1 as a quick and easy way to teach you how to install Check Point FireWall-1 software. Let's get started!

EXERCISE 1.1

Installing Check Point NG on Windows

1. Insert the CD into the CD-ROM drive. You will see the Welcome screen.

2. Click Next. The End User License Agreement will appear.

3. Agree to the License Agreement and choose VPN-1 & FireWall-1. Click Next.

4. On the Server/Gateway Components screen, choose Server/Gateway and click Next to start the Install Shield.

5. The Install Shield screen will show you the list of components you have selected to install. Click Next. SVN Foundation and VPN-1/FireWall-1 will be installed. When the installation is complete, click Next.

6. You are given a choice of product type. Per our discussion in the "Installation" section of this chapter, choose Enforcement Module and Management Server.

7. Choose Install Without Backward Compatibility and click Next.

8. Install the firewall in the default destination folder. Click Next.

9. Click Add to add a license. Copy to the Clipboard the whole `cplic` command from the e-mail message sent to you by Check Point, and then click Paste License. The form should populate. (If it doesn't, double-check the license you copied.) Click OK and then Next.

10. Click Add to add an administrator. Add an Administrator name and password. Choose Read/Write All for the permissions. Click OK and then Next.

11. Add the IP addresses of the administrator's machines that will be running the GUI client. Click Next.

12. In the Key Hit Session dialog box, type random characters at a random pace until the blue bar fills up and the software replies "Thank you!" As you enter characters, a bomb icon indicates an entry that is not random enough, and a light-bulb icon indicates an acceptable entry. Click Next.

13. To initialize the certificate authority, click Next. A message will appear, indicating that your certificate authority was initialized successfully. Click OK.

14. You'll see the SmartCenter Server fingerprint. Click Export to File if you want to export it and keep it for future reference. Otherwise, click Finish. You are done with the installation.

15. A thank you screen will appear, and you will be asked to reboot. Click Yes to reboot the machine. When it comes back up, your stand-alone Check Point FireWall-1 software will be up and running.

Solaris Installation

On the Check Point NG CD is a Unix Install Script that will determine the flavor of Unix on which you are installing FireWall-1; the script will then guide you through the installation. If you are installing Check Point NG on Linux, you can use the same Unix Install Script.

If you're installing from a downloaded copy, do a pkgadd on the decompressed FP3 SVN Foundation directory first and then add the FP3 VPN-1/FireWall-1 package. You can also download the bundled wrapper and install from that.

In the Unix installation, rather than clicking a Next button to proceed to the next step as you did in the Windows installation, you press the letter N. The navigation options appear at the bottom of the screen while you're performing the installation. Let's get started with Exercise 1.2.

EXERCISE 1.2

Installing Check Point NG on Solaris

1. Insert the CD into the CD-ROM drive. Type **./UnixInstallScript** from the cdrom directory. You will see the Welcome screen.

2. Press N to proceed. The End User License Agreement will appear.

3. Agree to the License Agreement and choose VPN-1 & FireWall-1 from the Product menu. Press N.

4. You are given a choice of installation type. Press 1 to choose Enterprise Primary Management and Enforcement Module. Press N.

5. Choose 2 to install without backward compatibility; press N. A validation screen will appear to confirm the products you have chosen to install. Press N to confirm that your choices are correct.

6. The software will be installed, IP forwarding will be disabled, and the cpconfig options will run. You will be asked to add licenses; for now, press N to choose not to add licenses.

7. Add an administrator name and password. Press W for Read/Write All permissions.

8. Press C to create a list of GUI clients. Enter the IP addresses of the administrator's machines. Press Ctrl+D when the list is finished.

9. Press N to not activate the SNMP Extension daemon.

10. Press Enter to not add groups. Press Y to confirm that no groups will be added.

11. To configure the random pool, type random characters at a random pace until the bar in brackets fills up and the software replies "Thank you". As you enter characters, a * icon indicates an acceptable entry.

12. Press Enter to initialize the certificate authority. A message confirming success will be reported back to you.

13. The fingerprint is displayed on the screen. Press Y to save it, and then enter **testfp** as the filename. The fingerprint will be saved in the /opt/CPshared/5.0/conf directory.

EXERCISE 1.2 *(continued)*

14. When asked if you would like to reboot, press N. You'll add the license before rebooting.

15. Copy to the Clipboard the whole `cplic put` command from the e-mail message sent to you by the Check Point User Center. Paste the command in the command line. The license should successfully be installed.

16. Reboot by issuing an `init 6` command. When the machine comes back up, your stand-alone Check Point FireWall-1 software will be up and running.

Upgrading to VPN-1/FireWall-1 NG

Now that you've performed a successful installation of FireWall-1 NG, it's time to understand how to upgrade from a previous version of VPN-1/ FireWall-1. At the time of this writing, many companies are looking to upgrade from an older version of VPN-1/FireWall-1 (usually 4.1 SP3 or higher) to NG FP3. You can upgrade to NG FP1 from version 4.0 and higher. If you are running a version older than 4.0, you must upgrade to version 4.0 first, and then upgrade to NG.

With the many enhancements in NG, it's better to create a fresh install of NG and then migrate your existing configuration files over to the newly created NG firewall. The upgrade technique discussed here will upgrade version 4.1 Service Pack 6 configuration files to NG configuration files. It is recommended that the 4.1 files are upgraded to Service Pack 6 before converting them to NG.

In many instances, companies are viewing the NG upgrade as an opportunity to upgrade the current platform on which their firewalls are running. For example, this is an chance to upgrade operating systems from Solaris 2.6 to 2.8, or to upgrade hardware from a Pentium II machine with limited hard drive space and memory to a Pentium IV with lots of hard drive space and much more memory.

In order to make the NG upgrade a smooth and convenient process, Check Point has developed an upgrade script that helps convert 4.1 configuration files to NG configuration files. This scripts automates the conversion by using the `confmerge` command on the `objects.C`, `fwauth.NDB`, and `rulebases.fws` files. (This script is not meant for people who are moving from a Windows machine to a Unix machine, or for people running Flood-Gate.) The script is in a zipped file called `upgrade.4.3.tgz` and can be downloaded from the `support.checkpoint.com` website. Here are the steps to use the *upgrade script*:

1. Create a new SmartCenterServer machine with the desired Feature Pack version of NG (FP1, FP2 or FP3), based on the installation guidelines previously discussed. This upgrade procedure will upgrade to FP3.

2. Download and unzip the `upgrade.4.3.tgz` file. This file opens into a directory named `upgrade`.

3. Place the 4.1 SP6 files on the SmartCenter Server under `upgrade/4.1`:

    a. `objects.C`.

    b. `fwauth.NDB`. On Windows machines, this file is only the pointer to the real database file—for example, `fwauth.NDB522`. In this case, take the real database file (`fwauth.NDB522`), rename it `fwauth.NDB`, and put it in the `\upgrade\4.1` directory.

    c. `rulebases.fws`.

4. Stop the FireWall-1 Services (`cpstop`), `cd` to the *<upgrade_directory>*, and issue the following command

    `in Windows (upgrade from 4.1 to FP3):`

    `upgrade.bat` *<upgrade_directory>*`\upgrade FP3 4.1`

    `In Unix, enter this command (upgrade from 4.1 to FP3):`
    `upgrade.csh` *<upgrade_directory>*`/upgrade FP3 4.1`

5. Restart the FireWall Services (`cpstart`) and log in to the GUI.

After you have successfully run the script, in order to transfer the remaining configuration files (such as `gui-clients`, `masters`, and so on), copy the following files from the VPN-1/FireWall-1 4.1 $FWDIR/conf directory to the VPN-1/FireWall-1 NG $FWDIR/conf directory:

> `xlate.conf, aftpd.conf, smtp.conf, sync.conf, masters,`
> `clients, fwmusers, gui-clients, slapd.conf, serverkeys,`
> `product.conf`

In addition to understanding which configuration files are important in upgrading to Check Point NG, it's important to understand which configuration files need to be saved for backup in case of a failure or loss of files. The next section talks about backup and restore options and identifies the critical configuration files needed for backup.

Backup and Restore

It is always a good idea to back up files in case of a failure. The files on the SmartCenter Server contain the bulk of the configuration information. In order to have a safe recovery process in case of an unfortunate failure, keep a backup of the following files:

$FWDIR/conf/Objects_5_0.C

$FWDIR/conf/rulebases_5_0.fws

$FWDIR/conf/InternalCA.*

$FWDIR/conf/ICA*.*

$CPDIR/conf/sic_cert.p12

$FWDIR/conf/fwauth.NDB

In addition to these files, you also need to back up and import the following:

Unix /opt/CPshared/registry/HKLM_registry.data (copy everything under SIC).

32-bit Windows HKEY_LOCAL_MACHINE\SOFTWARE\CheckPoint\SIC (export this key and then import it on the target machine).

From NG FP3, you should also copy all the files from $FWDIR/conf/crls.

Copying these files will save you the need to issue a new root certificate and new modules certificates. To restore the FireWall-1 NG SmartCenter Server with backup files, follow these steps:

1. Uninstall the SmartCenter Server and reboot.

2. Reinstall the FireWall-1 NG SmartCenter Server and reboot.

3. Reset SIC on the enforcement module(s) through cpconfig.

4. Stop the FireWall-1 NG SmartCenter Server with the `cpstop` command.

5. Copy the backup files to the `$FWDIR/conf` and `$CPDIR/conf` directories, respectively.

6. Start the FireWall-1 management machine with the `cpstart` ommand.

Note that this process will work only if both SmartCenter Servers are on the same OS.

Uninstalling

If you need to uninstall FireWall-1 from a machine, you must do so in a selective order. In Windows, you go to Add/Remove Programs in Control Panel, as shown in Figure 1.15, and first select all Check Point patches and hot fixes. Then, remove backward-compatibility components, followed by VPN-1 and FireWall-1 components and, finally, the SVN Foundation.

FIGURE 1.15 Choosing components to uninstall in Windows

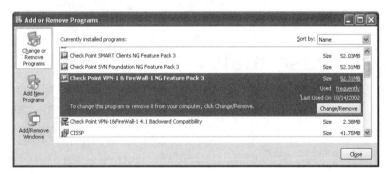

For Solaris, you can use a simple `pkgrm` command. You'll be provided with a list of packages that are installed on the Solaris machine, and you can select the packages that you want to uninstall. Remember that the same rule applies regarding the SVN Foundation (CPShared): Remove it last.

Summary

Installing Check Point VPN-1/FireWall-1 NG takes careful consideration and planning. Every deployment requires a planning process for selecting the proper OS, hardware, architecture, and Check Point features. It's important to think about the long term when planning for the processing power, memory, network interfaces, and hard drive space you'll need for the growth of the firewall deployment. The minimum hardware requirements we've listed are only required for the software to function and are not recommended for production firewalls.

After you acquire the necessary hardware and install an OS on your future firewalls, you should properly harden the OS. It's also important to check the routing and network configurations on the machines before installing firewall software. Configuration information, including IP addresses and licenses, should also be available prior to installing VPN-1/FireWall-1.

When you're upgrading from a previous version of VPN-1/FireWall-1, it's important to remember that version 4.0 is not supported even if you're using backward compatibility on NG versions newer than FP1. An NG Smart-Center Server will only manage 4.1 FireWall Modules and cannot integrate some NG features for those modules. You can smooth the upgrade process by using the Check Point upgrade script.

Exam Essentials

Know the minimum system requirements.   Although you will not want to install your firewall with minimum system requirements, it is important to know the operating systems that are supported by VPN-1/FireWall-1 NG and also the hardware required to run the software.

Be aware of the planning and preparation needed prior to installing.   It is important that you understand the preparation involved before installing FireWall-1 software. In addition to planning for your hardware, OS, and architecture, you must understand what it means to harden the OS and make sure all routing is working properly.

Understand the steps involved in installing FireWall-1 software. It is imperative that you know how to install Check Point's FireWall-1 software. Know each component involved in the installation and understand the architecture of the three major components: SmartCenter Server, FireWall (Enforcement) Module, and SMART Clients.

Understand how to upgrade from one system to the next. Understand the process of upgrading from earlier versions of Check Point VPN-1/ FireWall-1. Know the major changes that must take place.

Key Terms

Before you take the exam, be certain you are familiar with the following terms:

Certificate Key	hardening the operating system
Cpconfig	license key
CPShared	Management GUI Client
default filter	Management Server
demilitarized zone (DMZ)	Secure Internal Communications (SIC)
distributed environment	Secure Virtual Network (SVN) Foundation
enforcement point	SecurePlatform
Feature Packs (FPs)	SMART Clients
fingerprint	SmartCenter Server
FireWall Module	SmartDashboard
GUI client	

Review Questions

1. What should you be sure to do prior to installing the FireWall-1 software?

   A. Make sure you cannot ping any of the machines in the DMZ.

   B. Make sure all networking is working properly.

   C. Turn off IP forwarding in the OS.

   D. Reboot the switch the firewalls are plugged into.

   E. Reboot the servers and clients that will be involved in the installation.

2. What does it mean to harden the operating system?

   A. Put it through a more detailed installation and include all the bells and whistles.

   B. Customize the OS to be user friendly for future firewall administrators.

   C. Make the OS easier to use by adding extra help menus to it.

   D. Remove all unnecessary services and vulnerabilities to make the OS as secure as it can be prior to installing the firewall software.

   E. Strip down the OS so that no routing is allowed and nobody can access it.

3. What are the procedures when installing the SmartCenter Server?

   A. Add the license, add GUI client IP addresses, and then add the administrator and password.

   B. Add the license, add the Master's IP address, and then add putkeys.

   C. Set up SIC, add the GUI client IP addresses, and then add the license.

   D. Both A and C.

   E. None of the above.

4. What information do you *not* need prior to installing the FireWall-1 Enforcement Module?

  A. Proper routing on the box

  B. SIC password

  C. License

  D. Group names

  E. GUI client IP addresses

5. Which of these steps is *not* part of installing the VPN-1/FireWall-1 software?

  A. Add the license.

  B. Add administrators.

  C. Add subnets for IP addresses behind the firewall.

  D. Generate a random seed for cryptography.

  E. Add GUI client IP addresses.

6. Check Point FireWall-1 can be installed on which operating systems?

  1. Solaris

  2. Windows NT

  3. Red Hat Linux

  4. Windows 2000

  5. IPSO

  A. 1, 3, 5

  B. 2, 4, 5

  C. 1, 2, 3

  D. 3, 4, 5

  E. All of the above

7. Which steps are necessary to upgrade from 4.x to NG?

   A. Upgrade/patch the OS to support NG.

   B. Make sure the machine has enough RAM to support NG.

   C. Update your license to NG.

   D. Clear out old rule bases from 4.x.

   E. All of the above.

8. What command is used to uninstall the firewall on Solaris?

   A. pkg rm

   B. pkgrm

   C. uninstall

   D. cp uninstall

   E. cp pkgrm

9. Which operating systems can support the SmartDashboard? (Choose all that apply.)

   A. Windows Me

   B. Red Hat Linux

   C. Solaris

   D. IPSO

   E. Windows 2000

10. What is the recommended amount of memory for the Management Client?

    A. 16MB RAM

    B. 32MB RAM

    C. 64MB RAM

    D. 128MB RAM

    E. 256MB RAM

11. Which version of Solaris supports NG running in 64-bit mode?

    A. Solaris 2.6

    B. Solaris 2.7

    C. Solaris 2.8

    D. None of the above

    E. All of the above

12. You are going to perform a fresh installation of NG on a Windows 2000 machine. You have a 250-user license. This firewall will perform address translation and VPNs. Which of the following configurations could you use? (Choose all that apply.)

    A. GUI on a Windows Me machine, SmartCenter Server on Windows NT, and enforcement point on Windows 2000

    B. GUI on Windows 2000, SmartCenter Server on Solaris, and enforcement point on Windows 2000

    C. GUI on Solaris, SmartCenter Server and enforcement point on Windows 2000

    D. GUI, SmartCenter Server, and enforcement point on Windows 2000

    E. GUI on Linux, SmartCenter Server and enforcement point on Windows 2000

13. Which services would you remove when you harden your OS? (Choose all that apply.)

    A. rlogin

    B. FTP

    C. Telnet

    D. NetBIOS

    E. IP forwarding

14. Which types of licenses are supported in NG? (Choose all that apply.)

    A. Central licenses

    B. Enforcement licenses

    C. Local licenses

    D. Management licenses

    E. Firewall licenses

15. Check Point licenses can be generated at which URL?

    A. `license.checkpoint.com`

    B. `www.license.firewall.com`

    C. `usercenter.checkpoint.com`

    D. `www.checkpoint.com/licensing`

    E. `licensing.checkpoint.com`

16. You are going to install a SmartCenter Server, three enforcement points, and six Windows GUI clients. How many licenses do you need?

    A. 1

    B. 2

    C. 3

    D. 4

    E. 5

17. After you generate a license, an e-mail message will be sent to you with an attachment. This attachment can be imported during your installation so that you don't have to type in the long license string. What is the extension on the license file?

    A. `.cp`

    B. `.lic`

    C. `.fw`

    D. `.checkpoint`

    E. `.license`

18. You are installing a new NG firewall. In which order should the following components be installed?

1. SVN Foundation

2. Policy Server

3. SmartCenter Server

4. Enforcement point

   A. 1, 2, 3, 4

   B. 1, 3, 4, 2

   C. 2, 3, 4, 1

   D. 3, 1, 2, 4

   E. 4, 1, 2, 3

19. You are planning to upgrade a company's security. The company has (A) a SmartCenter Server running v. 4.1, (B) an enforcement point running 4.0, and (C) an enforcement point running 4.1. In which order would you plan your upgrades?

   A. Upgrade enforcement point B to 4.1, upgrade the SmartCenter Server to NG, and then upgrade both enforcement points to NG.

   B. Upgrade the SmartCenter Server to NG, and then upgrade both enforcement points to NG.

   C. Upgrade both enforcement points to NG, and then upgrade the SmartCenter Server to NG.

20. Which of the following will you see the first time you use a new GUI client to connect to the SmartCenter Server?

   A. Digital signature

   B. SIC certificate

   C. Fingerprint

   D. Internal certificate authority

Answers to Review Questions

1. B. By making sure networking is working prior to the installation, you eliminate the possibility of the OS being the problem if networking doesn't work after the FireWall-1 software is installed. Routing and networking are more difficult to troubleshoot after installing VPN-1/FireWall-1 software.

2. D. You harden or secure the OS to make sure the OS is not vulnerable. The firewall can be configured to be as secure as possible, but if the OS is not secure, the firewall is vulnerable.

3. D. The GUI clients and administrators are part of the SmartCenter Server installation. Setting up SIC and adding licenses are part of both component installations. Therefore, the answer includes choices A and C.

4. E. The SmartDashboard GUI logs in to the SmartCenter Server, so the Access Control List for the GUI clients is located and configured on the SmartCenter Server. The other choices are all components of the enforcement point installation.

5. C. Although you will eventually have to add subnets for IP addresses behind the firewall to configure your rule base, this step is not part of installing the Check Point software. The other choices are all part of the installation.

6. E. The supported platforms for FireWall-1 are Solaris, Windows NT, Red Hat Linux, Windows 2000, and Nokia IPSO. There are not many operating systems that Check Point NG does not support.

7. E. Because Check Point NG is a more advanced software, it requires more powerful hardware than previous versions of FireWall-1. In order to effectively upgrade, you must boost the RAM, upgrade the OS, update the license, and upgrade the rule bases.

8. B.   The `pkgrm` command is used to remove all the firewall packages in Solaris. The same command can be used in previous Check Point versions on the Solaris platform.

9. A ,C, and E.   The SmartDashboard will run on Windows machines with no additional license required. On Solaris, the GUI will run, but it requires an additional license that is available for an additional cost.

10. D.   The minimum requirement is 32MB, but the recommended amount of RAM is 128MB. For software like Check Point NG, the more memory is available, the better the software will perform. Even 1024MB is not too much memory to run Check Point NG.

11. C.   Solaris 2.8 is the first 64-bit OS supported by VPN-1/FireWall-1 software. Many companies are finding their upgrade to NG to be an opportunity to upgrade their firewalls to Solaris 2.8 in a 64-bit OS.

12. C, D.   The 250-user license means this is a stand-alone installation and not an enterprise installation. Therefore, both the SmartCenter Server and the enforcement point must be loaded on the same machine.

13. A, B, C, D.   IP forwarding is necessary for the OS to be a gateway and eventually a firewall. Without IP forwarding, no packets can pass through the firewall.

14. A, C.   NG supports central and local licenses. In previous versions, Check Point only supported local licensing. For companies with many firewalls, central licensing can make license management much easier.

15. C.   `License.checkpoint.com` was the old way to license Check Point products. The new website is `usercenter.checkpoint.com`.

16. D.   You need one license for the SmartCenter Server and one for each of the enforcement points. GUI clients do not require licenses unless they are running on Unix.

17. B.   The .lic file is a special license file that is included as an attachment when your newly generated license is e-mailed to you. This file can be used to quickly enter a license.

18. B.   The SVN Foundation should always be installed first. The SmartCenter Server should be installed before the enforcement point, and the Policy Server should be installed after the enforcement point.

19. A.   You need to be at version 4.1 to go to NG, so the first order of business is to upgrade the enforcement point to 4.1 and make sure you can push policy to it. After you succeed at that task, the SmartCenter Server is next. Always upgrade the SmartCenter Server first, because with backward compatibility, you can still push policies to 4.1 enforcement points. After successfully upgrading the SmartCenter Server, upgrade the enforcement points to NG.

20. C.   The fingerprint appears the first time you make a connection to the SmartCenter Server. It should be the same fingerprint you saw during the installation.

Chapter 2

Putting Up a Good Defense

THE CCSE EXAM TOPICS COVERED IN THIS CHAPTER INCLUDE:

- ✓ Configuring tracking on a VPN-1/FireWall-1 NG system.
- ✓ List the benefits and limitations of tracking potential hacking attempts against the firewall.
- ✓ SYN flood attacks and the components involved.
- ✓ Using SmartDefense to protect your network from known and unknown attacks.

The main purpose of a firewall is to act as a gateway between the Internet and your internal networks, but with Check Point's firewall product, you can do much more. In addition to controlling what comes into or goes out of your network, you can decide what protocols to statefully inspect, stop denial of service attacks, integrate your Lightweight Directory Access Protocol (LDAP) user database with the firewall, and write scripts so you will be notified of specific logging occurrences. These are just a few of the Check Point options at your disposal.

In this chapter, we will explore your ability to track information and discuss how to set alerts via built-in Check Point functionality or custom scripts. We'll also examine SmartDefense, a component that allows the firewall to detect and prevent certain attacks.

Tracking and Alerting

One important aspect of protecting your network with any security device, especially a firewall, is logging traffic; this log information can be used for troubleshooting, testing, auditing, administration, or litigation. Many companies invest large amounts of money in network monitoring packages to customize tracking and alerting on network devices. Check Point's built-in tracking and alerting options provide convenient logging, auditing, and alerting mechanisms—and you don't have to invest in a third-party product.

VPN-1/FireWall-1 not only allows traffic logging but also allows custom user-defined alerts so you are notified of important logging information. These alerts can be customized to your specific criteria and used for a variety of purposes. For example, you may want to be alerted if the Nimda virus spreads into your internal network. You can configure SmartDefense to match the Nimda or Code Red string originating from your internal network or your demilitarized zone (DMZ) and then track it with an alert that will instantly alert you when SmartDefense is hit with information about the packet including the source IP address. This alert will allow you to stop the spread of the virus.

SmartDashboard lets you select a variety of alert options. To configure a rule for alerting, right-click in the Track element of the rule; a menu similar to the one shown in Figure 2.1 will appear.

FIGURE 2.1   Tracking menu in a rule

As you can see in the figure, the alerting choices for a rule are Alert, SNMP Trap, Mail, UserDefined, UserDefined 2, and UserDefined 3. Every rule in the rule base has these tracking options, so you can configure an alert for every rule. You configure the *user-defined* alerts in the Alert Commands tab in the Global Properties of the firewall.

When the alerts are triggered, they are executed by the *alertd* process—the Check Point alerting daemon—which runs on the SmartCenter Server. The enforcement point detects the alert condition and either sends a notification to the log server or, if the SmartView Status is open, sends a pop-up alert to the SmartView Status, or both. If logs are directed to a machine other than the SmartCenter Server, the alertd process will be running on that machine and the alert will be executed there.

Because everyone's alerting needs are different, VPN-1/FireWall-1 allows you to create user-defined alerts that run your own scripts or applications to further customize the alerting functionality. These scripts can be written using

- C/C++
- Perl
- Bourne Shell
- C-Shell

 Real World Scenario

Custom User-Defined Alerts

Many companies have Intrusion Detections Systems (IDS) running on their networks to detect potential attacks. Network IDS Sensors are usually positioned on each subnet of the firewall to listen to traffic in promiscuous mode and detect attacks using either a signature-based or anomaly-based detection method. IDS sensors can detect attacks, but most products don't have the ability to stop attacks after they are detected. By the time an administrator is alerted to most attacks, the damage is already done. (It's like having a silent car alarm that sends you an alphanumeric page after someone has broken in and stolen your stereo. The text message should say, "Thank you. It has been a pleasure being your thief.")

Check Point's SmartDefense has the ability to detect an attack, block the attack, and send alerts about the attack. Using Check Point's alerting features, an administrator can configure SmartDefense to block known attacks and send a customized alert when an attack occurs. The customized alert can be an e-mail, an alphanumeric message, a screen pop-up, or whatever else the administrator would like to use.

Log and Alert Properties

In VPN-1/FireWall-1 NG, Check Point has predefined some alerts so you don't need to create your own scripts as often. You can see an example of such an alert in Figure 2.2. Notice that the Log and Alert tab of the Global Properties includes a series of events called track options; each track option has an event description and a pull-down menu, so you can choose the type of alert you would like to trigger if the event happens. It's important to remember that SNMP Traps will not work for any alerts if SNMP is not installed on the firewall.

FIGURE 2.2   Log and Alert Tab of the Global Properties

In the configuration shown in Figure 2.2, a successful VPN key exchange will only be logged—it will not generate an alert. However, a connection matched by the Suspicious Activity Monitor (SAM) will generate a pop-up alert. Each of these predefined events, known as track options, can have a separate alert customized to your needs.

Track Options

Track options are predefined events that provide alerts of your choice; they can be used as monitoring or troubleshooting tools. We'll discuss the custom configuration of the choices in the drop-down menus later in this chapter.

For now, let's look at the Track Options portion of the Log and Alert tab in Figure 2.2 so you'll understand what each track option means:

VPN Successful Key Exchange   Executes when a successful VPN key exchange occurs.

VPN Packet Handling Errors   Executes when an encryption or decryption error occurs. This track option provides a brief description of the error, the possible cause, and whether the packet was dropped or rejected.

VPN Configuration & Key Exchange Errors   Executes when a VPN configuration or key exchange error occurs.

IP Options Drop   Executes when a packet with IP options is encountered. These packets are always dropped because they are generally used for probing; so, it's a good idea to log them.

Administrative Notifications   Executes when an administrative or maintenance notification occurs.

SLA Violation   Executes when a Service Level Agreement (SLA) violation occurs. This track option is used with the Check Point SmartView Monitor.

Connection Matched by SAM   Executes when a packet blocked by the Suspicious Activity Monitoring (SAM) is encountered.

Dynamic Object Resolution Failure   Executes when a dynamic object fails to resolve.

Under the Track Options portion of the Log and Alert tab is a section called Logging Modifiers. This section contains a single option: Log Every Authenticated HTTP Connection. When this box is checked, the firewall logs every authenticated HTTP connection.

Time Settings

At the bottom of Figure 2.2, you can see the Time Settings section. The default time settings usually are sufficient, but it is a good idea to understand the settings in case you need to modify them:

Excessive Log Grace Period   This setting allows you to remove redundancy in the SmartView Tracker. The default of 62 seconds means that identical packets will not be logged within 62 seconds of each other, allowing you to minimize repetitive packets in your log.

Log Viewer Resolving Timeout   This setting denotes the amount of time FireWall-1 will spend attempting to resolve IP addresses into names. If names are not resolved when the timeout is reached, the SmartView Tracker will fail to open.

Virtual Link Statistics Logging Interval   Virtual links are used with the Check Point SmartView Monitor. This setting specifies the amount of time between virtual link information packets.

Status Fetching Interval   This setting allows you to configure the frequency rate at which the SmartCenter Server acquires status information from VPN/FireWall-1 NG, FloodGate, and other Check Point modules that it manages.

Alert Commands

Now we're going to look at the Alert Commands tab in the Global Properties; this tab is found below the Log and Alert tab. As shown in Figure 2.3, this tab lets you define what your alerts do.

FIGURE 2.3   Alert Commands tab of the Global Properties

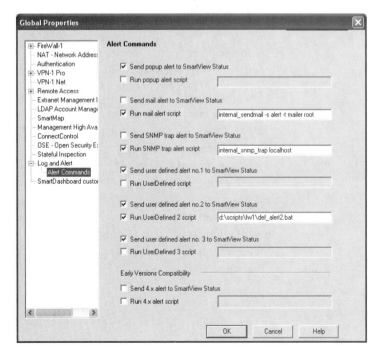

You configure alert commands by first clicking the check box next to the script and then specifying the script in the text box next to it. Above each script is a Send To SmartView Status check box. If you want to also send the alert to the SmartView Status GUI, check this box. The following are the different script options and the Track settings they pertain to in the rule base:

Run Popup Alert Script   This script will be executed when your rule specifies a Track setting of Alert. The SmartView Status GUI should be opened to receive these alerts.

Run Mail Alert Script   This script will be executed when your rule specifies a Track setting of Mail.

Run SNMP Trap Alert Script   This script will be executed when your rule specifies a Track setting of SNMP Trap. SNMP must be running on the firewall for an SNMP Trap to work.

Run UserDefined Script   This script will be executed when your rule specifies a Track setting of UserDefined.

Run UserDefined 2 Script   This script will be executed when your rule specifies a Track setting of UserDefined 2.

Run UserDefined 3 Script   This script will be executed when your rule specifies a Track setting of UserDefined 3.

Run 4.x Alert Script   This script will be executed when your SmartCenter Server is using backward compatibility and managing 4.x firewalls.

Previous versions of FireWall-1 had only one UserDefined alert option, so the same user-defined script had to be used on every rule that needed a customized alert. NG has upgraded the number to three scripts, which is a nice feature if you want to do heavy custom alerting. Scripts can be written to do anything: pop up a simple text message, send an alphanumeric page or e-mail to a cell phone or PDA, or even block a certain connection that meets predefined criteria.

You can find a pre-written alert script called *fwalert* in the $FWDIR/bin directory This script will pop up an alert in the SmartView Status GUI and provide a brief description of what caused the alert so you don't have to go to the log to retrieve the information.

SmartView Status Alerts

The SmartView Status GUI provides more built-in alerting opportunities to help monitor the well being of your Check Point components. In previous versions, the SmartView Status GUI was called the System Status Viewer and provided good health-check monitoring functionality. In Check Point NG, this GUI has evolved into a tool that monitors all Check Point components in greater detail with better alerting capabilities; so, its name has been upgraded to SmartView Status (Status Manager in versions prior to FP3).

Although the SmartView Status is covered in the CCSA Study Guide, we'll discuss its alerting capabilities in this section of the book. Figure 2.4 shows the System Alert tab of the SmartView Status GUI.

FIGURE 2.4 System Alert tab of the SmartView Status GUI

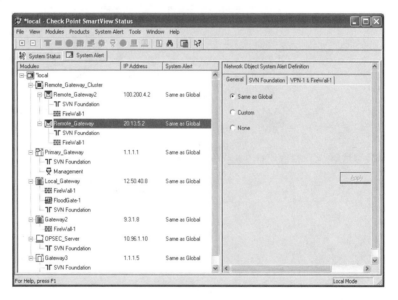

As you can see, each firewall is listed with an SVN Foundation and a VPN-1/FireWall-1 setting to the right of it. For the gateway highlighted in Figure 2.4, we've chosen the Same as Global option for the system alert settings. The Custom option lets you customize your system alert settings for this firewall; these settings may be different from the global settings for all the firewalls being managed by your SmartCenter Server. The global settings that can be set for the SVN Foundation are illustrated in Figure 2.5.

FIGURE 2.5   SVN Foundation system alert tab

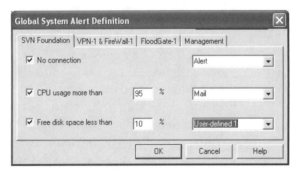

The global settings for the SVN Foundation system alerts relate more to hardware. Figure 2.5 shows that if the SVN Foundation loses connection or there is no connection, Alert is the chosen Track method. If the CPU usage exceeds 95 percent, the Mail script is executed; it could send alphanumeric pages to a group of administrators. If free disk space drops below 10 percent, the User-Defined 1 script is executed; it could send e-mails or alerts to all administrators. You can customize each of these alerts using the corresponding drop-down menu. The alerts are defined in the Alert Commands tab in the Global Properties of the Policy Editor, as discussed earlier in this chapter. Figure 2.6 shows the options for VPN-1/FireWall-1 system alerts.

FIGURE 2.6   VPN-1/FireWall-1 system alert tab

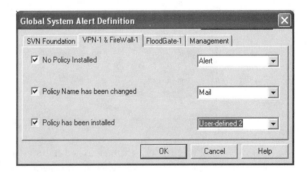

The VPN-1/FireWall-1 global system alerts are based on firewall policies. As Figure 2.6 shows, if the firewall detects that no policy is installed, an alert will be generated. If the policy name has been changed, the Mail alert script will be executed. This alert can come in handy when you're managing several firewalls, because it is possible to accidentally install the wrong policy on the wrong firewall. If this happens, an e-mail alert will be sent so administrators can quickly catch the mistake. When a policy has been installed, the User-Defined 2 alert script will be executed. This could be a script designed to let administrators know that someone from their group has changed or updated the policy. Just like the Global Properties for the SVN Foundation system alerts, these alerts are completely customizable.

You now understand the alerting capabilities of Check Point NG and how they are used. It's time to configure it for yourself and see it work. Exercise 2.1 will guide you through the configuration of an alert and you will be able to use the same guidelines to configure other alerts throughout your Rulebase.

EXERCISE 2.1

Using Alerts

The purpose of this exercise is to set up an alert in the rule base and see it work. You will configure a Stealth rule to send a pop-up alert. If it's configured correctly, an alert will pop up every time a connection attempt is made directly to the firewall. Follow these steps:

1. Create a Stealth rule at the top of your rule base with the Track element set to Alert. These are the specifications of the Stealth rule:

    Source: Any

    Destination: Your firewall

    Service: Any

    Action: Drop

    Track: Alert

2. Go to the Alert Commands tab in the Global Properties.

3. Click the Send Popup Alert to SmartView Status check box.

4. Open the SmartView Status GUI to monitor the alerts.

5. Test the alerts by attempting to FTP or telnet into the firewall specified in the rule.

You should see alerts pop up on your screen. Now test the same procedure with the Mail or UserDefined setting. You can write your own script or batch file to execute.

SmartDefense

Now that you understand alerts and tracking, it's important to learn about SmartDefense, another major component of Check Point firewall protection that was introduced in FP3. Individual components from previous versions of FireWall-1, including anti-spoofing, SYN flood protection, and prevention of web worms, are incorporated into this one component: SmartDefense. This separately licensed component can be updated via a subscription service to Check Point or if you have software subscription you can receive updates for free with each Feature Pack release. You don't have to understand the details of the attacks your system receives—just whether you want to detect and/or prevent them.

Configuring SmartDefense

SmartDefense is in essence an Intrusion Detection System (IDS), but don't let the marketing people at Check Point hear you say that. They categorize it as an "attack detection and prevention feature" which, in this author's humble opinion, is basically the same thing as an IDS. SmartDefense can detect and block attacks based on type and class such as port scanning, known ports checking, and the ping of death, just to name a few. SmartDefense uses Check Point's Stateful Inspection technology to inspect the traffic passing through the firewall and pinpoint attack signatures as well as analyzing the log files looking for specific patterns. Information gleaned by SmartDefense can be implemented and managed from one centralized GUI.

SmartDefense prevents and blocks type-based attacks such as web worms, Denial of Service (DoS), and Distributed Denial of Service (DDoS) attacks. It also provides real-time attack information. SmartDefense is triggered by selecting Policy ➢ SmartDefense in the SmartDashboard or by clicking on the SmartDefense tool bar icon illustrated in Figure 2.7.

FIGURE 2.7 The SmartDefense toolbar icon

Once SmartDefense is engaged, the SmartDefense Settings window will appear (see Figure 2.8). With every option selected in the window on the left, a description of that attack will appear in the window on the right along with the date the attack was last updated. You can specify which attacks to defend against by selecting the check box next to the attack.

FIGURE 2.8 SmartDefense Settings

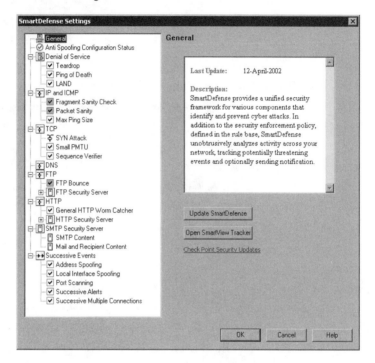

Clicking the Update SmartDefense button will automatically connect you to Check Point to download the latest information. After the update is completed a screen is displayed (like the one shown in Figure 2.9) which details exactly what has been updated.

The Check Point Security Updates link takes you to Check Point's Smart-Defense Subscription Service, where you can learn about each new attack in the Next Generation SmartDefense Advisories. The SmartDefense Subscription Service windows, illustrated in Figure 2.10, shows the Alerts Archive, Downloads Archive, and other services essential to running and keeping track of attacks SmartDefense can detect and prevent.

FIGURE 2.9 Update SmartDefense

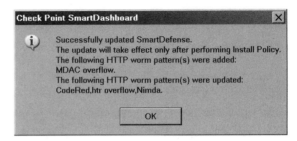

FIGURE 2.10 SmartDefense Subscription Service

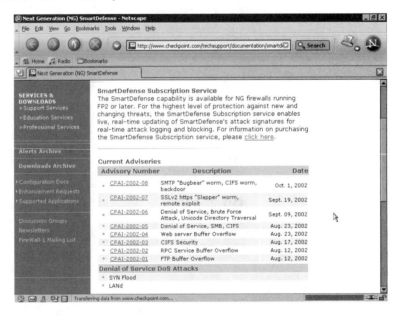

The advisories found in the subscription service describe and categorize the severity of the attack along with Check Point's solution for preventing it. As of the writing of this book, the information on the website is sparse; but I'm sure that as the website matures more information will be added.

In the following sections, we describe each of the SmartDefense settings, including anti-spoofing, Denial of Service, IP, and ICMP.

Anti-Spoofing

You don't configure SmartDefense to prevent anti-spoofing. That functionality still resides in Check Point's Gateway properties. The Anti Spoofing Configuration Status displayed in Figure 2.11 informs you whether any of your firewall interfaces are susceptible to spoofing.

FIGURE 2.11 Anti Spoofing Configuration Status

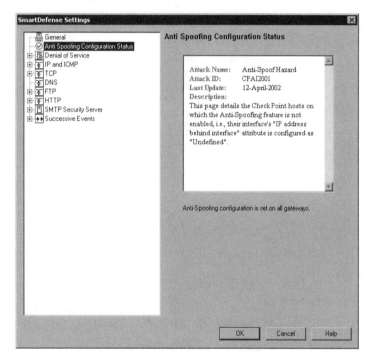

In the example illustrated in Figure 2.11, all firewall interfaces are configured correctly. If one or more of your firewall interfaces are not configured to prevent spoofing, then a warning like the one shown in Figure 2.12 will appear.

The gateway in which the interfaces are not defined correctly appears so you know where to go to make the proper configuration changes to protect your network from spoofed packets. Check Point makes fixing the interface definitions extremely easy by providing an Edit button in SmartDefense that takes you directly to the offending interface(s).

FIGURE 2.12 Incorrectly configured interfaces

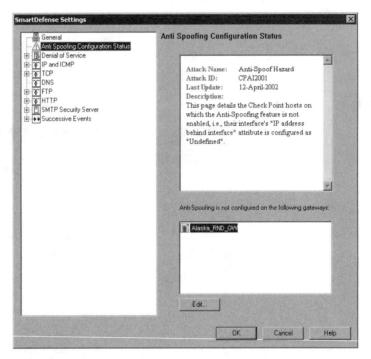

Denial of Service

There are a variety of attacks referred to as a *Denial of Service (DoS)* or *Distributed Denial of Service (DDoS)* attacks. A DoS attack involves one computer attacking another. A DDoS attack involves many computers attacking one computer or a group of computers belonging to one company (such as the June 2002 attacks on Fox News and some Disney websites) at the same time, with the goal of making the network unreachable or disrupting normal network operation.

Check Point lists the Teardrop, Ping of Death and LAND attacks in this category. Figure 2.13 shows these three attacks listed on the left side of the screen.

FIGURE 2.13 Denial of Service attacks

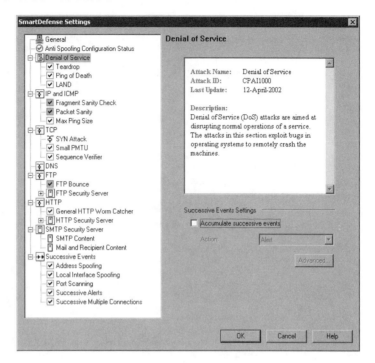

The Accumulate Successive Events option shown in Figure 2.13 was formerly known as CPMAD (Check Point Malicious Activity Detection). Checking the Accumulate Successive Events option under Successive Event Settings activates a process in which the firewall logs are filtered, looking for specific attack patterns. You can modify which attacks patterns you're looking for by toggling the check boxes on/off for specific attacks as described under the Successive Events section later in this chapter (see Figure 2.29). The Successive Events feature runs on the SmartCenter Server (formerly known as the Management Server). Its purpose is to analyze chunks of log data looking for specific patterns. It does not analyze the packets but the log information. Therefore, logs that don't make it to the SmartCenter Server will not be analyzed for these types of attacks. Clicking on the Advanced tab in SmartDefense Settings will display the Advanced Configuration window shown in Figure 2.14.

FIGURE 2.14 Advanced Configuration window

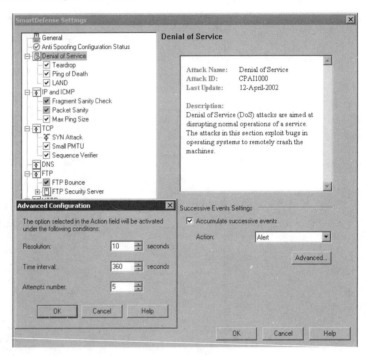

Configuring the options shown in the Advanced window controls the action of Accumulate Successive Events. Resolution, for instance, can be set at a specific interval of time in which log will be examined. For example, if a Resolution of 60 seconds was selected, that is the amount of logs that will be examined at one time looking for that specific pattern. Time Interval is an interval after which information about the attacks will be removed from the state tables. Attempts Number is the number of events that must occur during the Resolution time period for SmartDefense to respond. SmartDefense's response is defined by the Action option selected.

Three Denial of Service attacks are currently screened for in Smart-Defense. If SmartDefense detects any of these attacks, the attacks will be dropped by the firewall and you can choose how you wish to be notified for each attack specifically. Your options are: Log, Alert, Mail, SNMP Trap, User Defined Alert no. 1, User Defined Alert no. 2 or User Defined Alert no.3. Descriptions of each attack are listed below.

Teardrop

The Teardrop attack takes advantage of a TCP/IP weakness in which overlapping IP fragments are not handled correctly. This attack freezes your computer, forcing you to reboot. The default Track option in SmartDefense is Log.

Ping of Death

The Ping of Death attack involves sending an ICMP ping packet that exceeds 65535 octets in length, resulting in an overload that causes a computer to crash. The default Track option in SmartDefense is Log.

LAND

The LAND attack consists of spoofing a packet so that the source IP address and source port are the same as the destination IP address and destination port. The end result of this attack is the crash or automatic reboot of the computer. The default Track option in SmartDefense is Log.

IP and ICMP

The IP and ICMP group listed in the SmartDefense Settings screen allows you to run a comprehensive sequence of layer 3 tests, such as a Fragment Sanity Check, a Packet Sanity Check and a Maximum Ping Size Check (see Figure 2.13).

Fragment Sanity Check

The Fragment Sanity Check is a process that has been a part of FireWall-1 for a while. When a packet is too big, it's fragmented for transport across the network. The INSPECT engine in SmartDefense collects all the packet fragments and virtually reassembles them. This process allows the INSPECT engine to fully inspect all aspects of the packet including its source, destination, and service. This check is always performed your only option is to choose the Track method.

Packet Sanity

The Packet Sanity check in SmartDefense runs layer 3 and 4 checks that include verifying UDP and TCP header lengths and TCP flags, dropping IP options and verifying the packet size.

The Packet Sanity check is always performed by SmartDefense, but you can choose which Track method to use. Included in the configuration of the Packet Sanity check is the ability to Enable Relaxed UDP length verification.

Selecting this option lets the firewall ignore inconsistencies in the UDP length calculation methods caused by some applications. Inclusion of the Enable Relaxed UDP length verification shows foresight by Check Point because UDP length inconsistencies could cause errors and trigger false positives.

Max Ping Size

The Max Ping Size option in SmartDefense allows you to specify the size of the ICMP packets allowed to/through the firewall. Don't confuse this with the Ping of Death option: The Ping of Death is a malformed request packet, whereas Max Ping Size controls the maximum acceptable size of an ICMP echo request.

You can limit the requested data size by selecting the Ping Size, which is set by default to 64 bytes.

TCP

This SmartDefense grouping allows the firewall to test TCP parameters. Using the TCP settings, you can verify and analyze the protocol type and protocol flags, analyze protocol headers for SYN floods, and verify small PMTU and packet sequence numbers. Items covered in the TCP grouping include SYN Attack, Small PMTU, and Sequence Verifier (see Figure 2.13).

SYN Attack

The SYN Attack feature of the SmartDefense Settings protects against SYN flood attacks using SYNDefender Using SmartDefense, you can configure SYNDefender globally or on a gateway by gateway basis. Since SYNDefender is covered in great detail in the current Check Point courseware, we'll discuss it in great detail later in this chapter.

Small PMTU

The Small PMTU SmartDefense option deals with preventing an attack that utilizes TCP maximum segment size (MSS) and Maximum Transfer Unit (MTU) settings. When a TCP connection is set up, both sides communicate their MSS values to each other. The smallest MSS value between the two is used for the connection.

MSS is the link layer MTU minus 40 bytes for the IP and TCP headers.

Figure 2.15 illustrates the options available for Small PMTU.

FIGURE 2.15 Small PMTU

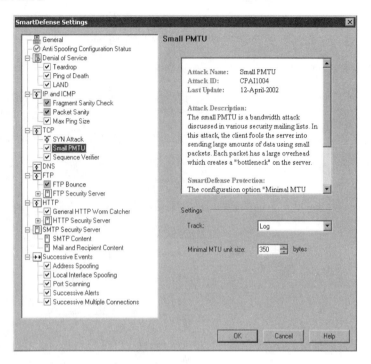

When a packet is destined for a network outside of yours, a Don't Fragment bit is set in the IP header. If a router, switch, or other device between the two hosts has a smaller MTU value than the one set between the two hosts, the device will attempt to fragment the packet. Once set, the Don't Fragment bit will not allow fragmenting to happen, so the device ends up sending a Destination Unreachable message back to the host. If this message is not sent, packets are dropped, a host of errors occurs, and the TCP handshake is never completed. This is how the attack is carried out. In this bandwidth attack, an attacker tricks a server into sending a lot of data but using small packets. This process clogs the server, which is in essence a Denial of Service attack. The Small PMTU setting in SmartDefense allows you to control the Minimal MTU Unit Size so you can avoid this type of attack.

Setting the Minimal MTU Unit Size value too small won't prevent an attack, but setting it too high could deny legitimate requests and degrade performance.

Sequence Verifier

A new feature in FP2 Global Properties (illustrated in Figure 2.16) let you check the sequence number of TCP packets to make sure they were in order.

FIGURE 2.16   Global Properties in FP2

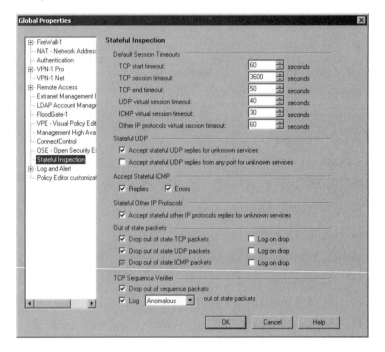

This functionality was moved to SmartDefense in FP3, as you can see in Figure 2.17.

Whether you're dealing with FP2 or FP3, the firewall checks the TCP packet sequence number against the TCP connection state. If a packet matches the TCP session but the sequence numbers aren't correct, the packet is either dropped or stripped of data. There are three tracking options for Sequence Verifier:

- *Anomalous*—Tracks only packets that don't normally appear in a valid/legitimate connection

- *Every*—Tracks every out-of-state packet

- *Suspicious*—Tracks only packets that are unrelated to the connection or packets that seem erroneous

FIGURE 2.17   SmartDefense Sequence Verifier

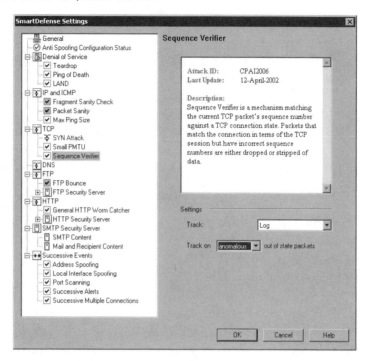

 Turning on Sequence Verifier in SmartDefense activates this option even on gateways that don't support SmartDefense.

 Sequence Verifier will not inspect load-shared connections, and it will not inspect connections after a failover (the connection will be allowed; its sequence will not be verified).

DNS

If the DNS SmartDefense option is selected, the firewall monitors traffic for compliance to RFC 1035: Domain Names - Implementation and Specification. In other words, it checks to see whether the DNS packets are formatted correctly. The DNS option in Smart Defense, illustrated in Figure 2.18, only looks at DNS over UDP (UDP port 53) for queries and not at DNS over TCP (TCP Zone Transfer - TCP port 53).

The DNS feature works only on UDP traffic, not TCP DNS traffic, and it only supports Query and Answer operations. Other DNS operations will be dropped, which will have a negative impact on Windows 2000 or greater domain controllers using Microsoft Active Directory and communicating through the firewall. The only solution is to turn off DNS verification.

FIGURE 2.18 DNS

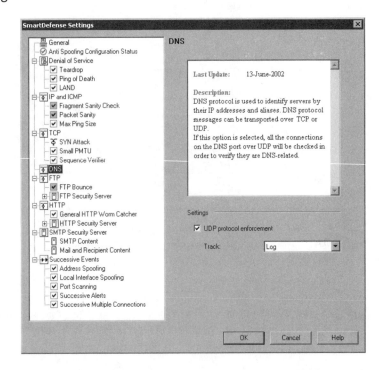

FTP

The FTP (File Transfer Protocol) SmartDefense group essentially has two purposes: It can protect your system against a specific FTP attack called FTP Bounce, and it lets you configure your FTP Security Server. Figure 2.19 illustrates the many FTP options for SmartDefense, including FTP Bounce and the features of the FTP Security Server.

FIGURE 2.19 SmartDefense for FTP

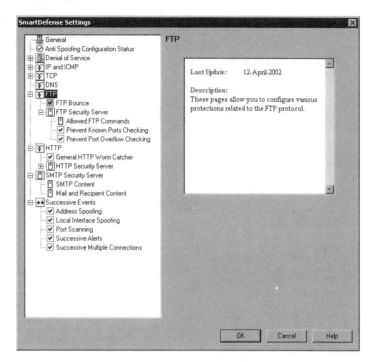

FTP Bounce

The FTP Bounce attack takes advantage of a design flaw in FTP. Port 20 is where the FTP PORT command negotiates a random high port for PASV transport of FTP data files. RFC 959, which describes FTP, dictates that the negotiated high port be allowed to any IP address and any port. The FTP Bounce attack takes advantage of this and the attacker can open a connection to a machine of their choosing for illegitimate purposes. You can select the Track option for notification if a FTP Bounce attack is detected.

FTP Security Server

The firewall FTP Security Server provides authentication and content security services (see Chapter 4,"Content Security," for more details on the FTP Security Server). Usually the FTP Security Server (shown in Figure 2.20) is invoked by rules in your rule base that specify an FTP Resource or User Authentication. Selecting the Configurations Apply To All Connections radio button forces all FTP connections through the FTP Security Server regardless of whether your rule base contains an authentication or resource rule.

FIGURE 2.20   FTP Security Server

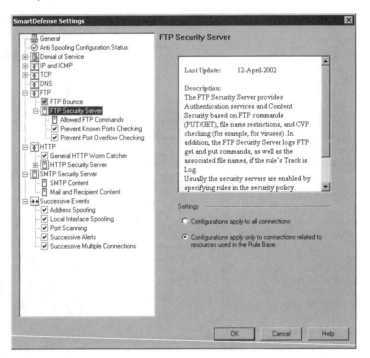

  As of this writing, no data is available concerning the kind of performance degradation selecting Configurations Apply To All Connections causes on the firewall.

Selecting the default option of Configurations Apply Only To Connections Related To Resources Used In The Rule Base will cause the FTP Security Server to be invoked only when a resource or authentication rule in the rule base triggers it.

You need to take into consideration three further settings when setting up the FTP Security Server: Allowed FTP Commands, Prevent Known Port Checking, and Prevent Port Overflow Checking:

Allowed FTP Commands   The Allowed FTP Commands option, illustrated in Figure 2.21, gives you granular control over the FTP commands the FTP Security Server will respond to. You can set Acceptable commands and Blocked commands.

FIGURE 2.21 Allowed FTP commands

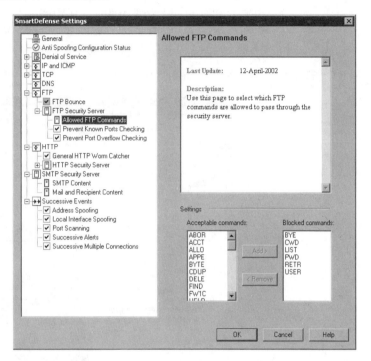

Prevent Known Port Checking The Prevent Known Port Checking
option allows you to specify whether you want the FTP Security Server to
allow connections to well-known ports. This option also provides another
line of defense against the FTP Bounce attack by not allowing a connection to a well-known port.

Prevent Port Overflow Checking Prevent Port Overflow Checking is
another component to help prevent the FTP Bounce Attack. Turning on
this option turns off the checks that prevent numerous instances of connections from/to the same port.

HTTP

The HTTP settings of the SmartDefense configuration are important because
they protect your system against attacks utilizing or found in HTTP or the
HTML language used on the Web. HTTP establishes connections to the Web
and transmits web pages using a web browser.

The HTTP group of settings has two purposes: It can protect your network against HTTP worms and it is where you can configure your HTTP Security Server. Figure 2.22 illustrates the list of options available in the HTTP portion of the SmartDefense Settings screen.

FIGURE 2.22   SmartDefense for HTTP

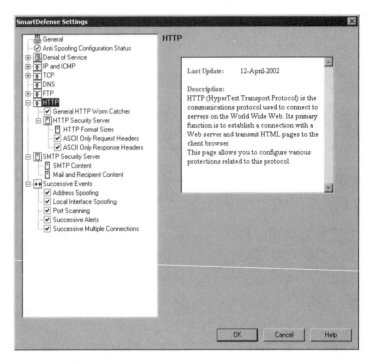

General HTTP Worm Catcher

A *worm* is a program or algorithm that replicates maliciously over a network by continually sending copies of itself to infect other machines. FireWall-1 allows you to define worm signatures in SmartDefense so that this traffic can be thwarted. By default, Code Red, Nimda, and htr overflow are defined in the settings, as you can see in Figure 2.23.

You can add new patterns by clicking the Add button, or you can import new patterns from Check Point's website. You can also manually enter new patterns using the following format:

```
:Attack1 (
  :worm_name (<name>)
  :pattern (<a regular expression>)
)
```

FIGURE 2.23 General HTTP Worm Catcher

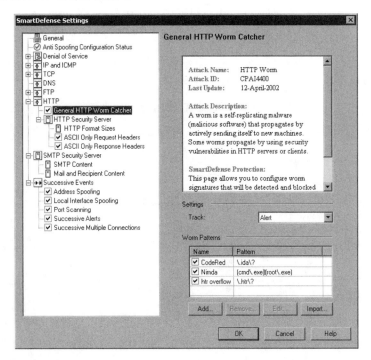

Worm detection takes place at the kernel level and does not invoke the HTTP Security Server. If you configured an URI resource in FP2 to prevent this type of traffic, then after your upgrade to FP3, you must remove that resource and configure worm blocking in SmartDefense.

If General HTTP Worm Catcher is enabled and the policy is installed, but the previous policy did not have this option turned on, then connections started before installation of the policy will be ended.

General HTTP Worm Catcher connections will not transfer in a high-availability configuration failover.

HTTP Security Server

Usually the HTTP Security Server is invoked by rules in your rule base that specify a HTTP Resource or User Authentication. Figure 2.24 illustrates the HTTP Server options in SmartDefense.

FIGURE 2.24 HTTP Security Server

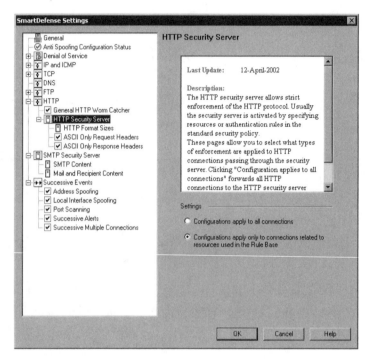

Selecting the Configurations Apply To All Connections radio button forces all HTTP connections through the HTTP Security Server, regardless of whether there is an authentication or resource rule in your rule base.

As of this writing, no data is available concerning the kind of performance degradation selecting Configurations Apply To All Connections causes on the firewall.

Selecting the default option of Configurations Apply Only To Connections Related To Resources Used In The Rule Base will cause the HTTP Security Server to be invoked only when a resource or authentication rule in the rule base triggers it.

The HTTP Security Server has three further configuration features you must take into consideration: HTTP Format Sizes, ASCII Only Request Headers, and ASCII Only Response Headers.

HTTP Format Sizes   The HTTP Format Sizes SmartDefense option, illustrated in Figure 2.25, allows you to set the following HTTP parameters:

- *Maximum URL Length* (default 2048 bytes)—Affects HTTP client request or redirect requests
- *Maximum HTTP Header Length* (default 1000 bytes)—Affects HTTP client request and HTTP server reply
- *Maximum Number Of HTTP Headers* (default 500)—Affects HTTP client request and HTTP server reply

Check Point's default value of 2k for HTTP Format size may prevent your users from accessing some websites. If this feature is used you will have to tweak this setting to find the optimal HTTP format size for your particular web traffic.

FIGURE 2.25   HTTP Format Sizes

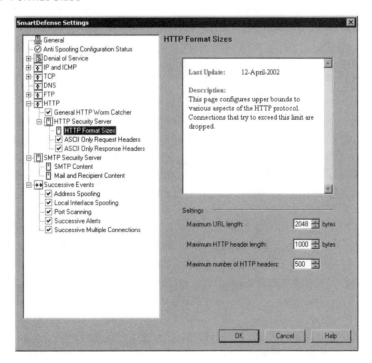

Any connections that exceed the limits you set will be dropped.

ASCII Only Request Headers The ASCII Only Request Headers option seen in Figure 2.25 checks to make sure all HTTP request headers are ASCII only, which prevents malicious content from entering your network through HTTP protocol headers.

ASCII Only Response Headers The ASCII Only Response Headers option checks to make sure all HTTP response headers are ASCII only.

There is an excellent white paper that goes into great detail about HTTP Header Exploitation. You can find it at `http://www.cgisecurity.com/lib/bill/William_Bellamy_GCIH.html`.

SMTP Security Server

SMTP SmartDefense maintains control over the SMTP protocol as it passes through or to the firewall. Usually the SMTP Security Server is invoked by rules in your rule base that specify a SMTP Resource. Selecting the Configurations Apply To All Connections radio button, shown in Figure 2.26, forces all SMTP connections through the SMTP Security Server regardless of whether your rule base includes an authentication or resource rule.

As of this writing, no data is available concerning the kind of performance degradation selecting Configurations Apply To All Connections causes on the firewall.

Selecting the default option, Configurations Apply Only To Connections Related To Resources Used In The Rule Base, will cause the SMTP Security Server to be invoked only when a resource or authentication rule in the rule base triggers it.

SMTP Content

The SMTP Content settings, shown in Figure 2.27, allow you to set limitations on SMTP variants.

FIGURE 2.26 SmartDefense for SMTP

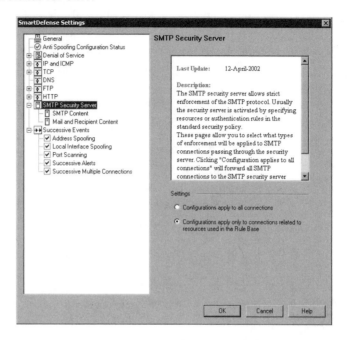

FIGURE 2.27 SMTP Content

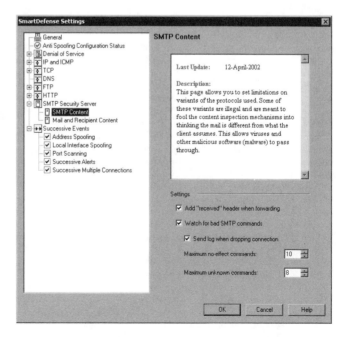

Add "Received" Header When Forwarding forwards SMTP headers to a Content Vectoring Protocol (CVP) server (check out Chapter 4 for more information on CVP servers). Watch For Bad SMTP Commands limits the commands the firewall will respond to. For example, the firewall will not recognize the WIZ or DEBUG commands, which are common SMTP attacks. The Maximum No-Effect Commands and Maximum Unknown Commands options define the number of commands that can be sent during the SMTP protocol exchange without producing an adverse affect.

Mail and Recipient Content

The Mail and Recipient Content Settings, shown in Figure 2.28, are fairly self explanatory. The one worthy of mentioning is Perform Aggressive MIME Strip, which can supercede any SMTP resource settings. If this option is selected, the entire message is scanned for MIME information. If it's unchecked, only the mail headers section and the MIME headers of each MIME part are scanned. If MIME information is located, it will be stripped.

Settings in Mail and Recipient Content are enforced only if a SMTP resource rule is set, regardless of whether Configurations Apply To All Connections is selected under SMTP Security Server.

Successive Events

Successive Events was formerly known as CPMAD (Check Point Malicious Activity Detection) in pre-NG FP2 and 4.x versions of FireWall-1.This feature runs on the SmartCenter Server.

Successive Events does not provide active detection. Instead, it reads the firewall logs and tries to match sections of the log against defined attack profiles (Successive Events also affects Denial of Service attack detection. See the Denial of Service section earlier in this chapter for more details). You have the option to turn off Successive Events, to define your own attack profiles, or to decide which attacks you wish to scan for. The Settings option shown in Figure 2.29 determines how much memory (Max Memory Allocation Size) is allocated to grab logs for profile matching. If more memory is required than is allocated, the Successive Events check will cease working without warning.

FIGURE 2.28 Mail and Recipient Content

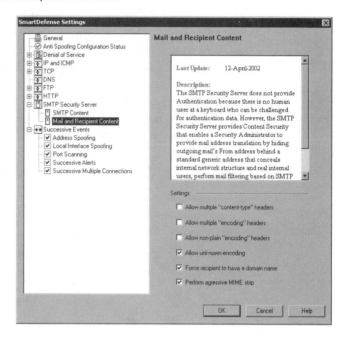

FIGURE 2.29 Successive Events

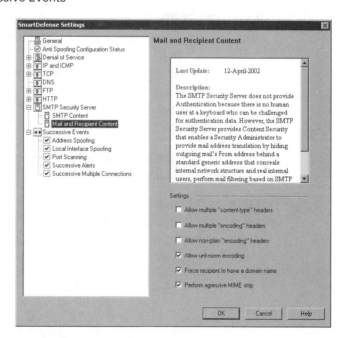

The Reset Accumulated Events Every option is set in seconds and sets how often the memory is cleared (or deleted from the SmartDefense internal tables) to begin collecting logs anew. Setting this option high reduces CPU usage. Unfortunately, setting it high also increases memory requirements. Logging Attempts Interval determines a set number of logs that are analyzed. For example, if you set this option to 20 seconds, it's unlikely that you would detect a slow port scan. Setting it higher increases the amount of memory required but also increases the likelihood that you will detect an attack.

Max Logging Attempts defines how many events must occur within the logging attempt interval for the firewall to consider it an attack and generate an alert.

WARNING

If you are using CPMAD with a pre-FP3 version, you'll find that upon FP3 upgrade, CPMAD stops functioning. You must update the pre-FP3 $FWDIR/conf/cpmad_rulebase.conf by either downloading the FP3 version of the file from Check Point's website or extracting the file from the FP3 CD.

Successive Events Options

There are currently five different options for Successive Events in FP3 as seen in Figure 2.29.

ADDRESS SPOOFING

Spoofing is masquerading the source IP address of a packet to make it appear as if it was coming from somewhere other than the real address. The firewall can detect these packets only based on its own IP addresses. For example, if your firewall has an internal network defined with the network address of 10.0.0.0/8 and the firewall sees a packet with an IP address from this network on its external interface, the firewall will drop the packet as a spoofed packet. If the firewall does not recognize the source IP address of a packet as a defined network the firewall protects, then even if the packet is spoofed, the firewall will allow it through. Address Spoofing is logged by default.

LOCAL INTERFACE SPOOFING

The Local Interface Spoofing attack is similar to a LAND attack (described in the Denial of Service section earlier in this chapter) except that the IP addresses it spoofs are the IP addresses of the gateway itself.

PORT SCANNING

SmartDefense will scan the firewall logs looking for a large number of communication attempts from the same source IP address to connect to ports on an explicit destination address.

SUCCESSIVE ALERTS

A Successive Alerts attack occurs when an excessive number of firewall alerts are produced which overloads the firewall.

SUCCESSIVE MULTIPLE CONNECTIONS

The Successive Multiple Connections option searches for an abnormal number of connections from a single source IP address destined for a specific destination IP address or destination port.

For all features of the Successive Events configuration—Address Spoofing, Local Interface Spoofing, Port Scanning, Successive Alerts, and Successive Multiple Connections—you can configure Advanced features by clicking the Advanced button of each Successive Event screen. Here you can specify how many logs are examined, how long the logs are stored in the INPSECT State tables before being cleared and how many attempts must be detected before SmartDefense considers an attack to have occurred. Each feature has the following options:

- *Resolution*—Determines the interval of successive logs that will be examined for an attack pattern

- *Time Interval*—An interval after which information about the attacks will be removed from the state tables

- *Attempts Number*—The number of events that must occur during the Resolution time period for SmartDefense to respond

SmartDefense's response for each selection of each Successive Event is defined by which Action option is selected.

Table 2.1 lists the default settings for each Successive Event interval.

TABLE 2.1 Successive Event Default Intervals

Type of Successive Event	Resolution Default	Time Interval Default	Attempts Number Default
Address Spoofing	300 seconds	3600 seconds	10 attempts
Local Interface Spoofing	10 seconds	360 seconds	15 attempts

TABLE 2.1 Successive Event Default Intervals *(continued)*

Type of Successive Event	Resolution Default	Time Interval Default	Attempts Number Default
Port Scanning	1 second	60 seconds	50 attempts
Successive Alerts	60 seconds	600 seconds	100 attempts
Successive Multiple Connections	10 seconds	60 seconds	50 attempts

SmartView Tracker

The SmartView Tracker, formerly known as the Log Viewer in pre-FP3 versions of NG, does not appear in the SmartDefense Settings screen. Instead, you can access it through the Open SmartView Tracker button in SmartDefense or by opening SmartView Tracker and double-clicking on SmartDefense in the Objects Tree. Figure 2.30 shows the SmartView Tracker.

FIGURE 2.30 SmartView Tracker SmartDefense filter

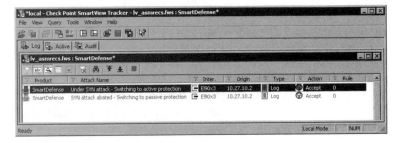

Figure 2.30 shows specific SmartDefense information. By double-clicking on the log that interests you—for example, the Under SYN Attack, you can view the details of the attack. Figure 2.31 shows an enlarged view of an SYN Attack log. It shows the name of the attack, where the attack originated, the action taken in regard to the attack, and a host of other important bits of information about the attack.

FIGURE 2.31 Record Details

Record Details		×
Number		27
Date		2Jun2002
Time		18:35:13
Product		SmartDefense
Attack Name		Under SYN attack - Switching to active protection
Interface		EI90x3
Origin		10.27.10.2
Type		Log
Action		Accept
Service		
Source		
Destination		255.255.255.255
Protocol	UDP	udp
Rule		0
NAT rule number		
NAT additional rule number		
Source Port		
User		
XlateSrc		
XlateDst		
XlateSPort		
XlateDPort		
Partner		
Community		
Information		

SYNDefender

Before we talk about SYNDefender options, let's review the building blocks of a *TCP/IP handshake*. Figure 2.32 illustrates the TCP/IP handshake, which is an analogy for how computers communicate with one another.

FIGURE 2.32 TCP/IP handshake

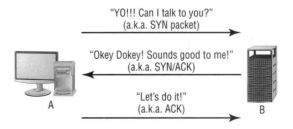

When computer A wants to talk to computer B, the initiator of the "conversation" (in this example, computer A) sends a SYN packet requesting a connection and specifying the port it wants to talk on. If computer B agrees to talk with computer A, it replies with a SYN/ACK packet and a queue for the connection. To complete the transaction, computer A sends an ACK packet to computer B; the TCP/IP handshake is complete, and the connection is opened. After the connection is opened, data can flow between the computers.

Crackers and hackers can attack your network by exploiting a weakness in the TCP/IP protocol itself. Such a DoS attack is called a *SYN flood*. A SYN flood is actually a combination of two different techniques: a SYN flood and IP spoofing. Figure 2.33 shows an example of a SYN flood.

FIGURE 2.33   A SYN flood

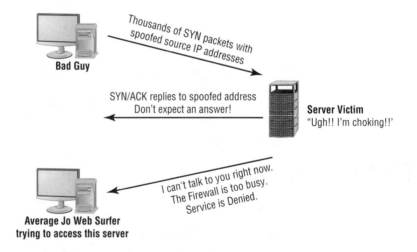

The attackers spoof their source IP address to some unreachable address (RFC 1918 addresses are usually good choices) and then send a flood of SYN packets with the spoofed source IP address to the server they want to take out of commission. Following the TCP/IP protocol, the victim responds to each SYN packet with a SYN/ACK packet. The problem lies in the fact that the victim is sending the SYN/ACK packets to an IP address that will never reply with an ACK packet to complete the handshake. The attackers' goal is to flood the victim with so many packets that the server's *backlog queue* (a TCP/IP stack table on a server that keeps track of open connections) fills up, waiting for ACK packets that will never come.

This situation leaves the victim unable to respond to legitimate requests for communication. If the bad guys continue the flood, they can keep the server out of commission indefinitely.

When the backlog queue limit is reached, an attempt to establish another connection will fail until one of the backlogged connections is established, is reset, or times out.

Why Use SYNDefender?

That's a good question. The answer depends on whom you talk to. Some people are of the philosophy that you don't need to use this feature unless you have been hit with a SYN flood. Others are of the mindset that you should prevent any type of attack if at all possible. Still others sit in the middle of the argument and use this feature to monitor but not necessarily prevent SYN floods. Regardless of your opinion, by the end of this section you will understand your different options and be able to make an informed decision about your security stance with regard to SYN floods.

Check Point offers the SYNDefender feature (available since version 3.x), which can protect your servers against a SYN flood attack. The next section describes the different methods and how to deploy them.

SYNDefender Modes

What does a SYN flood have to do with a Check Point firewall if the attack is destined for a server that you want publicly available to people on the Internet? Check Point's SYNDefender options put the firewall between the attackers and the server they want to attack, creating a buffer to thwart the attack.

Depending on your version of Check Point FireWall-1, you may have a variety of SYNDefender options; all of them are integrated into the INSPECT engine:

- Versions 4.0 and 4.1 support only *SYN Gateway* and *Passive SYN Gateway*.

- Version NG FCS supports *SYN Relay*, SYN Gateway, and Passive SYN Gateway.

- Versions NG FP1 and beyond supports SYN Relay and Passive SYN Gateway.

- Version FP3 can defend against a SYN flood either on a per-firewall basis or through SmartDefense.

In the following sections, we'll discuss Check Point's options for defending against SYN floods across all NG versions. The methods we will cover are SYN Gateway, SYN Relay, and Passive SYN Gateway.

SYNDefender was a global property in version 4.1: If activated, it affected every firewall you controlled. However, it is a gateway-specific property in NG up to FP2: You can choose to turn it on or off for each individual firewall you control. In FP3, you can do both. You can configure it on a firewall-by-firewall basis or globally configure it through SmartDefense.

For SYNDefender to be effective against a SYN flood attack, the reset timer must be short enough to keep the server backlog queue from filling up, but long enough to ensure that users with slow connections are able to connect. SYN Gateway solves this dilemma by having the firewall send an ACK packet to the server in response to the SYN/ACK packet that is sent to the client. This step completes the handshake between the server and the firewall, thereby removing the connection from the backlog queue and opening the connection to the server (as far as the server is concerned). Because the backlog queue is kept clear, the server can wait longer before resetting connections that have not actually been completed between the server and the client. The firewall acts as a buffer between the server and the Internet. SYN Gateway works as depicted in Figure 2.34.

When the client sends a SYN packet to the server, the firewall allows the packet through and makes note of it in its connections table (step 1). The server responds with a SYN/ACK packet, which the firewall allows through to the client (step 2), again making a note in its connections table. The firewall responds by sending an ACK packet to the server (step 3), thereby completing the TCP/IP handshake, and starts the reset timer. If the firewall receives an ACK packet from the client (step 4), then the handshake is completed on the client side too, and data begins flowing. If the firewall doesn't receive an ACK, or receives something other than the expected ACK (step 5), then the connection to the server is closed. This closure is accomplished by sending a RST packet to the server.

FIGURE 2.34 SYN Gateway at work

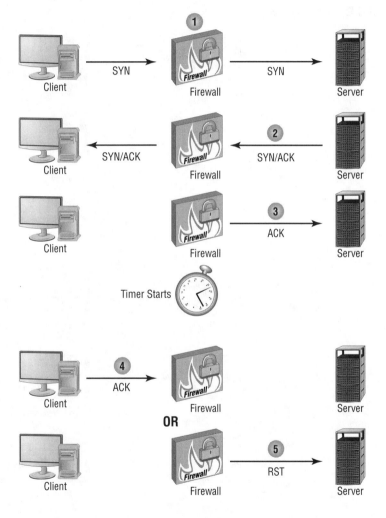

The effectiveness of SYN Gateway is based on quickly moving connection attempts out of the backlog queue. SYN Gateway is only available as an option for backward compatibility with 4.x versions of FireWall-1 up to and including FP3.

SYN Relay counters a SYN flood by making sure the TCP/IP handshake is valid before sending a SYN packet to the server. SYN Relay, illustrated in Figure 2.35, is a high-performance kernel-level process that acts as a relay mechanism at the connection level.

FIGURE 2.35 SYN Relay

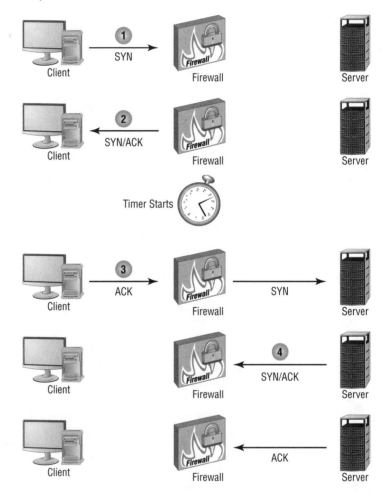

The firewall intercepts the client SYN packet destined for the server (step 1). The firewall does not pass the SYN packet to the server but acts on its behalf, sending a SYN/ACK packet to the client (step 2) and starting the reset timer. If the client sends an ACK packet, the handshake (step 3) is completed between the firewall and the client. The firewall then initiates the handshake on the server side; once it's completed (step 4), data begins to flow. Incidentally, SYNDefender correctly translates the connection sequence numbers, which are now different for each half of the connection. If the firewall doesn't receive an ACK packet before its reset timer expires, or if it receives a RST packet when an ACK or SYN/ACK packet is expected, it kills the connection immediately.

If the client tries to contact a server that has been taken out of commission by a SYN flood, it will first connect and then get a RST. (Normally the server would send a SYN/ACK.) This process will not adversely affect the client.

The advantage of using SYN Relay is that the server doesn't receive any invalid connection attempts. If the server has limited memory and/or is often overloaded, then this method of filtering invalid connection attempts can help in the event of a SYN flood attack.

If SYN Relay is deployed, users making valid connection attempts may experience a slightly longer setup time.

SYN Relay is *not* supported for pre-NG firewalls.

Passive SYN Gateway is like SYN Gateway, but it waits for the client's ACK packet before completing the handshake to the server. Therefore, the connection stays in the server's backlog queue but times out after the firewall's reset time period (which is configurable and usually much shorter than the backlog queue's timeout period). The connections are moved out of the backlog queue so quickly that they don't have time to fill up the queue. Passive SYN Gateway is depicted in Figure 2.36.

The client sends a SYN packet to the server, which the firewall allows through and notes in its connection table (step 1). When the firewall sees the SYN/ACK packet from the server bound for the client (step 2), it starts its reset timer. The firewall then proxies the SYN/ACK packet to the client (step 3). If the client sends an ACK packet (step 4), the firewall stops its timer and allows the packet through, and the connection is complete. If the client doesn't send an ACK packet in the allotted reset time (step 5), the firewall sends a RST packet to the server to free up the connection.

FIGURE 2.36 Passive SYN Gateway

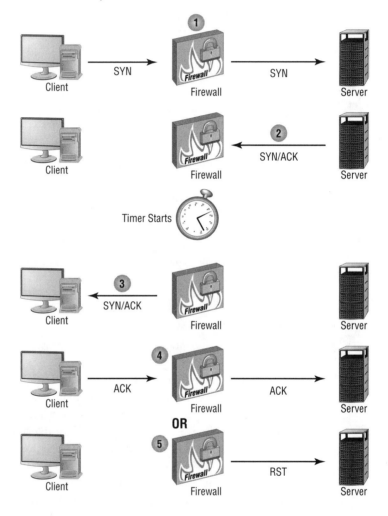

Passive SYN Gateway gives you an option that SYN Relay does not: You can configure the maximum protected sessions. You can set the number of connections (the default is 5000) that can be maintained in an internal connection table maintained by SYNDefender. If the table fills up, SYNDefender will not examine new connections.

Passive SYN Gateway offers two advantages:

- There is no delay in connection setup time for users establishing valid connections.

- Very little overhead is imposed on the firewall.

Configuring SYNDefender

Although the way SYNDefender works has not really changed between version 4.x and NG, its deployment method has changed. And, unfortunately, the deployment methods have changed from Feature Pack to Feature Pack since NG was released in August 2001. In 4.1, if SYNDefender was enabled and configured, it was enforced on all firewalls that your Management Server controlled. For example, you did not have the option to configure SYNDefender on an external firewall and turn it off on an internal firewall. NG now gives you that option: It lets you configure SYNDefender on a firewall-by-firewall basis.

In FP2, a backward compatibility option still allows SYNDefender to be configured if you have an NG Management Server controlling 4.x firewalls. By going to Policy ➤ Global Properties, as shown in Figure 2.37, you can configure SYNDefender backward compatibility options for 4.x firewalls.

FIGURE 2.37   How to open Global Properties

Keep in mind that the settings shown in Figure 2.38 apply only to fire-walled gateways prior to NG.

FIGURE 2.38 SYNDefender options for firewalled gateways before NG

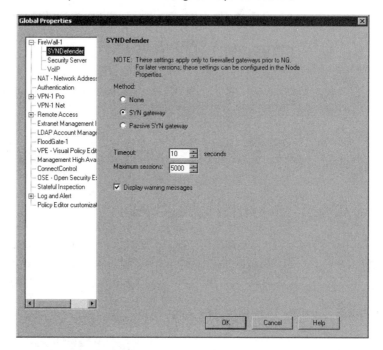

For NG versions FCS, FP1 and FP2, these properties are configured specifically for each Check Point gateway, by editing the gateway on which you want to deploy SYNDefender in the Policy Editor. SYNDefender is listed under the Advanced option, as shown in Figure 2.39. The default defense method is None.

If you select the SYN Relay option (see Figure 2.40), the Timeout for SYN Attack Identification option becomes available (the default setting is 10 seconds). It specifies how long the firewall waits for an ACK from the client before killing the connection.

FIGURE 2.39 Host-specific SYNDefender options

FIGURE 2.40 SYN Relay options

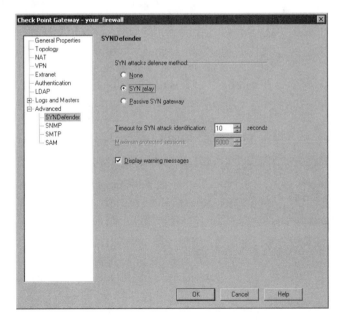

If you select Passive SYN Gateway (see Figure 2.41), the Maximum Protected Sessions option also becomes available.

FIGURE 2.41 Passive SYN Gateway options

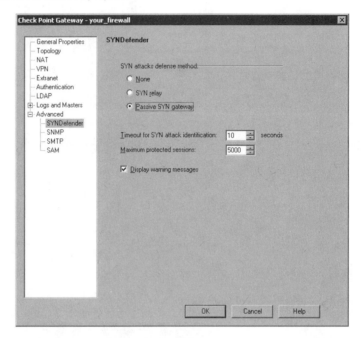

It specifies the max number of connection attempts the FW will accept before dropping all further connections from that specific source. This number can be modified to fit your specific needs. If you change the value, the new value will not take effect until the security policy is reinstalled. The Display Warning Messages option (which is turned on by default) prints console messages regarding SYNDefender status.

For AIX platforms, the new Maximum Protected Sessions value takes effect after you install the Security Policy and then stop and restart the firewall.

In FP3, SYNDefender options changed once again, as you can see from Figure 2.42.

FIGURE 2.42 Gateway-specific SYNDefender options

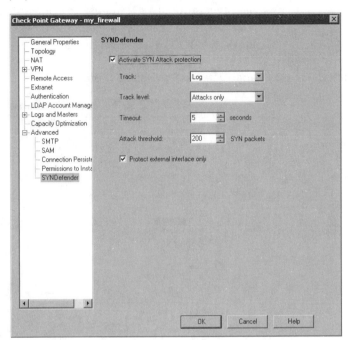

This gateway option is only available if the Override Module's SYNDefender configuration option is turned off in SmartDefense (see Figure 2.43). Selecting Active SYN Attack Protection will protect you against SYN floods on this specific gateway. Select the desired Track option and then the Track Level:

- *None*—This gateway will not be protected against a SYN flood.

- *Attacks Only*—SmartDefense will kick in and make sure the connection is valid before allowing the connection to the server. In essence, it works like SYN Relay.

- *Individual SYNs*—If this option is selected, the firewall does not simulate the packet but waits for the ACK before passing it on to the server. In essence, it works like Passive SYN Gateway.

The Timeout option determines how long SYNDefender waits for the ACK before deciding the connection is a SYN flood. Attack Threshold controls the maximum number of SYN packets being examined at one time by the INSPECT engine. Protect External Interfaces Only allows you to remove your internal interfaces from having to process SYN attack information since a majority of SYN floods are against the external interface.

SYNDefender can also be configured through SmartDefense. Figure 2.43 shows the SYN Attack screen in the SmartDefense Settings area.

FIGURE 2.43   SmartDefense SYNDefender options

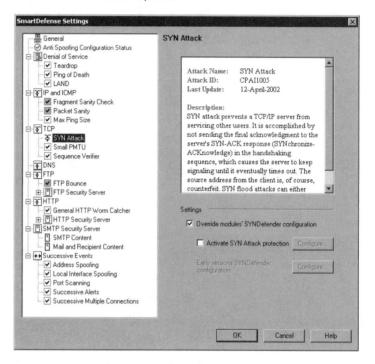

By default, SmartDefense can allow the gateway settings to take precedence or you can override the defaults by selecting Override Module's SYNDefender Configuration. Selecting this option activates the Activate SYN Attack Protection option. Selecting the Activate SYN Attack Protection check box triggers the Configure button, shown in Figure 2.44.

The options in Figure 2.44 are identical to the gateway-specific setting described earlier in this section. If Override Module's SYNDefender Configuration is not selected, the Configure button beside Early Versions SYNDefender Configuration is available. Figure 2.45 shows the Early Versions SYNDefender Configuration option.

FIGURE 2.44 Activate SYN Attack Protection options

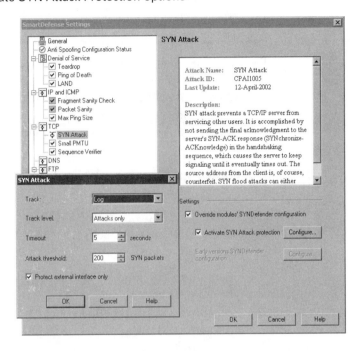

FIGURE 2.45 Early Versions SYNDefender Configuration

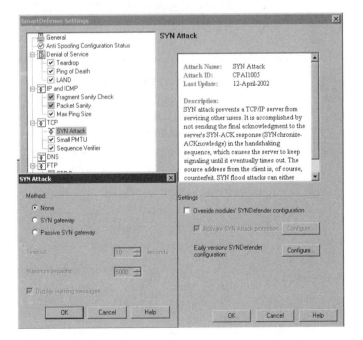

The settings in the Early Versions SYNDefender Configuration affect only pre-NG versions of FireWall-1.

If you are upgrading from earlier NG versions to FP3 and are licensing Smart-Defense, keep in mind that all previous SYNDefender configurations move to SmartDefense and SYNDefender defaults to Off. If you wish to configure SYN-Defender individually for each gateway, the Override Modules option under SYN Attack in SmartDefense must be turned off.

Guidelines for Deploying SYNDefender

Now that you understand how the different SYNDefender options work, you need to decide how to deploy SYNDefender. To ensure that you are deploying SYNDefender properly, per Check Point's guidelines, follow these recommendations:

- Because a SYN flood is a DoS attack and not a security breach, it may be more effective to deploy SYNDefender only after a SYN attack actually occurs. After all, if you are not currently under attack, why turn on SYNDefender?

- If you want to be notified when you come under attack, use Passive SYN Gateway with the Maximum Protected Sessions option set to 50 or less.

You may have to do some tweaking to get the correct timeout setting for your environment. If the timeout is too short, valid connections could fail. If it is too long, SYN flood attacks may affect your network. For this reason, Check Point recommends using Passive SYN Gateway as a monitoring tool along with information in SmartView Tracker to identify SYN flood attacks.

- If SYN flood attacks are a reality for you, then SYN Relay is the option of choice. It provides complete protection against a SYN flood, at the cost of increased memory usage and a slight delay in connection setup time.

- Check Point recommends that SYN Gateway *not* be used. However, that's a moot point, because SYN Gateway isn't an option in NG since FP1.

Other Important Information

You should know a few other important things about SYNDefender:

- Passive SYN Gateway doesn't protect a Nokia gateway. Use SYN Relay instead.

- On Windows platforms, SYNDefender only works when IP forwarding is enabled.

- When you're upgrading from 4.1, the SYNDefender method may change from SYN Gateway to None (this makes sense, because SYN Gateway isn't an option in NG). Be sure you check all your Global Property settings after an upgrade.

- SYNDefender doesn't work in a high-availability configuration because the SYNDefender kernel state table is not synchronized.

Summary

Configuring your firewall for alerts can provide you with helpful information for monitoring, troubleshooting, and protecting your firewall. Predefined tracking options are available, such as pop-up alerts, e-mail alerts, and SNMP Traps. Every rule in the firewall rule base can be set up with an alert as a tracking option if you choose. NG includes predefined events that you can configure for alerts in the Log and Alert tab of the Global Properties. VPN-1/FireWall-1 allows you to write custom scripts to enhance the tracking and alerting capabilities of your firewall; you can add these alerting scripts in the Alert Commands tab of the Global Properties. These scripts can be written in C/C++, C-Shell, Perl, or Bourne Shell.

SmartDefense provides attack detection and prevention capabilities for the Check Point firewall. With SmartDefense, administrators can block specific known attacks that a firewall would not be able to detect. A firewall rule base protects a corporate network with static, predefined rules. SmartDefense is an extension of the firewall that protects a corporate network dynamically, by detecting for known attacks and blocking them.

Using the alerting capabilities built into Check Point NG, administrators are able to receive custom alerts when attacks are detected and/or blocked by SmartDefense. These alerts can keep an administrator aware of what kinds of attacks are targeted for their LAN. Administrators can be alerted by e-mail, cell phone, pager, and other methods.

SYNDefender is a part of SmartDefense. The three methods available are SYN Relay, SYN Gateway, and Passive SYN Gateway, although SYN Gateway is no longer an option after NG FP1. SYN Relay will only allow valid connections to the server. SYN Gateway completes the handshake with the server while waiting for the connection to complete on the client side. Passive SYN Gateway starts the connection process to the server when it receives the first SYN packet, but doesn't complete the handshake on either side until the valid ACK packet is received from the client. In pre-NG versions of FireWall-1, SYNDefender was a Global Property; in NG, it is a gateway-specific property up until FP2 and then as of FP3 you can configure it either globally or gateway by gateway. Check Point recommends using Passive SYN Gateway for monitoring and SYN Relay as a way to prevent SYN floods.

Exam Essentials

Understand the purpose of tracking and alerting.   Tracking and alerting are used to monitor traffic passing into and out of the firewall. You may want to monitor some connections that match certain criteria more closely than others, and you have the ability to set up alerts for those types of connections. Each rule in the rule base can be set to an alert.

Know how to configure alerts.   You can set alerts on rules in the Track element of the rule base. The alerts you set can be configured with a script in the Alert Commands tab of the Global Properties in the SmartDashboard GUI. Each alert can use a custom script written in C/C++, C-Shell, Perl, or Bourne Shell.

Understand the components of a TCP/IP handshake.   A TCP/IP handshake has three components that occur in this order: SYN ➢ SYN/ACK ➢ ACK. This process completes a TCP/IP connection.

Know the difference between SYN Relay and Passive SYN Gateway.
SYN Relay allows only legitimate connections to make it to your protected server, but increases memory usage on the firewall. Passive SYN

Gateway doesn't add overhead to the firewall, but allows open connections to the server. There is a configurable reset timeout on the firewall that is usually shorter than the timeout on the server.

Know how to configure SmartDefense.   Knowing how to configure SmartDefense will help you protect your network now and in the future. As time goes on, more attacks and potential threats will need to be added to SmartDefense.

Key Terms

Before you take the exam, be certain you are familiar with the following terms:

alertd	SYN Gateway
backlog queue	SYN Relay
Denial of Service (DoS)	TCP/IP handshake
Distributed Denial of Service (DDoS)	Track options
fwalert	user-defined
Passive SYN Gateway	worm
SYN flood	

Review Questions

1. What is the FireWall-1 built-in alert?

   A. alert

   B. SNMP Trap

   C. Mail alert

   D. fwalert

   E. UserDefined

2. Which language can you *not* use to write customized alert scripts?

   A. C-Shell

   B. ActiveX

   C. C/C++

   D. Bourne Shell

   E. Perl

3. Which of the following alerts is *not* available for your use in the Track element in SmartDashboard?

   A. Mail alert

   B. UserDefined

   C. Logged alert

   D. SNMP Trap

   E. Alert

4. Which of the following would *not* be a good use of alerting?

   A. Setting up a Mail alert to execute when a firewall goes down

   B. Setting a UserDefined alert for every person who accesses the Internet through the firewall

   C. Setting up an alert when too many connections are dropped from the Stealth rule from the same source

   D. Setting up a Mail alert to execute when a Nimda attack is detected

   E. None of the above

5. Where do you configure an alert script in SmartDashboard?

   A. In the rule under Track

   B. At the NAT tab under Track

   C. In the Object Properties tab

   D. In the Alert Commands tab of the Global Properties

   E. None of the above

6. Where do you set up a Mail alert to trigger when a specific rule is executed?

   A. In the Global Properties

   B. In the Log and Alert properties

   C. In the rule under Track

   D. In the alert command properties

   E. None of the above

7. Which of the following must you be sure of when using SNMP Trap alerts?

   A. What SNMP stands for

   B. That SNMP is running on the firewall

   C. That the rule is implicit

   D. That the object is using static NAT

   E. None of the above

8. What tracking choice would you choose if you already had two custom scripts and wanted to add a third?

   A. SNMP Trap

   B. Mail alert

   C. Log

   D. Popup alert

   E. UserDefined 3

9. Which of the following alerts lets you send either an alphanumeric page to a cell phone or an e-mail?

   A. UserDefined alert

   B. SNMP Trap

   C. Mail alert

   D. Popup alert

   E. None of the above

10. Where can you configure predefined alerts?

    A. In the object properties

    B. In the Log and Alert tab in the Global Properties

    C. In the implicit rules

    D. In the rule base

    E. In the NAT tab of the rule base

11. Which is not a Check Point SYNDefender option?

    A. SYN Relay

    B. SYN Gateway

    C. Passive SYN Gateway

    D. Passive SYN Relay

12. Which of the following are necessary to create a SYN flood?

    1. SYN packet

    2. ACK packet

    3. SYN/ACK packet

    4. IP spoofing

    A. 1, 3

    B. 1, 2

    C. 1, 4

    D. 1, 2, 3

    E. 1, 2, 4

13. Which SYNDefender method completes the handshake to the server while waiting for the ACK packet from the client?

    A. SYN Gateway

    B. Passive SYN Gateway

    C. SYN Relay

14. In which SYNDefender method does the server receive a connection attempt only after a valid connection attempt is completed between the firewall and the client?

    A. SYN Gateway

    B. Passive SYN Gateway

    C. SYN Relay

15. What OSI Model layers do the packet sanity check verify?

    A. Physical and Data Link (1 and 2)

    B. Network and Transport (3 and 4)

    C. Session and Presentation (5 and 6)

    D. Data Link and Network (2 and 3)

    E. All layers (1-7)

16. Which portion of a server is overwhelmed by a SYN flood?

    A. TCP/IP stack

    B. TCP/IP handshake

    C. Backlog queue

    D. DoS

    E. Connection setup

17. Which SmartDefense option will search for an abnormal number of connections from a single source IP address destined for a specific destination IP address or destination port?

    A. Port Scan

    B. Ping of Death

    C. SYNDefender

    D. Successive Alerts

    E. Successive Multiple Connections

18. Which of the following is the term for masquerading the source IP address of a packet to make it appear as if it was coming from somewhere other than the real address?

    A. Ping of Death

    B. Teardrop

    C. Spoofing

    D. SYN Flood

    E. LAND attack

19. Where are worm signatures defined for HTTP worms such as Nimda and Code Red?

    A. SMTP Content tab

    B. HTTP Security Server tab

    C. HTTP Format Sizes

    D. General HTTP Worm Catcher tab

    E. None of the above

20. Which of the following are Denial of Service attacks that can be prevented by SmartDefense? (Choose all that apply.)

    A. SYN Flood

    B. LAND attack

    C. Teardrop

    D. Ping of Death

    E. All of the above

Answers to Review Questions

1. D.   fwalert is a built-in executable script that pops up a detailed alert on the screen when an alert is configured to do so. The other choices are not valid.

2. B.   ActiveX is not a supported scripting language for writing customized alerts. All the other options are.

3. C.   Logged alert does not exist as a choice in the Track element in the SmartDashboard. All alerts are logged, so a Logged alert is obviously a fictitious choice.

4. B.   Alerting should be used to monitor infrequent incidents that should be brought to someone's attention. Some companies would have millions of alerts per day if they set up an alert to go off every time a person accessed the Internet.

5. D.   Although the alert can be set in the rule under Track, the alert script is configured in the Alert Commands tab of the Global Properties.

6. C.   The Mail alert is set to trigger in a rule under Track. The script for the Mail alert is configured in the Alert Command properties.

7. B.   If SNMP is not running on the firewall, an SNMP Trap will not work.

8. E.   If there are already two scripts, then UserDefined and UserDefined 2 are taken. The UserDefined 3 alert would be the choice for the third custom script.

9. C.   The Mail alert allows you to write a script that sends an e-mail or an alphanumeric page. The other alerts can be configured to also send an e-mail or page with the proper script, but the Mail alert is the best answer for the question.

10. B.   The predefined alerts are configured in the Log and Alert tab in the Global Properties. There are no predefined alerts in the other choices.

11. D.   Passive SYN Relay is not an option. SYN Gateway is considered an option even though it is not available after NG FCS.

12. C.   To create a SYN flood, a multitude of SYN packets with spoofed unreachable IP addresses must be created.

13. A.   SYN Gateway is the only SYNDefender method in which the TCP/IP handshake is completed to the server *before* the handshake is completed with the client.

14. C.   SYN Relay is the only SYNDefender method in which the firewall validates the handshake with the client before completing any connection setup with the server.

15. B.   The Packet Sanity check runs Network layer and Transport layer (3 and 4) checks that include verifying UDP and TCP header lengths, dropping IP options, verifying packet size, and TCP flags.

16. C.   The backlog queue fills up while waiting for ACK packets to finish the TCP/IP handshake.

17. E.   Successive Alerts does not apply to connections from a single source IP address, so Successive Multiple Connections is the answer. This alert is handy because it pinpoints an IP address that an administrator can take action on.

18. C.   Spoofing an IP address is a process used for most hacks and attacks these days. If an IP address is not spoofed, the source of the connection can be traced back to the hacker.

19. D.   Worm signatures are configured on the General HTTP Worm Catcher tab under HTTP. Worm signatures can be imported or manually added.

20. E.   SmartDefense supports the prevention of all the DoS attacks listed. DoS attacks are one component of the many useful features of SmartDefense. A subscription to SmartDefense will add to this list and continue to protect against known attacks.

Chapter

3

Load Balancing

THE CCSE EXAM TOPICS COVERED IN THIS CHAPTER INCLUDE:

- ✓ Load balancing and the methods used to apply it.
- ✓ Setting up a logical server to load balance HTTP traffic.

oad balancing in "Check Point-ese" doesn't mean what most people think it does. When people hear *load balancing* and *firewalls* in the same sentence, they think of a scenario in which two firewalls share the function of filtering network traffic. But when Check Point talks load balancing, it's referring to a process in which the logical server decides which requests go to which server in a *server farm* (a group of mirrored servers). Load balancing is also referred to as *ConnectControl*, which is the name of the license string used to activate this feature. In this chapter, we'll discuss the various methods of load balancing, their advantages and disadvantages, and algorithms that accompany the methods.

Load Balancing Architecture Overview

Check Point's load balancing solution addresses the issue of public servers being overwhelmed by too many connections (see Figure 3.1).

In Figure 3.1, the example company has a website that takes a tremendous number of hits. Due to the busy state of the web server, not all the attempts reach the website. In the world of the Internet, if someone has to wait more than a few seconds to get to your website, they'll go somewhere else instead. Being a savvy firewall administrator, you implement the load balancing feature of the firewall to stave off high traffic and make your site constantly available to visitors.

Load balancing works with more than just HTTP traffic; it can support any TCP protocol.

FIGURE 3.1   Overwhelmed servers

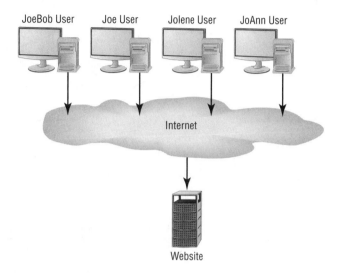

To take advantage of the load balancing feature, you must create mirrored servers. Mirrored servers are exact copies of each other. Each of these servers is represented by a Node object; they are then grouped together in a Simple Group in the SmartDashboard. Because the connection can't go directly to the firewall and it can't go directly to the web servers, it must go to the logical server. The logical server is *not* a physical server, but rather an object that represents a valid DNS-resolvable address that answers all requests from the Internet bound for the website. The logical server acts as the decision-maker to determine which server gets the connection. The best way to explain this process is to examine a picture like that in Figure 3.2.

The load balancing feature is built into the Check Point FireWall-1 software, but it is not active until the correct license string is applied to the firewall.

In the figure, when Joe User wants to visit your website, his connection is directed to the firewall's logical server address. This connection is then forwarded to one of the servers based on the algorithm you choose. Using load balancing this way, everyone always has access to your website.

FIGURE 3.2 Check Point load balancing

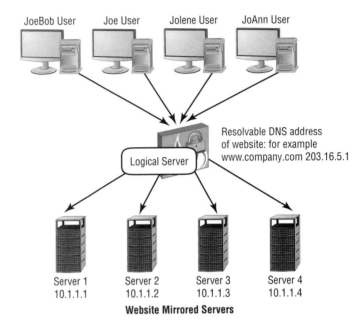

JoeBob User   Joe User   Jolene User   JoAnn User

Logical Server

Resolvable DNS address
of website: for example
www.company.com 203.16.5.1

Server 1   Server 2   Server 3   Server 4
10.1.1.1   10.1.1.2   10.1.1.3   10.1.1.4

Website Mirrored Servers

With the overview complete, let's delve deeper into how load balancing works.

Real World Scenario

Why Load Balancing?

Load balancing is a critical need of today's e-businesses. Making sure your public servers are available 24/7 is crucial to the success of an online venture. Let's say your company is a large online bookseller competing with Amazon.com, and your website is taking two million hits per day. One web server cannot handle that type of load. To solve this problem, you create multiple mirrored servers to share the load. Check Point offers you a feature called ConnectControl to balance the traffic between these servers, so your site is always available.

Check Point is not the only vendor offering this type of solution; others such as Alteon, Cisco, Foundry, and F5 also perform load balancing. The advantage of using Check Point is its ability to load balance from a central GUI.

Load Balancing Methods

Two components are involved in load balancing traffic: *load balancing methods*, which determine the way the traffic is allowed to flow through the firewall; and *load balancing algorithms*, which specify how the firewall makes its decision about which server gets the connection. Let's discuss methodology first.

There are two mechanisms for performing load balancing with FireWall-1: the *HTTP method* and the *Other method*. HTTP load balancing utilizes the ability of a browser to accept redirects to other websites. Figure 3.3 illustrates HTTP load balancing. Step 1 depicts the connection from the Internet reaching the logical server. In step 2, the lhttpd daemon sends a message back to the client's browser. Finally, in step 3, the lhttpd daemon tells the client's browser to connect to one of the servers in the server farm. From this point on, the connection is between the client and the server—the logical server's job essentially is done.

FIGURE 3.3 HTTP load balancing

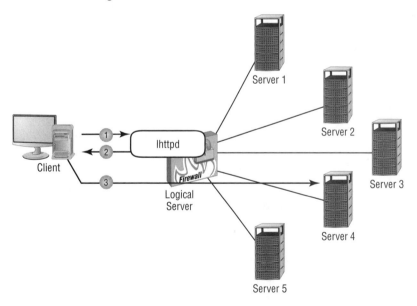

Unfortunately, the HTTP method only works for HTTP traffic. In addition, using HTTP redirect reveals to the customer the true IP address of the server in the server farm.

The other load balancing option is Other. This option uses a *dynamic address translation* mechanism to translate the destination address on the way in and the source address on the way out (see Figure 3.4).

FIGURE 3.4   Other load balancing

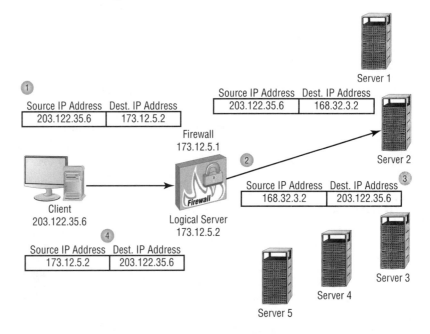

Other load balancing allows the firewall administrator to hide the true addresses of the web servers. The Other option can be used for any type of TCP traffic, including HTTP.

Load Balancing Considerations

When you're configuring HTTP load balancing, web servers in the server farm must have either legally routable addresses or Network Address Translation (NAT) set up for clients from the Internet to access the servers. This requirement is important because the connection eventually takes place between the client and the server *without* the intervention of the logical server.

There is also no option that lets you hide the true address of the web server; therefore, the IP address of the web server and *not* the logical server address is displayed in the URL field of your browser.

If you need to set up load balancing on HTTP logical servers that share the same IP address, keep in mind that the firewall always rewrites the HTTP logical server's name when several logical server names are tied to one IP address. The HTTP protocol has a feature that uses a server's name in the HTTP request. HTTP load balancing rewrites the logical server name to the physical server it represents.

You can solve all these problems by choosing the Other method for HTTP logical servers instead of the HTTP method. This way, the servers do not need legally routable addresses or NAT rules, because Other uses dynamic NAT to route the traffic. The true IP address of the servers will be hidden, because dynamic NAT will cause the browser to display only the logical server's IP address.

Load Balancing Algorithms

Now that you've learned about the methodologies the logical server/firewall uses to route traffic, you need to consider the algorithms used to decide which server in the server farm will get the load-balanced connection. Check Point provides five algorithms for the logical server; the administrator decides which of these algorithms to use. The algorithms are called *server load*, *round trip*, *round robin*, *random*, and *domain*. We'll describe these algorithms next.

The server load algorithm, shown in Figure 3.5, works in conjunction with a load agent that runs on each server in the server farm. The load agent is a small program that communicates to the firewall how busy the machine is. The machine with the lightest load is sent the next packet.

You can download this *load agent* from Check Point's website (only available for Solaris) or write one using the OPSEC APIs provided by Check Point on the OPSEC website (`www.opsec.com`). The load agent uses UDP port 18212 by default. The firewall checks the load on each server at the configured time and passes the connection to the server that has the lightest load.

The round trip algorithm uses `ping` to decide which server gets the request, as depicted in Figure 3.6. The round trip algorithm is much simpler than the server load algorithm, but not as intuitive—it cannot measure the load on the servers. Therefore, the round trip algorithm's decision is based solely on network factors rather than the server load. When you use round trip, the server with the least traffic will answer first. The server with the most traffic will be too busy to answer, and the packet will be delivered to the machine that answers first.

FIGURE 3.5 Server load algorithm

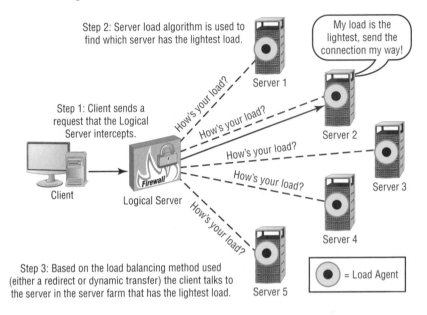

Step 2: Server load algorithm is used to find which server has the lightest load.

My load is the lightest, send the connection my way!

Step 1: Client sends a request that the Logical Server intercepts.

How's your load?

Step 3: Based on the load balancing method used (either a redirect or dynamic transfer) the client talks to the server in the server farm that has the lightest load.

Client

Logical Server

Server 1

Server 2

Server 3

Server 4

Server 5

⊙ = Load Agent

FIGURE 3.6 Round trip algorithm

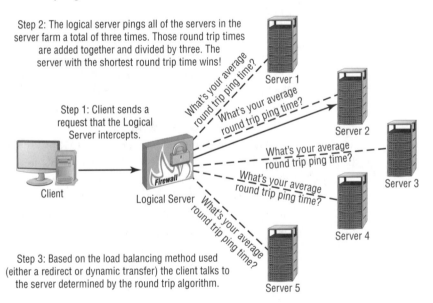

Step 2: The logical server pings all of the servers in the server farm a total of three times. Those round trip times are added together and divided by three. The server with the shortest round trip time wins!

Step 1: Client sends a request that the Logical Server intercepts.

What's your average round trip ping time?

Step 3: Based on the load balancing method used (either a redirect or dynamic transfer) the client talks to the server determined by the round trip algorithm.

Client

Logical Server

Server 1

Server 2

Server 3

Server 4

Server 5

The drawback to using the round trip method is that the server closest to the firewall usually gets the connection.

The round robin algorithm, shown in Figure 3.7, is not very intelligent. This algorithm begins with the first server in the server farm and gives it the first connection. The second connection goes to the second server in the server farm, the third goes to the third, and so on. When the algorithm reaches the bottom of the list, it starts over.

FIGURE 3.7   Round robin algorithm

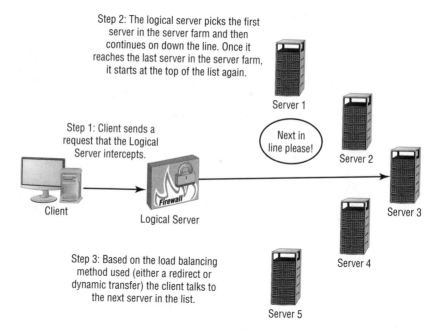

Next in the list of load balancing algorithms is random. Do you remember the method you used to choose teams when you were a kid? Eenie, Meanie, Minie, Mo! That is the same method the firewall uses. The random algorithm is illustrated in Figure 3.8.

Last is the domain algorithm. With this algorithm, the firewall chooses the closest server based on domain names. Figure 3.9 shows an illustration of the domain algorithm in action.

FIGURE 3.8 Random algorithm

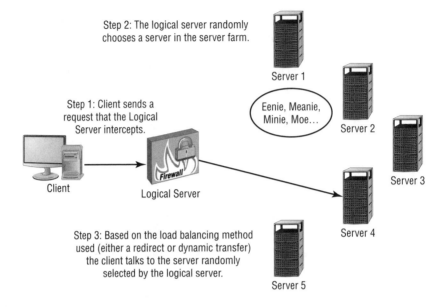

Step 2: The logical server randomly chooses a server in the server farm.

Step 1: Client sends a request that the Logical Server intercepts.

Eenie, Meanie, Minie, Moe…

Client

Logical Server

Server 1

Server 2

Server 3

Server 4

Server 5

Step 3: Based on the load balancing method used (either a redirect or dynamic transfer) the client talks to the server randomly selected by the logical server.

FIGURE 3.9 Domain algorithm

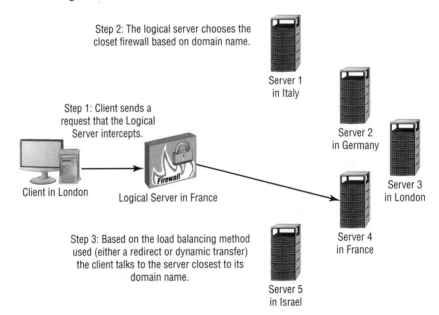

Step 2: The logical server chooses the closet firewall based on domain name.

Step 1: Client sends a request that the Logical Server intercepts.

Client in London

Logical Server in France

Server 1 in Italy

Server 2 in Germany

Server 3 in London

Server 4 in France

Server 5 in Israel

Step 3: Based on the load balancing method used (either a redirect or dynamic transfer) the client talks to the server closest to its domain name.

There is an issue with the domain algorithm. Check Point doesn't recommend using it, because it creates a noticeable delay for requests due to the required reverse DNS lookups. In today's e-business environment, any delay experienced by users accessing your website could be disastrous. This algorithm was originally designed for clients in Europe and the rest of the world, where they use country names at the end of their URLs (such as www.company.uk) For example, in Figure 3.9, if a client in the U.K. is trying to connect to a website for a global company based in France, the initial connection goes to the logical server in France. At this point, the closest server is in France, and it would be "logical" to send the connection to the server in France. Unfortunately, the domain algorithm will send packets back to the client in the U.K. and redirect them to the server located in the U.K., wasting precious time in the connection setup. This is an effective method only if all your servers are located in Europe and the client is also located in Europe.

To sum up, Check Point offers five algorithms—but in our opinion, only one is a true load balancing method. The server load algorithm is the only method that takes into account the actual load on each server. The rest of the algorithms don't consider how busy each server is in the server farm. As the administrator, you should check out all methods of load balancing (both Check Point and non–Check Point) before deciding which one is best for your situation.

Implementing Load Balancing

Now that you understand the theory and components of load balancing, it's time to explore how to configure load balancing on the firewall.

Creating the Necessary Objects

You need to create a network object for every server in the server farm. You do this by clicking Manage ➢ Network Objects to access the Network Objects Manager. Then, click New ➢ Node ➢ Host to bring up the Host Node General Properties screen, shown in Figure 3.10.

You identify each object by typing in a name and the IP address of the server and then clicking OK.

FIGURE 3.10 Creating a Workstation/Host Node object

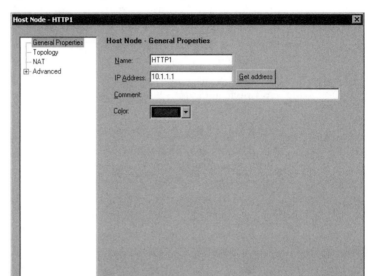

Some NG FP1 object names have changed significantly in NG FP2. Depending on which version of NG you are running, you could be creating a new Workstation object (as defined in FP1) or a new Host Node object (as defined in FP2). Object names didn't change much between FP2 and FP3, but the names of all the GUIs did.

Naming these objects similarly will make identification easier. For example, you might use the names HTTP1, HTTP2, HTTP3, and so on. Because the Objects Tree organizes names alphabetically, the objects will be listed together.

After you create a Host Node object for every server in the server farm, you need to pull the objects into a group object. You do so through the Network Objects Manager. Create a new group by clicking New ➤ Group ➤ Simple Group, which brings up the Group Properties dialog box shown in Figure 3.11.

FIGURE 3.11   Creating a server group

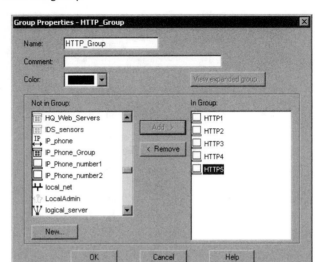

The name of the group should correspond to the names of the Host Node objects you created (for example, HTTP_Group). This approach keeps your naming convention consistent and makes it easy to identify which servers belong to which group. The Comment and Color fields are optional. The Host Node objects created should be listed in the left column. Select the objects that represent the servers in the server farm (by holding down the Ctrl key and clicking each one) and add them to the In Group column on the right by clicking the Add button.

The next task is to create the *logical server* object. This object represents the routable IP address that will be published (via DNS) to the whole world as your server IP address.

There are a few ways to create this object. You can go to the menu bar and select Manage ➢ Network Objects, and then select New ➢ Logical Server in the Network Objects Manager—but that's a lot of steps. We prefer to use the new Objects Tree to create objects. Figure 3.12 shows this process, which you can use to create most objects.

FIGURE 3.12 Creating a logical server object from the Objects Tree

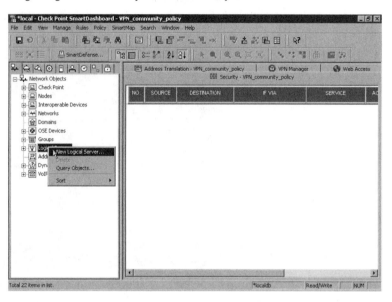

You can create most objects from the Objects Tree, not just logical server objects.

When you right-click on Logical Server and select New Logical Server, the Logical Server Properties window appears as shown in Figure 3.13. Enter a name in the Name field and the routable IP address in the IP Address field. Again, follow the same naming convention you started earlier. The IP address is the DNS-resolvable valid IP address registered in the public DNS, such as 172.21.101.100. Your firewall address is 172.21.101.1, but your web traffic has the address of 172.21.101.100. Any traffic to the firewall on 172.21.101.1 is dropped by the stealth rule, but traffic to the logical servers' IP address of 172.21.101.100 is accepted. The Comment and Color fields are not required, but they're a nice way to organize your objects.

FIGURE 3.13   Logical Server Properties window

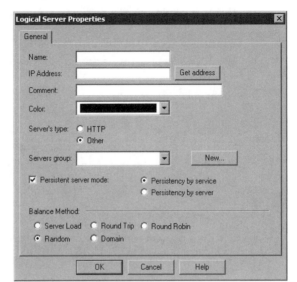

Next, select the Server's Type option. Select HTTP if you are load-balancing web servers. If you are using valid routable addresses for the servers in your server farm or if you do not care if the actual IP addresses of the load-balanced servers are known, then HTTP is the proper choice. For every other TCP protocol, select Other. You can use Other for HTTP traffic as well, if you wish to hide the true IP addresses of the servers in your server farm.

Persistent Server Mode should always be turned on. This option is the "superglue" of the logical server: It makes the connection stay with the same server or service for a time frame specified by you in the Global Properties. Persistent Server Mode is helpful with services such as FTP , which involve an active connection. You want the connection to stay with the same server throughout the duration of the session. That way, if there is a break in the session, you will be able to get back to that specific server to complete the download. With Persistent Server Mode turned on (it is on by default), two persistency options are available: You can choose to make the connection persistent based on either the service being used (HTTP, FTP, and so on) or the server selected by the algorithm.

If a client adds the URL of one of the load-balanced web servers to their browser's Favorites list and HTTP was the Server's Type method chosen, the URL reflects the true IP address of the web server. However, if the Other method was chosen, the client is really adding the URL of the logical server IP address, even if this is done after the load balancing has taken effect. This happens because Persistent Server Mode is active for each session. When the client clicks on an item in the Favorites list, a new session is created; this new session is directed to one of the servers in the server farm based on the selected algorithm.

Finally, you select the Balance Method from the five algorithm options described earlier in this chapter. You can see what a completed logical server object looks like in Figure 3.14.

FIGURE 3.14 Completed logical server object

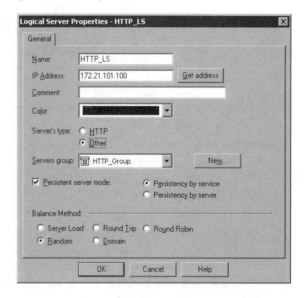

Configuring Global Properties

After you configure the server farm group and the logical server object, you must configure Global Properties that affect load balancing. In the Smart-Dashboard, go to Policy ➤ Global Properties and select the ConnectControl option in the Objects Tree. The window shown in Figure 3.15 will appear.

FIGURE 3.15 ConnectControl Global Properties window

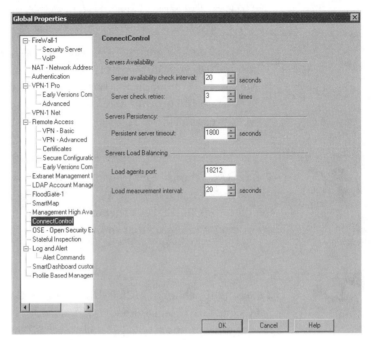

In Figure 3.15, three configurable options are listed:

Servers Availability   This option uses the Server Availability Check Interval to control how often the firewall pings the server to see if it is still available to take connections (the default is 20 seconds). If the firewall *doesn't* receive a reply, the Server Check Retries feature controls how many times it will continue trying before it gives up.

The firewall isn't very intelligent when it comes to determining whether the server is available. If the server replies to a ping, it will get a connection. If it doesn't reply, it won't get a connection. It cannot decipher whether the service that is needed is actually running.

Servers Persistency   This option ties in with Persistent Server Mode, which you set up in the logical server object. The Persistent Server Time-out specifies how long in seconds the connection will stay with the server or service (the default is 1800, or 30 minutes for those without a calculator). The Persistent Server Timeout is refreshable; therefore, every new connection to the persistent server will reset the timer.

Servers Load Balancing This option ties in with the server load algorithm. Here you configure the port on which the agents on the servers and the firewall communicate (Load Agents Port: default 18212), along with how often the firewall checks to see who has the lightest load (Load Measurement Interval).

The port you choose for the load agent must be identical on all the servers in the server farm and the firewall. Check Point does not recommend changing the port from 18212, because both the load balancing agent and the firewall are communicating on that known port.

If the SmartDashboard ➢ Global Properties ➢ ConnectControl➢ Servers Load Balancing, Load Measurement Interval value is set to 0, you will see the following error during a policy install: Internal error [12] while handling object Firewall_properties "Error."Error in field <lbalance_load_period_wakeup_sec> at object <Firewall_properties> -> "Error:"value. Reset the Load Measurement Interval to a value other than 0 to clear this error.

Ping is used extensively in load balancing, so you need to make sure Internet Control Message Protocol (ICMP) is allowed between the firewall and the servers. You can configure this by turning on Accept ICMP requests in the Global Properties (see Figure 3.16) or by explicitly writing a rule to allow ICMP between the firewall and the servers in the server farm. These explicit rules should allow echo_request from the firewall to the server group and echo_reply from the server farm to the firewall.

At configured times, the firewall pings each machine in a logical server group (these pings should be visible in the firewall logs). If the pings directed at a specific server fail the specified number of times, as configured in the Global Properties, the firewall will establish no new connections to that server until the machine is able to re-establish connectivity. If Persistent Server Mode is used (it should be), the firewall will continue to route traffic for existing connections until they time out, but no new connections will be established.

FIGURE 3.16 The Accept ICMP Requests option

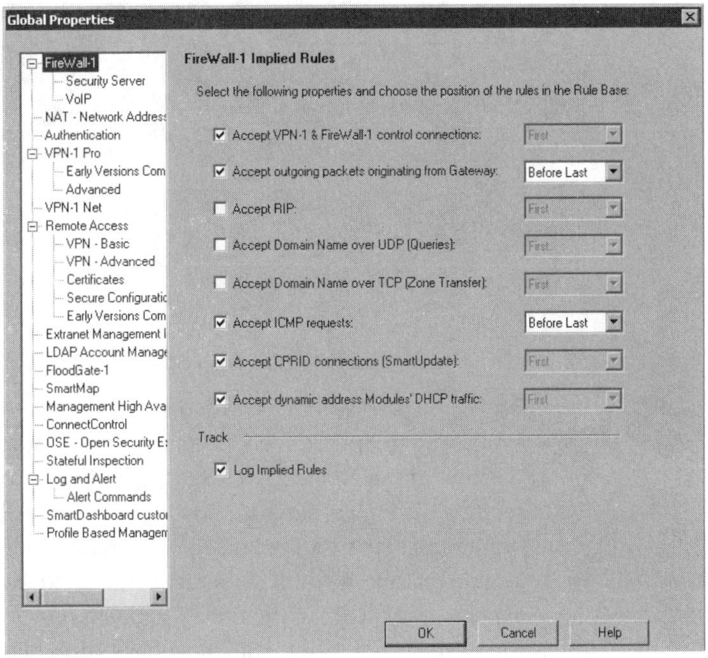

Configuring the Rule Base

Now that you've finished configuring the objects and the Global Properties, you need to set the rule base. How the rule base is configured depends on which option (HTTP or Other) you chose.

Configuring the Rule Base with the HTTP Option

If you selected the HTTP option when you created the logical server, then two rules are required to make load balancing work. In Figure 3.17, the first rule allows the connection to the logical server address via HTTP. The second rule allows the redirect from the client to a server in the server farm. The last rule is the cleanup rule; it is not required to make load balancing work, but it serves to log any connections that don't match previous rules.

FIGURE 3.17   HTTP load balancing rule base

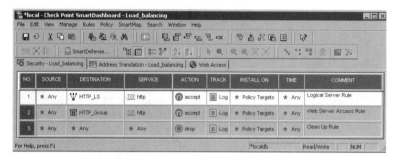

Remember that with the HTTP load balancing method, the logical server sends a message to the client and redirects the client to a server in the server farm. The rest of the connection takes place directly between the client and the server—the logical server is no longer involved. Keep in mind that the servers in the server farm must have legally routable addresses or have NAT performed for this method to work. As a result, the IP address of the physical web server appears in the URL of the browser. Using the Other load balancing option allows the client to see only the logical server IP address in the URL field.

Using the HTTP load balancing method gives you one extra option that the Other method does not: You can use two different actions, as shown in Figure 3.18.

FIGURE 3.18   HTTP load balancing using two actions

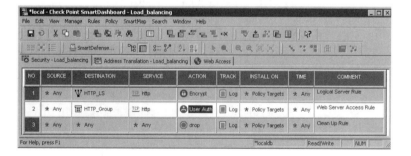

The action of the rule that connects to the logical server must be either Accept or Encrypt.

To complete the exercise for this section, you will need the firewall initially configured in the exercises from Chapter 1 as well as at least three Windows PCs and a hub. One PC will be a client on the outside of the firewall and must have a web browser installed. The other two PCs will be configured as web servers. The lab setup should be configured as depicted in Figure 3.19.

FIGURE 3.19 Configuration for load balancing labs

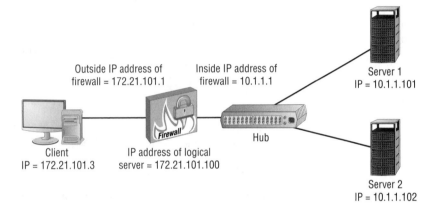

Outside IP address of
firewall = 172.21.101.1

Inside IP address of
firewall = 10.1.1.1

Server 1
IP = 10.1.1.101

Hub

Client
IP = 172.21.101.3

IP address of logical
server = 172.21.101.100

Server 2
IP = 10.1.1.102

EXERCISE 3.1

Load Balancing with HTTP

1. Make sure a network connection exists between your servers and the inside interface of your firewall.

2. Create a Host Node object to represent each server (10.1.1.101 and 10.1.1.102).

3. Create a Simple Group called HTTP_Group that contains the server objects created in step 1.

EXERCISE 3.1 *(continued)*

4. Create a logical server object with the following attributes:

   - IP address: 172.21.101.100

   - Persistent Server Mode: off (in real life, Persistent Server Mode should always be turned on; in this exercise it is turned off to demonstrate the logical server load balancing back and forth to each server in the server farm)

   - Server's Type: HTTP

   - Servers Group: HTTP_Group

   - Algorithm: Round Robin

5. Create a rule to allow traffic from the outside of your firewall to your logical server object via HTTP. Be sure logging is turned on for this rule.

6. Below the rule created in step 5, create a rule to allow traffic from the outside of your firewall to your group of servers via HTTP. Be sure logging is turned on for this rule.

7. Below the rule created in step 6, create the cleanup rule.

8. Turn on Accept ICMP Requests in the Global Properties.

9. Verify and install your policy.

10. Test by opening a browser on the client and setting the home page to 172.21.101.100. Continually click the Home button to watch the connection bounce between the two servers. Note the connections bouncing between the servers in the Log Viewer.

Configuring the Rule Base with the Other Option

If you selected the Other option when you created the logical server, then only one rule is necessary to make load balancing work. Rule 1 in Figure 3.20 illustrates the logical server rule for Other load balancing. Because Other uses dynamic address translation, you only need a rule that allows connections to the logical server via whatever protocol is being used. The last rule is the cleanup rule; this rule is not required to make load balancing work, but it serves to log any connections that don't match previous rules.

FIGURE 3.20 Other load balancing rule base

To complete the exercise for this section, you will need the firewall initially configured in the exercises in Chapter 1, as well as at least three Windows PCs and a hub. One PC will be a client on the outside of the firewall. The other two PCs will be configured as FTP servers. The setup for Exercise 3.2 should be configured as shown previously in Figure 3.19.

EXERCISE 3.2

Load Balancing with FTP

1. Create a logical server object with the following attributes:

   - IP address: 172.21.101.101

   - Persistent Server Mode: off (in real life, Persistent Server Mode should always be turned on; in this exercise it is turned off to demonstrate the logical server load balancing back and forth to each server in the server farm)

   - Servers Group: HTTP_Group (created in the previous exercise)

   - Server's Type: Other

   - Algorithm: Round Robin

2. Remove the rules from the previous lab.

3. Create a rule to allow traffic from the outside of your firewall to your logical server object via FTP. Be sure logging is turned on for this rule.

4. Below the rule created in step 3, create the cleanup rule.

5. Turn on Accept ICMP Requests in the Global Properties (this should already be on from the previous exercise).

6. Verify and install your policy.

7. Test by opening a DOS window on the client and FTPing to 172.21.101.11 numerous times. Note the entries in the Log Viewer that show the connection alternating between the servers.

Daemons that Affect Load Balancing

Two daemons affect load balancing, and both are tied to the *fwssd* execut-able. The fwssd executable is in charge of Security Server functions and includes the daemons *in.pingd* and *in.lhttpd*. These Security Server daemons are defined in the $FWDIR/conf/fwauthd.conf file ($FWDIR is the directory in which the firewall software is installed). This file was created when the firewall was installed and contains the Security Server daemons and the ports on which they run. Figure 3.21 depicts the contents of the fwauthd.conf file.

FIGURE 3.21 Contents of fwauthd.conf file

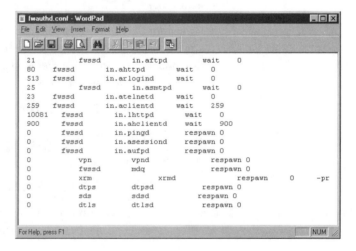

You learned about the lhttpd daemon earlier in this chapter. You can see from the fwauthd.conf file that this daemon runs by default on port 10081; but what does the *in.pingd* daemon have to do with load balancing? The in.pingd daemon's responsibility is to ping the servers to make sure they are still up and running. There is a known problem with FP1 in which the in.pingd process of fwssd consumes excessive CPU resources when logical servers are defined in the Security Policy. The only known fix is to upgrade to FP2 and above.

There are multiple security servers but each security server is not a separate executable. Each security server or service listed in the `fwauthd.conf` file links to the fwssd executable.

Load Balancing Tables

The load balancing tables are among the many state tables Check Point uses to keep track of connections traversing the firewall. Following are descriptions of the tables that pertain to load balancing. You can view these tables by typing **fw tab -t [*table name*] -s** at a command prompt on the firewall. Replace *[table name]* with one of the following options to view a summary of the connections being tracked by that particular table:

Type fw tab -s to view a summary of every FW-1 table.

check_alive   This table holds a list of either load balanced servers or client authentication machines running in wait mode that should be pinged to verify they are still working.

logical_requests   This table contains connections that need to be forwarded to another server as a result of a logical server performing load balancing. Connections are held in this table until the firewall determines which server gets the request.

logical_servers_table   This table holds a list of logical servers—but only the logical servers that are actually used in a rule. Each machine will appear once, even if the machine is used in more than one logical server.

logical_cache_table   Each connection is recorded in this table so it will always be directed to the same security server (if Persistent Server Mode is turned on).

Non-Firewall Configuration

After all the objects are created and rules are implemented on the firewall, you need to make some non-firewall changes. Regardless of which method you are using, if you want someone to get to your servers from the Internet, you have to publish DNS information. For example, if you were load-balancing your web traffic, you would publish the IP address of your website as the IP address of your logical server.

You also need to make sure that traffic gets to your firewall. Because the logical server is usually a publicly routable IP address that you own, you should set up an ARP or add a route. The easiest method is to add a route from the upstream router to the firewall's external interface. Unfortunately, not everyone owns their upstream router or is allowed to make configuration changes to it. Therefore, the fallback option is to publish an ARP. Publish the IP address of the logical server to the external NIC of the firewall so that whenever an ARP broadcast goes out asking who owns the IP address of the logical server, the firewall's external NIC will reply, "Send it my way!"

ConnectControl in conjunction with high availability is now supported by Check Point, as well as load balancing with full cluster configurations.

Summary

Load balancing with FireWall-1 ensures that your servers are always available on the Internet. Installing the ConnectControl license feature enables the load balancing feature. Load balancing includes two main components: the load balancing methods (which includes the lhttpd daemon) and the five algorithms.

The lhttpd daemon is used with the HTTP logical server option to redirect HTTP connections to a server in the server farm. The Other method uses dynamic address translation for protocols other than HTTP (although HTTP also can be used with the Other method). The server chosen for the connection depends on the algorithm chosen.

The logical server object requires a legally routable IP address. Persistent Server Mode should be configured (either by service or server), along with the algorithm and the server farm group. The Global Properties allow you to control how often the firewall checks to see if the server is up and running, the persistency timeout, and the load agent's port and measurement interval.

You need to make non-firewall configuration changes to ensure that packets make it to the firewall. The IP address of the logical server must be published via DNS. Routing concerns are addressed in one of two ways. If you own the upstream router, the easiest configuration is to add a static route that directs traffic for the logical server IP address to the firewall. The other option is to publish an ARP to the external interface of the firewall so the firewall will answer for logical server traffic.

Exam Essentials

Know the purpose of load balancing.   Load balancing's purpose is to make your servers available 24/7. Using the load balancing feature of the firewall allows you to ensure that your website is always available. In addition, if you have multiple servers, you do not want one server handling all your traffic. By using load balancing, the work of the servers is distributed as evenly as possible among all the servers.

Know the components of load balancing.   The two components are the lhttpd daemon and the five algorithms.

Know the difference between the HTTP and Other load balancing methods.   HTTP uses the lhttpd daemon to redirect traffic and therefore requires two rules to implement. The Other method uses dynamic address translation and therefore requires only one rule to implement.

Know the five load balancing algorithms.   The five load balancing algorithms are server load, round robin, round trip, random, and domain. These algorithms indicate to the firewall which server in the server farm gets the connection.

Know how to create rules for HTTP and Other load balancing.   The number of rules defined depends on the method chosen. HTTP dictates that two rules be defined: One rule ensures a connection to the logical server, and the other rule allows the redirect to happen to the server farm. Each rule can have a different action. The Other method requires only one rule, because it uses dynamic address translation to make the connection.

Key Terms

Before you take the exam, be certain you are familiar with the following terms:

ConnectControl	load balancing
domain	logical server
dynamic address translation	Other method
fwssd	Persistent Server Mode
HTTP method	random
in.lhttpd	round robin
in.pingd	round trip
lhttpd	server farm
load agent	server load

Review Questions

1. How many rules are needed to implement HTTP load balancing using the HTTP method?

   A. 1

   B. 2

   C. 3

   D. 4

2. Which of the following is *not* a load balancing algorithm?

   A. Round robin

   B. DNS

   C. Round trip

   D. Server load

   E. Random

3. Which load balancing algorithm pings each server three times and then averages the reply times from the server to the firewall to determine which server gets the next connection?

   A. Round trip

   B. Round robin

   C. Random

   D. Server load

   E. Domain

4. Which load balancing algorithm arbitrarily picks which server gets the next connection?

   A. Round trip

   B. Round robin

   C. Random

   D. Server load

   E. Domain

5. Which load balancing algorithm sends connections to one server after another down the line?

   A. Round trip

   B. Round robin

   C. Random

   D. Server load

   E. Domain

6. Which load balancing algorithm uses agents on each server to determine the server with the lightest load?

   A. Round trip

   B. Round robin

   C. Random

   D. Server load

   E. Domain

7. Which load balancing algorithm uses reverse DNS lookups to determine which server gets the next connection?

   A. Round trip

   B. Round robin

   C. Random

   D. Server load

   E. Domain

8. How many rules are needed to implement HTTP load balancing using the Other method?

A. 1

B. 2

C. 3

D. 4

9. You have a situation in which your website traffic has increased dramatically. Implementing Check Point's load balancing solution would solve your dilemma. Which of these tasks are needed to implement load balancing?

A. Adding a static route or publishing an ARP

B. Publishing DNS information

C. Creating a server group

D. Obtaining a ConnectControl license

E. All of the above

10. Which process does the firewall use to check the availability of the servers for load balancing?

A. fwauthd

B. lhttpd

C. in.pingd

D. aclientd

11. What process does the Other load balancing method use to get traffic to the server farm?

A. HTTP redirect

B. DNS

C. Dynamic address translation

D. Round trip algorithm

12. Load balancing is a Check Point solution that does which of the following?

    A. Allows two Check Point firewalls to share their load

    B. Allows a failover capability in a high availability solution

    C. Allows the firewall to decide which server in the server farm gets the connection

    D. Lets you perform VRRP with the Nokia platform

13. Your website has had increased traffic over the last few months, to the point that clients can't access your content because your server is too busy. Which Check Point module would you choose to remedy this situation?

    A. High Availability

    B. ConnectControl

    C. Encryption

    D. Authentication

    E. Enforcement

14. Which daemon is used to redirect web traffic with the ConnectControl module?

    A. http

    B. httpd

    C. lhttpd

    D. lbhttpd

15. If you want to set up load balancing for HTTP traffic and you want to hide the true addresses of the web servers in your server farm, which method should you choose?

A. Round robin

B. Server load

C. Other

D. HTTP

E. Random

16. Which option forces a connection to stay with a particular server to which it has been load balanced until the timeout is reached?

A. Persistent Server Timeout

B. Servers Availability Check Interval

C. Server Check Retries

D. Servers Load Balancing

E. Load Measurement Interval

17. On what default port does the server load agent communicate with the firewall?

A. 18210

B. 18211

C. 18212

D. 18213

E. 18214

18. By default, how many times over what period of time does the firewall ping a server in the server farm before deciding that it is unreachable?

    A. Every 10 seconds for 5 tries

    B. Every 20 seconds for 3 tries

    C. Every 30 seconds for 5 tries

    D. Every 20 seconds for 10 tries

    E. Every 10 seconds for 3 tries

19. Which load balancing table contains connections that must be forwarded to another server because HTTP load balancing is being used?

    A. check_alive

    B. logical_requests

    C. logical_servers_table

    D. logical_cache_table

    E. load_balancing_table

20. Which command is used to access the state tables to view connection information?

    A. fwssd

    B. fw lb

    C. fw lhttpd

    D. fw tab

    E. cp tab

Answers to Review Questions

1. **B.**   The first rule allows the connection to the logical server, and the second rule allows the redirect to the server farm.

2. **B.**   DNS is not a load balancing algorithm. The other four are valid algorithms. The domain algorithm is missing.

3. **A.**   Round trip uses `ping` to determine the shortest round trip time between the firewall and each server. The server with the shortest time will receive the connection.

4. **C.**   Random doesn't use any method to determine which server is the busiest. It just closes its eyes (so to speak) and picks one out of the group to receive the next connection.

5. **B.**   Like all the other algorithms with the exception of server load, round robin doesn't take the number of connections to a particular server into consideration. It just picks the next server in the list and sends the connection to it.

6. **D.**   In our opinion, server load is the only true load balancing method because it takes into consideration the amount of traffic on the server and sends the connection to the server with the lightest load.

7. **E.**   This is the worst algorithm of the bunch. The reverse DNS lookups create too much latency. Most web users won't wait more than three seconds for a page to load.

8. **A.**   Only one rule is needed when you use Other, because it uses dynamic address translation.

9. **E.**   All these options are essential to making load balancing possible.

10. **C.**   The in.pingd daemon is responsible for pinging each server in the server farm. If a ping reply is received from the server, the firewall will send a connection regardless of whether the appropriate service is actually running.

11. C.   It will dynamically translate the destination IP address on the way in and the source IP address on the way out.

12. C.   Many people confuse load balancing with high availability (HA). Options A, B, and D describe an HA solution. Only C describes Check Point load balancing.

13. B.   ConnectControl is the module needed to perform load balancing.

14. C.   It's important to understand that the lhttpd daemon controls the HTTP redirect method of load balancing.

15. C.   Options A, B, and E are all load balancing algorithms, not methods. Option D redirects the user to a web server, and the actual IP address of the web server is revealed. Only option C hides the true IP address of the server in the server farm.

16. A.   The Persistent Server Timeout default is 1800 seconds. Once a connection is load balanced to a particular server (based on the server or the service), it will stay "stuck" there until the 1800 seconds (or whatever value you set) runs out.

17. C.   You can change the default port of 18212 on the firewall, but you must also configure it for each server in the server farm. Check Point recommends that you don't change the default port option.

18. B.   The firewall will ping the server once. If it doesn't receive a reply, it will try another ping after 20 seconds. If it still doesn't receive a reply, after 20 seconds it will give one more attempt before ceasing to send any connections to the server.

19. B.   The logical_requests table holds these connections until the logical server determines which server gets the request. The check_alive table holds a list of the load-balanced servers, logical_servers_table holds a list of logical servers that are used in a rule, and logical_cache_table keeps track of the persistent connections and their timeouts.

20. D.   The fw tab -s command lists a summary of all connection tables. Using fw tab followed by the name of the table (such as logical_requests) will list only the connections for that particular connection table.

Chapter

4

Content Security

THE CCSE EXAM TOPICS COVERED IN THIS CHAPTER INCLUDE:

- ✓ Know the Content Security process and know the components involved.
- ✓ Configuring Java Blocking.
- ✓ Blocking Web browser access to restricted sites on a URL.
- ✓ Using a UFP server to restrict access to FTP sites on the Internet.
- ✓ Configuring an HTTP Security Server.
- ✓ Configuring a CVP Server.
- ✓ Implementing a TCP Security Server.

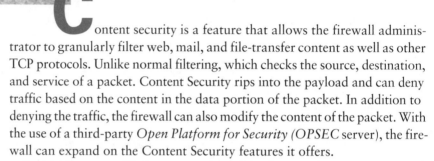

Content security is a feature that allows the firewall administrator to granularly filter web, mail, and file-transfer content as well as other TCP protocols. Unlike normal filtering, which checks the source, destination, and service of a packet. Content Security rips into the payload and can deny traffic based on the content in the data portion of the packet. In addition to denying the traffic, the firewall can also modify the content of the packet. With the use of a third-party *Open Platform for Security (OPSEC* server), the firewall can expand on the Content Security features it offers.

In this chapter, we'll give an overview of the Content Security process and then delve into the specifics of HTTP, SMTP, and FTP Content Security. You'll also be introduced to a new NG Content Security feature: the TCP resource.

To complete the exercises for this chapter, you will need the firewall initially configured in the exercises in Chapter 1, a Windows PC, and an Internet connection. The PC requires a web browser and will act as the internal client to view the content. You'll need access to the Internet to receive files and web content.

Content Security Overview

Content Security is a proxy-like service that runs on the firewall for HTTP, SMTP, FTP and TCP. When traffic comes to the firewall in step 1 (as shown in Figure 4.1), it hits the network interface card (NIC) and is immediately picked up by Check Point's INSPECT engine (step 2). The INSPECT engine checks the rule base, determines whether this traffic matches a rule that deals with Content Security, and in step 3, *folds* the connection up to the *Security Servers*.

FIGURE 4.1   Basic Content Security process

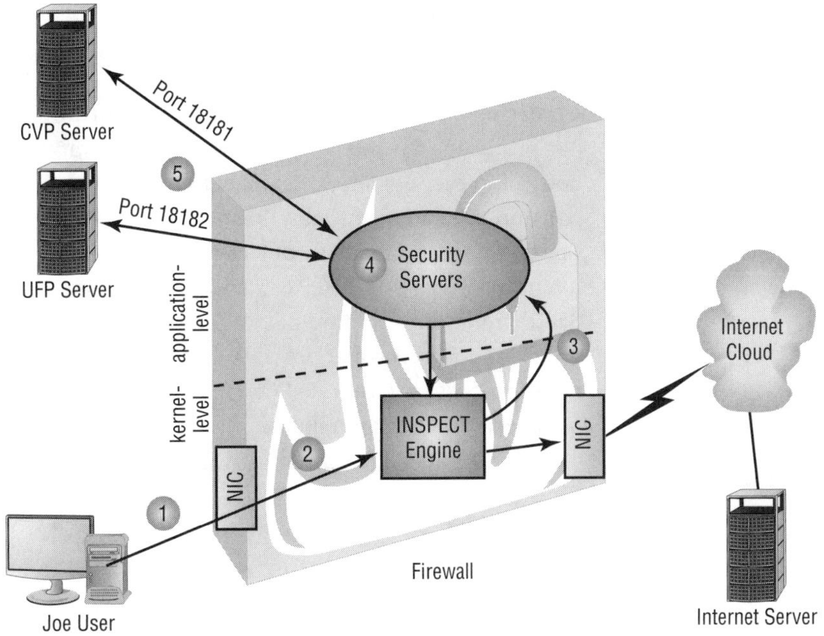

When a client opens a connection to the server, the Security Server kills the
connection and opens a new connection to the server. The connection is killed
at the kernel level using NAT. The kernel translates the destination address to
one of its local interface addresses and to the Security Server special port
(defined for each Security Server in fwauthd.conf). NATing the connection in
the kernel to the module address is called *folding*.

The rule base inspection happens at the kernel level (that's why it's so fast),
but the Security Servers work in application layer space and are therefore
slower. Once the connection is being handled by the Security Servers in step 4,
the Security Servers accept, reject, or modify the traffic based on the rule. The
firewall can do everything described so far without any external help. If you
need more functionality than the Content Security features of the firewall
offer, you can combine them with an OPSEC server as depicted in step 5.

⊕ Real World Scenario

Why Content Security?

Increasing numbers of firewall administrators are responsible for more than just protecting the internal network from bad traffic on the Internet: They are becoming responsible for controlling the content of the data packets and policing the use of company resources by employees. This is where the Content Security features of FireWall-1 come in handy. You can configure the firewall to control FTP GET and PUT commands, control the content of SMTP traffic by stripping out dangerous attachments (like the Melissa virus), and strip Java and ActiveX code out of web pages, as well as apply other processes. FireWall-1 can also use other vendor applications to enhance filtering capabilities.

The OPSEC servers used in conjunction with Content Security fall into two categories:

Content Vectoring Protocol (CVP) Servers   A CVP server's basic function is virus scanning. If a data stream hits the firewall and matches a Content Security rule, the packets are folded up to the Security Servers and can be sent to a CVP server on a specific port to be scanned for viruses.

URL Filtering Protocol (UFP) Servers   A UFP server's basic function is scanning web traffic. Traffic is routed from the firewall in the same way as the CVP server, but it scans web traffic and uses a different port to communicate with the firewall.

After scanning the traffic with a CVP or UFP server, if the connection is allowed through the firewall, the Security Server opens a second connection to the final destination (the firewall acts as a *proxy*).

In version 4.1, the packet leaving the Security Server had the source IP address of the firewall. In NG, the outbound kernel translates this source IP address to the IP address of the client that originally opened the connection. If the client is configured for Hide or Static NAT, the source IP address will be translated to whatever is configured in the rule base.

If the client uses the HTTP Security Server as a proxy, connections will leave the firewall with the firewall as the source IP address—no NAT will take place to the IP address of the original client. This is the default behavior of the Security Servers. In versions 4.0 and 4.1, connections always left the firewall with the source IP address of the firewall. To change the behavior to that of previous versions, use dbedit to change the following properties from true to false in $FWDIR/conf/objects_5_0.C:

http_transparent_server_connection

ftp_transparent_server_connection

We've covered the 20,000-foot view of Content Security. Now, let's look at the specifics.

Security Servers Overview

The way Security Servers operate has changed from previous versions of FireWall-1. Previously, there was a separate service for each Security Server. In the NG version of Check Point FireWall-1, the *fwssd* executable is in charge of all Security Server functions.

 Changing the architecture so that only one executable is in charge of a function or set of functions offers an advantage: It increases performance and eases debugging and troubleshooting (you no longer need to kill daemons or stop the firewall to debug and troubleshoot).

There are five Security Servers. Some are responsible for Content Security and some for User Authentication, and some fulfill both roles. Table 4.1 lists the Security Servers and their roles in User Authentication and Content Security.

TABLE 4.1 Security Servers and Their Roles

Security Server	User Authentication	Content Security
telnet	Yes	No
rlogin	Yes	No
HTTP	Yes	Yes
FTP	Yes	Yes
SMTP	No	Yes

We explore the Security Servers further in the following sections of this chapter. User Authentication is a topic covered in the CCSA book and will not be discussed in this book; therefore the roles of Telnet, rlogin, HTTP and FTP as they relate to User Authentication will not be covered.

HTTP Security Server

The HTTP Security Server (also known as a URI resource) controls schemes, methods, URLs, paths, and queries. It can also scan for viruses via CVP or screen URLs against a vendor-maintained database via UFP. The URI resource can be used to gather verbose logging information on web surfing habits and to protect against web attacks such as Code Red. The HTTP Security Server can also scan URI traffic based the firewall administrator's definition of the URI resource. It can scan on a case-by-case basis, against a file the firewall administrator defines, or against a database maintained by a third-party vendor.

You can increase the number of Security Server processes associated with filtering URI traffic by adding more instances of in.ahttpd in the $FWDIR/conf/fwauthd.conf file.

FTP Security Server

The FTP Security Server controls GET and PUT commands, filename restrictions, and virus checking (via CVP). It can also monitor FTP traffic via logging.

You can increase the number of Security Server processes associated with filtering FTP traffic by adding more instances of in.aftpd in the $FWDIR/conf/fwauthd.conf file.

SMTP Security Server

The SMTP Security Server's functions are based on the TO and FROM fields. This Security Server can perform the following Content Security actions:

- Provide mail address translation by hiding outgoing mail's FROM address behind a standard generic address

- Perform mail filtering based on SMTP/IP addresses
- Strip MIME and file attachments of specified types
- Drop mail messages that are larger than a defined size
- Resolve the DNS address for mail recipients and their domain on outgoing connections (referred to as *MX resolving*)
- Send numerous mail messages in a single connection
- Control the load generated by the mail dequeuer by controlling the number of connections per site and controlling overall the number of connections generated by the mail dequeuer
- Send mail to a CVP server for virus or content checking

SMTP provides a secure sendmail application that prevents direct online connection attacks. This application also can serve as an SMTP address translator by rewriting information in the FROM field to hide real user-names while maintaining connectivity by restoring the correct addresses in the response.

You can increase the number of Security Server processes associated with filtering SMTP traffic by adding more instances of in.asmtpd in the $FWDIR/ conf/fwauthd.conf file.

Additional Security Server Information

Security Servers have a tendency to use a lot of CPU cycles. Because there is no executable file for each Security Server (each Security Server links to the fwssd executable), you cannot grep for information or check the Windows Task Manager to look for CPU utilization. To find out if you need to increase the number of Security Servers for a specific protocol, look for the relevant Security Server's Process ID (PID) in the $FWDIR/tmp directory (for example, the SMTP Security Server's PID is written in the in.asmtpd.pid file). Once you know the PID number, you can grep for the PID or look for the number in the Windows Task Manager Processes tab; then, you can modify $FWDIR/ conf/fwauthd.conf accordingly.

RFC2518 describes HTTP Extensions for Distributed Authoring (WEB-DAV), which is required for e-mail access over HTTP for applications such as Hotmail. As of FP3, the HTTP Security Server supports intelligent inspection of this type of traffic.

Content-Filtering Protocols

As mentioned earlier, Check Point utilizes two different protocols to filter the content of HTTP, FTP, SMTP, and TCP traffic: CVP and UFP. Each protocol runs on a specific port and offers a different functionality, as described in the following sections. The Application Program Interface (API) information for each of these protocols can be found at www.opsec.com. Check Point encourages vendors to program their content filtering products to interface with FireWall-1.

Content Vectoring Protocol (CVP)

Content Vectoring Protocol (CVP) allows FireWall-1 to send a connection on port 18181 to a CVP server to perform content checking. This API scans HTTP, FTP, SMTP, or other TCP data streams for viruses and malicious Java and ActiveX code. Some of the products also perform security for e-mail message content, but the CVP's main function is virus scanning.

Products certified by Check Point for CVP can be found at http://www.opsec.com/solutions/sec_content_security.html.

FireWall-1 also supports CVP in a load sharing or chaining configuration.

URL Filtering Protocol (UFP)

URL Filtering Protocol (UFP) allows FireWall-1 to send data on port 18182 to a UFP server to perform URL filtering. This API allows organizations to monitor and/or eliminate network traffic to Internet sites deemed inappropriate or otherwise undesirable, as well as control the content viewed by the end user.

Products certified by Check Point for UFP can be found at http://www.opsec.com/solutions/sec_url_resource_management.html.

Creating Content Security Objects

Now that you understand the theory and components involved in Content Security, it's time to explain how to configure Content Security objects on the firewall.

Creating CVP and UFP Objects in FireWall-1

In order for the firewall to work with a CVP and/or UFP server, it must be able to communicate with that server. To accomplish this task, follow these steps:

1. Create a Host Node object to represent the IP address of the server, as shown in Figure 4.2 (you don't need to define anything but the General Properties).

FIGURE 4.2   Creating a Host Node object

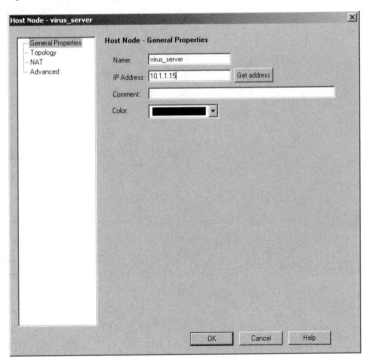

2. Create the OPSEC application object by going to Manage ≻ OPSEC Applications in the SmartDashboard. Choose New ≻ OPSEC Application to open the OPSEC Application Properties window shown in Figure 4.3.

FIGURE 4.3 OPSEC Application Properties for a CVP server

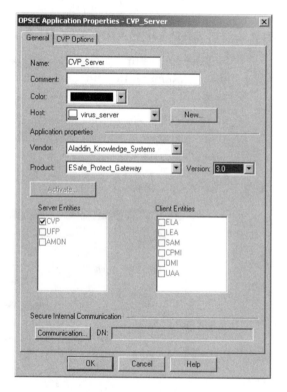

3. To create a CVP server object, first type a name for the object in the Name field (you cannot use a previously used name, and the name cannot contain any spaces or reserved words). Make the name something that is recognizable for that specific server, for example CVP_ server. The Comment and Color fields are optional. The Host field uses the pull-down menu to pull the Host Node object from the Network Objects Manager (in this example, represented by the virus_ server object you just created). Under Application Properties, the specific vendor is identified along with the specific product and version

number. The Server and Client Entities for that product are automatically selected.

Server and Client Entities

CVP and UFP are self-explanatory, but the rest of the entities are defined as follows:

- Application Monitoring (AMON) allows the OPSEC server to report its status to Check Point.

- Event Logging API (ELA) allows OPSEC applications to log events to VPN-1/FireWall-1.

- Log Export API (LEA) allows OPSEC applications to receive real-time and historical auditing log data generated by VPN-1/FireWall-1.

- Suspicious Activities Monitor (SAM) integrates OPSEC IDS applications with VPN-1/FireWall-1.

- Check Point Management Interface (CPMI) is the GUI access protocol for NG.

- Object Management Interface (OMI) was the GUI access protocol for pre-NG versions of VPN-1/FireWall-1.

- UserAuthorityAPI (UAA) integrates FireWall-1 user authentication information with OPSEC applications.

---

1. Secure Internal Communications (SIC) must be established between the SmartCenter Server and the OPSEC application. You do this by loading the OS-specific OPSEC SIC utility application on the CVP server and initializing the communication between the SmartCenter Server and the CVP server.

2. After communication has been established, you need to set the CVP options (see Figure 4.4). The Service option is the default predefined TCP service *FW1_cvp*; if you look in the Services Manager, you will see that this service runs on port 18181. You should select Use Early Versions Compatibility Mode only if you are communicating with a non-NG firewall/management server.

FIGURE 4.4 CVP Options window

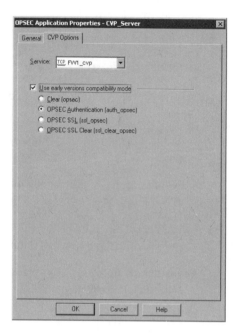

The process for creating a UFP server object is nearly identical to that for creating a CVP server object:

1. Create the Host Node object to represent the IP address of the UFP server.

2. Create the OPSEC application. Under the General tab of the OPSEC Application Properties window, the Vendor and Product options reflect the UFP options as shown in Figure 4.5.

3. The UFP Options tab is a bit different from the CVP Options tab, as shown in Figure 4.6. The Service option is the default predefined TCP service *FW1_ufp*; if you look in the Services Manager, you will see that it runs on port 18182. The Get Dictionary option lets you pull the categories from the UFP server. Use the Use Early Versions Compatibility Mode check box only if you are communicating with a non-NG firewall/management server.

FIGURE 4.5 OPSEC Application Properties for a UFP server

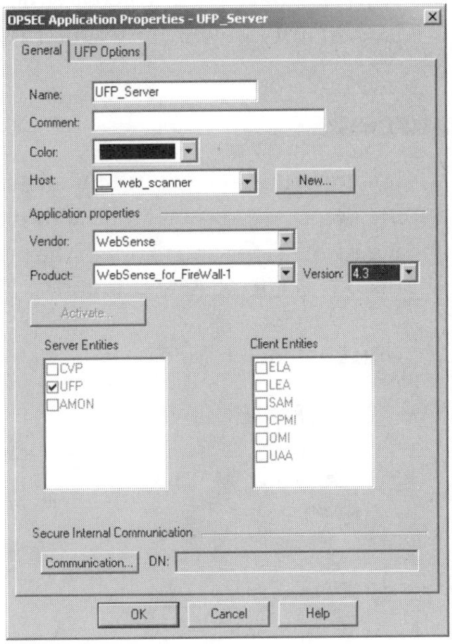

FIGURE 4.6 UFP Options window

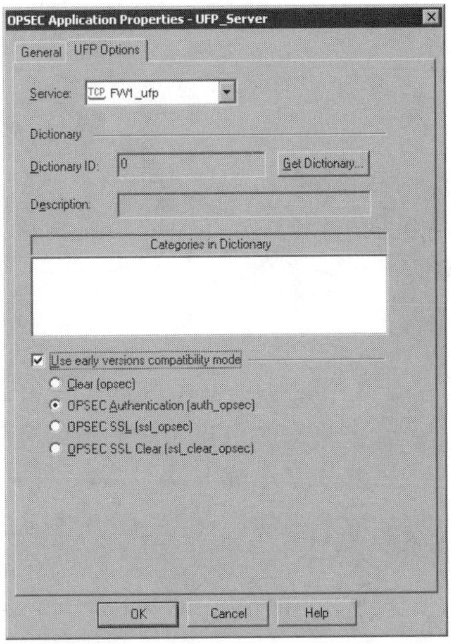

Once you've created the Host Node objects and OPSEC application objects, you're ready to create the resource objects needed to enforce Content Security in your FireWall-1 rule base.

URI Resources

It's important for you to understand the theory behind URL Content Filtering before we show you how to physically make it happen on the firewall. Figure 4.7 steps you through the process of content-filtering web traffic (also known as URL Content Filtering). This process involves the following steps:

FIGURE 4.7 URL Content Filtering

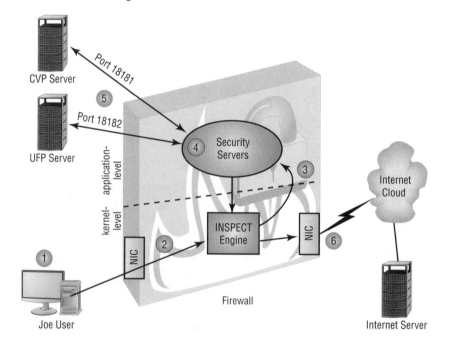

1. Joe User wants to visit a particular web site, so he opens a web browser and types in the specific URL.

2. The request reaches the firewall. The INSPECT engine intercepts the packet and then matches it against the rule base.

3. The request matches a resource rule in the rule base and is folded up to the Security Server process.

4. The Security Server makes decisions based on how the URI resource has been configured.

5. One of the decisions the Security Server can make is to send the connection to a UFP or CVP server for additional filtering. In order for this to happen, the UFP or CVP server must return the packet to the firewall.

6. After filtering is complete, and if the connection is allowed, the Security Server opens a connection to the web server identified by Joe User in step 1.

URI stands for Uniform Resource Identifier. Most people are familiar with the term Uniform Resource Locator (URL); a URL is a specific case of a URI.

Creating URI Resource Objects

Figure 4.8 illustrates the URI Resource Properties dialog box where you'll set up properties for resources, connection methods, exception track, and URI match specification types. To access the URI Resource Properties window, go to Manage ➢ Resources and click on New ➢ URI.

FIGURE 4.8 URI Resource Properties window

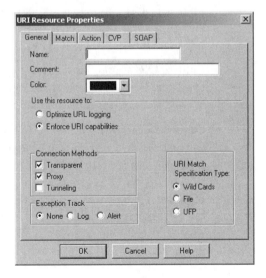

General Tab Options

Under the General tab, you can define a *URI resource* three ways: Wild Cards, File, or UFP. All three options can include interaction with a CVP server but only UFP can include interaction with a UFP server. Regardless of which URI Match Specification Type you use, all URI resources (for that matter, all resource objects) have commonalities—they all define the object's name and methodology under the General tab. The option you select under URI Match Specification Type on the General tab affects what appears under the Match tab. Under the Match tab for each resource object, you specify what you're looking for. Under the Action tab, you define what you want to do if you find what you're looking for. Each resource object also has a CVP tab, where you define whether you want to send this connection on to a CVP server for virus scanning. We'll discuss the General tab, Action tab, CVP tab, and SOAP tab (specific to URI resource objects) first. After we look at these tabs we'll examine the Match tab and URI Match Specification Type options in greater detail.

LOGGING OPTIONS

Let's talk about the specific URI resource options available under the General tab. Two options appear under Use This Resource To, as described here:

Optimize URL Logging   If this option is selected, all other options for the URI resource are grayed out. The Security Policy is enforced when URL logging is integrated with UFP caching. URL logging uses Check Point's TCP streaming technology, which enables the firewall module to take over some of the Security Server functions. Basically, this option gives you more detailed logging of web traffic.

Enforce URI Capabilities   If this option is selected, all other options are available. Everything you define will be checked by the Security Server. We'll discuss this option in great detail later in this section.

Optimize URL Blocking   This option was new in NG FP2 and was moved to SmartDefense in FP3 (see Chapter 2 for more information on Smart-Defense). The purpose of Optimize URL Blocking (as it was called in FP2) or General HTTP Worm Catcher (as it is referred to in FP3) is to look for patterns of HTTP attacks such as Code Red. There is no automatic update of the pattern blocking if you used this feature in FP2 and then upgrade to FP3. You should remove any rules configured in FP2 for pattern blocking and configure them through the SmartDefense settings in FP3.

CONNECTIONS METHODS

In the URI Resource Properties dialog box (Figure 4.8), you can choose from three Connection Methods:

- **Transparent**   Matches all connections that are not in proxy mode and is relevant only if a proxy to the web browser is *not* defined.

- **Proxy**   Matches connections in proxy mode and is relevant only if a proxy to the web browser *is* defined.

- **Tunneling**   Matches connections using the HTTP CONNECT method and is relevant only if the HTTP Security Server is defined as the proxy to the web browser.

As of FP2, the HTTP Security Server handles the Transparent and Proxy connections differently. If a rule is matched and the Action of the rule is Accept, proxied or tunneled connections are not allowed. They are allowed only if the rule matched is an Authentication or Resource rule. The functionality was changed to prevent the CONNECT method from looping to the HTTP Security Server and then to another destination.

FP2 also allowed FTP over HTTP proxied connections with User Authentication even if a resource rule wasn't defined. FP3 locked this down so that FTP over HTTP proxied connections are not allowed unless there is an explicit URI resource rule with an Action of Accept.

The CONNECT method only specifies the hostname and port number to connect to. When the Tunneling option is specified, the firewall doesn't examine the content of the request or even the URL—it only checks the hostname and port number. Therefore, if Tunneling is specified, all Content Security options under the Match tab (with the exception of the Host field) are grayed out.

EXCEPTION TRACK

The Exception Track area at the bottom of the URI Resource Properties dialog box defines what to log. We always turn on logging because it gives detailed information, such as which link in the web site the user visited or tried to visit. We don't recommend turning on Alert, because too many alerts will be generated due to the amount of web surfing that takes place on corporate networks.

Action Tab Options

In the Action tab of the URI Resource dialog box, shown in Figure 4.9, you define what happens to the traffic if it matches your specifications. The Replacement URI field is our favorite feature for HTTP scanning. If this value is defined and the Action of the rule that incorporates this resource is Drop or Reject, then this URI is given to the user instead of the URI they requested. For example, if a user tried to visit pornographic sites during work hours, you could redirect them to a custom web page that outlines the Human Resources policies that prohibit this kind of activity.

FIGURE 4.9 URI resource Action tab

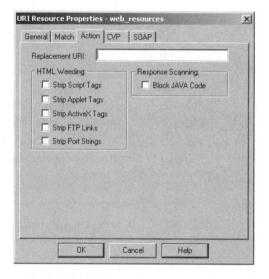

If a UFP server, defined on this URI resource, sends a URL for redirection, it will override this replacement URI.

HTML Weeding options allow you to strip specified code from an HTML page. The user will not be aware that the code has been stripped (Java applets already in the cache are not affected by this option).

The truth is, the code is not really stripped from the web page; as you can see in Figure 4.10, the code is still there. The firewall takes the HTML header information and modifies it so the browser doesn't run the code (note the highlighted changes in Figure 4.10).

FIGURE 4.10 Source code that results from HTML weeding

```
A:hover (color:"#FF3300";)
-->
</STYLE>
<LINK REL="stylesheet" type="text/css" href="/library/flyoutmenu/default.css" />
<scrip! language="JavaScrip!">
<!--
        var userAgent = navigator.userAgent;
        var MSIEIndex = userAgent.indexOf("MSIE");
        if (userAgent.indexOf("Win")  != -1 &&
                userAgent.indexOf("MSIE") != -1 &&
                userAgent.substring((MSIEIndex + 5),(MSIEIndex + 6)) > 4)
                window.location.replace("ms.htm");

function initPage()
{
        var userAgent = navigator.userAgent;
        var MSIEIndex = userAgent.indexOf("MSIE");
        if (userAgent.indexOf("Win")  != -1 &&
                userAgent.indexOf("MSIE") != -1 &&
                userAgent.substring((MSIEIndex + 5),(MSIEIndex + 6)) > 3)
        {
                FTDownLevelDiv.style.display = "none";
                drawFooter();
        }
}
//-->
</script>
</HEAD>
<BODY onloa!="loadPage(100);initPage();" BGCOLOR="#FFFFFF" TOPMARGIN="0" LEFTMARGIN="0" MARGINWII
<scrip! language="JavaScrip!" src="/library/toolbar/toolbar.js"></script>
<scrip! language="JavaScrip!" src="/library/toolbar/en-us/globalMNP.js"></script>
<scrip! language="JavaScrip!" src="/library/toolbar/en-us/localMNP.js"></script>
```

CVP Tab Options

In the CVP tab of the URI Resource dialog box, shown in Figure 4.11, you define what happens if you want the traffic sent to a CVP server.

FIGURE 4.11 CVP tab

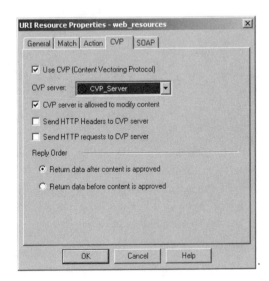

First you must select the Use CVP (Content Vectoring Procotol) check box; otherwise all other options are grayed out. The CVP Server Is Allowed To Modify Content option lets the CVP server know whether it can modify the content if necessary (for example, to clean out a virus). HTTP headers and requests can also be sent to the CVP server for content checking. Reply Order options determine how the content will be filtered. If Return Data After Content Is Approved is selected, no data is sent back to the firewall until the entire data stream is filtered. If Return Data Before Content Is Approved is selected, the data is scanned packet by packet.

SOAP Tab Options

In the SOAP tab (new to FP3 and unique to the URI resource object), shown in Figure 4.12, you define how you want Simple Object Access Protocol (SOAP) traffic handled.

FIGURE 4.12 SOAP tab

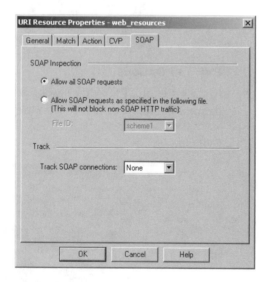

SOAP is an XML/HTTP-based protocol for sharing data over the Internet platform independently using HTTP. SOAP relies on XML to encode the information to be shared and then adds HTTP headers. This new FP3 feature allows a URI resource to parse SOAP traffic and validate its integrity according to a user-defined scheme.

SOAP is a call-response protocol. The client calls the server across the Internet, passing commands called *methods*. The server then provides a response. Both calls and responses are XML documents. FireWall-1 detects these SOAP packets and then decides to accept them all if Allow All SOAP Requests is selected, or to accept them only if a user-defined scheme is met (if Allow SOAP Requests As Specified In The Following File is selected). This option will not block non-SOAP traffic.

The SOAP file must have one of 10 predefined names: scheme1, scheme2, scheme3, and so on. These files already exist in the $FWDIR/conf/XML directory but are blank by default. The file contents are defined very specifically with the namespace and method separated by a space. If the syntax is not correct, the SOAP packets are dropped; so, it's a good idea to copy and paste the namespace and method information directly from your logs. Here is an example of two lines from a user-defined scheme:

```
http://test.org/text/ GetScript
http://test.org/text/ Total
```

If you're using Management High Availability, these files must be duplicated on all SmartCenter Servers.

Now that we've looked at the common options shared by all URI resources, let's backtrack and visit the URI Match Specification Type option; this option distinguishes the three different ways the firewall can filter web traffic. We'll begin with filtering by wildcards.

Filtering by Wildcards

The Wild Cards URI Match Specification Type allows firewall administrators to define specific web sites they wish to block or filter. You begin this process by selecting Wild Cards under the URI Match Specification Type in the General tab of the URI Resource Properties, as shown in Figure 4.13.

FIGURE 4.13   Wild Cards URI Match Specification Type

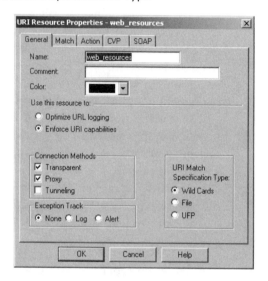

With Wild Cards selected, the Match tab appears as shown in Figure 4.14.

FIGURE 4.14   Match tab when the Wild Cards URI Match Specification Type is selected

Firewall administrators are able to determine which schemes and methods they wish to filter. Keep in mind that the Schemes field is relevant only when the HTTP Security Server is defined as a proxy to the browser. The Other field lets you define methods and schemes not listed.

At the heart of the Wild Cards option is the ability to define a specific web site, link on a web site, or specific query on a web site that you wish to filter or block. For example, a company's security policy states that all ActiveX code will be removed from web content so it doesn't endanger the internal network. You can accomplish this task by creating a Wild Cards URI resource in which the Host, Path, and Query fields are defined with a wild-card asterisk (*) and the Action tab specifies the Strip ActiveX Tags option. Once the rule base enforces this resource, ActiveX content will be removed from any web site visited.

The next example uses blocking. Suppose a company's security policy prohibits employees from visiting a competitor's web site to look for jobs. You can create a Wild Cards URI resource in which the Host field is the competitor's web site (either the URL or the IP address), the Path field lists the specific portion of the web site that lists job openings, and the Query field is filled in with a wildcard (*) to cover any type of query, as shown in Figure 4.15. Once the rule base enforces this resource, employees will be able to visit the competitor's site but unable to click on the job listings.

FIGURE 4.15   Wild Cards URI resource example

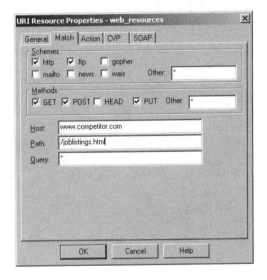

When you're defining the Host field, you can use a wildcard, IP address, or fully DNS resolvable name. If you wish to define a hostname and a port number, the port number must be specifically defined (for example, www.mydomain.com:8080).

The HTTP Security Servers sometimes see the IP address instead of the host-names because the Security Server uses reverse DNS lookups to resolve the IP address to a hostname; if it doesn't resolve, the URI resource will not match.

The Path value can include a pathname, including a filename and wild-cards, as the examples in Table 4.2 show.

TABLE 4.2 Path Name Examples for the Wild Cards URI Resource

Path	Description
/dir/home/*	Includes all the files in the /dir/home directory.
/dir/home/	Does not include any of the files in the /dir/home directory.
/dir/home	If /dir/home were a file, it would be included in /dir/home.

Filtering by File

The File URI Match Specification Type allows firewall administrators to create and maintain a list of web sites they wish to block and/or filter. Before creating this resource object, you must create the list in a specific format using a text editor. The format looks like this:

URL or IP address <Tab>*path* <Tab>*category*<Enter>

Table 4.3 lists the formats for addresses, paths, and categories.

TABLE 4.3 Formatting Addresses, Paths, and Categories

Field	Description	Example
IP Address	URI's IP address or URL	207.46.197.100

TABLE 4.3 Formatting Addresses, Paths, and Categories *(continued)*

Field	Description	Example
Path	URI's path	/personal (defines only everything under personals at 207.46.197.100)
Category (in hex)	Not functional, but must be defined in order for the file to work	Any hexadecimal character (a–f or 0–9)

The format of this file is critical—if you don't follow it explicitly, the resource will not work. Each web site you wish to filter or block has its own line in the file, with no white space between categories. You *must* end each line by pressing the Enter key. The practical limit for this file is 50 web sites—if you have more than 50 web sites in your list, you should consider purchasing a UFP server to manage your web filtering. The file should be saved in ASCII.

You should initially save the file on whichever machine houses the Smart-Dashboard you will use to create this resource (don't forget where you stored it; you'll see why this is necessary in a moment). Now you can create the resource object by selecting the File option under URI Match Specification Type under the General tab of the URI Resource Properties, as shown in Figure 4.16.

FIGURE 4.16 Filtering by file

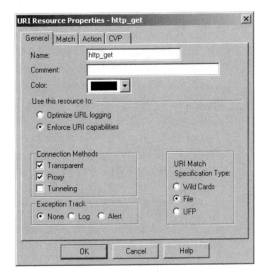

With File selected, the Match tab view appears as shown in Figure 4.17.

FIGURE 4.17 Match tab when the File URI Match Specification Type is selected

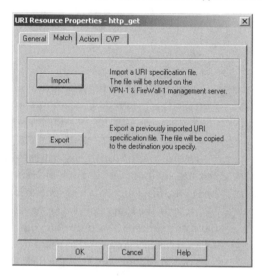

Clicking the Import button will prompt you to open the file you've created. (That's why it is important to remember where you stored the file, and why it must be on the same machine that houses the SmartDashboard you're using to create the resource.) Once imported, the ASCII file is saved with the name of the resource. For example, suppose you've created a text file named badwebstuff.txt. Then you've imported the file in your URI resource, which is named badstuff. The file is saved on the SmartCenter Server with the filename badstuff, not the original text filename, badwebstuff. This file is stored in $FWDIR/conf/lists and is also referenced in the $FWDIR/conf/fwrl.conf file. If you need to update the file, you can edit it directly on the SmartCenter Server. You also have the option of going to any Smart-Dashboard and exporting the list from the resource object, modifying it, and re-importing it.

For example, if you wanted to block corporate users from visiting the personal pages on Yahoo!, the line in the file would look something like this:

personals.yahoo.com<Tab><Tab>a<Enter>

Users would be allowed to go to Yahoo!, but would be unable to go to the personal pages. You didn't need to define a specific link on that web site, but the space had to be accounted for in the file so the extra tab character had to be included in the spot in which the link would have been defined.

Filtering with a UFP Server

The UFP URI Match Specification Type allows firewall administrators to use an OPSEC server to keep track of sites they wish to block or filter. Before you create the resource object, you must create a Host Node object and pull it into an OPSEC application object as described in the section "Creating CVP and UFP Objects in FireWall-1" earlier in this chapter. Then, you can create a resource and select the UFP radio button under the URI Match Specification Type in the General tab of the URI Resource Properties, as shown in Figure 4.18.

FIGURE 4.18 Filtering with UFP

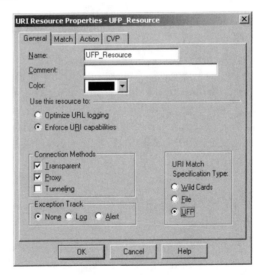

With UFP selected, the Match tab appears as shown in Figure 4.19.

The OPSEC server is pulled into the UFP Server field, and the categories you wish to filter/block are listed in the Categories field. You have caching options to speed up web browsing. The choices are No Caching, UFP Server, and VPN-1 & FireWall-1(one or two requests). Because the investment has been made for a UFP server, it makes sense to use this caching feature on the UFP server to speed up web browsing for users.

FIGURE 4.19 Match tab when the UFP URI Match Specification Type is selected

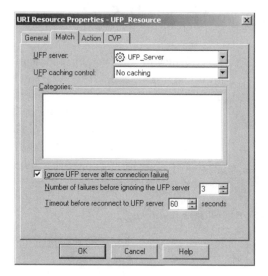

There is one more option under the Match tab—Ignore UFP Server After Connection Failure—but we consider this option useless. You can define the number of failures and the timeout for reconnection; if the firewall still cannot contact the UFP server after that time period, then the firewall will ignore the UFP server and allow the traffic to proceed unfiltered.

Global Properties

Security Server Global Properties also affect the HTTP Security Server (see Figure 4.20).

The HTTP Next Proxy setting defines the hostname and port number of an HTTP proxy server that sits behind the firewall (if you have one). If defined there, these settings affect pre-NG firewalls. You define your HTTP Next Proxy settings in your Gateway object under Authentication for NG firewalls.

FIGURE 4.20   HTTP Security Server Global Properties

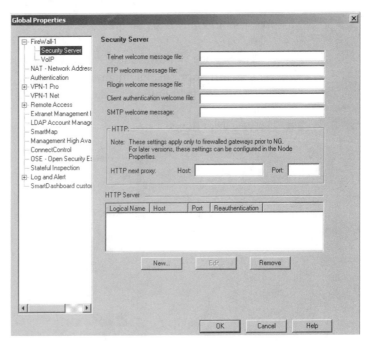

Only an IP address can be used in the HTTP Next Proxy field if the internal web browsers are configured to proxy to an IP address (which they should be). If the browsers are configured to use a hostname instead of an IP address, the HTTP Security Server doesn't allow the connections to the proxy.

The HTTP Server option allows you to define specific hostnames and port numbers for the purpose of restricting incoming HTTP traffic. You can control access to specific ports on specific hosts and whether users must reauthenticate when accessing a server on this list.

Writing Resource Rule(s)

After creating the Host Node (if necessary), OPSEC application (if necessary), and URI resource objects, you need to create rule(s) to enforce the Content Security parameters. You add resources to the rule base's Service column by right-clicking in the column and selecting Add With Resource.

You can add only one resource per rule.

The Service With Resource window appears; it includes the various Content Security options. Highlighting the service you wish to filter populates the Resource field pull-down menu, as shown in Figure 4.21

FIGURE 4.21 Service With Resource window

After selecting a resource from the pull-down menu, populate the Source and Destination columns in the rule as needed, and select the Action to achieve your objective. Selecting Accept as the Action will filter out the unwanted content but allow the rest of the content to reach the user. A rule base such as the one depicted in Figure 4.22 allows web traffic out of the network but filters out malicious Java and ActiveX code.

FIGURE 4.22 Rule base to filter out malicious content

Depending on your resource object, selecting Drop or Reject as the Action will either stop users from accessing that web site or redirect them to another web site. Such a rule base could prevent access to certain sites while allowing access to others, or it could redirect a user to another web site if the resource was set up that way. Figure 4.23 shows the rule base in which rule 1 rejects access so that rule 2 can allow the connection to be redirected to a replacement URI.

FIGURE 4.23   Rule base to block access

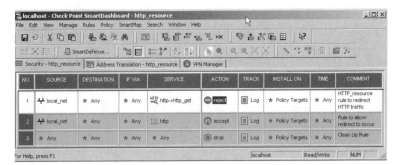

Here are some guidelines for adding Content Security rules to your rule base:

- When using an OPSEC application server, a rule allowing the connection from the firewall to the server is required to allow for file transfers between the firewall and the OPSEC server. This rule is usually taken care of by the Accept VPN-1 & FireWall-1 Control Connections global property. If this implied rule is not enabled, an explicit rule must be written to include the appropriate ports as defined here:

  - Use the FW1_cvp service (port 18181) for a CVP server.

  - Use the FW1_ufp service (port 18182) for a UFP server.

- Content Security rules *do not* replace rules allowing FTP, HTTP, or SMTP connections. Therefore, Content Security rules must go before other rules that accept these services.

- Content Security rules that reject HTTP, FTP, or SMTP must be placed before Content Security rules that filter these connections.

Now that you understand the theory behind URI Content Filtering as well as what it takes to configure it on the firewall, you should be ready to put your knowledge into action with the following exercise. Figure 4.24 shows you the configuration you'll need for Exercise 4.1.

FIGURE 4.24 Configuration for Exercise 4.1

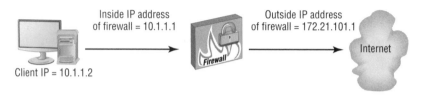

Inside IP address
of firewall = 10.1.1.1

Outside IP address
of firewall = 172.21.101.1

Internet

Client IP = 10.1.1.2

EXERCISE 4.1

URL Filtering to Remove Malicious Code

1. Create a network object called local_net that represents the internal network, with a network address of 10.1.1.0 and a subnet mask of 255.255.255.0.

2. Create a URI resource object by going to Manage ≻ Resources and clicking on New ≻ URI.

3. In the General tab, populate the listed fields with the following information:

   Name: bad_stuff

   Use This Resource To: Enforce URI Capabilities

   URI Match Specification Type: Wild Cards

   Exception Track: Log

4. Click the Match tab. Select all Schemes and Methods options. Enter a wildcard (*) in the Host, Path, and Query fields.

5. Click on the Action tab. Select all the HTML Weeding options, and select Block JAVA Code.

6. Locate a web site that contains HTML code to filter out (such as a site that contains either Java or ActiveX code). Make note of this page for use in testing this URI resource.

7. Create a new blank rule base.

8. Add a resource rule with the following parameters:

Source: local_net

Destination: any

Service with Resource: http ➤ bad_stuff

Action: Accept

Track: Log

9. Below the resource rule, add an HTTP access rule with the following parameters:

Source: local_net

Destination: any

Service: http

Action: Accept

Track: Log

10. Add the Cleanup rule as the last rule in the rule base.

11. Verify and install the policy.

12. Clear your browser's cache and then go to the web site identified in step 6. The Java and/or ActiveX content should not be viewable and/or functional. View the source code in your web browser and try to identify the changes that were made to the HTML code. Hint: Look for instances in which the last letter of a command/word was changed to an exclamation point (!).

13. View the Info field in the SmartView Tracker. You should see verbose information about the HTTP connection.

SMTP Resources

Filtering e-mail is another Content Security option; you can do this by creating SMTP resource objects. With SMTP Content Filtering, the firewall acts as a *mail relay*, filtering the mail content before forwarding it on to your internal mail server. This process is outlined in Figure 4.25 and works as follows:

FIGURE 4.25   SMTP Security Server process

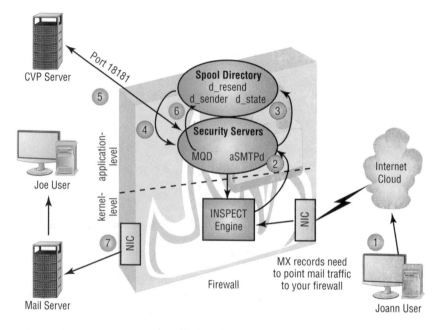

1. Joann User sends an e-mail to Joe User. With the implementation of SMTP Content Security, Mail eXchange (MX) records would have been modified to point all mail traffic to the firewall.

2. The *aSMTPd* daemon on the firewall listens for mail traffic on port 25. `in.asmtpd` (the aSMTPd daemon as it's listed in `$FWDIR/conf/fwauthd.conf`) performs a separate rule match for every recipient. The aSMTPd daemon listens for only a small subset of sendmail commands (EHLO, MAIL, RCPT, DATA, SIZE, EHOL, RSET NOOP, QUIT, and HELP), to prevent the more common sendmail exploits.

3. The aSMTPd daemon sends the mail to the spool directory—specifically the d_state subdirectory.

4. The *mail dequeuer (MQD)* daemon checks the spool directory for messages and performs the necessary actions as defined in the SMTP resource (such as MIME stripping, rewriting headers, blocking mail above a specific size, and so on).

5. One of the actions performed could include sending the mail to a CVP server to be checked.

6. If no errors are detected in the message, MQD will transfer the message to the d_sender spool subdirectory.

7. MDQ pulls mail from the spool and tries to send the message to the recipient (internal mail server). If there are problems with the delivery of the mail, MQD will send the messages to the d_resend spool subdirectory (the *resend queue*); the firewall will attempt to resend the message when it's not too busy.

SMTP Content Security performance is enhanced in NG because the MQD daemon runs in multithreaded mode by default.

SMTP Content Filtering is a complex process, but it is important to understand it so you comprehend what you are configuring on the firewall instead of just learning the steps.

SMTP Performance

NG has made tremendous strides in improving the SMTP Content Security processes. A new spool-handling mechanism makes sure that mail is handled using First In/First Out (FIFO). This process gives new mail priority over old mail that is waiting to be resent.

Pre-NG versions of the firewall suffered from performance problems. The most pronounced was that the MQD daemon opened a connection for every file. These problems have been addressed in NG by making more SMTP load control parameters configurable. Some parameters can be configured through the GUI by going to SMTP under the Advanced option of the firewalled gateway object; others require modification of the $FWDIR/conf/ *smtp.conf* file. Figure 4.26 illustrates the SMTP load control options.

FIGURE 4.26 Firewalled gateway SMTP load control options

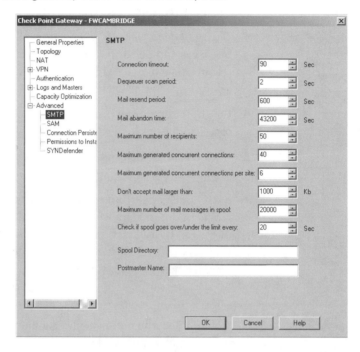

In the GUI, you can configure the Maximum Generated Concurrent Connections and Maximum Generated Concurrent Connections Per Site, among other options. Some of the settings in the GUI are duplicated in the $FWDIR/conf/smtp.conf file, as shown in Figure 4.27.

FIGURE 4.27 Contents of the smtp.conf file

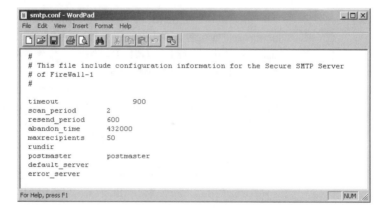

To solve the pre-NG issue of MQD opening a connection for every file, add a `max_mail_per_conn` line in the `smtp.conf` file and set its value to 20 or greater.

You have two options for SMTP Content Security: You can filter mail with or without the help of an OPSEC CVP server. Let's examine these options in more detail.

Filtering Without a CVP Server

The firewall can scan and modify mail without the help of a CVP server, but it cannot perform virus scanning without a CVP server. In this section, we'll explore the filtering capabilities the firewall has without using a CVP server.

In the SmartDashboard, go to Manage ➢ Resources and open the Resources Manager. Click on New ➢ SMTP to open the SMTP Resource Properties page shown in Figure 4.28.

FIGURE 4.28   SMTP Resource Properties

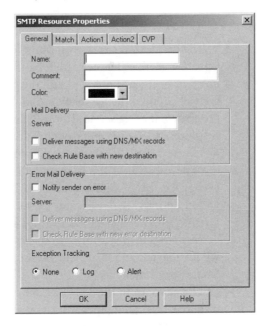

Like any other object, you give the SMTP resource a Name, Comment, and Color. Two sections dictate mail delivery: Mail Delivery and Error Mail

Delivery, and each must be defined. Under Mail Delivery, you enter the internal mail server's IP address in the Server field (if this field is left empty, mail is forwarded to the IP address specified under `default_server` in the $FWDIR/conf/smtp.conf file; see Figure 4.27). Deliver Messages Using DNS/MX Records is a new field in NG; it solves a lot of version 4.x problems with mail delivery. If this option is turned on, the MX record is used to set the destination IP address of the connection. The message will be sent only when the IP address is resolved. The Check Rule Base With New Destination option works in conjunction with the MX option. If it's checked, the rule base will be checked again with the new resolved IP address, and all resource actions will be determined based on the last matched rule.

MX resolving is DNS resolving for mail. The firewall receives a recipient's name and resolves its domain. If the mail message has recipients in multiple domains, the original message is split by domains. When you're using MX resolving, you can add two variables to $FWDIR/conf/smtp.conf: max_mx_node_per_mail (5 should be the default) and max_ips_per_mx_node (1 by default). The maximum number of results is determined by multiplying these two values.

The Error Mail Delivery options define where messages are sent if there is a problem delivering the mail. If Notify Sender On Error is not checked, then no error notification is sent and the rest of the options are grayed out. If it is checked, then the Server field should be populated with the IP address of the error-handling server. (If this field is left empty, mail is forwarded to the IP address specified under `error_server` in the $FWDIR/conf/smtp.conf file. If the `default_server` and `error_server` values are not specified, the error notification is sent to the originator of the mail.) The Deliver Messages Using DNS/MX Records and the Check Rule Base With New Error Destination options work the same as the corresponding options under Mail Delivery. We always set Exception Tracking to Log at minimum; this option determines whether information about an e-mail that matches this resource will be logged, and it provides verbose information in the Info field in the SmartView Tracker.

The next tab in the SMTP resource is the Match tab. As with the URI resource, this tab defines what you are searching for. If the mail you are filtering matches what is defined under this tab, then the actions defined under Action1, Action2, and CVP will be performed. Figure 4.29 illustrates the SMTP Resource Properties Match tab.

FIGURE 4.29 SMTP Resource Properties Match tab

The Sender and Recipient fields can be filled in with wildcards that help to designate the sender and/or recipient. The * wildcard specifies a string of any length (for example, *@domain.com), the + wildcard specifies a single character (jo+@domain.com), and the & wildcard specifies either side of the @ sign (&&mydomain or joeuser@&). You can also fill these fields with a specific user (such as **janeuser@mydomain.com**). If the mail matches what you define here, the defined actions will be performed.

The Action1 tab allows the headers of the mail message to be re-written. Figure 4.30 shows the Rewriting Rules for an SMTP resource.

For example, on this tab you could change the Sender header information to remove the fully qualified name of the mail server (for example, changing **&&mailserver.mydomain.com** to **&&mydomain.com**). The left side of the field is the information you're looking for, and the right side of the field is the result you want to see from the modification. Be sure you don't include embedded spaces in the transformed data. The Action1 tab lets you modify the Sender and Recipient fields along with any other header recognized by sendmail (CC, BCC, and so on).

FIGURE 4.30 Rewriting Rules for an SMTP resource

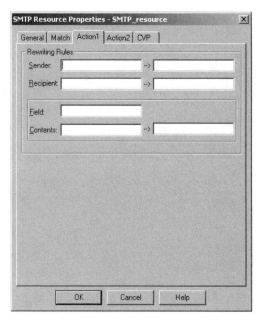

 Stripping To (Sender) and From (Recipient) fields is not recommended, because doing so makes it impossible to deliver the mail.

Whereas the Action1 tab looks at mail header information, the Action2 tab (Figure 4.31) focuses on the body of the mail. The Attachment Handling section allows the administrator to control what type of attachments to allow into or out of the network. Allowed MIME types include text, multipart, message, image, audio, video, and application. (For more information on MIME types, read RFC 1521; you can find it at `http://www.ietf.org/rfc/rfc1521.txt?number=1521.`)

 If you strip MIME of type text, the text in the body of the message is *not* stripped; only attachments of MIME type text are removed.

You can strip out entire groups of files by using the Strip MIME of Type option, or you can strip specific filenames using Strip File by Name. For example, you could remove all executables and Word documents by entering {∗**.exe,**∗**.doc**} in the Strip File by Name field.

FIGURE 4.31 Action2 tab of an SMTP resource

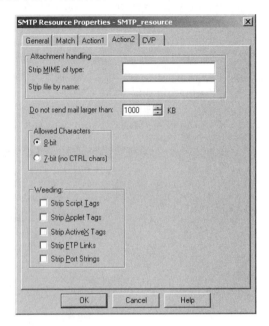

When entering multiple files to strip in the Strip File by Name field, the field must start and end with brackets { } and the file types must be separated by commas.

The Do Not Send Mail Larger Than field lets you control the size of e-mail attachments (this value can also be configured for each gateway, as shown in Figure 4.26 in the Don't Accept Mail Larger Than field. The default value is 1MB. The Allowed Characters option is set to 8-bit by default. This value allows 8-bit ASCII e-mail, which is what the majority of sendmail applications use. The 7-bit option allows only 7-bit ASCII but no control characters.

The Weeding options are new to NG; they arose from the fact that a majority of e-mail today is HTML based. These options let you filter out malicious content as described earlier in the URI Resource section.

Filtering With a CVP Server

The firewall is capable of many more functions with the help of a CVP server. The process of setting up an SMTP resource to utilize CVP scanning requires that you first define a Host Node and pull it into an OPSEC application object, as described in the earlier section "Creating CVP and UFP Objects in FireWall-1." Then, you create an SMTP resource object as described in the previous section "Filtering Without a CVP Server." The only difference in creating a resource that filters with a CVP server is that the information under the CVP tab (Figure 4.32) of the resource is defined.

FIGURE 4.32 CVP tab of an SMTP resource object

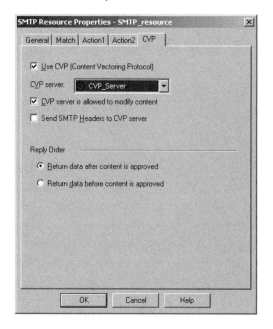

Unless Use CVP (Content Vectoring Protocol) is selected, all other options are grayed out. Selecting this option allows you to pull in an OPSEC CVP server and define how it will interact with FireWall-1. We always turn on CVP Server Is Allowed to Modify Content so that mail sent to the CVP server and found to be infected with a virus can be cleaned of the virus and sent on its way. The Send SMTP Headers to CVP Server option enables the SMTP mail headers to be forwarded to the CVP server for content checking.

The Reply Order option determines when the mail is sent back to MQD to be forwarded to the recipient. If Return Data After Content Is Approved is chosen, the CVP server will receive and check the entire message before sending it back to the Security Server. If Return Data Before Content Is Approved is chosen, each data packet of the message is inspected and the CVP server returns the packet to the Security Server before approving the content of the entire message. For example, if a CVP server finds a virus in a data packet, it may replace the data within the packet before returning it to the Security Server for content checking.

Writing SMTP Resource Rules

The same general rules outlined for creating URI resource rules apply here as well, but you must take one important thing into consideration: Although the SMTP Content Security feature acts as a mail relay, you don't want it to relay mail for everyone on the Internet. Having a server that relays mail for the entire Internet could land you on the *Realtime Blackhole List* (RBL; `http://mail-abuse.org/rbl`). This list exists for the purpose of limiting the transport of known-to-be-unwanted mass e-mail (a.k.a. SPAM).

People who send SPAM scour the Internet looking for misconfigured mail servers that will allow them to "relay" their SPAM and make it look like it came from someone else's mail server. The RBL also finds such servers, but for a different purpose: It puts these servers on its list, which many, many people subscribe to in an effort to prevent SPAM. Once you are on this list, mail originating from your server will begin to be dropped by other mail servers subscribing to the RBL (and once you're on the list, it's not easy to get off). So, you need to set up rules to prevent this situation. A resource should be created for inbound e-mail access and outbound e-mail access. The inbound resource's Match tab should specify the * wildcard in the Sender field, and the Recipient field should contain the destination domain (such as `&@mydomain.com`). The outbound resource's Match tab should specify the domain (such as `&@mydomain.com`) in the Sender field and the * wildcard in the Recipient field. These rules look something like those shown in Figure 4.33.

These rules ensure that no one can use your mailserver as a relay for SPAM.

FIGURE 4.33   Rules to block mail relay

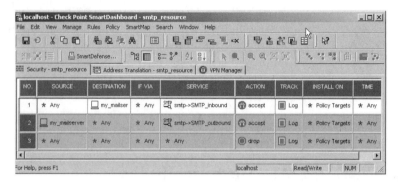

FTP Resources

Scanning FTP traffic is yet another Content Security option. The firewall controls *FTP GET* and *PUT* commands as well as scanning for viruses. This process is outlined in Figure 4.34.

FIGURE 4.34   FTP Security Server process

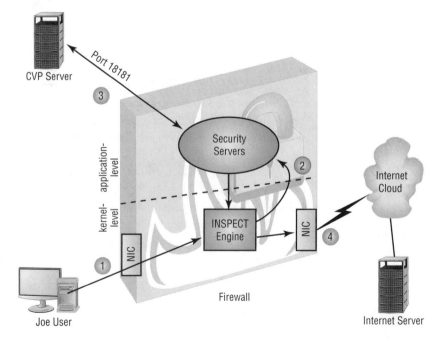

In the scenario presented in Figure 4.34, Joe User wants to FTP his resume to a potential employer. (Joe is being a smart guy and trying to bypass the SMTP scanning he knows his company is doing.) The steps are as follows:

1. Joe creates an FTP session to his potential employer's FTP site on the Internet.

2. Based on a match of an FTP Content Security rule, the INSPECT engine folds the connection to the Security Server. Compared to URI and SMTP resources, FTP Content Security is relatively simple: It can only control sending and retrieving of files and scanning for viruses. Once the connection is associated with the Security Server, it determines whether Joe is getting files or sending files. In this scenario, the FTP resource is blocking the sending of files, so Joe's connection is denied.

3. If the resource had allowed *FTP PUT* and was also configured to scan for viruses, the FTP data stream would have been sent to the CVP server for checking and then sent back to the firewall.

4. If no viruses were found, the connection would have been proxied out to the Internet.

FTP Performance

The firewall FTP Security Server is configured for security and therefore can limit some FTP commands that could be potential risks. These commands are listed in Table 4.3.

TABLE 4.4 FTP Commands that can be blocked by an FTP Security Server

FTP Commands	
ABOR	ACCT
ALLO	APPE
BYE	BYTE
CDUP	CWD
DELE	FIND
FW1C	HELP

TABLE 4.4 FTP Commands that can be blocked by an FTP Security Server *(continued)*

FTP Commands	
LIST	MACB
MAIL	MDTM
MKD	MLFL
MODE	MRCP
MRSQ	MSAM
MSND	MSOM
NLST	NOOP
PASS	PASV
PORT	PWD
QUIT	REIN
REST	RETR
RMD	RNFR
RNTO	SITE
SIZE	SOCK
STOR	STOU
STRU	SYST
TYPE	USER
XCUP	XCWD
XMD5	SMKD
XPWD	XRMD

You can configure these individual commands to be blocked in Smart-Defense under FTP ➢ FTP Security Server ➢ Allowed FTP Commands.

The FTP Security Server provides protection from Known Ports Checking and Port Overflow Checking, both of which are configured in SmartDefense. Please review Chapter 2 for more information about SmartDefense.

You have two options for FTP Content Security: You can filter FTP traffic with or without the help of a CVP server. Let's examine these options in more detail.

Filtering Without a CVP Server

The firewall can control FTP GET and PUT commands without the help of a CVP server, but it cannot perform virus scanning without a CVP server. In this section we'll explore the filtering capabilities the firewall has without using a CVP server.

In the SmartDashboard, go to Manage ➢ Resources to open the Resources Manager. Then click on New ➢ FTP to open the FTP Resource Properties page, shown in Figure 4.35.

FIGURE 4.35   FTP Resource Properties

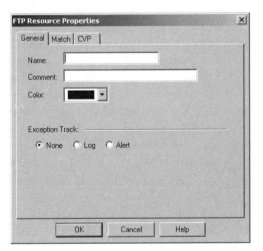

Like any other object, you give the resource a Name, Comment, and Color. We always set Exception Track to Log, because this setting gives much more information in the Info field of the SmartView Tracker.

The next tab in the FTP resource is the Match tab. As with the URI and SMTP resources, this tab defines what you are searching for. The FTP resource is a little different from the SMTP and URI resource objects in that it has no Action tab. If the FTP traffic you are filtering matches what is defined in the Path field (Figure 4.36), then the Methods options determine whether files can be sent or retrieved.

FIGURE 4.36 FTP resource Match tab

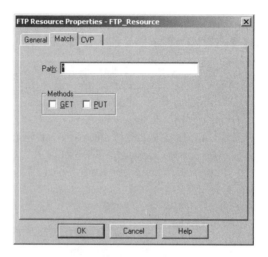

The Path field should contain the full pathname of the file, because filename matching is based on appending the filename in the command to the current working directory (unless the filename is already a full pathname) and then comparing the result to what was entered in the Path field. The Path field *must* include the / character to separate directories. If the Path field contained only the directory name (for example, `mydirectory` instead of `/mydirectory`), then the command appended to the path wouldn't match. The Path field wildcard rules are the same as those for a URI resource's Path field (see Table 4.2). The only Methods options available for an FTP resource are shown in Table 4.4.

TABLE 4.5 FTP Methods

Method	Purpose
GET	Getting a file from the server to the client
PUT	Sending a file from the client to the server

When specifying the pathname in an FTP resource, you can use only lower-case characters and a directory separator (/).

Using an FTP resource would have prevented an embarrassing situation for a large telco (which shall remain nameless) a few years ago. To the company's surprise, it found 4GB of pirated software on its public FTP server. If it had had a Check Point firewall and had implemented an FTP resource, it could have prevented this from happening.

Filtering With a CVP Server

The firewall can scan FTP traffic for viruses with the help of a CVP server. The process of setting up an *FTP resource* to utilize CVP scanning requires that you first define a Host Node object and pull it into an OPSEC application object, as described in the earlier section "Creating CVP and UFP Objects in FireWall-1." Then, you create an FTP resource object as described in the previous section, "Filtering Without a CVP Server." The only difference in filtering with a CVP server is how the information under the resource's CVP tab (Figure 4.37) is defined.

FIGURE 4.37   CVP tab of an FTP resource object

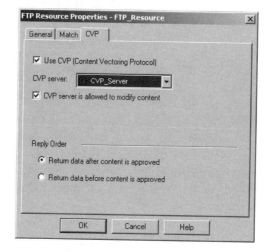

Unless Use CVP (Content Vectoring Protocol) is selected, all other options are grayed out. Selecting this option allows you to pull in an OPSEC CVP server and define how it will interact with FireWall-1. We always select CVP Server Is Allowed to Modify Content so that FTP data sent to the CVP server and found to be infected with a virus can be cleaned of the virus and sent on its way.

The Reply Order options determine when the FTP traffic is directed back to the Security Server. If Return Data After Content Is Approved is chosen, the CVP server will receive and check the entire file before sending it back to the Security Server. If Return Data Before Content Is Approved is chosen, the CVP server inspects each data packet of the file and returns it to the Security Server before approving the content of the entire file. For example, if a CVP server finds a virus in a data packet, it may repair the data within the packet before returning it to the CVP server for content checking.

Writing FTP Resource Rules

The same general rules outlined for creating URI and SMTP resource rules apply here as well. Figure 4.38 shows an FTP resource rule that prevents users from FTPing files out of the network but allows them to retrieve files.

FIGURE 4.38 FTP resource rule

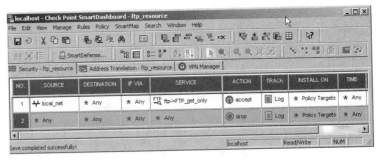

Now that you understand the theory behind FTP Content Filtering as well as what it takes to configure it on the firewall, you should be ready to put your knowledge into action with the following exercise. To begin Exercise 4.2, you'll need the setup illustrated in Figure 4.39.

FIGURE 4.39 Configuration for Exercise 4.2

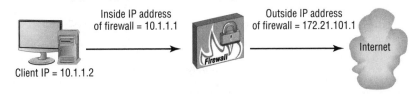

Inside IP address
of firewall = 10.1.1.1

Outside IP address
of firewall = 172.21.101.1

Internet

Client IP = 10.1.1.2

EXERCISE 4.2

FTP Filtering to Prevent Sending Files

1. Create a network object called local_net that represents the internal network, with a network address of 10.1.1.0 and a subnet mask of 255.255.255.0.

2. Create an FTP resource object by going to Manage ➢ Resources and clicking on New ➢ FTP.

3. In the General tab, populate the listed fields with the following information:

    Name: FTP_get

    Exception Track: Log

4. In the Match tab, populate the listed fields with the following information:

    Path: *

    Methods: GET

5. Locate an FTP site on the Internet that will allow you to download and upload files. Make note of this site before continuing.

6. Create a new blank rule base.

7. Add a resource rule with the following parameters:

    Source: local_net

    Destination: any

    Service with Resource: ftp ➢ FTP_get

    Action: Accept

EXERCISE 4.2 *(continued)*

8. Below the resource rule, add an FTP access rule with the following parameters:

    Source: local_net

    Destination: any

    Service: ftp

    Action: Accept

9. Add the Cleanup rule as the last rule in the rule base.

10. Verify and install the policy.

11. (Note that you must test via the command line. FTP through a browser does not work with this feature.) Go to the FTP site identified in step 5 and download a file; you should be allowed to do so. Now try to FTP the file back to the site; you should see a message stating that the "Security Server forbids that action."

12. View the Info field in the SmartView Tracker.

 You can use three other FTP services with FTP Content Security: ftp-pasv, ftp-bidir, and ftp-port. By using these services, you can force the firewall to allow only ftp-pasv, ftp-bidir, or ftp-port. Selecting FTP allows them all.

TCP Resources

A new resource is available in NG: the *TCP resource.* It supports all TCP services and has two uses:

- The *TCP resource* can be used with a CVP resource by supporting a genericd. This generic daemon is not associated with the Security Server but can receive data packets and send them to a *CVP server.*

- The TCP resource can be used with a *UFP server* in which the UFP server screens the URLs without using the Security Server. When this type of TCP resource is configured, the IP address of the URL is sent to the UFP server, therefore performing IP-based-only URL screening.

Before you use a TCP resource with a UFP server, make sure the UFP server supports IP-based URLs and can categorize specific TCP protocols.

To enable a TCP service for use with a TCP resource, follow these steps:

1. Open SmartDashboard, go to Manage ➢ Services, and select a TCP service. In this example, we will use AOL.

2. Click the Edit button. The TCP Service Properties window will appear, as shown in Figure 4.40.

FIGURE 4.40   AOL properties

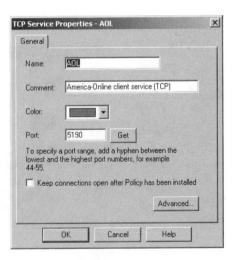

3. Click the Advanced button to display the properties screen shown in Figure 4.41. Select Enable for TCP Resource.

4. While still in SmartDashboard, go to Manage ➢ Resources and create a new TCP resource. You can define a TCP resource to utilize a UFP or CVP server, as shown in Figure 4.42.

FIGURE 4.41 AOL advanced properties

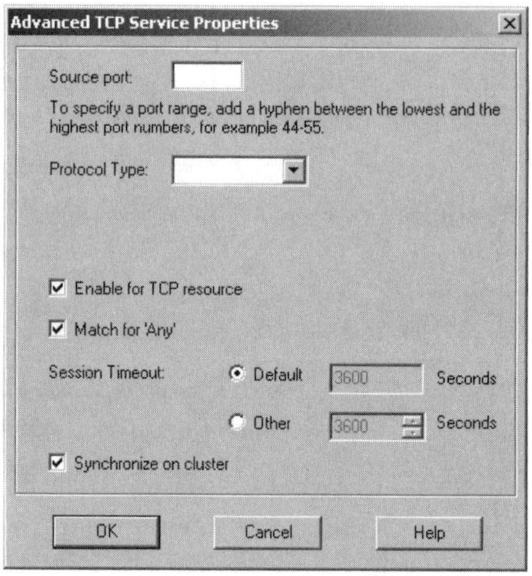

FIGURE 4.42 TCP resource properties

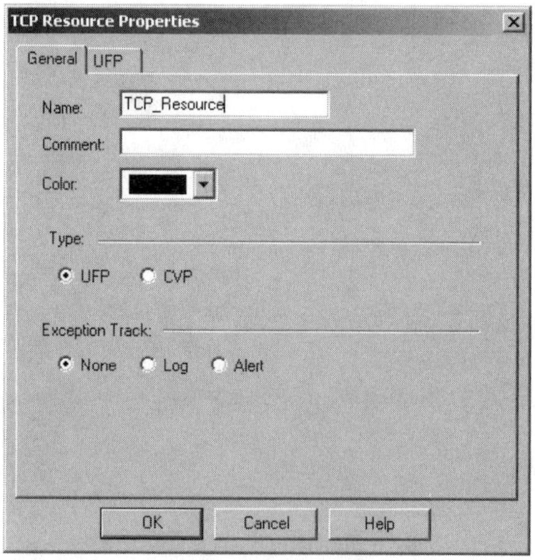

5. If you select UFP, click on the UFP tab to define the server just as it would be configured for an URI resource. If you select CVP, then the UFP tab is replaced by a CVP tab; under the CVP tab, you configure the server just as described earlier in this chapter for a FTP, URI, or SMTP resource.

6. After creating the TCP resource, it's time to add it to a rule. Right-click on the Service column and select Add With Resource. You will now see AOL as a Service option, and you can choose the TCP resource you created to filter AOL traffic (see Figure 4.43).

FIGURE 4.43   Service With Resource window

Changing Security Server Welcome Messages

By default, Check Point identifies itself whenever any Security Server service is used, whether it's Content Security or User Authentication. One such message for a connection with an FTP resource is displayed in Figure 4.44.

FIGURE 4.44   FireWall-1 FTP Security Server message

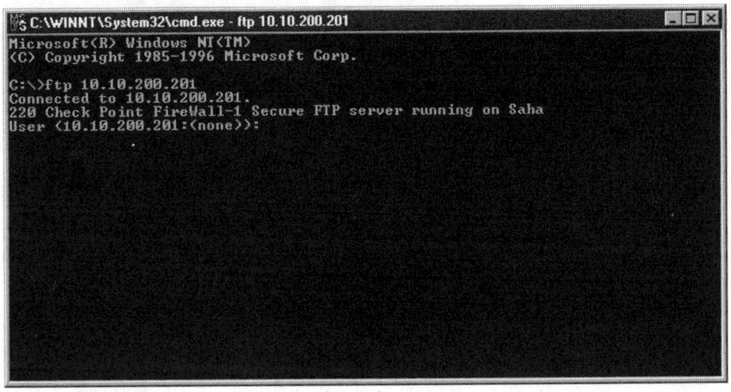

In our opinion, giving away any information—including what type of firewall you're running—is not a good idea. Therefore, when we're configuring a Check Point firewall, we always turn off these messages and replace them with appropriate legal text.

To remove the Security Server banners, go to your SmartCenter Server. Make sure all instances of the GUI are closed on the SmartCenter Server and on any Smart Clients. Once you are sure all GUI sessions are closed, open a command prompt on the SmartCenter Server and type **dbedit**. Then, follow the process depicted in Figure 4.45. At the end of each line, be sure to press Enter.

FIGURE 4.45   Removing Security Server banners using dbedit

Once you have accomplished this edit, it's a good idea to add some text that will cover you in case of illegal entry into your network. This step is necessary due to a legal case in Canada a few years back in which a hacker caused some damage, was caught red-handed, and was prosecuted. Because the network message he received when he penetrated their network said

"Welcome", he was acquitted. Create your message in an ASCII file and save it in $FWDIR/conf. (That way it will always be backed up with the rest of your firewall files.) Add the Security Server message by going to Policy ≻ Global Properties in SmartDashboard and clicking on the Security Server link under FireWall-1 (see Figure 4.46).

FIGURE 4.46 Adding Security Server messages

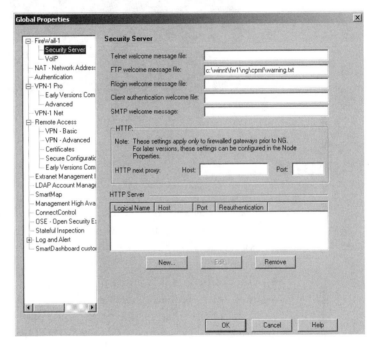

Note that the fully qualified path for the file is entered in the FTP Welcome Message File field. Also note that all the Security Servers except SMTP require a path to the file, but for SMTP, you type the message directly in the SMTP Welcome Message field. After you've made these edits, the Security Policy must be re-installed. With the Security Server banners removed and the appropriate text added, the access looks different (see Figure 4.44) than it does in Figure 4.47.

FIGURE 4.47 An access attempt with Security Server banners removed and new text added in

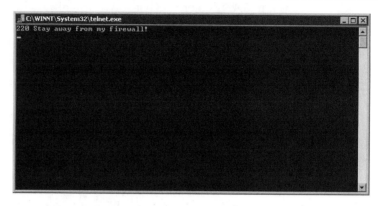

Summary

Content Security is a feature that allows a firewall administrator to configure granular checking of HTTP, FTP, SMTP, and TCP traffic. It is a proxy-like service that utilizes the Security Server process (`fwssd.exe`) along with the definitions in the `$FWDIR/conf/fwauthd.conf` file to inspect these specific traffic types. Content that can be filtered includes malicious code, viruses, and e-mail attachments.

Many of the filtering functions can be performed by the firewall alone, but functionality is greatly enhanced if an OPSEC server is also used. Two types of OPSEC servers work in conjunction with the Content Security features of the firewall: Content Vectoring Protocol (CVP) runs on port 18181 and mainly filters viruses but can also perform content filtering; URI Filtering Protocol (UFP) runs on port 18182 and performs URL filtering.

You must define each OPSEC server to the firewall by first creating a Host Node object that ties the server to an IP address. This object is then pulled into an OPSEC application object. Secure Internal Communications (SIC) must be configured so the OPSEC server and firewall can communicate.

URI resources allow the firewall administrator to filter URL traffic three ways: by defining a resource for each URL you wish to filter (Wild Cards URI Match Specification Type), by creating/maintaining a list yourself (File URI Match Specification Type), or by utilizing a UFP server to maintain the web sites to filter (UFP URI Match Specification Type). An URI resource can also utilize a CVP server to scan for viruses.

An SMTP resource allows the firewall administrator to filter SMTP traffic by re-writing headers, weeding out HTML, stripping out attachments, and scanning for viruses with a CVP server, to name just a few. If you use this resource, be sure to write rules that stop your firewall from acting as a mail relay for the entire Internet.

An FTP resource allows the firewall administrator to control FTP GET and PUT commands as well as scan for viruses.

Resource objects are added to the Service column of a resource rule and should be added above rules that allow generalized access. In other words, Content Security rules do *not* replace rules allowing FTP, HTTP, SMTP, or TCP services and therefore should go above rules that accept these services. Content Security rules that reject or drop HTTP, SMTP, FTP, or TCP services must be placed above Content Security rules that filter these connections. Only one resource can be defined in each rule.

A TCP resource can be created for any TCP service the firewall supports by first enabling the TCP resource in the Advanced tab of the service. TCP resources can be used with a UFP or CVP server. TCP resources do not use the Security Server.

It's vital to change Security Server welcome messages so you don't give away information about your security structure. You can do so by using `dbedit` to modify the `objects_5_0.C` file to remove the default security banners, and then adding your own verbiage in the Global Properties.

Exam Essentials

Know the Content Security processes.   Know that there is only one Security Server process (`fwssd.exe`) and that the different services attached to this service are defined in the `$FWDIR/conf/fwauthd.conf` file. Additional instances of each Security Server daemon (for example; in.asmtpd) can be added to this file to increase performance.

Know the types of services that can be filtered with FireWall-1's Content Filtering options.   The services that can be filtered with Content Filtering are HTTP, FTP, SMTP, and (new to NG) TCP.

Know what types of content a URI resource can filter. A URI resource can filter out HTML codes (script tags, ActiveX tags, and so on), block Java code, scan for viruses, and redirect users to alternate web sites.

Know the three URI Specification Types and how they function. The three types are Wild Cards, File, and UFP. The Wild Cards option allows you to create resources for individual web sites or for all web sites to filter out a specific piece of code (such as Java). The File option lets you create a list of web sites to filter (with a practical limit of 50 sites); this list must be maintained manually. The UFP option is configured so that the firewall looks to a UFP server to determine which web sites to filter.

Know what types of content an FTP resource can filter. An FTP resource can control FTP GET, PUT, PASV, BIDIR, and PORT commands, as well as scan for viruses utilizing the FTP Security Server and (potentially) a CVP server.

Know what types of content an SMTP resource can filter. An SMTP resource can modify mail headers, drop mail attachments above a specified size, and scan for viruses, among other tasks.

Know how to remove the Security Server banners. You can do this by using `dbedit` to modify the `objects_5_0.C` file and changing `undo_msg` from `false` to `true`.

Know how to create a TCP resource. Modify the TCP service properties and turn on Enable the TCP resource. Then, create a TCP resource and associate it with that service.

Key Terms

Before you take the exam, be certain you are familiar with the following terms:

aSMTPd	HTML weeding
Content Security	mail relay
Content Vectoring Protocol (CVP)	MDQ
Content Vectoring Protocol (CVP)	OPSEC
CVP server	Realtime Blackhole List
folding	Security Server
FTP GET	`smtp.conf`
FTP PUT	TCP resource
FTP resource	UFP server
FW1_cvp	URI Filtering Protocol (UFP)
FW1_ufp	URI Match Specification Type
`fwr1.conf`	URI resource
`fwssd`	

Review Questions

1. What port does the Content Vectoring Protocol use?

   A. 18181

   B. 18182

   C. 18212

   D. 18121

2. Which FireWall-1 service uses port 18182?

   A. FW1_tcp

   B. FW1_cvp

   C. FW1_uri

   D. FW1_ufp

   E. FW1_ftp

3. Which file must you modify to remove the FireWall-1 security banners?

   A. fwauthd.conf

   B. fwssd.exe

   C. objects_5_0.C

   D. fwrl.conf

   E. No file needs to be modified; security banners are modified through the GUI

4. Which of the following is not a URI Match Specification Type?

   A. URI

   B. UFP

   C. File

   D. Wild Cards

5. What is the proper way to edit the `objects_5_0.C` file?

   A. Use a text editor like vi.

   B. Use Notepad or WordPad.

   C. Use `dbedit`.

   D. You should not modify the `objects_5_0.C` file.

6. Which file should be edited if you want the SMTP Security Server to control the maximum number of recipients to which one e-mail can be sent?

   A. `fwr1.conf`

   B. `smtp.conf`

   C. `objects_5_0.C`

   D. `fwauthd.conf`

   E. `fwssd.exe`

7. Which SMTP Security Server daemon is responsible for sending mail to the spool directory on the firewall?

   A. MQD

   B. smtp.conf

   C. fwssd.exe

   D. aSMTPd

   E. fw1_cvp

8. Which of these Security Server processes perform both Content Security and User Authentication services?

   1. TELNET

   2. RLOGIN

   3. FTP

   4. HTTP

   5. SMTP

A. 1, 2

B. 3, 4

C. 4, 5

D. 2, 3, 4

E. All of the above

9. Which of the Content Security options cannot work with a CVP server?

   A. HTTP

   B. SMTP

   C. FTP

   D. TCP

   E. None of the above

10. Which OPSEC application property allows a CVP server to write log files to the FireWall-1 SmartCenter Server?

    A. AMON

    B. LEA

    C. SAM

    D. CPMI

    E. ELA

11. Which tab of an SMTP resource object allows you to configure FireWall-1 to strip out MIME attachments?

    A. General

    B. Match

    C. Action1

    D. Action2

    E. CVP

12. If you had the following types of rules in your rule base, what order would you put them in to be most effective?

1. Cleanup rule

2. Stealth rule

3. Resource rule that redirects users to an alternate web site

4. Resource rule that filters SMTP traffic for viruses

5. Rule that allows HTTP and SMTP traffic

A. 1, 2, 3, 4, 5

B. 2, 3, 4, 5, 1

C. 3, 4, 5, 1, 2

D. 4, 5, 1, 2, 3

E. 5, 1, 2, 3, 4

13. Which objects must be created for an SMTP resource to work with a CVP server?

1. Host Node object

2. OPSEC application

3. FTP resource

4. SMTP resource

A. 1, 2

B. 2, 4

C. 1, 3, 4

D. 1, 2, 4

E. 1, 2, 3, 4

14. Which resource can control GET, PUT, and HEAD commands?

A. URI

B. SMTP

C. TCP

D. FTP

15. Which process allows a CVP or UFP server to communicate securely with a FireWall-1 SmartCenter Server?

    A. fwssd.exe

    B. smtp.conf

    C. ELA

    D. SIC

    E. fwauthd.conf

16. Which URI resource option is used to stop malicious web code such as Code Red?

    A. Optimize URL Blocking

    B. Tunneling

    C. Enforce URI Capabilities

    D. Transparent

    E. Optimize URL Logging

17. Which is not a predefined scheme that can be selected when creating a URI resource object?

    A. FTP

    B. GOPHER

    C. HTTP

    D. WAIS

    E. JAVA

18. Which is a valid path if you want to match all the files in a directory?

    A. /files

    B. /dir/files/

    C. /

    D. /files/*

    E. /files*

19. What is the practical limit for the number of sites in a file to be used with a File URI Match Specification Type?

   A. 5

   B. 10

   C. 25

   D. 50

   E. 100

20. Which option is in the correct format for a File URI Match Specification Type?

   A. `mywebsite.com<Tab>1<Enter>`

   B. `www.mywebsite.com<Tab><Tab>3<Enter>`

   C. `www.mywebsite.com<Tab>j<Enter>`

   D. `192.34.12.1<Tab><Tab>11`

   E. `24.5.38.121<Tab>/home.html<Tab>m<Enter>`

Answers to Review Questions

1. A. This is the default port used by the CVP OPSEC applications to communicate with the firewall.

2. D. This is the default port used by the UFP OPSEC applications to communicate with the firewall.

3. C. Remember that you must reinstall the policy after modifying `objects_5_0.C` for the changes to take effect.

4. A. UFP, File, and Wild Cards are URI Match Specification Types.

5. C. `dbedit` is the new NG utility you should use to modify the `objects_5_0.C` file. It forces users to log in to make edits; their activity is recorded in the audit log in SmartView Tracker.

6. B. Parameters affecting the performance of the SMTP Security Server are modified in the `smtp.conf` file. Maximum Generated Concurrent Connections and Maximum Generated Concurrent Connections Per Site are just two of the other parameters defined in this file.

7. A, D. The aSMTPd daemon sends the mail to the spool, and the MQD daemon retrieves and sends it to and from the spool.

8. B. Only FTP and HTTP Security Server processes perform both Content Security and User Authentication. TELNET and RLOGIN only do User-Authentication, and SMTP only does Content Security.

9. E. All Content Security options can work with a CVP server, but HTTP and TCP are the only options that can work with a UFP server.

10. E. AMON allows the OPSEC application to be monitored, LEA allows the OPSEC application to receive log data from the firewall, SAM integrates applications that detect suspicious activity, and CPMI is the GUI interface.

11. D. This tab also allows you to strip files by name, specify which ASCII text format is allowed, drop mail that's larger than a specified size, and perform HTML weeding. These functions could conceivably be handled by a CVP server that also filtered mail content.

12. B. This question should have been relatively easy, because the cleanup rule is always the last rule in the rule base. The important part to remember is that resource rules that reject or drop traffic (like the redirect rule) go before resource rules that only filter traffic. All resource rules go above those rules that generally allow access for those same services.

13. D. The Host Node object is needed to tie the CVP server to an IP address. The Host Node object is pulled into the OPSEC application object, which is then pulled into the SMTP resource object.

14. A. If you didn't read the entire question, you might have answered D because FTP can control GET and PUT commands. However, only a URI resource can control GET, PUT, HEAD, and POST commands.

15. D. Secure Internal Communications (SIC) sets up the framework for the CVP and/or UFP server to securely communicate with the Smart-Center Server. This connection is encrypted and authenticated.

16. A. This option will check and, if necessary, drop URL requests containing patterns that match the Code Red signature. This FP2 functionality is built into the kernel of the firewall and doesn't require a Security Server. This functionality was moved to SmartDefense in FP3.

17. E. JAVA is something that can be blocked, not a scheme to be matched.

18. D. This option will match all files in the `files` directory. If options A or C were files, they would be included. Option B does not include any of the files in the directory. Option E only includes files whose names begin with *files*.

19. D. The practical limit is 50 sites. If you need to maintain a file of more than 50 web sites to filter, then you should consider purchasing a UFP server.

20. B. Only option B is in the correct format, which is crucial if you want it to work. Option A doesn't have the URL in the correct format, and it is missing the Tab to account for the path. Options C, D, and E don't use a hexadecimal character in the category spot, and D is missing the Enter at the end of the line.

Chapter

5

Voice Over IP

THE CCSE EXAM TOPICS COVERED IN THIS CHAPTER INCLUDE:

✓ The methods for using Voice over IP (VoIP).

✓ Configuring the VPN-1/FireWall-1 NG firewall to pass VoIP traffic in a H.323 configuration.

✓ Configuring the VPN-1/FireWall-1 NG firewall to pass VoIP traffic in a SIP configuration.

In this chapter, we're introducing a new feature that has been available since Check Point NG FP2. Those of you working with FireWall-1 for a time may say "you could pass *Voice over IP* (VoIP) traffic with previous versions of FW-1," and you would be correct. In the past, you could configure the firewall to pass VoIP connections by opening specific ports. But this approach did not statefully inspect the VoIP traffic—it just allowed the traffic to go through the firewall. In versions FP2 and beyond you can configure the firewall to securely pass VoIP traffic that uses either the H.323 or SIP protocol. We'll discuss both H.323 and Session Initiation Protocol (SIP) protocols in this chapter. Although it will be difficult to create a VoIP test lab at home because of the extra hardware required, you will learn how to configure the firewall for each VoIP protocol.

Introduction to Voice over IP

Most people are more familiar with the term *Internet telephony* than Voice over IP (VoIP) but they mean basically the same thing. Internet telephony refers to the transmission of telephone calls, whereas VoIP is a broader term that encompasses voice, facsimile, and/or voice-messaging applications over the Internet as opposed to the *public switched telephone network (PSTN)*.

Internet telephony is gaining in popularity because it provides the integration of voice and data at a substantial cost savings compared to the traditional PSTN. With Internet telephony, you can bypass long-distance carriers by using the Internet to carry your long-distance calls.

Everyone is accustomed to using a telephone, but do you understand what happens when you pick up the handset to make a long distance call? First the local telephone company sees that you're making a long-distance call and transfers the call to your long-distance telephone company. The long-distance company sends the call to the local provider on the other end. The long distance company then charges you based on where and when you called, as well as how long the call lasted. Figure 5.1 represents the basic call process through the PSTN. Calls leaving your analog phone are converted to digital. They travel in a digital format at 64Kbps until they reach their destination, where they are then converted back to analog.

FIGURE 5.1   Traditional phone call process

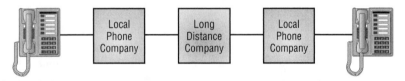

With VoIP, the process is different: Your call goes through the Internet (packet-switched/connectionless network) as opposed to the proprietary circuit-switched networks of the telephone companies. VoIP methods also convert your analog voice signal to a digital format as well as compressing/translating the signal into Internet Protocol (IP) format for transmission over the Internet. Once the voice packets reach the other side, a compatible system must be available to reverse the process. This process is outlined in Figure 5.2

FIGURE 5.2   VoIP call process

When you want to make a call using VoIP, you first dial the number. Signaling determines if the person you're calling is available or busy. If the line is not available, VoIP can switch you into voicemail. If the line is free, the call is established and the conversation begins. At this point, the analog signal produced by the microphone is encoded into digital format to be transmitted across the network with acceptable voice quality. A gateway may have to convert the encoded signal again into another format that the end-point understands, such as another VoIP protocol or the PSTN.

Regardless of which methodology you eventually decide to use (if you decide to use VoIP at all), each method must support the same functionality as the PSTN: call setup and tear-down, call-holding, call transfer, call for-warding, call waiting, and conferencing.

 Real World Scenario

VoIP in Action

The Internet has already helped us make the world smaller by enabling us to contact people across the country or across the world with e-mail, instant messaging, and chat rooms. The same concept exists for corporations, because a company can efficiently do business in a different country or con-tinent without traveling there. VoIP has the potential to make the world even smaller by allowing corporations to hold live meetings and conference calls with multiple people in multiple countries at a fraction of the cost of today's long-distance rates. A corporation can setup IP based or analog phones to take advantage of Virtual Private Network (VPN) tunnels already in place. This way, the phone company can be bypassed and voice data can be tun-neled over the Internet through a VPN tunnel.

Not only can companies save on long-distance rates with VoIP, they can also reduce travel expenses because face-to-face video conferencing meet-ings can include people from all over the world without requiring anyone to fly. With VoIP, an automotive engineer in Detroit can have a face-to-face meeting with a group of people in Japan and then have a face-to-face meet-ing with people in Germany 10 minutes later. All of a sudden, rather than flying an engineer from Detroit to Japan and then from Japan to Germany, and allocating resources for travel time and expenses, a company can achieve the same result in a matter of hours for less than the cost of today's long distance rates.

Although no standards are set, many companies are currently researching VoIP and strategizing their deployment. Some companies have begun the migration to VoIP but most are waiting until the market is more mature.

VoIP Methods

VoIP incorporates *signaling*, compression and encoding standards. Most users refer to the VoIP methods by the signaling standards that control them. Two popular signaling standards are currently in use:

- *H.323*, an *International Telecommunications Union (ITU)* standard

- *Session Initiation Protocol (SIP)*, an *Internet Engineering Task Force (IETF)* standard

Neither of these signaling standards has been exclusively adopted by the Internet community.

Visit `http://www.itu.int/home/index.html` for more information about H.323, and `ftp://ftp.isi.edu/in-notes/rfc3261.txt` for more information about SIP.

Which should you use? That question may be moot in the near future because the protocols may be converging. H.323 v3 has addressed some of its shortcomings, which were initial advantages to using SIP. SIP seems to be addressing some of its shortcomings as well. Whether these methods converge or not, FireWall-1 currently supports both standards. In the following sections, we'll discuss each standard in more detail.

H.323

H.323 is the most popular IP telephony protocol and has been approved by the world governments as the international standard for voice, video and data conferencing. H.323 has the flexibility of sending multimedia communications over the Internet and integrating well with the PSTN.

When H.323 was developed in the mid-1990s, its creators hoped to produce a next-generation protocol. Version 1 of H.323 was developed with a focus on multimedia communications and interoperability with other multimedia protocols and services. The version 1 standard was accepted in October 1996.

The emergence of VoIP applications and IP telephony has set the guidelines for a revision of the H.323 specification. With the development of VoIP, new requirements emerged, such as providing communication between a PC-based phone and a phone on a traditional switched circuit network; but the lack of a standard for VoIP made most of the products with these requirements incompatible. Such requirements subsequently forced the need for a standard for IP telephony. Version 2 of H.323, a packet-based multimedia communications system, was defined to accommodate these additional requirements and was accepted in January 1998.

The power of H.323 lies in its extensibility, flexibility of centralized and/or decentralized control, ease of integration with Internet protocols, worldwide acceptance, and technical capability to provide voice, video, and data convergence. In today's market, H.323 is the leader in multimedia communications and carries billions of minutes of voice, video, and data conferencing traffic over IP networks every month.

SIP

Session Initiation Protocol (SIP) is the IETF protocol for IP telephony. It only supports IP-based phones. It has a smaller footprint than H.323 so it's faster and more scalable. The problem lies in the fact that it's a newer protocol, and therefore fewer products exist that use it. However, SIP addresses some of the shortcomings of H.323 by making users easier to identify, making it easier to connect two circuit-switched networks across an IP network, and decreasing the delay in call setup time.

SIP identifies users with a Hierarchical URL. This URL is based on a user's phone number or host name and looks similar to an e-mail address (for example, SIP: joeuser@abc.com). Figure 5.3 illustrates the SIP call process.

FIGURE 5.3   SIP call process

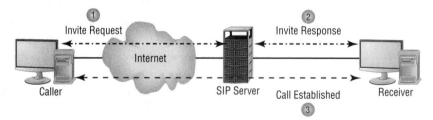

When a call is made, the caller initiates it with an invite request. This request contains the information necessary for the person you're calling to join the session: the media types and formats for the call, the destination for the media data, and perhaps requests for using H.261 video and/or G.711 audio. The invite request is sent to the user's SIP server. Because you include your available features in the invite request, the negotiation of the connection takes place in a single transaction thus call setup time is decreased (approximately 100 milliseconds).

The SIP server may or may not be a proxy server. A SIP proxy server receives the request and figures out the user's location using its internal algorithms. A non-proxy SIP server functions as a redirect server in that it sends back to the user the SIP URL that the user uses to query. In both the redirect and proxy server cases, the server's address is obtained by querying the Domain Name Service (DNS).

Once the SIP URL is found, the request finally makes it to the person you're trying to call. If the person picks up the call, the receiver's client responds to the invite request with the capabilities of its software (video-conferencing, whiteboarding,and so forth), and the connection is established.

SIP has two features that really make it unique:

- It can split an incoming call so that multiple extensions can be rung at once. When the invite request comes in, the SIP server can return to the initiator of the call a Web Interactive Voice Response (IVR) page, which contains extensions of different departments or users in a list. All you have to do is click on the link to call the appropriate person or department.

- It can return different media types.

SIP is simple and easy to deploy because its only job is to identify the user and set up the call; it relies on other protocols and applications to manage the call. It utilizes existing DNS instead of having to create a separate database for telephony. It also interfaces with circuit-switched networks (the PSTN) more easily than H.323. Does this mea SIP is the way to go? Not necessarily. It is not widely available, and (the biggest drawback at this point) it must "de-throne" Microsoft. Every version of Windows that ships has an H.323 client as part of the package (it's free!). Whether a company will purchase another client all depends on its needs and what it wants to accomplish with IP telephony.

While H.323 is the accepted VoIP protocol today, many people think that SIP will be the VoIP protocol of the future. Most of the larger vendors are developing SIP-based solutions if they haven't already. It will be beneficial to understand both protocols to make a decision on what kind of VoIP solution to deploy.

VoIP Issues

Now that you have a general understanding of how calls are handled with VoIP, we'll address some issues that affect a VoIP setup: bandwidth, voice quality and security.

Bandwidth

Bandwidth usage in VoIP depends on the type of compression used when the VoIP protocol converts the analog signal to digital. There are quite a few voice compression standards (a.k.a. voice encoders), such as G.723, G.726, G.728 and G.729.

For more information about voice compression options, visit `http://www.imtc.org`.

The greater the compression rate, the poorer the voice quality. Therefore you must maintain a delicate balance in which you conserve bandwidth as much as possible without sacrificing too much voice quality. Bandwidth consumption can also be made more efficient if the VoIP hardware is configured to look for pauses in conversation and not transmit data when a caller is not talking.

Voice Quality

Voice quality is a factor of bandwidth, but there is another component to consider: You want the calls to traverse the connection as quickly as possible, and all the packets must be received in the same order they were generated (as opposed to normal IP traffic, which doesn't care about the order in which packets are received). Because of this requirement, you should make sure calls receive priority on your network. You can accomplish this using the *Differential Quality of Service (DiffServ QoS)* protocol.

Check Point offers a product called *FloodGate* that uses DiffServ QoS. Visit `http://www.checkpoint.com/products/accelerate/floodgate-1.html` for details.

Latency in the transmission of the voice data can also cause problems. Administrators can control this issue in a LAN environment; but if the traffic has to traverse the Internet, then latency is out of the administrators' control. Latency can cause delays (accumulation, processing, and network delays), lost packets, echoes, and jitter.

Delay causes problems, two of which are: *echo* and *talker overlap*. You've probably experienced both if you have a cellular phone. Echo is caused by signal reflection of your voice back at you. This becomes a significant issue if the round-trip delay (the time between when you speak and when you hear yourself speak) is greater than 50 milliseconds (ms). Each VoIP system needs to control echo and perform some type of echo cancellation. Talker overlap (you and the person you're talking to step on each other's words) is caused by a one-way delay of greater than 250ms. The other person begins speaking because they hear a pause (which is actually a delay) and assume you've finished talking. Table 5.1 lists some causes of delay.

TABLE 5.1   Causes of Delay in VoIP Connections

Delay	Cause
Accumulation (a.k.a. algorithmic) delay	The requirement to collect voice sample frames to be processed by the voice coder (these are the voice compression standards mentioned earlier)
Processing Delay	The process of encoding voice samples and collecting them into packets for transmission over the network
Network Delay	The physical medium and protocols that are used to transmit the voice data, and buffers used to remove jitter on the receivers' side of the connection
Jitter	The fact that packets must be collected and held long enough to allow the slowest packet to arrive in time to be played in sequence

Lost packets also affect voice quality. IP networks do not guarantee service like Asynchronous Transfer Mode (ATM) networks do, so there will be more lost packets. The VoIP protocol or scheme you choose to implement must compensate for echoes, delays, and lost packets.

Security

When it comes to security, your VoIP equipment is just as vulnerable as all the other devices in your WAN. If your VoIP solution is running on a server, then the vulnerabilities that exist on the operating system will also be VoIP vulnerabilities. We discussed operating system security in Chapter 1, and the same issues apply to a server-based IP solution. In addition to hardening the operating system, here are some more steps you can take to secure the passing of voice over an IP network:

- Separate traffic from the rest of the LAN by using a separate subnet or VLAN
- Limit administrative access to the VoIP servers by allowing only designated administrators to access them
- Limit the types of protocols that can reach the VoIP servers
- Encrypt voice traffic in a Virtual Private Network (VPN) if possible

VoIP security is where the firewall comes into play. With FireWall-1 you can set up your VoIP traffic to be in its own subnet on a separate interface on the firewall and securely pass voice traffic through the firewall to the Internet. You can limit who accesses the servers on the separate subnet and what protocols are allowed in and out. You can also choose to have your VoIP traffic encrypted and travel through a VPN. Check Point supports both of the protocols we've discussed so far. Next, let's see how to configure VoIP to traverse FireWall-1.

The next section covers how to setup VoIP. To learn how to configure a VPN, turn to Chapter 6, "Virtual Private Networks."

Configuring FireWall-1 and VoIP with H.323

Analog (conventional) telephones and digital (soft) telephones can be used in conjunction with a H.323-based VoIP solution. Conventional phones do not have IP addresses but can be connected to a H.323 gateway which converts the analog signal to digital so that it can participate in VoIP. Digital phones can be either a physical telephone that has an IP address or a computer with the appropriate software that enables it to act as a telephone. Both of these configurations are referred to as "soft phones."

The IP addresses of the gateway (if necessary) and the soft phones should be their own subnet along with the H.323 gatekeeper computer.

The gatekeeper H.323 component is the focal point for all calls within a VoIP network. It provides important services such as addressing, authorization, and authentication for the gateway and the IP phones behind it. The gatekeeper can also provide bandwidth management, accounting, billing, charging, and call-routing services.

The first step in configuring the firewall to inspect VoIP traffic is to define host node and/or network objects that represent the IP phones, the gateway computer (optional) and the gatekeeper computer. The gatekeeper and the gateway should be created as host objects. Each IP phone can be a host node object as well or you could create a network object that represents the IP address range of your VoIP network. The only portion of the H.323 architecture in which you do not have to create objects is the analog phones. Since they don't have IP addresses, they are represented by the gateway object. If you do not have analog phones then you have no need to create a gateway object.

Creating the Gateway

If you have analog phones in your VoIP network you must create a VoIP Domain H.323 Gateway object as outlined in the following steps:

1. Go to Manage ➤ Network Objects and choose New ➤ VoIP Domains ➤ VoIP Domain H.323 Gateway.

2. In the General tab, define the gateway's Name, Comment, and Color. Choose the network object that represents the IP addresses of your VoIP subnet in the Related Endpoints Domain pull-down menu. Keep in mind that if different H.323 protocols are carried on different interfaces, then a separate host node object has to be created to represent each interface. These host node objects should then be grouped together and defined in the VoIP Installed field. If there is a single interface carrying the protocols that make up H.323 then only one host node object (which represents the H.323 gateway) should be defined in the VoIP Installed At field.

3. In the Routing Mode tab, you'll see two options: the Call Setup and Call Setup And Call Control. Call Setup (Q.931) handles the setup and termination of the calls whereas Call Setup And Call Control does that as well as negotiating the parameters necessary for multimedia. At least one of the choices must be checked, depending on the VoIP product that you are using.

Most people are not familiar with the H.323 protocol but have experienced using it if they've ever used Microsoft's NetMeeting product.

Creating the Gatekeeper

The gatekeeper object must be created to securely pass H.323 traffic through your firewall. To create a gatekeeper object, follow these steps:

1. Go to Manage ➤ Network Objects Go to the Network Objects window and choose New ➤ VoIP Domains ➤ VoIP Domain H.323 Gatekeeper.

2. In the General tab, shown in Figure 5.4, define the gatekeeper's Name, Comment, and Color. The network object or address range object that represents your soft phones subnet and/or the object that represents your gateway (if you're using analog phones) should be defined in the Related Endpoints Domain field. If you are using a combination of analog and digital phones then combine the gateway and the network range in a Simple Group and define it here. The host node object that represents your H.323 gatekeeper machine should be defined in the VoIP Installed At field.

FIGURE 5.4 Gatekeeper General Properties

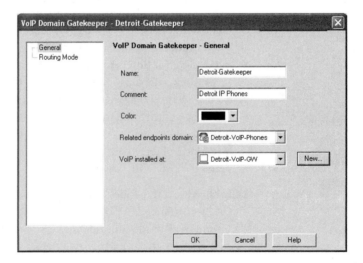

3. Under the Routing Mode tab of the gatekeeper properties, you can choose from three allowed routing modes. This option identifies which connections will be rerouted from your VoIP gatekeeper to the VoIP gatekeeper on the other end. At least one of the following choices must be checked depending on the VoIP equipment that is being utilized:

Direct   The H.225 and Q.931 protocols, which allow gatekeeper to gatekeeper communication and call setup and breakdown respectively, are rerouted if this check box is selected.

Call Setup (Q.931)   H.245 which is the control protocol used by H.323 for multimedia communication will be rerouted from gatekeeper to gatekeeper along with the Q.931 protocols.

Call Setup (Q.931) and Call Control (H.245)   Connections that deal with video, audio and controls connections associated with video and audio will be rerouted gatekeeper to gatekeeper.

VoIP is a large set of protocols that are not easily understood. A good resource to learn more about VoIP is http://www.voip-calculator.com/.

Configuring Global Properties

In the VoIP page of the Global Properties window, shown in Figure 5.5, you can change the VoIP parameters from their default settings. If the Log VoIP Connection option is checked, every VoIP (SIP and H.323) connection will be logged including the telephone number information. Under the H.323 section, Allow to Re-direct Connections is a H.323 function that allows call forwarding and call waiting to occur. Disallow Blank Source Phone Numbers is what we commonly know as blocking CallerID. Enable Dynamic T.120 enables the T.120 protocol which most recognize as the whiteboarding feature of NetMeeting.

FIGURE 5.5   VoIP Global Properties

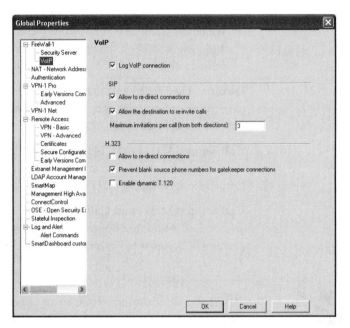

Configuring the Rule Base

Now that you have created your network objects and configured your VoIP global parameters, it's time to configure the rule base to filter H.323 traffic. The concept in creating the rule is to allow traffic to pass from gatekeeper to gatekeeper or from gateway to gateway using the H.323 service. You have more than one H.323 service to choose from: H.323_any provides all the required services for VoIP, and H.323_ras includes only the RAS part of the H.323 protocol. If you wish to use more than just H.323_ras then you will have to define additional services for this rule or create additional rules to allow the other protocols (e.g. T.120 orH.450) necessary for the call to be completed.

For our purposes in this book, Figure 5.6 displays a good example of an H.323 VoIP rule. The gatekeepers of Detroit and Madrid are listed in both the Source and Destination columns of the rule. The Service is H.323_any, and the Action is Accept.

FIGURE 5.6 H.323 VoIP rule

NO.	SOURCE	DESTINATION	SERVICE	ACTION
1	Detroit-Gatekeeper Madrid_VoIP_GW	Detroit-Gatekeeper Madrid_VoIP_GW	TCP H323_any	accept

You now have an understanding of how to configure the firewall for H.323-based VoIP systems. Now look at the next section where you will learn how to configure SIP-based VoIP systems.

Configuring FireWall-1 and VoIP with SIP

There are a few different ways to configure VoIP with SIP. You can configure SIP using a SIP proxy on one or both ends of the connection, or you can use a SIP redirect server to provide DNS services to map IP addresses to SIP URLs. You can also configure SIP without using proxies. Figure 5.7 depicts these three proxy scenarios.

FIGURE 5.7 Three SIP scenarios

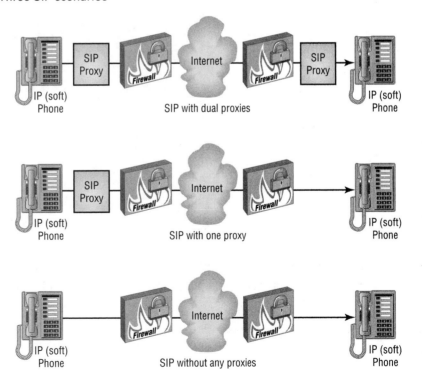

Configuring Objects

Before configuring specific VoIP objects to the firewall, you must define Address Range or Network objects that represent the network of IP-based phones. You could also create Host Node objects to represent each phone and then put all the Host Node objects into a group. To create an Address Range object, follow these steps:

1. Go to Manage ➢ Network Objects and choose New ➢ Address Range.

2. Define the range of IP addresses that represent your IP phones, as shown in Figure 5.8.

FIGURE 5.8 Creating an Address Range object

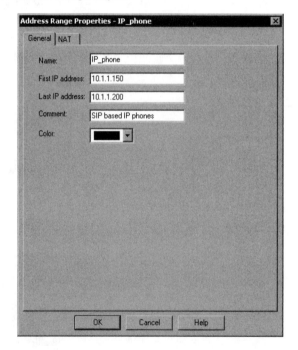

To create a group, follow these steps:

1. Go to Manage ➢ Network Objects and choose New ➢ Node ➢ Host.

2. Define an object to represent each individual phone, as depicted in Figure 5.9.

FIGURE 5.9 Creating a Host Node object creation

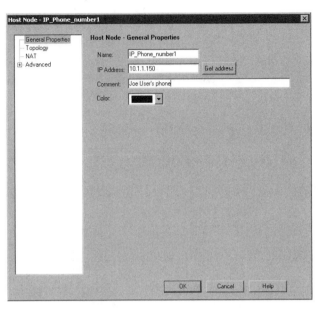

3. Go to New ➢ Group ➢ Simple Group and define the group name.

4. Select the Host Node objects you created and move them into the In Group column, as shown in Figure 5.10.

FIGURE 5.10 IP_Phone_ Group object

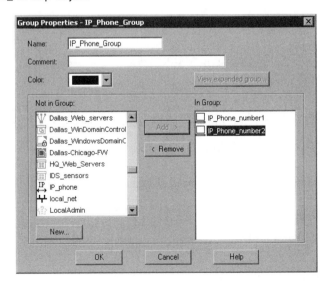

5. At this point, if you're using a SIP proxy or a SIP redirect server, you must configure a VoIP Domain SIP object by going to Manage ➢ Network Objects and clicking New ➢ VoIP Domains ➢ VoIP Domain SIP. This step is demonstrated in Figure 5.11. (We gave the object a name and then pulled the previously defined Address Range object into the Related Endpoints Domain pull-down menu. Alternatively, we could have pulled in the group object.)

FIGURE 5.11 SIP Domain object

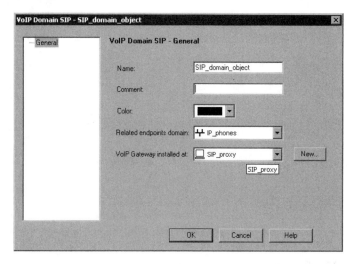

6. Pull in the host node object that represents the SIP proxy.

VoIP Global Properties exist as well and should be configured. Figure 5.12 shows the VoIP Global Properties options:

Allow To Re-direct Connections   This option must be selected if either a SIP re-direct or proxy server is being utilized. Turn this option off only if no proxies or redirect servers are involved.

Allow The Destination To Re-Invite Calls   If this option is turned on, users can take advantage of SIPs ability to initiate a new call while a call is already in progress.

Maximum Invitations Per Call (From Both Directions)   This option is related to the previous one: It quantifies the maximum number of additional calls that can be placed while the initial call is still in progress.

FIGURE 5.12 VoIP Global Properties

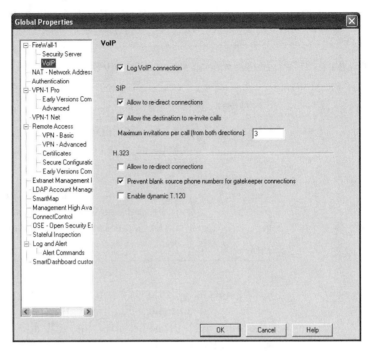

Configuring the Rule Base

Creating the objects is the easy part. The tough part is creating the rules because so many different scenarios can come into play.

If the scenario does not include any proxies, you need only one rule. Figure 5.13 shows that the Source and Destination columns must include your SIP network range and the SIP network range you wish to communicate with.

FIGURE 5.13 SIP rule base with no proxies

Note that the Service column is populated with the SIP UDP service. For any of the SIP rules, you can select the sip service or the sip_any service. The differences between these two services are described in Table 5.2.

TABLE 5.2   Explanation of sip and sip_any Services

Service	How It Works
sip	If the Source or Destination column is Any, then the firewall is not able to redirect the connection unless the gateway is configured as a SIP proxy.
sip_any	If the Source or Destination column is Any, the firewall is able to redirect the connection even if it isn't a SIP proxy, but *only* if the SIP Domain is external to the network protected by the firewall.

If the scenario includes a proxy on only one side of the connection, then a rule is needed to allow communication from the VoIP Domain SIP object (the SIP proxy), to the network object, IP address range, or destination as shown in Figure 5.14.

FIGURE 5.14   SIP rule base with one proxy

If the scenario includes proxies on both sides of the connection, then a rule is needed to allow the SIP proxies to communicate as shown in Figure 5.15.

FIGURE 5.15 SIP rule base with two proxies

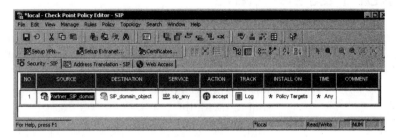

After determining what rules are needed for your scenario and configuring your rule base, all that is required is to verify and install your policy and start talking.

Summary

Voice over IP is a growing trend in today's high-tech world. Companies are looking at enhancing their current telephone systems to provide more services and features with lower long-term costs. VoIP enables a telephone call to transmit over a TCP/IP network like the Internet, thereby better integrating voice and data and saving on cost.

In addition to bandwidth and voice quality issues, there are security considerations when deploying a VoIP solution, as is the case for any device that sits on a LAN that is IP based and connects to the Internet.

The NG INPSECT engine addresses security issues faced by VoIP such as call hijacking and denial of service attacks. The firewall can be used to physically segment the VoIP network from the rest of the data LAN, limit administrative access to VoIP equipment and servers, limit the types of protocols that can access VoIP servers and equipment and encrypt VoIP traffic through a VPN.

Check Point NG supports two VoIP protocols: H.323 and SIP. Different VoIP architectures using these protocols will determine which objects need to be created and how your rule base is configured.

Exam Essentials

Know the basics of how VoIP works. VoIP provides a more economical method for making phone calls by passing the phone call over the Internet using TCP/IP. By knowing what VoIP is and how it works, you will be able to intelligently approach the concept of protecting a VoIP solution with the Check Point NG firewall.

Understand what H.323 and SIP do. H.323 and SIP are the most common protocols for VoIP and the two protocols supported by Check Point NG. By understanding H.323 and SIP, you'll be able to recognize the advantages and disadvantages of each. You'll also be able to make a decision about which protocol to use in your own VoIP environment.

Know how to configure H.323 and SIP in Check Point NG. You should be able to configure H.323 and SIP in CheckPoint NG after completing the steps in this chapter. Knowing how to configure both protocols in the firewall will help you on the exam and also help you conceptualize what needs to be done when setting up a VoIP solution.

Key Terms

Before you take the exam, be certain you are familiar with the following terms:

bandwidth

Differential Quality of Service (DiffServ QoS)

echo

FloodGate

gatekeeper

gateway

H.323

International Telecommunications Union (ITU)

Internet Engineering Task Force (IETF)

Internet telephony

IP phones

public switched telephone network (PSTN)

Session Initiation Protocol (SIP)

signaling

soft phones

talker overlap

Voice Over IP

Review Questions

1. What two signaling protocols does FireWall-1 support?

   A. PSTN

   B. PBX

   C. H.323

   D. VoIP

   E. SIP

2. How many rules are needed to setup SIP with no proxies?

   A. One

   B. Two

   C. Three

   D. Four

   E. Five

3. Which of these issues affect voice quality with VoIP connections? (Choose all that apply)

   A. Bandwidth

   B. Latency

   C. Delay

   D. Lost packets

   E. Echo

4. In which SIP scenario do you *not* need to create a VoIP Domain SIP object?

   A. A scenario in which there is a SIP proxy at both ends of the connection

   B. A scenario in which there is a SIP proxy on only one end of the connection

   C. A scenario in which there is no SIP proxy on either end of the connection

   D. A scenario in which there is a SIP proxy on one end of the connection and a SIP Redirect server on the other end of the connection.

   E. A scenario in which there is a SIP Redirect Server at both ends of the connection

5. What type of object(s) do you use to define a Related Endpoints Domain? (Choose all that apply.)

   A. Network object

   B. Address Range object

   C. Host Node object

   D. Group object

   E. VoIP Domain object

6. Echo is caused by a round-trip delay of greater than how many milliseconds?

   A. 50

   B. 100

   C. 150

   D. 200

   E. 250

7. Talker overlap is caused by a one-way delay of greater than how many milliseconds?

   A. 50

   B. 100

   C. 150

   D. 200

   E. 250

8. Which is *not* a SIP feature?

   A. Splitting incoming calls to ring multiple extensions

   B. Returning IVR page(s)

   C. Utilizing existing DNS for SIP URLs

   D. Utilizing analog phones

   E. Using only one connection to setup a call

9. Which protocol interfaces most easily with the PSTN?

   A. G.723

   B. H.323

   C. DiffServ QOS

   D. SIP

   E. VPN

10. Which problem is caused because packets have to be collected and held long enough for the slowest packet to arrive and be played in order?

    A. Accumulation delay

    B. Processing delay

    C. Network delay

    D. Jitter

    E. Echo

11. What is a soft phone?

    A. Phone with a soft handset

    B. Computer with a modem

    C. Computer with software enabling the computer to be a phone

    D. Phone without an IP address

    E. Phone with an IP address

12. What benefits does H.323 offer? (Choose all that apply.)

    A. Flexibility in centralized and decentralized control

    B. Worldwide availability

    C. Flexibility in integration

    D. Extensibility

    E. All of the above

13. Which service does a gatekeeper *not* offer?

    A. Authentication

    B. NAT

    C. Authorization

    D. Accounting

    E. Billing

14. When configuring a VoIP Domain H.323 Gatekeeper object, which type of object is created for the VoIP Installed At field?

    A. Gateway

    B. Group

    C. Network

    D. Host

    E. Address Range

15. Which of these security features should be considered when deploying a VoIP solution?

    A. Bandwidth

    B. Deploy the solution in its own segment, separate from the corporate LAN

    C. Voice Quality

    D. Install it on a hardened server

    E. All of the above

16. Which protocol will enable a full phone call without limitations?

    A. H.323_ras

    B. HTTP

    C. H.323_any

    D. FTP

    E. None of the above

17. Which H.323 device is the focal point for all VoIP phone calls?

    A. Gateway

    B. Host

    C. Virtual Machine

    D. Domain

    E. Gatekeeper

18. SIP relies on which other protocols/applications to manage calls?

    A. DNS

    B. PSTN

    C. HTTP

    D. All of the above

    E. None of the above.

19. What does PSTN stand for?

    A. Packet switched technology network

    B. Public segment telephone network

    C. Public switched telephone network

    D. Public switched technology network

    E. None of the above

20. What is the most widely used protocol for VoIP today?

    A. H.323

    B. HTTP

    C. SIP

    D. H.225

    E. FTP

Answers to Review Questions

1. C, E. FireWall-1 only supports H.323 and SIP. PSTN and PBX have to do with public telephone service. VoIP is the general term for all IP telephony.

2. A. Only one rule is needed because you don't have to account for communication with any SIP proxies or SIP redirect servers.

3. A, B, C, D, E. Each of these factors affects voice quality. Some issues are addressed through the VoIP scheme that is used; others (such as bandwidth) can be addressed by using another protocol, such as DiffServ QoS.

4. C. There is no need for a VoIP Domain SIP object in SIP scenarios in which no proxy or redirect server is involved.

5. A, B, C, D. You can create a Network object or an Address Range object to define the range of IP addresses that represent your IP phones, or you can create individual Host Node objects and pull them into a group to represent the IP addresses of your IP phones.

6. A. Echo, a problem that causes you to hear your own voice echoed back to you during a conversation is caused by a round-trip delay of greater than 50 ms.

7. E. Talker overlap, a problem that causes you to talk over another person's words, is caused by a one-way delay of greater than 250ms.

8. D. SIP can only be used with IP-based phones, not analog phones.

9. D. One of the advantages of SIP over H.323 is the fact that it interfaces with the PSTN more easily.

10. D. Jitter is caused by having to wait for the packet to arrive and be played in order.

11. C, E.   Soft phones are based on computer software that enables a computer to be an IP phone as well as IP based telephones. These phones can be part of an H.323 or SIP VoIP solution.

12. E.   All of these benefits are true for H.323. It was originally designed to be a multimedia communications protocol, but with version 2 it was upgraded to be a VoIP standard protocol.

13. B.   The gatekeeper does not offer NAT but does offer the rest of the services listed. NAT can be performed on the firewall if necessary, but the gatekeeper would not be the appropriate place.

14. D.   The physical gatekeeper machine is represented by a Host object.

15. E.   All of these should be considered when architecting a VoIP solution.

16. C.   H.323_any will provide all the services needed to make a full phone call. H.323_ras will have limitations. The other protocol choices are not H.323 based.

17. E.   The gatekeeper is the focal point for all VoIP phone calls. It is created as a host machine in the SmartCenter server and then configured as a VoIP Domain Gatekeeper object.

18. D.   SIP uses DNS to identify the user, the PSTN to help with call setup and your browser to display an IVR page if necessary.

19. C.   Public switched telephone network (PSTN) is the name given to the current network that converts analog calls to digital, transports them, and then converts the calls back to analog on the other end.

20. A.   H.323 is the most widely accepted and most widely used protocol today because it's included with every Microsoft operating system. SIP is gaining popularity because it addresses the shortcomings of H.323. There is no exact standard selected yet for VoIP.

Chapter

6

Virtual Private Networks

THE CCSE EXAM TOPICS COVERED IN THIS CHAPTER INCLUDE:

- ✓ Basic encryption terminology and theory.
- ✓ Encryption components used to implement a VPN.
- ✓ Configuring an IKE site-to-site VPN with shared secrets.
- ✓ Configuring an IKE site-to-site VPN with certificates.
- ✓ Deploying an internal and external certificate authority.

I n this chapter, we'll cover the basics of encryption theory as a foundation to prepare you for understanding *virtual private networks* (VPNs) and how they work. This discussion will lead into the topic of how VPNs are configured in Check Point's product line. But first, an update on the product line.

Throughout the book, we've been referring to FireWall-1 or VPN-1/FireWall-1, which is the way the product has been marketed over the last few years and that functionality still exists. In the middle of the year 2002, Check Point changed its marketing terminology; these changes have a direct effect on how we will refer to the product in this chapter, but in no way affect any of the functionality previously discussed. Check Point has two core products: FireWall-1 (just firewall functionality) and VPN-1/FireWall-1 (firewall and VPN functionality). When Check Point FP2 came out, the company changed the product options to the following: FireWall-1, VPN-1 Net, and VPN-1 Pro. Table 6.1 will help you keep this information straight.

TABLE 6.1 Check Point's Core Products as of FP2

Product	Functionality
FireWall-1	Firewall solution that provides access control, content security, authentication, centralized management, and so on
VPN-1 Net	Dedicated VPN solution with simplified management Includes very minimal firewall functionality
VPN-1 Pro	Integrated solution that includes VPN functionality as well as FireWall-1 functionality

For a more thorough listing of Check Point products, go to `http://www.checkpoint.com/products/index.html`.

NG has a new way of configuring VPNs. In the 4.x version of VPN-1/FireWall-1, VPNs were configured manually. This method, which is now referred to as Traditional Mode in NG, is the method we are covering in this section. A more automated method of configuring VPNs called Simplified VPNs was introduced in FP1; we discuss it at length in Chapter 7.

Now that we've made these distinctions, let's move on to the theory behind how Check Point performs VPNs.

VPN Basics

A variety of components must come together for a VPN to happen. When most people use the term *encryption* or *VPN*, they think of the actual scrambling of data—but that is only one part of the puzzle. You may find it easier to remember the components by equating them with PAIN—not the physical kind, but an acronym that indicates the core pieces of encryption. The meaning of the PAIN acronym is spelled out for you in Table 6.2.

T A B L E   6.2   Meaning of the PAIN Acronym

Letter	Meaning	What This Element Does
P	Privacy	Scrambles the message so that only the intended recipient can read it
A	Authentication	Verifies that the message or keys you have received are from the correct entity
I	Integrity	Checks the message to make sure nothing has changed in route to you
N	Non-repudiation	Identifies the sender absolutely

We'll explore these core components of VPNs and the different methods available to carry them out. Let's start with privacy.

Privacy

Encryption (a.k.a. privacy) is the process of scrambling data so that no one can read it. This can be accomplished using two different encryption methods: symmetric or asymmetric.

Symmetric Encryption

Symmetric encryption is best described graphically, as shown in Figure 6.1.

FIGURE 6.1 Symmetric encryption

The original message shown in Figure 6.1 is referred to as being in *cleartext* because it's readable. When this original message is combined with the secret key the result is the encrypted message (referred to as *ciphertext*). The message can only be decrypted by someone who holds the same secret key. When the process is reversed, the encrypted message together with the secret key will produce the original cleartext message.

The process is relatively simple and very quick, but it has some drawbacks; the most basic is that the same key used to encrypt is also used to decrypt. The secret key must be created and then securely delivered to the person with whom you want to share encrypted messages. The safest way is to put it on a floppy disk and physically carry it to the person, but it is not always possible to do so. It's not secure to send this key via e-mail, because anyone could intercept it and read all of your encrypted messages. Even if you're able to physically get the key to the person, it is good security practice to change the key on a regular basis. When you're exchanging messages with one person, this is not a big deal—but with multiple people, it would be a daunting task. With symmetric encryption you should have a separate key for each person with whom you want to share encrypted information. If you used the same key for everyone, then everyone would be able to read all the messages sent. So you need to generate one key for every person with whom you wish to encrypt. As the number of keys grows, key management becomes an issue.

We're not saying that symmetric encryption doesn't have a place in a VPN. However, you'll have to address the problem of key management. This leads us to asymmetric encryption.

Asymmetric Encryption

Asymmetric encryption uses two keys for encrypting/decrypting data. This is also referred to as public/private key encryption. Figure 6.2 depicts asymmetric encryption.

FIGURE 6.2 Asymmetric encryption

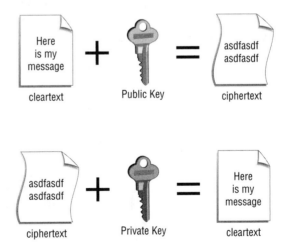

The public/private key pair is generated by the person who wants to encrypt. The private key is secured by the generator of the keys, and the public key is handed out freely to whoever wants to share encrypted information with the generator of the keys (the Pretty Good Privacy [PGP] program originally worked this way). The person who wishes to encrypt a message gets a copy of the public key and encrypts the message with it. Only the holder of the private key will be able to decrypt the message.

The public key is mathematically related to the private key; it is impossible to reverse-engineer the public key to get the value of the private key. For more details about the mathematics involved in encryption, see *Applied Cryptography* by Bruce Schneier (John Wiley & Sons, 1995).

As is true for symmetric encryption, the keys should be regenerated on a regular basis or any time you think they have been compromised. Although asymmetric encryption reduces number of keys that must be managed, as an encryption process it is 1,000 times slower than symmetric encryption. What we need is a methodology that combines the assets of asymmetric and symmetric encryption. That's where the Diffie-Hellman key exchange method comes into play.

Diffie-Hellman Key Exchange Mechanism

The *Diffie-Hellman* key exchange uses the public/private key pair to generate a secret key. This process is illustrated in Figure 6.3.

FIGURE 6.3 Diffie-Hellman key exchange

In step 1, users exchange public keys. When you're using asymmetric encryption, the exchange of public keys is all that is required to begin encrypting. But Diffie-Hellman combines asymmetric and symmetric processes. Each user's private key is combined with their encrypting partners' public key using the Diffie-Hellman key calculation, as shown in step 2. As we stated earlier, the public and private keys that each user creates are mathematically related; that's how the users can exchange keys, apply the Diffie-Hellman key calculation, and both end up (in step 3) with mathematically identical keys.

Different mathematical groups can be used to generate the identical keys. The Diffie-Hellman standard supports three groups: DH groups 1, 2, and 5. The larger the group number, the larger the prime number used to generate the key pair. The larger groups are more secure but require more CPU cycles to generate the keys. Check Point also gives you the ability to expand the database of groups by adding custom groups.

The process depicted in Figure 6.3 solves two problems. First, you have generated the secret key necessary to perform symmetric encryption without having to physically exchange the secret key with your encrypting partner. Second, you can use that key to symmetrically encrypt data much more quickly than you can using asymmetric encryption alone. The best aspects of both encryption techniques are combined to yield a process that's better than each individual technique. The encryption processes we've described fill out the P in PAIN, but they are useless unless you get the correct key from your encrypting partner. The next section addresses how to verify that the key is from the correct source and explains the *AIN* in PAIN.

Authentication, Integrity, and Non-repudiation

In this next section, we will discuss how authentication, integrity, and non-repudiation come into play as well as tie together the entire PAIN acronym.

One-Way Hashes, Digital Signatures, and Certificate Authorities

Verifying the person you receive keys from is important—you do not want to send important information to the wrong party! This verification can be accomplished with the use of digital signatures (which are based on keys) and one-way hash functions.

A *hash* is a one-way mathematical function that operates to ensure a message's integrity. It's one-way because the process is irreversible. The hash functions most routinely used are MD4, MD5, and SHA1. A one-way hash works by taking a variable-length input and putting it through a mathematical algorithm that produces a fixed-length output called a hash value or *message digest*.

A one-way hash function is also known by many other names, such as contraction function, fingerprint, compression function, cryptographic checksum, message integrity check (MIC), message authentication code (MAC), and manipulation detection code (MDC).

The purpose of the one-way hash is to determine if the message you receive has changed from the original message sent. The output of the hash, or message digest, is combined with the sender's private key to generate a *digital signature*, as depicted in Figure 6.4.

FIGURE 6.4   One-way hash plus a private key equals a digital signature

The digital signature is combined with the sender's public key and the original variable-length input and sent to the recipient. This process authenticates the sender's identity, as shown in Figure 6.5.

FIGURE 6.5   A message is sent

The recipient repeats the process by putting the message through the same one-way hash function. This time the recipient combines the message digest with the sender's public key (the original was combined with the sender's private key) to produce a digital signature like the process shown in Figure 6.6.

FIGURE 6.6   Recipient checks the message

Because of the mathematical relationship between the public/private key pair, the digital signature sent with the message should match the digital signature the recipient generated. If the signatures don't match, the public key sent should be rejected.

Check Point specifically uses RSA public/private key pairs and hash functions for integrity and authentication. Thus RSA key pairs are used to sign and verify certificates, and the Diffie-Hellman process is used to generate secret keys to encrypt/decrypt the data.

If you receive the public key directly from the source, then you must trust the source. If you receive the public key from somewhere else (such as a certificate authority), then you must trust that source. It all boils down to the fact that eventually, you have to trust someone or some entity. This leads us into the discussion of the purpose and role of a certificate authority.

Certificate Authorities

A *certificate authority* (CA) is a trusted third party that has the responsibility of verifying the identity of generators of public keys as well as being a repository to hold those keys. You may already trust a CA and not even realize it. If you've ever purchased something on the Web, then odds are you've trusted a CA. Inside any browser is a list of trusted root CAs. Figure 6.7 shows a list of root CAs from Netscape. By default, all browsers trust the root CAs they were built to trust.

A *root CA* is the highest level in a CA hierarchy. Any certificate generated by a CA below the root will be trusted by anything that trusts the root CA. Figure 6.8 shows a CA hierarchy.

For example, if your browser received a certificate generated by the Detroit CA and your browser already trusted the root CA that created the Detroit CA certificate, then by default your browser would automatically trust the certificate from Detroit.

There are different classes of certificates with varying levels of trust. The more proof of identity required (and the more money paid), then the higher the class of certificate.

FIGURE 6.7 Trusted root certificate authorities list in Netscape

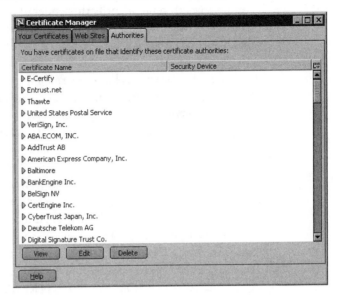

FIGURE 6.8 CA hierarchy

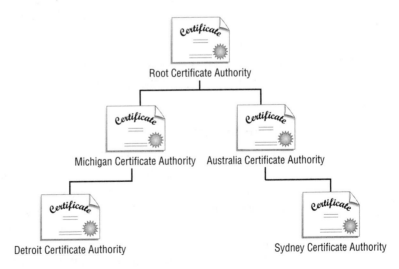

A certificate from a CA could include a variety of different identifying entities such as a *distinguished name* (DN), public key, IP address, e-mail

address, CA identifier, expiration date, and digital signature. Each of these components serves to identify the sender of the information. The certificate's security is based on the secrecy of the password protecting the certificate and the difficulty associated with accessing the physical device on which the certificates are stored.

Certificates are not valid forever. Some expire, and others are invalidated for a variety of reasons. For those that are invalidated before their expiration date, a *certificate revocation list* (CRL) is required. The CRL provides a place where entities can go to make sure all the certificates they possess are still valid. The CA and CRL go hand-in-hand to ensure the integrity of the certificates and public keys.

How does the CA tie in with authentication, integrity, and non-repudiation (the *AIN* in PAIN)? Instead of directly exchanging certificates with each entity with which you want to establish a VPN, most people take advantage of a CA to hold their public keys. The CA verifies the identity of the public key generator and then adds its own digital signature to the public key. This process ensures that the public key was indeed generated by the person or entity in question. You can go to a centralized place (the CA) to get all the public keys needed to set up VPNs with your VPN partners instead of having to contact each one individually. Two entities in Check Point can identify themselves using certificates: encrypting gateways and SecureClient/SecuRemote in a Remote Access VPN (which are discussed in detail in Chapters 9 and 10).

We can't emphasize enough that you eventually have to trust someone—either the generator of the public key or the CA that is holding the key.

The Complete PAIN Process

The processes we've just covered are tied together in Figure 6.9. Each VPN participant obtains the digitally signed public key of their VPN partner from the CA. Each participant then combines their private key with their VPN partner's public key (using Diffie-Hellman) to generate the basic session key (a.k.a. shared secret key). The basic session key is used to generate a new session key for each VPN session.

The session key generated by VPN Partner #1 is placed into a data packet that is encrypted with the basic session key and sent to VPN Partner #2. Only VPN Partner #2 can decrypt the packet to reveal the session key. Now that both partners have a session key for a VPN session, they can begin encrypting/decrypting data between them. The gray layer in the figure indicates asymmetric processes and the white areas depict symmetric processes.

FIGURE 6.9 Entire PAIN process

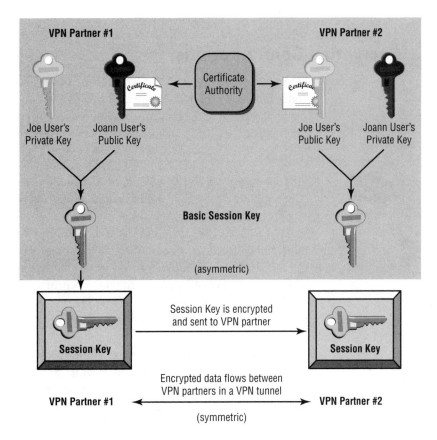

The *P* for privacy takes place when the session key is used to encrypt data sent to either VPN partner and decrypt data received from either VPN partner. Because the same key is used for both decrypting and encrypting data, this part of the process uses symmetric encryption.

The *A* for authentication is taken care of when the CA receives and verifies that the public keys are genuine. The CA then authenticates the validity of the key. When each partner receives the key, it is digitally signed by the CA; this step provides the *N* for non-repudiation, meaning the CA can't refute that the key came from the CA. The *I* for integrity finishes the equation when the digital signature is reverse-engineered to ensure no data was tampered with in transit. Because the AIN portion of the process primarily uses asymmetric encryption, it's much slower; but this portion is not required to be performed as frequently. If everything passes inspection, then you have PAIN!

Encryption Configurations

Before we discuss the specific schemes used by VPN-1, it's important to understand how Check Point categorizes VPNs. Intranet and extranet VPNs are site-to-site because they take place between two firewalls. Remote VPNs are client-to-site because they take place between a firewall and a VPN client.

VPN clients will be discussed in detail in Chapters 9, "SecuRemote," and 10, "SecureClient, The Policy Server, and Clientless VPNs."

An intranet VPN, as defined by Check Point, exists between two Check Point firewalls that are under the control of one company and one Smart-Center Server for example, a corporation that has a large corporate office and small satellite offices, each of which is protected by a firewall and managed by the same SmartCenter Server. These firewalls are all controlled by the central office, and all information that flows between the offices is encrypted.

An extranet VPN exists between two firewalls that are controlled by different companies and different SmartCenter Servers for example, the large automotive companies and their suppliers, each of which is protected by its own firewalls. Each supplier needs to securely communicate with the automotive companies, so they set up extranet VPNs between their firewalls. (These do not all need to be Check Point firewalls, but it certainly makes things easier to configure if they are.)

In this chapter we are specifically concerned with site-to-site VPNs between Check Point firewalls, as shown in Figure 6.10. This figure outlines some very important concepts. It shows that the data that flows between the two firewalls is encrypted; it also shows that the data behind the firewalls is *not* encrypted. This is an important concept to grasp: The firewall is doing the encryption, but everything is still in cleartext until it reaches the firewall.

FIGURE 6.10 Site-to-site VPN

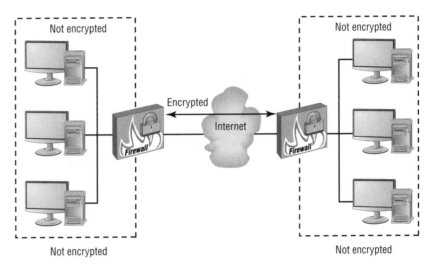

The figure shows encryption domains, as well. *Encryption domains* are the defined networks or hosts that need to have their traffic encrypted. (Although these terms may not seem to tie together right now, they will all make sense when we begin configuring VPN-1 Pro to create VPN tunnels.)

 Real World Scenario

VPNs in Action

You can use different VPN configurations to securely transfer your data. Many companies deploy gateway-to-gateway VPNs between corporate headquarters and remote offices, saving on leased lines and even incorporating VoIP to save on long-distance charges. Using VoIP for long distance is an intranet VPN.

VPNs can also be configured between business partners to secure their communication. The Automotive Network eXchange (ANX) is an example of this type of extranet VPN.

In future chapters, you'll learn how traveling or home users can encrypt information bound for their companies' networks using remote access VPNs.

Now that we've covered the basics, it's time to get into the specifics of how Check Point utilizes these encryption concepts.

IKE Encryption Scheme

A long time ago (about four years in real time), Check Point supported many different encryption schemes: Manual IPSec, Simple Key Management for Internet Protocols (SKIP), FWZ (Check Point's own proprietary scheme), and Internet Key Exchange (IKE). As the industry began to settle on a standard and it became apparent that different vendors' VPN products needed to work together, the schemes were whittled down to only one: IKE.

IKE is a hybrid protocol that combines the Internet Security Association and Key Management Protocol (*ISAKMP*) and the *Oakley Key Exchange Protocol*. ISAKMP is responsible for the generation and maintenance of Security Associations, and Oakley is responsible for key exchanges. Both ISAKMP/Oakley and IKE are described in the IETF standard for encryption using the IP Security Protocol (IPSec). (The terms IKE and IPSec are frequently used interchangeably.)

You can find more on IPSec and its related protocols in RFCs 2401-2411 and 2451.

IPSec provides the access control, integrity of the packet, authentication, rejection of replayed packets, encryption, and non-repudiation (there's that PAIN acronym coming into play). IPSec does so by using the protocols *Authentication Header* (AH) and *Encapsulating Security Payload* (ESP). Each protocol—IPSec, AH, and ESP—is incorporated into its own header in the IPSec packet. IKE is also a tunneling protocol, which means it encrypts the entire original packet and adds new headers to the encrypted packet. See Figure 6.11 for an example.

Tunneling encrypts the entire original packet and adds new headers, which increases packet size and the likelihood of packet fragmentation. In-place encryption was Check Point's proprietary FWZ scheme supported in versions before FP2. It only encrypted the payload, and left the headers alone; therefore packet size did not increase. Although FWZ is no longer supported as of FP2, this information could still be used for a valid NG test question.

FIGURE 6.11   IPSec packet

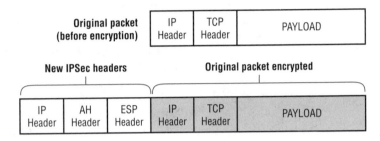

The new IP header uses the IPSec protocol and replaces the true source and destination of the packet (which are now encrypted) with the source and destination IP addresses of the firewalls involved in the VPN tunnel.

The AH header provides data integrity and authentication by using a message digest (instead of a digital signature, which is too slow for this process) and a *Security Parameters Index* (SPI). The SPI is like a pointer that tells your VPN partner which methods were selected for this VPN session. The SPI references the *Security Association* (SA), which was negotiated by the VPN participants. A good analogy to describe the SA is a large spreadsheet that contains all the possible combinations for key exchange, encryption, data integrity, and so forth that could be used for this connection. The SPI is the pointer that tells each partner which parts of the spreadsheet will be used for this specific tunnel.

The ESP header provides confidentiality as well as authentication. It gives a reference to the SPI as well as an Initialization Vector (IV), which is another data integrity check.

IKE supports a variety of different encryption algorithms, but VPN-1 supports only DES, Triple-DES, CAST, and AES. These algorithms are explained in Table 6.3.

TABLE 6.3   Encryption Standards Support by IKE and VPN-1

Algorithm	Description
DES	Data Encryption Standard (standard in the U.S. for the last 20 years). A symmetric key encryption method that uses 56-bit keys.
Triple DES	A variation on DES that addresses the problem of short, easily breakable keys. Encrypts with three different DES keys in succession, which increases the effective key strength to 168 bits.

TABLE 6.3 Encryption Standards Support by IKE and VPN-1 *(continued)*

Algorithm	Description
CAST	Named for its inventors, Carlisle Adams and Stafford Tavares. Similar to DES and supports variable key lengths from 40–128 bits.
AES	Advanced Encryption Standard. The new Federal Information Processing Standard (FIPS) standard. Also known as Rijndael (pronounced "rhine-doll") for its inventors, Vincent Rihmen and Joan Daemen.

For a more detailed explanation of encryption, IPSec, and cryptography, we recommend *Applied Cryptography* (John Wiley & Sons, 1995), *RSA Security's Official Guide to Cryptography* (McGraw-Hill, 2001) and *IPSec Securing VPNs* (McGraw-Hill Osborne Media, 2001).

Encryption is not an easy topic to grasp, especially in an abbreviated format within a study guide. But this background information is essential before we go into detail about how IKE negotiates keys and eventually encrypts data. Let's forge ahead and tackle the IKE phases of key negotiation.

ISAKMP Phase 1: SA Negotiation

In Phase 1 of the SA negotiation, the firewalls involved in the VPN negotiate an SA that is used to encrypt and authenticate Phase 2 exchanges. Phase 1 is a CPU-intensive process, and by default VPN-1 performs it only once every 1,440 minutes (24 hours). VPN-1 supports two modes for Phase 1: *aggressive mode*, which exchanges three packets; and *main mode* (the default mode in NG), in which six packets are exchanged. The three-packet difference is due to a cookie exchange that precedes the actual SA negotiation. The cookie exchange identifies the parties involved in the VPN, thus preventing man-in-the-middle attacks (to which the Diffie-Hellman key exchange is vulnerable). The SA that is negotiated includes the keys, authentication, and encryption methods.

Phase 1 negotiates the following:

- The encryption algorithm (the choices are DES, 3DES, AES, and CAST)

- The hash algorithm (the choices are MD5 or SHA1)
- The Diffie-Hellman group (the choices are Group 1, 2, or 5). The addition of DH group choices in NG increases the likelihood that a VPN tunnel can be established with non-Check Point firewalls.

Diffie-Hellman groups are used to determine the length of the base prime numbers used during the key exchange. The strength of any key derived depends in part on the strength of the Diffie-Hellman group on which the prime numbers are based. The larger the group, the stronger the key—but, conversely, the more CPU-intensive the computation.

The second step in Phase 1 is the exchange of public keys and the use of the Diffie-Hellman key calculation to generate the shared secret key. The shared secret key is used to authenticate each firewall's identity. This is accomplished by hashing and encrypting the firewall's identity with the shared secret key. If the identity of each firewall is authenticated, then we move on to Phase 2.

IPSec Phase 2: SA Negotiation

Phase 2 uses the IKE SA negotiated in Phase 1 to negotiate an IPSec SA for encrypting IPSec traffic. VPN-1, by default, initiates a Phase 2 negotiation every 3,600 seconds (1 hour). The first step in Phase 2 negotiates the IPSec protocol combination that will be used (the choices are AH only or a combination of AH and ESP).

As of NG FP2, AH is not supported. If you're upgrading from versions prior to FP2, be sure to change the encryption properties to use ESP only.

When the firewalls come to an agreement, two SAs are determined: one for inbound connections and one for outbound. The Oakley portion of ISAKMP/Oakley refreshes the keys on a regular basis. The negotiated SAs and the keys are handed off to the IPSec driver, and the VPN tunnel begins.

Perfect Forward Secrecy

Perfect Forward Secrecy (PFS) is a layer of protection that can be added to Phase 2. Using this option adds a Diffie-Hellman key exchange to Phase 2 negotiations (it normally occurs only in Phase 1). If your Phase 1 keys were compromised, an attacker could decrypt Phase 2 exchanges to get your IPSec keys (VPN session keys). This scenario is prevented by adding a Diffie-Hellman key exchange to Phase 2. Even if an attacker got your Phase 1 keys, they would need to get your Phase 2 keys to uncover the IPSec keys necessary to decrypt your traffic. Because Phase 2 occurs every hour, it's highly unlikely that the attacker would have time to decipher your Phase 2 keys before they were renegotiated.

IKE Using Pre-shared Secrets or Certificates

The authentication portion of IKE can be carried out two ways: either using a *pre-shared secret* (a password that both VPN parties agree upon) or using certificates. If certificates are used, then you can use two different methods: Each SmartCenter Server can generate its own certificate that can be manually exchanged, or you can go to a certificate authority for the certificates. Your choices are VPN-1 Certificate Manager (Check Point's proprietary twist on Entrusts' Certificate Server), Entrust PKI, or OPSEC PKI.

A public key infrastructure (PKI) is a set of protocols, services, and standards that supports applications that use public key cryptography.

Now that we've introduced and explained all the pieces behind VPNs, let's piece it all together to configure a VPN with Check Point VPN-1 Pro.

Configuring an IKE VPN

IKE VPNs can be configured using either a pre-shared secret (a shared-password) or certificates. You have four options for CAs (two internal and two external) when creating a VPN with certificates. This section will discuss how to configure your firewall object and the firewall object for your VPN partner for pre-shared secrets and certificates; we'll then explain how to configure the Global Properties for IKE VPNs and finish up by configuring the rule base.

IKE VPNs Using a Pre-Shared Secret

Creating an IKE VPN using a pre-shared secret is the simplest way to set up a VPN. The configuration steps begin with your own firewall object:

In this chapter, we focus on configuring a VPN on a standalone firewall in Traditional Mode. In Chapter 7, Simplfied VPNs, we'll discuss VPNs in Simplified Mode.

1. Go to Manage ➢ Network Objects and select your firewall object. Click the Topology option in the list to display the topology properties of your firewall, as shown in Figure 6.12. This is where you define your encryption domain. The encryption domain should include every network, gateway or host with which you want a VPN partner to connect. It should be all-encompassing for all VPN partners and then limited for each individual VPN partner in the rule base. Figure 6.12 shows the All IP Addresses Behind Gateway Based on Topology Information radio button selected: This option will include all networks behind the internal interfaces of the firewall as defined under Topology. If the Manually Defined option is selected, then you will need to create an object for each host, gateway, or network you want included in your encryption domain and pull all the objects into a Simple Group.

If you have many networks behind your firewall and you want only one to be in the encryption domain, select Manually Defined and select that specific network object. If you leave the default All IP Addresses Behind Gateway Based On Topology Information option, the partner with which you are setting up the VPN could have knowledge of all IP addresses behind your firewall.

2. After you've defined the topology, move to the VPN properties (see Figure 6.13) to configure the VPN parameters for the firewall.

FIGURE 6.12   Firewall topology for an IKE VPN

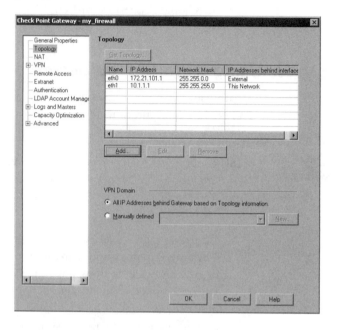

FIGURE 6.13   Firewall VPN properties

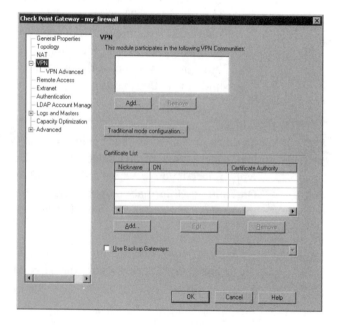

3. FP3 integrates more of the Simplified VPN architecture (see Chapter 7 for more information) into individual objects. So, to configure individual IKE properties for this specific firewall, click the Traditional Mode Configuration button to reveal the Traditional Mode IKE Properties shown in Figure 6.14.

FIGURE 6.14   Traditional Mode IKE properties

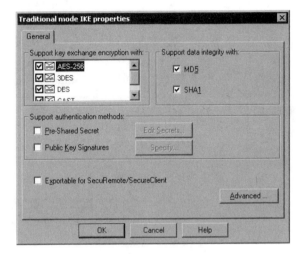

In this window, a lot of the theory we discussed in the "VPN Basics" section comes into play. The encryption methods AES, DES, 3DES, and CAST are listed under Support Key Exchange Encryption With; you can select which methods your firewall will support. Having multiple methods to choose from increases the likelihood that an IKE tunnel can be configured with a non–Check Point VPN product. SHA1 and MD5 are the hash methods available under Support Data Integrity With.

4. Check Point gives two options for authentication; they're listed in Table 6.4.

TABLE 6.4   IKE supported authentication methods

Authentication Method	Deployment
Pre-Shared Secret	Using this method, each firewall in the VPN must agree on a single password that is defined as the pre-shared secret. It is used initially to authenticate the connection before keys and encryption methods are negotiated.
Public Key Signatures	This method utilizes a certificate authority as a centralized place for each VPN partner to obtain the other's public key.

5. From the IKE Properties screen, select Pre-Shared Secret and click Edit Secrets to display the Shared Secret window shown in Figure 6.15.

FIGURE 6.15   Shared Secret window

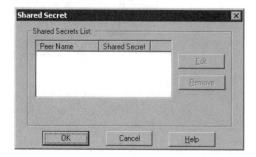

6. The Shared Secret window on your firewall will be empty, which is fine. Click OK three times to finish configuring your firewall object.

7. As you open each VPN partner firewall, each firewall object that has been created to set up a VPN will be listed in the Shared Secret window. Select a firewall and click the Edit button to display the Enter Secret field shown in Figure 6.16.

FIGURE 6.16 Enter Secret field

8. Enter the agreed-upon password and click the Set button. Repeat this process for each VPN partner with the corresponding pre-shared secret. The pre-shared secret must also be set in the VPN partner's firewall objects that are created. Your VPN partner must go through these processes on their firewall. After setting the pre-shared secret, click Set and then click OK to return to the Traditional Mode IKE Properties window.

9. Click the Advanced button to display the Traditional Mode Advanced IKE Properties window shown in Figure 6.17.

FIGURE 6.17 Traditional Mode Advanced IKE Properties window

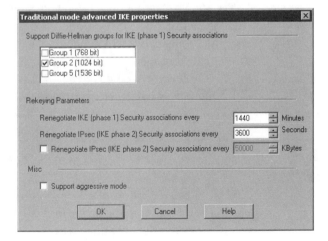

The different strengths of Diffie-Hellman groups are listed under Support Diffie-Hellman Groups (the default is Group 2). The group selected here is used only in Phase 1 IKE negotiations.

The Rekeying Parameters options specify how often keys are exchanged in Phases 1 and 2. Because the Phase 1 IKE SA negotiations use asymmetric encryption and are much slower than Phase 2 IPSec SA negotiations, Phase 1 negotiations happen less frequently (every 1,440 minutes—once every 24 hours) than Phase 2 (every 3,600 seconds—once per hour). You have the option of changing either of these parameters, but it must match your VPN partner's setting; otherwise your keys will be out of sync and the encryption tunnel will fail. You also have the option of renegotiating the Phase 2 IPSEC SA based on the number of bytes transferred in the VPN tunnel. The default is to renegotiate every 50000KB (50MB). Renegotiating based on the amount of traffic through the tunnel as opposed to a defined time frame causes a bigger load to be put on the firewall CPU.

Finally, you must consider whether to choose Support Aggressive Mode under Misc. If this option is turned off, the six-packet exchange that includes cookies to authenticate each VPN party is carried out. If the option is turned on, only a three-packet exchange occurs, and you are susceptible to man-in-the-middle attacks.

NG FP3 introduced a VPN Advanced tab, shown in Figure 6.18.

These are not totally new options to FP3 (although some are new), things have just been rearranged slightly.

The VPN Advanced options include Support NAT Traversal Mechanism (UDP Encapsulation). If this option is selected, SecuRemote/SecureClient encrypted connections will be enclosed in UDP packets so these connections can burrow through devices that perform address translation, which could disrupt the encrypted connection.

If Support Key Exchange for Subnets is selected, Phase 2 negotiates encryption keys for subnets as opposed to negotiating them for individual hosts.

Clientless VPNs will be discussed in Chapter 9.

Under Restart Options, Perform an Organized Shutdown of Tunnels upon Gateway Restart allows the firewall to securely close each VPN tunnel before restarting the firewall services.

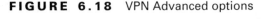

FIGURE 6.18 VPN Advanced options

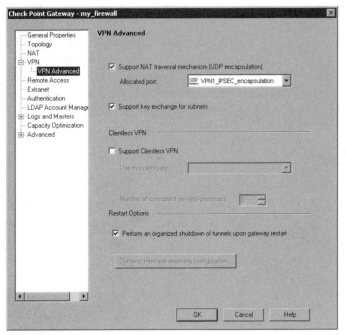

The Dynamic Interface Resolving Configuration button is active only if Enable Dynamic Interface Resolving per Gateway is selected in the Global Properties under either VPN-1 Pro ➢ Advanced or Remote Access ➢ VPN - Advanced. This setting is necessary only if one of the VPN gateways has a dynamic external interface.

Configuring an IKE VPN with Certificates

Creating an IKE VPN using certificates is the second way to set up a VPN. The configuration steps begin with defining certificate authorities:

If you're using Entrust PKI or OPSEC PKI as your certificate authority, you may have to contact the CA manufacturer and load specific software.

1. Go to Manage ➢ Servers. You will see one CA object already created. This is your *internal certificate authority* (ICA), as shown in Figure 6.19. It was created when the software was loaded and is tied to your Smart-Center Server. The ICA is responsible for overseeing the generation, signing, and revocation of certificates for VPN-1. The ICA establishes the SIC between Check Point components, generates certificates for users and administrators, authenticates SecuRemote/SecureClient traffic, and generates certificates for gateway-to-gateway VPNs as we're describing here.

FIGURE 6.19 Internal CA

2. Edit the ICA. Click the Local Management Server tab and then the View button to reveal the ICA information, which includes the expiration date, key usage, and MD5 and SHA1 Fingerprints (see Figure 6.20).

3. From the Local Management Server tab, you can also establish the location of the CRL. It can be stored on an LDAP (Lightweight Directory Access Protocol) server or an HTTP server, as shown in Figure 6.21.

4. The Save As option allows you to save your certificate to a file with a *.crt extension. This file can be shared with a VPN partner to set up a certificate-based IKE VPN. You can define more characteristics, such as CRL caching and valid branches of the CA, under the Advanced tab.

FIGURE 6.20   Internal CA characteristics

FIGURE 6.21   Local Management Server tab

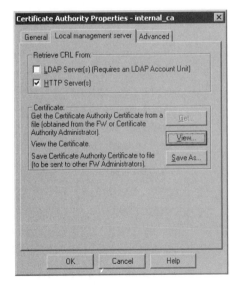

5. To create a new CA, click New ➤ Certificate Authority. The Certificate Authority Properties screen will appear, as shown in Figure 6.22.

FIGURE 6.22 Certificate Authority Properties window

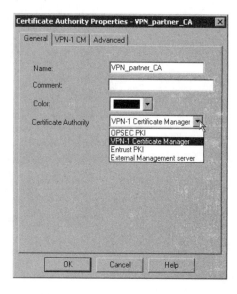

6. As with any other object, a Name is given and you can define a Comment and Color. The Certificate Authority pull-down menu lists the four choices for creating a CA server object:

VPN-1 Certificate Manager   This was Check Point's proprietary twist on Entrust's Certificate Manager. This product line was dropped in December 2001 but is listed to handle backward compatibility requirements.

Entrust PKI   This OPSEC partner offers a PKI solution. See www.entrust.com for more details.

OPSEC PKI   This option encompasses non-Entrust OPSEC PKI solutions. For a listing of current OPSEC-certified PKI solutions, go to http://www.opsec.com/solutions/sec_pki.html.

External Management Server   This option is for Check Point certificates that you import from other Check Point SmartCenter Servers.

NG's implementation of IKE supports X.509 digital certificates from these sources. Keep in mind that you can have only one certificate from each CA, and each CA must have a unique DN.

7. If you're setting up a VPN with another Check Point firewall using Check Point certificates, you select External Management Server from the pull-down menu. Then, under the External Management Server tab, click Get to import the certificate your VPN partner gave you. The certificate file should be in a `*.crt` format just like the one you exported to give to your VPN partner. The contents of a `*.crt` file looks like the one shown in Figure 6.23.

FIGURE 6.23   Firewall certificate

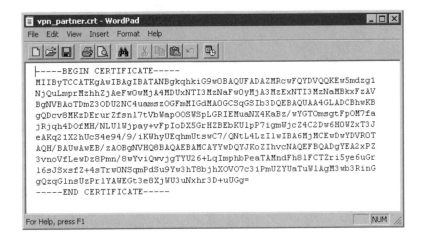

```
-----BEGIN CERTIFICATE-----
MIIByTCCATKgAwIBAgIBATANBgkqhkiG9w0BAQUFADAZMRcwFQYDVQQKEw5mdzg1
NjQuLmprMzhhZjAeFw0wMjA4MDUxNTI3MzNaFw0yMjA3MzExNTI3MzNaMBkxFzAV
BgNVBAoTDmZ3ODU2NC4uamszOGFmMIGdMA0GCSqGSIb3DQEBAQUAA4GLADCBhwKB
gQDcv8MKzDErurZfsn17tVbWapOOSWSpLGRIEMuaNX4KaBz/wYGTOmsgtFpOM7fa
jRjqh4DOfMH/NLUlWjpay+vFpIoDX5GrHZBEbKU1pP7igmWjcZ4C2Dw6HOWZxT3J
eAKq21X2hUcS4e94/9/iKWhyUEqhmUtswC7/QNtL4LzIlwIBA6MjMCEwDwYDVR0T
AQH/BAUwAwEB/zAOBgNVHQ8BAQAEBAMCAYYwDQYJKoZIhvcNAQEFBQADgYEA2xPZ
3vnoVfLewDz8Pmn/8wYviQwvjgTYU26+LqImphbPeaTAMndFh81FCTZri5ye6uGr
16sJSxsfZ+4sTrwONSqmPdSu9Yw3hT8bjhXOVO7c3iPmUZYUaTuWlAgM3wb3RinG
gQzqGlnsUzPrlYAWEGt3e8XjWU3uNxhr3D+uUGg=
-----END CERTIFICATE-----
```

Other certificate file formats that will be accepted by the firewall include `*.cer`, `*.b64`, and `*.mme`.

8. Once you get the certificate, a window like the one in Figure 6.24 will appear. It asks whether you want to accept the certificate.

9. The CA created for your VPN partner will be used instead of the pre-shared secret when configuring your partner's firewall object. Go to Manage ➢ Network Objects, select your firewall object, and move to VPN ➢ Traditional Mode Configuration where the VPN parameters for the firewall are configured.

FIGURE 6.24 Certificate acceptance window

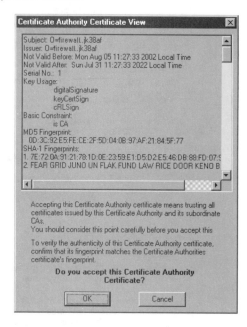

10. Select Public Key Signatures and click Specify to display the Allowed Certificates window shown in Figure 6.25.

FIGURE 6.25 Allowed Certificates window

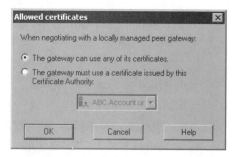

11. You have two choices: The Gateway Can Use Any of Its Certificates (the firewall will automatically select a CA from the list of CA servers you have defined) and The Gateway Must Use a Certificate Issued By This Certificate Authority (the firewall will use certificates issued by the CA selected from the pull-down menu).

12. To modify your VPN partner's firewall object, go to Manage ➤ Network Objects and select your VPN partners firewall.

13. In the VPN window, as shown in Figure 6.26, select Matching Criteria.

FIGURE 6.26   VPN properties

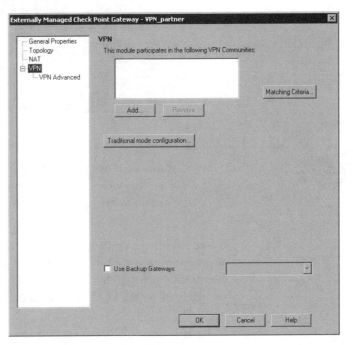

14. You'll see the Certificate Matching Criteria window shown in Figure 6.27. Using the pull-down menu, select the CA server object that represents your VPN partner's CA.

15. Now you must make a decision about the matching criteria. The first option will check to see if the information you enter here matches the distinguished name (DN) that is attached to the certificate (Check Point certificates are defined by their DN). The second option tries to match the IP address in the certificate to the IP address of the firewall (this option is irrelevant for Check Point certificates because they are tied to DNs, not IP addresses). The third option tries to match the e-mail address in the certificate with the one you define (this option is also irrelevant for Check Point certificates).

FIGURE 6.27 Certificate Matching Criteria window

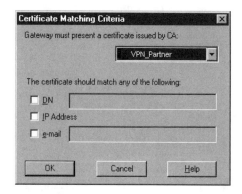

 WARNING

You can define all three options for matching against the certificate, but it takes only one to work. In other words, you can define all three fields, and even if two of the three fields don't match, as long as one matches it will pass the test.

You can choose not to match any criteria. If you do, you will see a warning message that states, "Are you sure you don't want any criteria for matching peers?" but you will be allowed to continue. Choosing not to match the certificate removes an authentication layer from the process.

 WARNING

In a gateway-to-gateway VPN, if each gateway has a pre-shared secret *and* a certificate defined, then the IKE key negotiation will default to using the pre-shared secret. If you're switching from a pre-shared secret VPN to a certificate-based VPN, first turn off the pre-shared secret and then run these commands from a command line prompt on the firewall to restart the VPN driver so it will use the new certificate not the old pre-shared secrets: **vpn drv off** and then **vpn drv on**.

Configuring Global Properties for IKE VPNs

After configuring your firewall object and your VPN partner's firewall and CA server object, the Global Properties must be defined. The settings under VPN-1 Pro ➢ Early Versions Compatibility, shown in Figure 6.28, affect only 4.1 firewalls that are controlled by an NG SmartCenter Server.

FIGURE 6.28 Early Versions Compatibility window

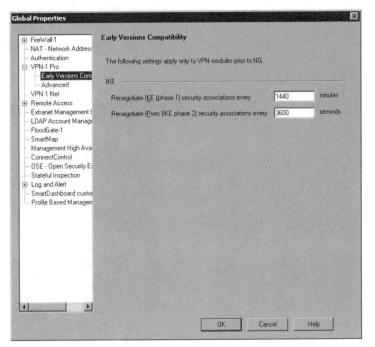

Note that Phase 1 and Phase 2 negotiation parameters affected every firewall controlled by a single Management Server in version 4.1, whereas each firewall can be individually configured in NG. This gives you much more flexibility in configuring VPNs with Check Point firewalls and other vendors. Figure 6.29 shows the VPN-1 Pro ➢ Advanced properties window.

The Enable Backup Gateway and Enable Load Distribution for Multiple Entry Point Configurations (Site to Site Connections) options deal with SecuRemote in a multiple entry point configuration (an advanced topic that we will not cover in this book). Enable Decryption on Accept (Relevant Only to Policies in Traditional Mode) will decrypt incoming packets even if the rule doesn't include encryption in the action. (This property applies only to Traditional Mode policies like the ones we're describing here.)

The CRL Grace Period options give you a time buffer to take into account time changes between the different components in a VPN. For example, a certificate could be created and timestamped by your firewall and then sent to a VPN partner whose clock is a minute or two slower than your firewall clock. When the VPN partner receives the certificate, it will look as if your certificate is not yet valid because your VPN partner's firewall hasn't reached that time yet. These buffer settings take this possibility into account. That's why it's so important, when setting up VPN and PKI type configurations, to synchronize your components with a permanent time source.

FIGURE 6.29 VPN-1 Pro Advanced Global Properties

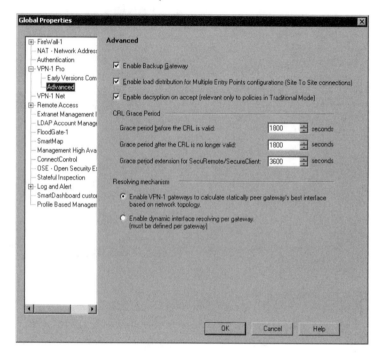

WARNING If a firewall's clock is wrong, the CRL may appear invalid to a VPN partner. When the VPN tunnel is trying to be established, the IKE negotiations will fail and report "Invalid Certificate" in the logs. The problem isn't that the certificate is invalid, but that a valid CRL was not found. Correcting the firewall's clock will correct this situation.

The grace period for SecuRemote/SecureClient is much larger because PC time drift is a more significant issue for traveling users (who are generally using laptops). The Resolving Mechanism options define how to resolve the

VPN peer's gateway address, whether statically or dynamically, based on its configuration.

WARNING Multiple interface resolving is not supported if Allowed Peer Gateway is selected in the Encrypt properties of a rule.

After configuring objects and the Global Properties, you must configure a rule base to allow the encrypted tunnel to occur. The process for setting up a rule base for an IKE VPN with pre-shared secrets does not differ from the process for setting up rules for an IKE VPN with certificates.

Configuring the IKE VPN Rule Base

After reading all the theory and configuring the Global Properties, CA server, and firewall objects, configuring the rule base will seem simple. There are two different schools of thought about how to configure the rule base. One way is to create one rule that includes the encryption domain or portion of the encryption domain for each firewall in both the Source and Destination columns, as shown in Figure 6.30.

FIGURE 6.30 Example using one encryption rule

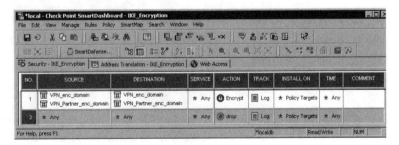

This approach is effective to limit the total number of rules in your rule base, but it forces you to allow the same services to be encrypted as you want decrypted from your VPN partner. To provide more flexibility, you can split your encryption rule into two rules (in our opinion, this is preferred) as shown in Figure 6.31.

FIGURE 6.31 Example using two encryption rules

With this model, you have the option to offer different services for your VPN partner than you allow. You can also limit access so your VPN partner can access only a small portion of your encryption domain rather than all of it. Encrypt is selected in the Action column; you can configure its properties by right-clicking the Encrypt icon and selecting Edit Properties. The Encryption Properties window will appear, as shown in Figure 6.32.

FIGURE 6.32 Encryption Properties window in the rule base

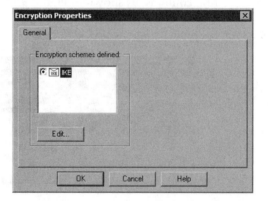

IKE is pre-selected for you because it's the only available option. Clicking Edit allows you to configure the characteristics of the IKE Phase 2 properties as noted in Figure 6.33.

FIGURE 6.33 IKE Phase 2 Properties window

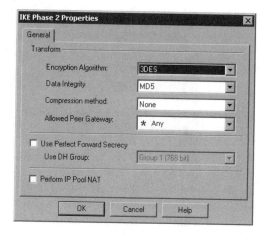

The Phase 2 encryption algorithm is defined with the following choices: 3DES, AES-128, AES-256, DES, CAST, DES-40CP, CAST-40, and NULL. You can choose from MD5 or SHA1 for Data Integrity. The Compression Method option is irrelevant because compression is not support for gateway-to-gateway VPNs. Your VPN partner or partners are defined in the Allowed Peer Gateway pull-down menu. If you choose to add a Diffie-Hellman key exchange to Phase 2, select Use Perfect Forward Secrecy and then select the desired DH group. (Perform IP Pool NAT is an MEP function and is not described in this text.)

Services such as FTP require back connections on different ports. VPN-1 takes care of automatically encrypting these back connections so that extra rules don't have to be added to the rule base.

With either one or two VPN rules and your encryption properties defined, all you need to do is verify and install the rule base and you will have a VPN tunnel. That is, *if* the Global Property Enable Decryption On Accept is turned on. This option was described earlier in the chapter; it makes the firewall attempt to decrypt packets even if the action of the rule is Accept. This option is relevant only in traditional policies like the one we are configuring. With this option turned off, you must add another rule above the encryption rule to allow the encrypted traffic to flow between the firewalls (as shown in Figure 6.34).

FIGURE 6.34 Rule base with Enable Decryption On Accept turned off

NO	SOURCE	DESTINATION	SERVICE	ACTION	TRACK	INSTALL ON	TIME	COMMENT
1	my_firewall VPN_partner	my_firewall VPN_partner	IPSEC	accept	Log	Policy Targets	Any	
2	VPN_Partner_enc_domain VPN_enc_domain	VPN_enc_domain VPN_Partner_enc_domain	Any	Encrypt	Log	Policy Targets	Any	
3	Any	Any	Any	drop	Log	Policy Targets	Any	

Because IPSec encrypts the entire packet and adds new headers with the firewalls as the source and destination IP addresses, your firewall and your VPN partner's firewall must both be listed in the Source and Destination columns. The service is the pre-defined IPSec group, which includes the IKE, AH, and ESP protocols. The action is Accept, *not* Encrypt!

Many people get confused and think this rule needs to be set to Encrypt. The rule that allows the IKE/IPSec traffic to flow between the two firewalls should be set to Accept. Once the firewall accepts the traffic, the second rule takes care of encrypting/decrypting the packets.

After you verify and install the rule base, the VPN tunnel is ready to go. The first packet that has a source IP address in the encryption domain with a destination address of the VPN partner's encryption domain will start the negotiation process, which will exchange the cookies, determine the SAs in Phases 1 and 2, and finally begin encrypting. You can see this whole process in the following three figures, which show the SmartView Tracker screen shots below. Figure 6.35 shows the first part of the log entry.

The gray-shaded portion of Figure 6.35 shows the key install process between two firewalls. The SrcKeyID and DstKeyID field values are the SPI values that the firewalls are sharing with each other. The Encryption Scheme is also identified.

Figure 6.36 illustrates the next portion of the SmartView Tracker (it was too large to fit across one page, so we broke it into three views).

The highlighted portion of the log shows the cookie information exchanged during Phase 1 of the IKE key negotiation as well as the authentication message digest from Phase 2. The Encryption Methods column shows which encryption methods were agreed upon during the negotiation process.

FIGURE 6.35 SmartView Tracker information that contains the key exchange and encryption

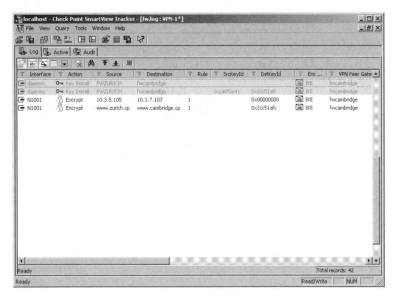

FIGURE 6.36 SmartView Tracker information that contains the key exchange and encryption

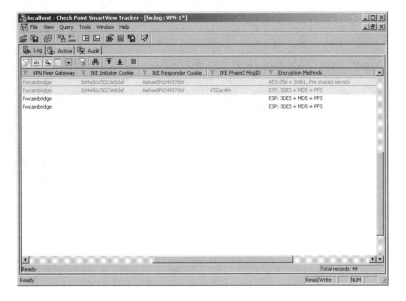

The Information field of the log depicting the key exchange process is shown in Figure 6.37. The first entry is Phase 1; the second entry is the completion of Phase 2, with the keys being generated based on subnets in the encryption domain.

FIGURE 6.37   SmartView Tracker information capture that contains key exchange and encryption

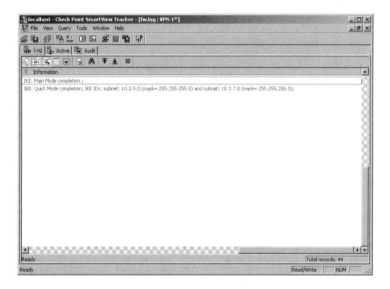

Setting Up an IKE VPN

Now it's time to use everything you've learned in this chapter. The following hands-on exercise will put to the test your ability to set up an IKE VPN using pre-shared secrets. You need to have four machines: the firewall you have been using throughout this book to carry out the exercises (known in this exercise as Firewall A), the machine that has been acting as the Web/FTP/Telnet server, and another pair of machines just like the first two. The machines will be networked like those illustrated in Figure 6.38.

FIGURE 6.38 Lab topology for the VPN exercise

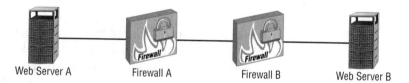

Web Server A   Firewall A   Firewall B   Web Server B

EXERCISE 6.1

Creating an IKE VPN Using Pre-Shared Secrets

1. Create a new stand-alone firewall (Firewall B) following the installation instructions in Chapter 1.

2. On the SmartCenter Server for Firewall A, edit Firewall A (your firewall) and turn on the pre-shared secret. Make sure the VPN Domain (under the Topology tab) is set to All IP Addresses behind Gateway Based on Topology Information.

3. Create Network objects to represent the internal networks of Firewall A and B.

4. Create an External Management Gateway object for Firewall B, turn on the pre-shared secret, and set it as **abc123**. Under the Topology tab, pull in the Network object created in step 3 as the manually defined encryption domain.

5. Create a rule in which the Source and Destination columns contain both Firewall A's and Firewall B's Network objects with an action of Encrypt.

6. On Firewall B SmartCenter Server, create objects and rules identical to those created on Firewall A in steps 2 through 5.

7. After verifying and installing the rule bases on both firewalls, test the VPN tunnel by initiating traffic from Web Server A to Web Server B and vice versa.

Summary

Encryption and VPNs are huge topics to absorb in one sitting. The theory of encryption/VPNs in a nutshell includes symmetric encryption (using the same key to encrypt as to decrypt data) and asymmetric encryption (using a different key to encrypt than is needed to decrypt the data). It also includes RSA keys to authenticate and sign certificates and keys generated by Diffie-Hellman to actually encrypt the data. One-way hashes in conjunction with public keys produce digital signatures, both of which serve to authenticate the keys and the integrity of the message. The keys and certificates are stored with a trusted third party called a certificate authority. This provides the PAIN necessary to carry out encryption.

All these processes are pulled together with the IETF standard for encryption and key exchange called IKE. IKE is a combination of ISAKMP and Oakley for key exchange and IPSec for encryption that Check Point deploys in NG. IKE uses two phases: one to negotiate a security association (SA) for IKE and the second to negotiate the SA for IPSec. Once the SA is negotiated, packets are exchanged that contain a Security Parameters Index (SPI) to let each gateway know which portions of the SA are needed to encrypt/decrypt the data. An added feature with IKE is Perfect Forward Secrecy (PFS), which includes a Diffie-Hellman key exchange in Phase 2 and thereby adds a layer of security.

NG provides two ways to configure an IKE VPN in a Traditional Mode policy. The first uses a pre-shared secret: Both gateways decide on a secret password to authenticate the key exchange. The second way has the gateways exchange certificates or obtain certificates from a CA as the basis to begin the key exchange. Regardless of which method you use, the rule base is the same. At least one rule is required in which both encryption domains are listed in the Source and Destination columns of the rule and Encrypt is the listed action.

Exam Essentials

Know the meaning of the encryption terminology, the function of each term, and how they relate to one another. You should know the definitions of the following encryption terms: cleartext, ciphertext, symmetric encryption, asymmetric encryption, Diffie-Hellman, certificate authority, certificate revocation list, one-way hash, and digital signature.

Know the difference between the different VPN scenarios. An intranet VPN is set up between firewalls controlled by the same SmartCenter Server or company. An extranet VPN is set up between business partners or suppliers in which the Firewalls are managed by different entities. A remote access VPN is a VPN tunnel set up between SecuRemote or SecureClient and a VPN-1 gateway.

Know the difference between a pre-shared secret and a certificate. A pre-shared secret is a single entity shared between two firewalls participating in an IKE VPN. A certificate is a single entity belonging to a single firewall in an IKE VPN, which much be exchanged with a certificate belonging to the other firewall(s) participating in the IKE VPN.

Know how to configure a site-to-site VPN using pre-shared secrets. A VPN using pre-shared secrets requires the pair of firewalls involved in the VPN to decide on a secret password that will authenticate and begin the IKE key negotiations.

Know how to configure a site-to-site VPN using certificates. A VPN using certificates requires a certificate from VPN-1 Certificate Manager, an OPSEC CA, an Entrust CA, or another Check Point SmartCenter Server's certificate.

Know how to configure an internal CA. To configure an internal CA, you need to create a server object of type External Management Server and import your VPN partner's certificate in a `*.crt` file format.

Know how to configure an external CA. To configure an external CA, create a server object of type OPSEC PKI or Entrust PKI (VPN-1 Certificate Manager is no longer sold) and get the certificate from the appropriate PKI server. You may have to load software from the PKI vendor for this to work.

Key Terms

Before you take the exam, be certain you are familiar with the following terms:

asymmetric encryption	IKE
Authentication Header	internal certificate authority
certificate authority	IPSec
certificate revocation list	ISAKMP
ciphertext	message digest
cleartext	Oakley Key Exchange Protocol
Diffie-Hellman	Perfect Forward Secrecy
digital signature	pre-shared secret
distinguished name	Security Association
Encapsulating Security Payload	Security Parameters Index
encryption	symmetric encryption
hash	virtual private network

Review Questions

1. Which of the following is *not* a description of a portion of the PAIN acronym?

   A. Scrambling the message so that it cannot be read in transit

   B. Checking to make sure the message has not changed in transit

   C. Identifying the sender of the message absolutely

   D. Verifying that the message came from the correct person

   E. Composing the original message

2. Using the public key to encrypt the data and the private key to decrypt the data describes which of the following?

   A. Diffie-Hellman

   B. One-way hash

   C. Symmetric encryption

   D. Asymmetric encryption

   E. Digital signature

3. The Diffie-Hellman key calculation produces which of the following?

   A. Digital signature

   B. Private key

   C. Public key

   D. Symmetric key

   E. Basic session key

4. How many DH groups does Check Point NG support by default?

   A. 1

   B. 2

   C. 3

   D. 4

   E. 5

5. Which of the following is *not* an irreversible mathematical process to ensure message integrity?

   A. One-way hash

   B. MAC

   C. MDC

   D. SPI

   E. MIC

6. What does Check Point VPN-1 use for integrity and authentication? (Choose all that apply.)

   A. CAST

   B. RSA encryption

   C. One-way hash function

   D. AES

   E. DES

7. Which is *not* an entity of a certificate?

   A. Expiration date

   B. E-mail address

   C. Digital signature

   D. Private key

   E. Distinguished name

8. This picture describes which type of VPN?

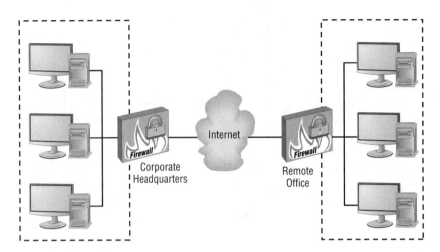

- **A.** Intranet VPN

- **B.** Extranet VPN

- **C.** SecuRemote/SecureClient VPN

- **D.** Remote access VPN

- **E.** Internet VPN

9. What standard does IKE use for encryption?

- **A.** FWZ

- **B.** IPSec

- **C.** SKIP

- **D.** Symmetric

- **E.** Asymmetric

10. Which type of encryption uses the same key to encrypt that it uses to decrypt?

A. SKIP

B. Asymmetric

C. Ciphertext

D. Certificate authority

E. Symmetric

11. Which encryption algorithm does Check Point VPN-1 *not* support?

A. DES

B. AES

C. 3DES

D. CAST

E. FWZ-1

12. If Phase 1 of IKE is using aggressive mode, how many packets are exchanged?

A. 2

B. 3

C. 5

D. 6

E. 1

13. Which Phase 1 mode prevents man-in-the-middle attacks?

A. Pre-shared secret

B. Aggressive

C. Perfect Forward Secrecy

D. Main

E. DH groups

14. By default, how often does Phase 2 negotiations occur?

   A. 3,600 seconds

   B. 1,440 seconds

   C. 50MB of data

   D. 2 hours

   E. 1,440 minutes

15. The authentication portion of IKE is carried out using which of the following? (Choose all that apply.)

   A. IPSec

   B. Pre-shared secret

   C. Digital signature

   D. PFS

   E. Certificates

16. Which is *not* an option for creating a certificate authority server object?

   A. External Management Server

   B. OPSEC PKI

   C. Entrust PKI

   D. OPSEC Certificate Manager

   E. VPN-1 Certificate Manager

17. Under which heading is the encryption domain defined in a Check Point Gateway object?

   A. General

   B. Topology

   C. Authentication

   D. VPN

   E. Extranet

18. If Enable Decrypt on Accept is turned on in the Global Properties, what is the minimum number of rules required to set up the VPN terminal?

   A. 1

   B. 2

   C. 3

   D. 4

   E. 5

19. Which is *not* a function of the ICA?

   A. Generate certificates for gateway-to-gateway VPNs

   B. Establish SIC between Check Point components

   C. Perform public key encryption with OPSEC PKI

   D. Generate certificates for users and administrators

   E. Authenticate SecuRemote/SecureClient traffic

20. Which is *not* a certificate authority certificate file format?

   A. .mme

   B. .B64

   C. .cer

   D. .crt

   E. .p12

Answers to Review Questions

1. E.   Option A describes the Privacy portion, B describes the Integrity portion, C describes the Non-repudiation portion, and D describes the Authentication portion.

2. D.   Asymmetric encryption uses the public key to encrypt the data, but only the holder of the private key can decrypt the data.

3. E.   The Diffie-Hellman key calculation combines the user's private key with their VPN partner's public key to produce the basic session key (a.k.a. shared secret key).

4. C.   Check Point supports three DH groups: 1, 2, and 5 by default but customized groups can be created as well.

5. D.   Every option except D is an irreversible mathematical process to ensure message integrity. The Security Parameters Index (SPI) is a reference that tells the VPN partners where in the SA to look for the information to encrypt/decrypt the data.

6. B, C.   Check Point uses RSA encryption to create and verify digital signatures and Diffie-Hellman to generate encryption keys to encrypt the data. One-way hashes are used to check the integrity of the message.

7. D.   Each of the components except D could be included as an identifier in a certificate. The private key should *never* be exposed outside the computer on which it was created.

8. A.   An intranet VPN is set up between two firewalls under control by the same SmartCenter Server or the same company.

9. B.   IKE uses ISAKMP/Oakley for key management and IPSec for encryption.

10. E.   Symmetric encryption uses the same key to encrypt as it uses to decrypt. It's a very fast encryption process, but key management is an issue.

11. E.   As of NG FP2, Check Point VPN-1 no longer supports FWZ-1.

12. B.   Aggressive Mode exchanges only three packets, whereas Main Mode exchanges six packets (including initiator cookies to identify each party in the VPN).

13. D.   The cookie initiator exchange (the extra three packets in Main Mode) identifies each party of the VPN, therefore preventing man-in-the-middle attacks.

14. A.   By default Phase 2 occurs every 3600 seconds. If you select the check box below this option then Phase 2 will be negotiated every 50MB of data by default. Negotiating based on the MB of data traveling through the VPN tunnel is very CPU intensive.

15. B, E.   The two authentication methods that VPN-1 uses are pre-shared secrets and certificates.

16. D.   There is no such option as an OPSEC Certificate Manager. Even though VPN-1 Certificate Manager is no longer sold, it is still included for backward compatibility.

17. B.   Although all the options are valid headings in the Check Point Gateway object, the encryption domain is defined under the Topology heading, *not* the VPN heading like it was in version 4.1.

18. A.   Only one rule is needed if Enable Decrypt on Accept is turned on and if you include both encryption domains in the Source and Destination columns of the rule.

19. C.   The internal certificate authority (ICA) helps to communicate within Check Point. Public key encryption with an OPSEC PKI is not a function of the ICA.

20. E.   All the options except E are valid certificate formats. The .p12 format is for an individual user certificate, not a CA certificate.

Chapter

7

Simplified VPNs

THE CCSE EXAM TOPICS COVERED IN THIS CHAPTER INCLUDE:

- ✓ Configuring VPNs using the Simplified VPN Setup.
- ✓ Compare and contrast star, meshed, and star/meshed Simplified VPN topologies.
- ✓ Understand how to configure VPN-1 Net Simplified VPNs.
- ✓ Understand VPN Routing.

aving read Chapter 6, "Virtual Private Networks," you should now be well versed in the ways of VPNs; it's time to show you how to perform VPN processes in a more automated fashion using Simplified VPNs (referred to as One-Click VPNs in FP1). Keep in mind that the manual way of doing things described in Chapter 6 gives you more granular control over the way your VPN works. The "simplified" method involves less work but is more rigid in its configuration options.

In this chapter, we'll discuss the specifics of Simplified VPNs, including sites, communities, and topologies. We'll show you how to configure Simplified VPNs using meshed and star configurations and finish up the chapter with incorporating VPN-1 Net and the new FP3 VPN routing feature.

What Is a Simplified VPN?

A *Simplified VPN* is Check Point's way of trying to make things easier for the firewall administrator. This feature was introduced in FP1 but wasn't fully integrated until FP2. Check Point has taken things farther in FP3 by fully integrating VPN-1 Net within Simplified VPNs and adding VPN Routing capabilities. For Simplified VPNs to work, all gateways involved must be running at least NG FP2.

If you have a centralized SmartCenter Server that controls multiple enforcement points, you can use Simplified VPNs to write all your encryption rules. Simplified VPNs work only if all the firewalls involved are under the control of one SmartCenter Server (although rumor has it that Simplified VPNs will be expanded in future Feature Pack releases to include both Check Point and non–Check Point controlled externally managed gateways). Figure 7.1 shows an example of a Simplified VPN configuration.

FIGURE 7.1   Simplified VPN configuration

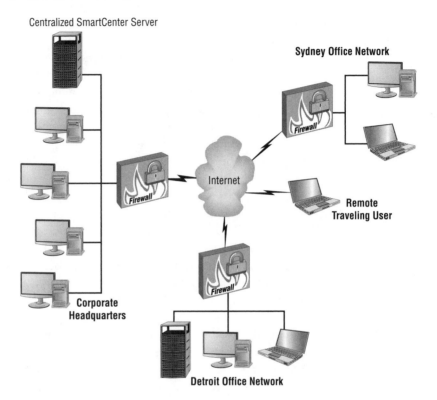

In this figure, the Sydney, Detroit, and Corporate Headquarters firewalls are all under the control of the corporate SmartCenter Server.

Simplified VPNs vs. Extranet VPNs

Manual VPN methods allow you to set up intranet, extranet, and remote access VPNs with very granular control. Extranet Management (covered further in Chapter 8, "Extranet Management") only allows you to set up extranet VPNs—that is, VPNs between your firewall architecture and the firewall architecture of another company (basically, a firewall under your control and a firewall under the control of someone else). Simplified VPNs only allow the configuration of remote access and intranet VPNs—*not* extranet VPNs (at least, not yet).

VPN Sites and Communities

Each Simplified VPN consists of VPN sites and VPN communities. A *VPN site* consists of the firewall and the firewall's encryption domain, shown in Figure 7.1. Each office network is considered a VPN site. For example, Corporate Headquarters and all the computers/networks behind the corporate firewall (if defined as part of its encryption domain) would be considered a VPN site. An unlimited number of VPN sites can then be grouped into a VPN community. Each *VPN community* shares common VPN settings, such as IKE/IPSec properties. Defining the VPN community automatically creates implied encryption rules (called a *Simplified mode policy*) between the VPN sites in the community so that you don't have to write explicit encryption rules (called a *Traditional mode policy*) as you did in Chapter 6. This is not to say that you do not have to write rules for a VPN to exist; access rules must be defined to let the firewalls know what type of traffic will be sent through the VPN tunnels. However, you don't have to create specific encryption rules. Essentially, the Simplified VPN process eliminates VPN rules from the Security Policy rule base you've been accustomed to configuring. That is, no rules with an action of Encrypt can be created in a Simplified Policy. The rules that require encryption will have an action of Accept and a VPN community defined in the If Via column of the rule base.

This chapter explores setting up Simplified VPNs with VPN-1 Pro (Simplified policy in the rule base) and VPN-1 Net (rudimentary access rules and encryption properties are defined in the Global Properties). We'll also cover the new VPN Routing feature available in FP3, which allows indirect encrypted tunnels to occur between gateways by means of a centralized VPN-1 module/hub. This centralized VPN-1 module acts as a router, decrypting the traffic from one VPN gateway and re-encrypting it and sending it to another VPN gateway. Before we discuss these specific scenarios, you need to understand the types of topologies that can be defined.

Simplified VPN Topologies

VPN-1 (whether using VPN-1 Pro, VPN-1 Net, or configuring a VPN router) recognizes two basic topologies: *mesh* and *star*. If a VPN community is set up with a mesh topology, then each VPN connection between each VPN site in the VPN community is enabled, as shown in Figure 7.2.

FIGURE 7.2   Simplified VPN mesh topology

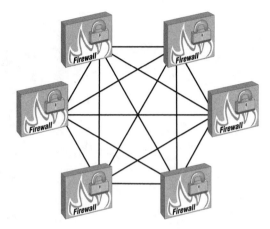

In the star topology, each satellite VPN site interacts only with a central-ized gateway, as shown in Figure 7.3.

FIGURE 7.3   Simplified VPN star topology

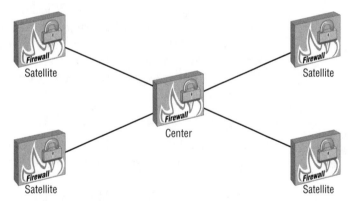

The star topology can be made a little more robust by combining it with a mesh topology. Figure 7.3 is considered a star topology with a non-meshed center. This same type of topology can exist with multiple firewalls at the center and is referred to as star, center meshed (see Figure 7.4).

FIGURE 7.4 Simplified VPN with star topology and a meshed center

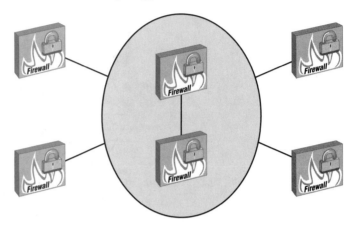

Figures 7.2 through 7.4 are only basic representations of these types of topologies; each firewall icon represents many different objects in a VPN site. You can add objects other than networks and hosts to a VPN site. Objects that can be added to the center of a star topology include *interoperable devices* (devices that don't run Check Point but participate in a VPN with Check Point products) and objects such as internally managed gateways and gateway clusters (FP2), externally managed gateways, and Check Point VPN-1 gateways (any version). Only FP2 VPN-1 modules can be added as satellites in a star topology, and only FP2 VPN-1 modules can be included in a mesh topology.

Keep in mind that the Simplified VPN topologies have no effect on clear connections between VPN community members.

Objects can also be added to more than one VPN community, but a VPN link between any pair of gateways can be defined only once. This constraint limits your VPN configurations because in a star topology, VPNs between two *satellite* VPN sites cannot be set up even if you write a rule to do so. If you wish to create a VPN tunnel between two satellites in your star topology, you can do one of the following:

- Add the two satellites to another star topology, with one being central and the other a satellite.

- Add the two satellites to a mesh topology.

Now that you have the theory behind Simplified VPNs down cold, let's walk through the click-by-click steps to configure one.

Using Simplified VPNs

Suppose your company has 10 firewalls across the United States managed by one SmartCenter Server, that each requires VPN tunnels to be set up, and that none of them requires any specialized type of tunnel between two specific points. A Simplified VPN is a quick way to set up this type of scenario. After defining gateway objects to represent each firewall and defining each gateways encryption domain, you need to decide whether a star, mesh, or combination topology is required. You create a VPN community based on that topology, create a Simplified Policy, and verify/install your rule base. Then you will have a 10-way VPN tunnel set up if you selected a mesh configuration and 9 tunnels to a central gateway if you selected a star topology.

Configuring a Simplified VPN

Configuring a Simplified VPN begins with making sure each participating gateway's encryption domain has been defined correctly. If you can't remember where encryption domains are defined on each gateway, double-click on a Check Point Gateway object from the Objects Tree, Objects list, or Network Objects Manager, and then click on the Topology option in the pane on the left. Doing so displays the Topology information for that gateway, as you can see in Figure 7.5.

You can either define the encryption domain based on the firewalls' interfaces or by manually defining it.

Refer to Chapter 6 for more information about configuring encryption domains.

To begin configuring your Simplified VPN, click on the Lock tab in the Objects Tree, shown in Figure 7.6; you will be transported to the VPN Communities Objects Tree. You can also choose Manage ➢ VPN Communities to open the VPN Communities Manager.

FIGURE 7.5 Check Point's Gateway Topology window

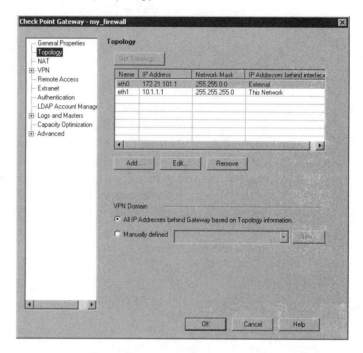

FIGURE 7.6 Simplified VPN tab in the Objects Tree

In the VPN Communities tree, you see three types of VPN Communities—Site To Site, Remote Access, and Extranet Manager—as shown in Figure 7.7.

FIGURE 7.7   Different types of VPN communities

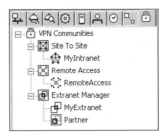

Extranet Manager deals with Extranet Management, which will be discussed in Chapter 8. The Remote Access option deals with SecuRemote and SecureClient, which are the topics of discussion in Chapters 9 and 10. In this chapter we're interested in the Site To Site option. First let's explore creating a meshed topology Simplified VPN.

Meshed Simplified VPN Configuration

Configuring a Simplified VPN in a mesh configuration is relatively simple. Begin by right-clicking on Site To Site and selecting New ➢ Meshed from the menu. Doing so displays the Meshed Community Properties window shown in Figure 7.8.

FIGURE 7.8   Meshed Community Properties window

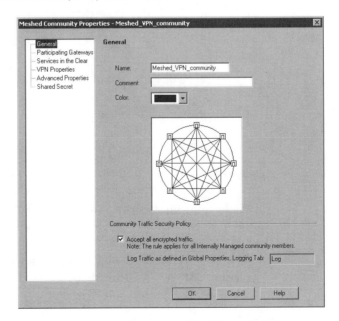

Like any other object you create in Check Point, you have to give the VPN a Name; otherwise you won't be able to move past the General window. As always, the Color and Comment fields are optional. Selecting Accept All Encrypted Traffic will allow this community to accept and decrypt traffic from all other internally managed VPN-1 modules in the community. Log Traffic As Defined In Global Properties, Logging Tab pulls from Global Properties ≻ Log and Alert where your options are either Log or None. The gateways that will participate in the VPN are defined on the *Participating Gateways* page, shown in Figure 7.9.

FIGURE 7.9 Participating Gateways window

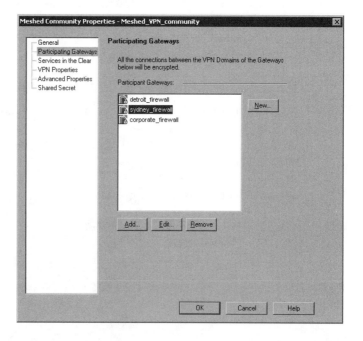

Click the Add button to display all the gateways you have configured, with their encryption domains already defined. Each selected gateway will be displayed in the Participating Gateways window. All connections between the VPN domains of these gateways will be handled based on the properties you define in the rest of the Meshed Community Properties windows.

The Services In The Clear window (Figure 7.10) allows you to specifically define services between the Participating Gateways that will not be *encrypted*. Any service defined in the Services Manager can be pulled in here.

FIGURE 7.10 Services In The Clear window

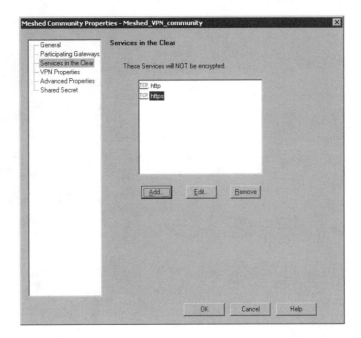

 Services In The Clear is not supported if one of the members of the community is a version prior to FP3.

In the VPN Properties window, shown in Figure 7.11, you define key exchange encryption and data integrity methods for both Phase 1 and 2 SA negotiations.

These properties will affect VPN connections between each Participating Gateway. These options were explained in detail in Chapter 6.

 Even though SmartDashboard allows you to add dynamically addressed VPN-1 modules to a VPN community with aggressive mode turned on, this configuration is not supported.

FIGURE 7.11 VPN Properties window

The Advanced Properties options, shown in Figure 7.12, were explained in detail in Chapter 6, with the exception of Support Site To Site IP Compression, Reset All VPN Properties, and Disable NAT Inside The VPN Community.

If Support Site To Site IP Compression is checked, stateless and reversible compression of IP packets will be allowed between Participating Gateways. FP3 includes a new feature: the Reset All VPN Properties button resets all VPN properties to their default values, including properties that don't show up in SmartDashboard (specifically edits to the objects_5_0.C file which affect VPNs). Disable NAT Inside The VPN Community is also a new FP3 feature; it lets you shut off any NAT rules for Participating Gateways, but only within the VPN tunnels.

If one of the members of the community is a version previous to FP3, the Disable NAT Inside The VPN Community option is not supported.

The Shared Secret window shown in Figure 7.13 allows you to set the pre-shared secret for each internally managed Participating Gateway that has a VPN tunnel with an externally managed gateway.

FIGURE 7.12   Advanced Properties

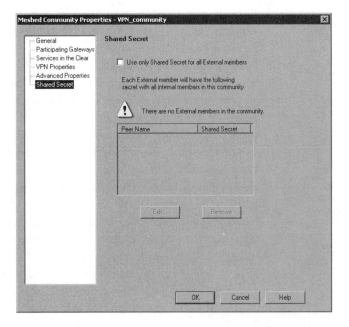

FIGURE 7.13   Shared Secret window

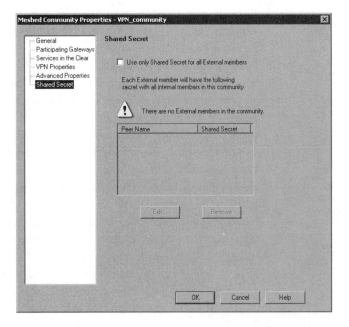

If one of the members of the community is a version previous to FP3, the shared secret that can be defined for externally managed gateways is not supported. Also, when you convert to a Simplified Policy using FP3 your pre-shared secrets are lost. Make note of your pre-shared secrets before conversion so that you can redefine them here.

In this particular example, no externally managed gateways are participating in this VPN community. This window is a fix to an aggravating problem that appeared in FP2. For example, suppose you had a Simplified VPN configured between a number of gateways and you wanted to change the pre-shared secret between a pair of gateways. In FP2, the only way to accomplish this was to remove the two gateways from the community so you could access the pre-shared secret functionality within each individual gateway. This was the only solution because when the gateways were added to a VPN community, the pre-shared functionality was hidden. This window also allows you to force this VPN community to used only pre-shared secrets between all external members (another feature that was hidden when a gateway was added to a VPN community in FP2).

Star Simplified VPN Configuration

To create a star VPN community, click on Site To Site and select New ➢ Star, which in turn displays the Star Community Properties window shown in Figure 7.14.

After you define a Name (the Color and Comment fields are optional), selecting Accept All Encrypted Traffic will allow this community to accept and decrypt traffic from all other internally managed VPN-1 modules in the community. Log Traffic As Defined In Global Properties, Logging Tab pulls from Global Properties ➢ Log and Alert, where your options are Log and None.

The *Central Gateways* option in the tree on the left displays the Central Gateways section of the Star Community Properties (shown in Figure 7.15). Here, you pull in the Central Gateway or select the Mesh Center Gateways option at the bottom of the window. The Central Gateway or gateways that you define will encrypt all connections between themselves and the Satellite Gateways defined under the Satellite Gateways option. To qualify as a central gateway, each object must have VPN-1 Pro or VPN-1 Net installed, must have FP1 or greater installed (exclusively for internally managed gateways), and must be a host, gateway, interoperable device, or gateway cluster.

FIGURE **7.14**   Star Community Properties window

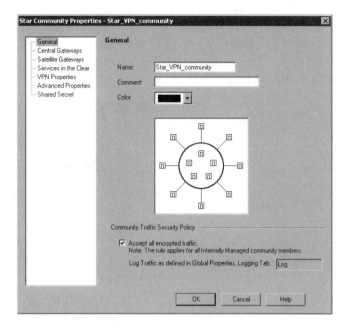

FIGURE **7.15**   Central Gateways window

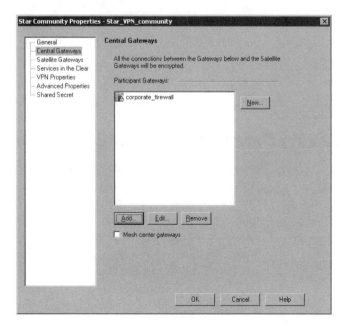

Satellite gateways are pulled in just like central gateways (see Figure 7.16). To qualify as a satellite gateway, each object must have VPN-1 Pro or VPN-1 Net installed, must have FP1 or greater, and must be a host, gateway, gateway cluster, interoperable device, or Check Point profile gateway.

FIGURE 7.16 Satellite Gateways window

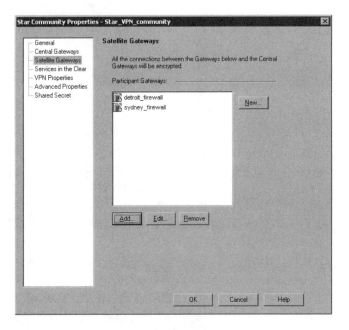

After you define the VPN Properties, Advanced Properties, and Shared Secret windows as you did for the Meshed Community Properties, all connections between the central gateway(s) and the satellite gateway(s) will be encrypted.

Creating Gateways from within VPN Community Properties

If you began creating a VPN community and suddenly realized you had forgotten to create a gateway object that needed to participate in the community, don't worry. You can create new gateway objects from within the VPN community you are defining (keep in mind that you already should have set up the hardware for this firewall, loaded the software, and put the firewall on the network). Whether in Participating Gateways Properties (in a meshed community), or Central and/or Satellite Gateways Properties (in a star community), you can click the New button to create a new gateway object. Doing so brings up the Check Point Installed Gateway Creation window shown in Figure 7.17.

FIGURE 7.17 The Check Point Installed Gateway Creation window

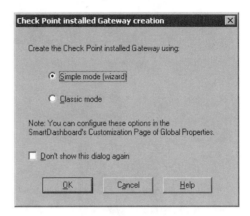

If Classic Mode is selected, this window will take you into creating a Check Point gateway object just as if you were doing it through the Network Object Manager or through the Objects Tree. If you select Simple Mode (Wizard), you will walk through a wizard that prompts you for the gateway information. The first window in the wizard is shown in Figure 7.18.

FIGURE 7.18 The Gateway's General Properties window

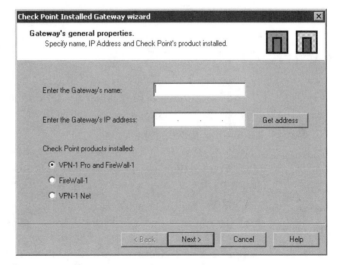

Enter information in the Enter The Gateway's Name and Enter The Gateway's IP Address fields as well as which product it is running. Click on Next and then Finish (Figure 7.19), and you're done. This gateway will inherit the properties defined in the VPN community to which it belongs.

FIGURE 7.19 Finished Gateway's Definition Wizard window

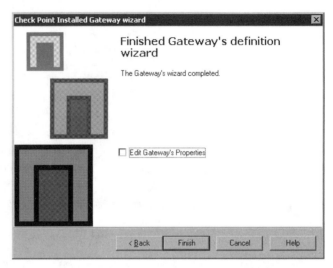

If you want to define some other properties for the gateway (such as Secure Internal Communications [SIC], if this is an internally managed gateway), select Edit Gateway's Properties before you click Finish. Doing so will take you to the gateway's properties, just as you would see them through the Network Objects Manager.

VPN Global Properties

Now that you have created VPN communities, our focus will turn to the Global Properties that affect Simplified VPNs. We'll begin with the VPN-1 Pro window shown in Figure 7.20.

Here, you can determine which type of policies you wish to create each time you create a new policy in SmartDashboard. If you select the first radio button, all new policies you create will incorporate the If Via column of Simplified VPNs and you will be unable to create any *Traditional mode* policies like the one you created in Chapter 6. If you select the second radio button, you will only be able to create Traditional mode policies and not *Simplified mode* policies. Selecting the third radio button will present you with a choice every time you create a new policy (as shown in Figure 7.21). We personally prefer having a choice, so we always leave it to the default option of Traditional Or Simplified Mode Per New Security Policy.

FIGURE 7.20   VPN-1Pro Global Properties

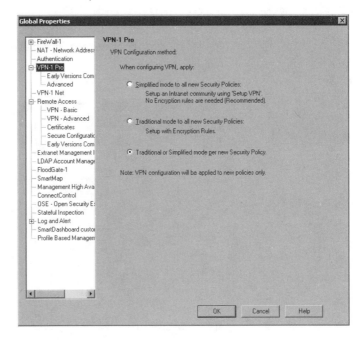

FIGURE 7.21   New Policy Package choices

The SmartDashboard Customization properties affect how VPNs are viewed in the SmartDashboard GUI (see Figure 7.22). VPN Topological View allows you to determine the number of VPN community members that should be displayed as icons instead of a full mesh.

FIGURE 7.22 SmartDashboard Customization window

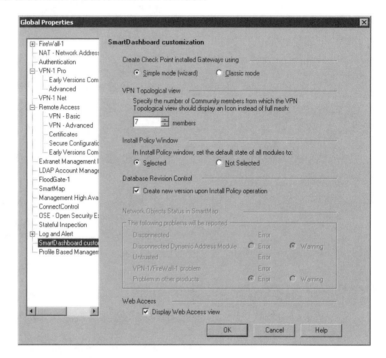

Of the other VPN Global Properties, some were discussed in Chapter 6, Extranet Management Interface will be discussed in Chapter 8, Remote Access will be discussed in Chapters 9 and 10, and VPN-1 Net will be discussed later in this chapter.

Creating the Simplified VPN Rules

Creating Simplified VPN rules is an oxymoron, because we've said you don't have to create any explicit encryption rules to make the VPN tunnels happen with a VPN community. However, you do have to create a new

Simplified Policy and define access rules (unencrypted connections) and rules that specify a VPN community in the If Via column with Accept as the action (which forces this traffic through a VPN tunnel where it is encrypted). In the SmartDashboard, click on File ➤ New to display the New Policy Package window (Figure 7.21). Give the policy a name (remember, no spaces and no dashes) and select Security And Address Translation. This option reveals the VPN Configuration methods: You can choose to create a Traditional mode policy (you write the encryption rules) or a Simplified mode policy (no encryption rules are explicitly written; they are assumed based on your VPN community definitions). After selecting Simplfied Mode and clicking OK, the new Simplified Policy is now displayed in SmartDashboard.

You can tell the difference between a Traditional mode policy and a Simplified mode policy by looking at the rule base. A Simplified Policy has a new column called If Via and a new tab called VPN Manager, as well as an implied VPN rule, as shown in Figure 7.23. If you look at the options available in the Action column, you will also notice that the Encrypt options are gone.

FIGURE 7.23   Simplified Policy in the SmartDashboard

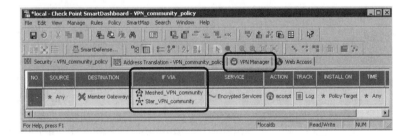

The *If Via* column is used to define access rules between VPN sites participating in a VPN community. If Via is not an acronym. It's easier to understand if you "read" a rule: For example, a source of my network with a destination of another network going through (If Via) using HTTP is allowed (accepted). The addition of a VPN community in the If Via column forces all traffic matching that rule to be encrypted/decrypted even though the Action is Accept. Remember that rules created in the rule base with nothing defined in the If Via column do not affect the VPN community. To see how the VPN is configured, click on the VPN Manager tab in the SmartDashboard to display your VPN communities, as shown in Figure 7.24.

FIGURE 7.24 VPN Manager tab in SmartDashboard

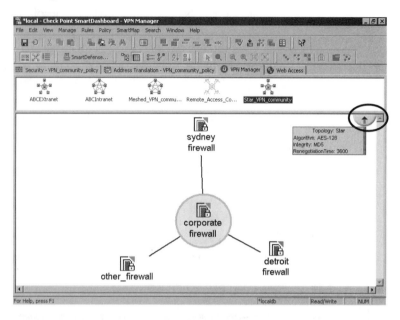

All VPN communities are listed here, including extranet management (discussed in Chapter 8) and remote access VPNs (discussed in Chapters 9 and 10). Select the specific VPN community in the upper window of the VPN Manager to display the topology of the VPN community in the lower pane. In Figure 7.24, selecting the circled portion of the picture will tell you all about that VPN community: the type of topology (star, meshed, star/center-meshed), the encryption algorithm, the data integrity method, and the key renegotiation time as depicted in Figure 7.25.

FIGURE 7.25 VPN community information

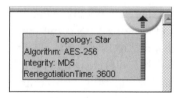

Aside from completing the access rules in the Security tab of the Smart-Dashboard and verifying/installing your policy, you've finished your Simplified VPN.

In Simplified mode (FP2), you could configure star and mesh intranet topologies as well as remote access topologies, but you could not configure extranets. Traditional mode was required in order to create extranet rules as well as specific VPN rules. This is no longer true in FP3. Remote access, extranet, and site-to-site Simplified VPNs can be configured in VPN communities.

VPN-1 Net

$\mathbf{V}$PN-1 Net is the Check Point product that gives you VPN capabilities with limited access control options. A separate license is required; it's based on the number of VPN tunnels (5–5000 VPN tunnels) that will be configured.

Setting up VPN tunnels using VPN-1 Net requires very few steps. From the central SmartCenter Server, you create each gateway that will participate in the VPN community with VPN-1 Net selected under Check Point Products, as shown in Figure 7.26.

FIGURE 7.26 Gateway General Properties

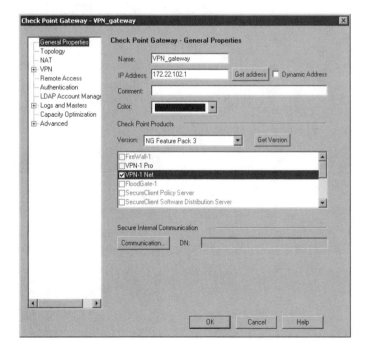

You can add the gateway directly to the VPN community through the VPN tab of the gateway (see Figure 7.27).

FIGURE 7.27 VPN tab of the Gateway General Properties

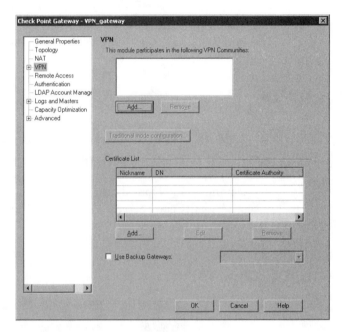

Clicking the Add button under VPN opens the Add This Gateway To Community window (Figure 7.28), where you can select a VPN community to which this gateway will belong.

FIGURE 7.28 Add This Gateway To Community window

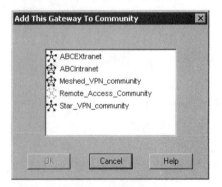

If the gateway is added to a mesh community you're finished. If the gateway is added to a star community, then you will be asked to choose whether this particular gateway will be a central gateway or a satellite gateway. Don't forget to attach the VPN-1 license through SmartUpdate before continuing.

All that's left to configure is the VPN-1 Net Global Properties (see Figure 7.29).

FIGURE 7.29   VPN-1 Net Global Properties

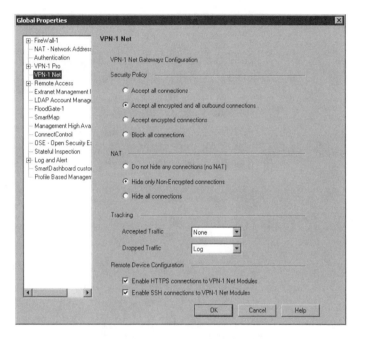

The Security Policy settings are reminiscent of the non-trivial policies associated with SecureClient in version 4.x. Accept All Connections will allow both cleartext and encrypted connections to flow between all the VPN-1 Net firewalls in the VPN community. If Accept All Encrypted And All Outbound Connections is selected, then encrypted connections will flow between all VPN-1 Net firewalls in the VPN community and only cleartext outbound connections will be allowed. Selecting Accept Encrypted Connections will let encrypted connections flow between all VPN-1 Net firewalls in the VPN community, but no cleartext connections will be allowed. The last option is rarely used, because selecting Block All Connections will not allow any traffic to flow between the VPN-1 Net firewalls in the VPN community.

You can configure NAT for a VPN-1 Net firewall, but there are only three options:

- *Do Not Hide Any Connections*—No NAT will take place.

- *Hide Only Non-Encrypted Connections*—Hide NAT (behind the external interface of the firewall) will only occur if the connection is not encrypted. This option is best combined with the Accept All Encrypted And All Outbound Connections Security Policy option.

- *Hide All Connections*—All connections will be NAT'd behind the external interface of the firewall including encrypted connections.

You can choose whether to log or not log accepted traffic in the Smart-View Tracker. Dropped traffic can be logged, logged and alerted, or not logged.

FP3 adds the Remote Device Configuration options to VPN-1 Net Global Properties. These options allow encrypted connections to these VPN-1 Net modules for management purposes, which comes in handy especially if this is a Nokia appliance normally managed via SSH or HTTPS.

VPN Routing

The new FP3 VPN Routing feature was designed so that encrypted connections can come in to a central VPN-1 module, be decrypted, and then be encrypted again and sent out a different VPN tunnel. *VPN Routing* is supported only in VPN communities. You can use this feature a variety of ways, including enabling remote offices to have full connectivity but not allowing them direct access to other remote offices, or for end-to-end encryption between SecureClients (supported in FP4). This is sometimes referred to as a *hub and spoke* configuration (see Figure 7.30).

In this configuration, each spoke should be able to open a VPN tunnel to the hub but not directly to another spoke without going through the hub first. The ability to architect this solution comes from the capability of VPN-1 to forward VPN traffic like a router configuring hops. Each VPN tunnel is routed to the next hop, where it is decrypted and then encrypted once again for the trip to the next VPN hop.

FIGURE 7.30   Hub and spoke configuration

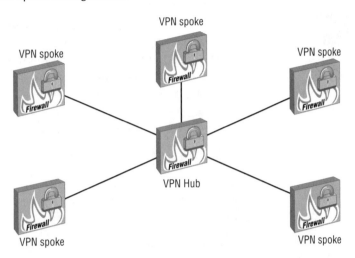

To configure these routes, you must add routing rules to the $FWDIR/
conf/vpn_route.conf routing table file. This file resides on the Smart-
Center Server and affects VPN hops for all VPNs (see Figure 7.31).

FIGURE 7.31   vpn_route.conf file

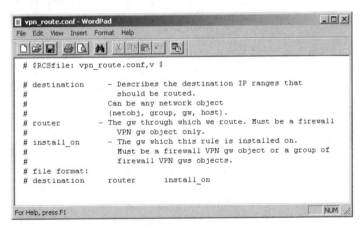

Trivial routing rules (specifying the next hop to be the VPN-1 module and including a destination in its encryption domain) are automatically added and need not be configured. For example, traffic that originates behind and passes through the VPN hub destined for a site behind a spoke doesn't require a routing rule specifying the spoke as the next hop.

The syntax for the VPN routes is as follows:

`(destination)(VPN-1 next hop)(install-on gateway)`

All the objects or groups in the `vpn_route.conf` file must already exist in the Network Objects database. Objects must be used in this file—*not* IP addresses.

If you have configured IP pool NAT on a VPN-1 module that is a VPN-1 hub (router), then the IP addresses in the IP NAT pool need to be defined as part of the encryption domain of the VPN-1 hub. If you don't do this, then connections that go through the VPN-1 router will fail.

Consider anti-spoofing when defining the VPN routes. Symmetric routing must be configured too, so that connectivity is maintained along the path. A VPN gateway won't accept just any packet from a VPN tunnel, the same way the firewall won't accept just any packet to any interface. Therefore, routing rules—whether manual or automatically configured—should specify the source from which VPN traffic will be allowed.

The use of Security Servers on a VPN-1 router is not supported.

An access rule in the Simplified mode policy allows the VPN traffic and VPN Routing traffic to be handled by the rule base as a single connection. Because only one rule is matched in VPN Routing, if more than one VPN community is involved in VPN Routing, the rule must contain all VPN communities that are included in the VPN route.

VPN Routing doesn't affect OS level routing. If your firewall contains multiple external interfaces, configure OS level routing so that traffic follows the route required for your VPN tunnels.

In the SmartView Tracker, multiple logs are generated for VPN Routing traffic. Encrypt and decrypt logs are generated for traffic from one spoke to another, and logs are generated for traffic from connected star communities.

Certain limitations (scheduled to be fixed in future Feature Pack releases) currently affect VPN routing. These include no support for SecureClient, no support for Multiple Entry Point (MEP) on the spokes but not on the hub, and VPN Routing support only in Simplified mode.

Summary

Simplified VPNs (or One-Click VPNs, as they were referred to briefly in FP1) are an automated method for creating encryption rules. VPN sites refer to a gateway and its encryption domain. A VPN site is not an object that is created. The VPN site terminology is used for the sole purpose of defining VPN communities. A VPN community is a group of VPN sites that will have VPN tunnels set up between them. A Simplified VPN can be configured in a star, meshed, or star/meshed combination configuration.

A star topology has a gateway or gateways at its center and satellite gateways that surround it. Once the VPN community is defined, encryption takes place between the satellites and the center gateway(s). Encryption does *not* take place between the satellite gateways. If a star topology has multiple gateways in the center, then it is referred to as a star with a center-meshed topology. The other topology is called a mesh topology. With this type of configuration, VPN tunnels are set up between all participating gateways.

After creating VPN communities, rules are needed to define access, but explicit VPN rules are not required. Access rules do not affect the VPN community, but specific rules listing the VPN community in the If Via column of the rule base SmartDashboard are needed for the VPN tunnel to occur. Even though the Action in a rule with the If Via column defined is accept, encryption will automatically occur.

VPN communities can be used for site to site, remote access, and extranet management VPNs, where the gateways are Check Point VPN-1 Pro or VPN-1 Net. VPN-1 Net is a Check Point product that supports VPNs and very limited access control.

New to FP3 is the ability to configure VPN Routing and allow traffic to flow from VPN-1 spokes through a VPN-1 hub and back out to another VPN-1 spoke.

Exam Essentials

Know what makes up a Simplified VPN. A Simplified VPN consists of VPN sites grouped together into VPN communities.

Know the differences between the VPN topologies. Star topologies have one firewall at the center and satellite firewalls surrounding it. Encryption takes place between the center firewall and the satellite firewalls but not between satellite firewalls. A meshed topology has at least two participants, and VPN tunnels are set up between all participants. Star with center meshed has multiple firewalls at its center; encryption takes place between the satellites and the firewalls in the center.

Know how the rule base is affected with Simplified VPNs. Access rules do not affect the VPN communities, but rules must be written in a Simplified Policy with the VPN community defined in the If Via column of the rule base for encryption to take place. The Action in the rule can be Accept, User Auth, Client Auth, or Session Auth; but if the If Via column is populated with a VPN community, the connection (if matched) will be encrypted.

Understand how to configure VPN-1 Net Simplified VPNs. Gateways are defined as having VPN-1 Net Check Point product installed and then the gateway is added to a VPN community. VPN-1 Net Global Properties are defined that determine whether the traffic is encrypted or not and whether it is NAT'd.

Understand VPN Routing. VPN Routing is a new FP3 feature that allows a hub and spoke architecture to be defined so that VPN traffic can travel between different gateways if routed through a central VPN-1 hub.

Key Terms

Before you take the exam, be certain you are familiar with the following terms:

Central Gateways	Simplified VPN
If Via	star
interoperable devices	Traditional mode
mesh	VPN community
Participating Gateways	VPN Routing
Satellite Gateways	VPN site
Simplified mode	

Review Questions

1. In which Feature Pack of Check Point VPN-1 was the Simplified VPN concept introduced?

   A. FCS

   B. FP1

   C. FP2

   D. FP3

   E. FP4

2. Which types of VPN-1 Security Policies can be created? (Choose all that apply.)

   A. Extranet

   B. One-Click

   C. Intranet

   D. Traditional

   E. Simplified

3. Which types of VPNs can be configured using a policy created with Traditional mode? (Choose all that apply.)

   A. Extranet

   B. Meshed

   C. Star

   D. Intranet

   E. Remote access

4. What type of Simplified VPN topology is represented by the following illustration?

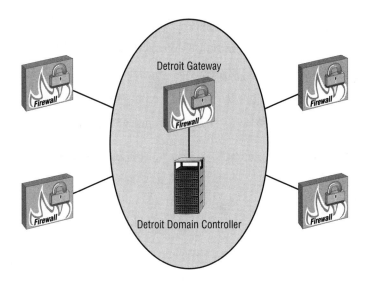

A. Star

B. Meshed

C. Star with center meshed

D. Meshed with star center

E. Star with star center

5. Which of the following statements is true for a VPN site?

A. Created when setting up SecuRemote/SecureClient

B. A group of gateways that encrypt to each other

C. The encryption domain of a specific firewall

D. Created when a VPN community is defined

E. A specific firewall and everything included in its encryption domain

6. Where are default VPN properties for VPN communities defined? (Choose all that apply.)

   A. Global Properties under VPN-1 Pro

   B. Global Properties under VPN-1 Net

   C. Global Properties under Remote Access ➤ VPN

   D. Meshed Community Properties

   E. Star Community Properties

7. Which types of objects can be added to a VPN site? (Choose all that apply.)

   A. Interoperable devices

   B. Network objects

   C. Gateways

   D. Gateway clusters

   E. External hosts

8. Which of the following statements are true for host node objects? (Choose all that apply.)

   A. Added to more than one VPN community

   B. Can be defined as a participant in a VPN community

   C. Can be added to a VPN site

   D. Can be defined as a satellite in a VPN community

   E. Can be a part of an encryption domain

9. What does the Check Point Installed Gateway Creation wizard have you define? (Choose all that apply.)

   A. Gateway name

   B. Gateway IP address

   C. Encryption properties

   D. Encryption domain

   E. SIC

10. Which ways can you define the encryption domain for a gateway participating in a VPN community? (Choose all that apply.)

   A. Automatically define the encryption domain with a wizard.

   B. Manually define the encryption domain.

   C. Define the encryption domain with the VPN community.

   D. Define the encryption domain under the VPN Manager tab in the SmartDashboard.

   E. Define the encryption domain based on the gateway's interface topology information.

11. What type of policy is used to create rules using the If Via column?

   A. Simplified

   B. Remote access

   C. Traditional

   D. Intranet

   E. VPN Manager

12. What type of Simplified VPN topology is represented by the following?

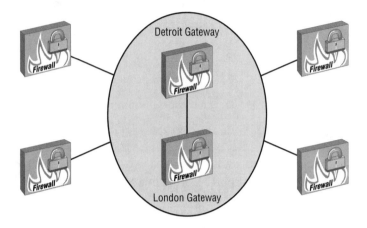

A. Star

B. Meshed

C. Star with center meshed

D. Meshed with star center

E. Star with star center

13. What is the name of the file that needs to be configured for VPN routing to occur?

A. `vpn_route.conf`

B. `vpn_conf.conf`

C. `vpnroute.sys`

D. `vpn_route.sys`

E. `rc2.d`

14. When defining a star topology for a VPN community, which of the following are defined? (Choose all that apply.)

   A. Central gateways

   B. Intranet gateways

   C. Participating gateways

   D. Extranet gateways

   E. Satellite gateways

15. IKE properties belong in which phase of encryption?

   A. Phase 1

   B. Phase 2

   C. DH keys

   D. IPSec

   E. IP compression

16. Which option enables stateless and reversible compression of IP packets between participating gateways in a meshed or star with center-meshed topology?

   A. Enable IKE Compression

   B. Support IP Comp (using DEFLATE)

   C. Enable IPSec Compression

   D. Support Site To Site IP Compression

   E. Enable Stateless IP Compression

17. What is the default renegotiation time for Phase II?

   A. 3600 milliseconds

   B. 3600 seconds

   C. 3600 minutes

   D. 3600 hours

   E. 3600 days

18. Which of the following is not a Security Policy option for a VPN-1 Net gateway?

    A. Accept All Encrypted And All Inbound Connections

    B. Accept All Connections

    C. Accept All Encrypted And All Outbound Connections

    D. Block All Connections

    E. Accept Encrypted Connections

19. When defining a meshed topology for a VPN community, which of the following are defined?

    A. Central gateways

    B. Intranet gateways

    C. Participating gateways

    D. Extranet gateways

    E. Satellite gateways

20. Which types of Simplified VPN topologies are supported in VPN-1? (Choose all that apply.)

    A. Star

    B. Star with star center

    C. Meshed

    D. Star with center meshed

    E. Meshed with star center

Answers to Review Questions

1. B.   The concept was first introduced in FP1 but not fully integrated until FP2.

2. D, E.   Only Traditional (the way things were done in version 4.1) and Simplified (the new way to do things in version NG) policies can be created. One-Click is a term used to describe Simplified VPNs, but it was only used briefly (for FP1).

3. A, D, E.   Traditional and Simplified policies can be used to create intranet, extranet, or remote access VPNs (this is true with FP3). With FP2, extranet VPNs could only be created using Traditional policies.

4. A.   Because the center of this topology contains only one gateway, it is considered a star topology.

5. E.   A VPN site consists of the firewall and the firewall's encryption domain.

6. D, E.   The VPN properties for VPN communities are defined specifically for each VPN community. VPN properties defined in the Global Properties mostly affect Traditional Policies.

7. A, B, C, D, E.   All of these objects can be part of a VPN site.

8. A, C, E.   Explanation: A host node object can not encrypt but it can be part of an encryption domain which is part of a VPN site which is a component of a VPN community.

9. A, B.   The wizard asks you to define the gateway name, IP address, and the product it's running. To define anything else, you must click on Edit Gateway's Properties before closing the wizard. If you've already closed the wizard, proceed to the Network Object Manager to make any additional configuration changes.

10. B, E.   There are only two ways to define an encryption domain under the Topology section of a gateway object. You can define it based on all of the internal interfaces of the gateway or you can manually define it.

11. A.   Simplified Policies are the only way to create the VPN tunnels for a VPN community.

12. C.   Because the center of this topology contains two gateways, it is considered a star with center meshed topology.

13. A. $FWDIR/conf/vpn_route.conf needs to be configured for VPN routing to occur.

14. A, E.   Star topologies require that a central gateway or gateways be defined, along with satellite gateways.

15. A.   IKE is part of the Phase I key exchange.

16. D.   The Support Site To Site IP Compression option enables site-to-site IP compression.

17. B.   Phase II keys are renegotiated every hour (3600 seconds). Renegotiation times for Phase I and Phase II can be configured under the Advanced Properties of a VPN community.

18. A.   Only A is not a Security Policy option for VPN-1 Net gateways.

19. C.   Meshed topologies require that participating gateways be defined.

20. A, C, D.   The star and meshed topologies are supported, as well as a combination of the two that may or may not include multiple firewalls at the center of the configuration.

Chapter 8

Extranet Management

THE CCSE EXAM TOPICS COVERED IN THIS CHAPTER INCLUDE:

- ✓ Extranet management and how it works.
- ✓ Configuring extranet management.
- ✓ Establishing an extranet community.
- ✓ Configuring an extranet management rule base.

ou'll recall from Chapter 6, "Virtual Private Networks," that an *extranet VPN* is a private network that enables a company to have secure, one-on-one encrypted communications with its partners, suppliers, and customers. An extranet usually provides authorized, encrypted access to specific information to enable the secure exchange of data or facilitate transactions. The data that is accessed is usually part of an extended network that is protected behind the firewall and is available only to select partners outside the company. Throughout this chapter, we will refer to these select partners as *extranet partners*.

In prior versions of Check Point VPN-1/Firewall-1, an extranet VPN was configured as a site-to-site VPN. When configuring site-to-site extranet VPNs, each side of the VPN must define its encryption domain, its extranet partner's encryption domain, and the network objects that will be shared between partners. Then, the partners exchange encryption keys and create specific rules for that specific encrypted traffic. If you are setting up more than a few extranet VPNs, the configuration is a lengthy process; in addition, the management of each VPN is challenging, because your VPN must depend on a different firewall administration group that's on the other side of the VPN, which must be configured by another company. Coordination between two groups at two different companies is a difficult task in itself—try setting up multiple extranet VPNs with multiple IT administration groups at multiple companies.

As the number of extranets grows, so does the potential for human error and the complexity of management. Real-world extranets may be configured from New York to Tokyo, Los Angeles to Hong Kong, Miami to Rio de Janeiro, and so on. Configuration occurs in different time zones with different people, different skill sets, and different corporate cultures. IP addresses and topologies are constantly changing, so extranet maintenance is ongoing. Extranet setup is further complicated when you're deploying *PKI-based extranets,* where public keys and distinguished names need to be exchanged on both sides of the VPN.

Check Point's Extranet Management Interface (EMI) simplifies the difficulties involved in creating extranet VPNs and makes them easier to manage and update. Even in large-scale, PKI-based extranet deployments, the EMI can greatly reduce the changes, the maintenance, and the number of objects and rules you need to configure to create extranet VPNs. In this chapter, you will learn how the Check Point NG Extranet Management Interface works, how to configure it, and how to set it up in your rule base.

How Does EMI Work?

Check Point's EMI eases the configuration of each extranet by enabling the firewall to securely import network objects from the firewall on the other end of the extranet VPN. By creating network objects for export, your extranet partner will be able to securely import your network objects, and you will be able to securely import your partner's network objects. In essence, you will be able to create one managed extranet object, import multiple objects from your extranet partners, and use those objects in one encryption rule. Without the EMI, you would need to create multiple objects and multiple rules for multiple extranet VPNs. EMI will not only ease the difficulty of coordinating with other groups at other companies, but also reduce the number of rules in the rule base and decrease the potential for human error.

If you are faced with the challenge of managing several site-to-site VPNs, you know how difficult it is to set up each extranet partner's objects and accommodate changes. EMI provides an easy-to-use graphical interface for defining and updating the topology and security information of imported objects. In addition, the built-in internal certificate authority (ICA) on the SmartCenter Server reduces the amount of configuration required to establish each extranet VPN.

 Real World Scenario

Extranet Management Standards Increase the Need for Extranets

Large corporations are setting up extranet VPNs like crazy. This surge in extranet VPN use results from a push for encryption standards to ensure certain corporations are compliant with security requirements.

> For example, mandatory standards such as HIPAA (Health Insurance Portability and Accountability Act), which requires a set of network security standards to secure patient record information, have health care companies scrambling to become compliant. With the HIPAA standards in place, a health insurance company would have an extranet VPN with every hospital and, potentially, every doctor's office that it deals with. This may result in hundreds or even thousands of extranet VPNs being created in hospitals and insurance companies in the U.S. over the next couple of years.
>
> Many doctors' offices don't have an in-house firewall or LAN administrator to help manage an extranet VPN. Check Point NG is helping to address this huge challenge for hospitals and health insurance companies with the Extranet Management Interface.

Licensing EMI

EMI is a new Check Point NG feature that requires an additional license. Each side of the extranet must be equipped with VPN-1/Firewall-1 and must have the Extranet Management Interface licensed and enabled. To take advantage of the EMI features, you must have one of these three types of licenses installed on your SmartCenter Server:

- One partner
- Up to five partners
- Unlimited partners

Licenses can be combined. If you hold a five-partner license and two one-partner licenses, you can set up extranets with up to seven partners. If you find yourself in a situation where you need more than five extranet licenses now, and you plan to increase your number of extranets, it's probably a good idea to invest in the unlimited partners license.

How Is EMI configured?

Now that you understand how EMI works and how it's licensed, let's discuss how to configure it. The procedure for setting up an extranet VPN using EMI is complex, but can be summarized into three major steps:

1. Establish an extranet community environment.

2. Create an extranet partner and import network objects.

3. Setup extranet rules with network objects imported from your extranet partners.

We'll explain these three steps in great detail in the next few sections of this chapter.

Establishing an Extranet Community

The first step in configuring an extranet VPN is to create an extranet community. An *extranet community* is a group (similar to an encryption domain) that contains the *extranet-enabled gateway* and the *export network objects* that will be exported to your extranet partner. An extranet-enabled gateway is an existing gateway that is able to participate in an extranet VPN using EMI. Export network objects represent the section of your network that will be shared in an extranet VPN with each of your extranet partners. These objects will be securely imported by your extranet partner's firewall and used in your partner's extranet encryption rule.

Three steps are involved in establishing an extranet community:

1. Create at least one extranet-enabled gateway.

2. Define your extranet community's general properties.

3. Define the export network objects that your extranet partners will be able to import.

This section will explain these steps in detail. When you are finished, you will be able to test your knowledge by performing an exercise to establish an extranet community.

Creating an Extranet-Enabled Gateway

By creating an extranet-enabled gateway, you enable the functionality of the EMI. When a gateway is extranet enabled, the following are true:

- You, as an administrator, will have the ability to install extranet rules on the extranet-enabled gateway.

- You will be able to create export network objects that are part of the extranet-enabled gateway's VPN domain.

- The IP address and certificate DN, necessary for establishing an IKE VPN, can be exported to extranet partner sites.

- An Extranet Resolution Server will launch the next time you install the Security Policy. This feature facilitates the secure exchange of network objects and will be discussed later in the chapter.

- Implied rules that enable Check Point–specific communication with the Extranet Resolution Server will be added and installed on your gateway. This topic will also be discussed later in the chapter; you can also look at the implied rules in your SmartDashboard GUI.

Usually, when you're using EMI, your firewall architecture will be in a distributed configuration. If this is the case, make sure your SmartCenter Server has an IKE certificate from the ICA. In the VPN tab of the SmartCenter Server's Properties, select the ICA as the certificate authority; your SmartCenter Server will then be ready to perform an IKE VPN so your firewalls can be configured for extranet VPNs.

Any Check Point NG gateway or cluster in your architecture that will be protecting shared resources can be configured as an extranet-enabled gateway. To configure your gateway or cluster object, perform the following procedure:

1. Verify that your gateway or cluster network object has Firewall-1 and VPN-1 Pro enabled under Check Point Products on the General page of the object's properties.

2. On the Topology page of the object's properties, verify that the encryption domain, under the VPN Domain section of the screen, has been configured to include the IP addresses of the network objects you wish to export.

3. In the VPN page of the object's properties, click the Traditional mode configuration button and make sure the IKE properties are enabled with your desired encryption and data integrity algorithms. Enabling all the algorithms will not hurt, and will give you flexibility for each VPN.

4. On the Certificate list of the VPN page, if a certificate does not exist, create one by clicking Add. Generate the certificate from the ICA.

5. On the Extranet page of the object's properties, check the Extranet Enabled Gateway check box, as shown in Figure 8.1.

FIGURE 8.1   Extranet Enabled Gateway

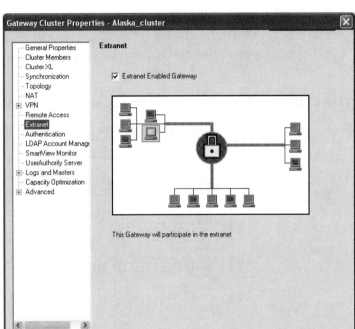

 As you may know, when you're configuring a gateway cluster as an extranet-enabled gateway, you don't need to configure each member gateway. The cluster object represents all the member gateways, and the configuration won't be available on individual objects.

After defining your extranet-enabled gateway, install the Security Policy so that your changes are saved and compiled. Once your extranet-enabled gateway is defined and the policy is installed, go to the Extranet Management Interface tab of the Global Properties shown in Figure 8.2. Two settings can be adjusted for your specific configuration:

Check Partners For Updates Every   This setting specifies how often the gateway will check extranet partners for changes to their network objects. The interval is set to check for updates every 60 minutes by default and can be set between 5 and 86,400 minutes. For the most part, the default will be sufficient, because extranet partners' objects don't change several times per day.

SSL Grace Period This setting defines the grace period for the extranet resolution protocol SSL CRLs. The extranet resolution protocol is defined in the next section.

FIGURE 8.2 Extranet Management Interface Global Properties

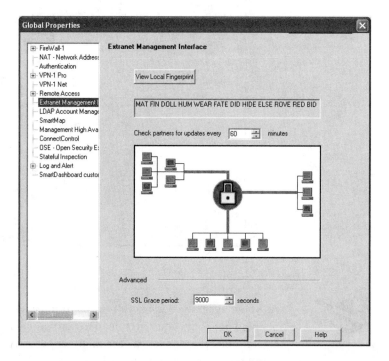

At the top of the EMI tab, you'll see a View Local Fingerprint button. Clicking this button will display your extranet fingerprint, which is calculated on the public key of your ICA. This fingerprint and the IP address of your extranet-enabled gateways must be sent in a secure manner to your extranet partners. Your extranet partners will also send you an IP address and fingerprint in a secure manner.

After changing the Global Properties, you should install the Security Policy to compile and save. Now that you have successfully configured an extranet-enabled gateway, you will learn how to define your extranet's general properties.

Defining your Extranet General Properties

Defining your extranet is simple. You need to create it only once, and then you will be able to use it for all your extranet VPNs. Go to the VPN Communities choice on the Manage menu in the SmartDashboard, where the MyExtranet object appears. Edit the properties of this object, and you will see that it has no partners defined.

Figure 8.3 shows an example of an Extranet Community object after partners have been added. (This screen shot was taken in SmartDashboard Demo Mode so you can get an idea what a populated extranet community looks like.) Notice the General and Exported Objects tabs, and that all the extranet partners are named in the center.

FIGURE 8.3 Extranet Community Properties

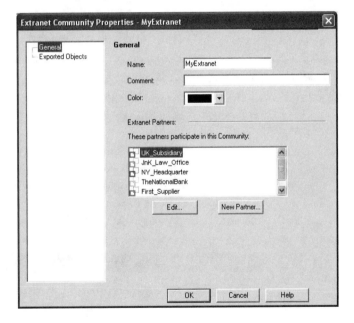

The next section will discuss the Exported Objects tab and how to define the export objects you will make available to your extranet partners.

Defining Export Objects

Exported network objects represent a section of your network that you will share with your extranet partners through a VPN tunnel. These objects can only be workstations, networks, address ranges, or groups that consist of workstations, networks, or address ranges. All of these objects must have a static IP address (dynamic objects are not supported) and must be protected by an extranet-enabled gateway as a part of the encryption domain.

To create the export network objects, use the same procedure you use to create regular network objects. If you are creating several objects, you may want to color-code them to distinguish among servers, networks, and other resources. If the objects already exist in your database, you do not need to re-create them.

After creating the objects, you can define them as export network objects in the Exported Objects tab of the Extranet Community Object properties. Objects can be added, removed, or edited by clicking the appropriate button. You can select multiple objects at one time by holding down the Shift key for consecutive objects or the Ctrl key for non-consecutive objects. Once added, these export objects will take effect and be available to your extranet partners for import after you install the policy.

Objects that have NAT defined for automatic NAT will be exported with the NAT address. Objects that are defined manually in the NAT rule base will retain their original object properties.

As always, you must install the Security Policy to compile and save your configuration. Once you have installed your policy, your extranet community is established. To help you become more comfortable with this procedure, it is time to do an exercise so you have some hands-on experience in establishing an extranet community. Exercise 8.1 walks you through the procedure.

EXERCISE 8.1

Establishing an Extranet Community

This exercise provides you with the steps involved in establishing your extranet community. The details of these steps have been discussed earlier. By reading the information and then following along in this exercise, you will be able to clearly understand the procedure involved in creating an extranet community. Follow these steps:

1. Go to the gateway's properties to define an extranet-enabled gateway. Verify that Firewall-1 and VPN-1 Pro are both selected under Check Point Products.

2. On the Topology tab, under VPN Domain, verify that the export objects you plan to define will be within the VPN domain.

3. On the VPN tab of the gateway's properties, click the Traditional mode configuration button and enable all the encryption and data integrity algorithms.

4. On the Certificate list of the VPN page, if a certificate does not exist, add one. Make sure the certificate is created from the ICA.

5. Go to the Extranet tab in the gateway's properties and select the Extranet Enabled Gateway check box.

6. On the Extranet Management Interface tab of the Global Properties, keep the Check Partners For Updates setting at the default of 60 and the SSL Grace Period setting at the default of 9000.

7. Click View Local Fingerprint at the top of the EMI tab on the Global Properties screen; the fingerprint will display. Click OK.

8. Click Manage ➤ VPN Communities and edit your extranet community. Add a comment and choose an appropriate color.

9. Click on the Exported Objects tab on your Extranet Community properties screen. Define exportable objects by clicking Add and choosing your export object.

10. Install your Security Policy.

Now that you understand how to establish your extranet community, the next step in establishing the extranet is to define extranet partners and import their network objects while they import yours. The next section will teach you how to define extranet partners and import their network objects.

Defining Partners and Importing Objects

Creating extranet partners requires coordination on your side and your extranet partner's side. Make sure your partner has properly established an extranet community and defined export objects as you have. Unless your partner's extranet community is properly configured and installed, communication will fail. For configuration and verification, you will need to provide to your partner (in a secure way) the IP address of your extranet-enabled gateway and your gateway's fingerprint from the EMI tab of the Global Properties. Your extranet partner will need to provide you with the same information in a secure manner. An encrypted e-mail or a face-to-face meeting is a good way to perform the secure exchange.

You need to create a secure communication with your partner so that you can import your network objects and your partner can import yours in a secure manner. The next section explains how the network objects are securely imported.

Understanding the Secure Import

The secure communication needed to accommodate the importing of network objects requires the establishment of trust between you and your partner by exchanging Check Point EMI public keys and verifying their fingerprints. Each EMI fingerprint is calculated on the SmartCenter Server's ICA and its distinguished name. Once trust is established, export network objects can be imported into the extranet partner's firewall, and you will be able to import your partner's objects.

Trust is established and the import is performed by using the *Extranet Resolution Protocol*. The Extranet Resolution Protocol is a certificate-based secured protocol. When you created your extranet-enabled gateway, after installing the Security Policy, the Extranet Resolution Server was started and implied rules that allow Check Point–specific communication with the Extranet Resolution Servers were added and installed on the gateway. Each extranet-enabled gateway houses two *Extranet Resolution Servers*. The first server, which is used to securely export your public keys to extranet partners, is the *Public Key Distributor* that runs on port 18262. The other server, which is used to securely export your network objects, is the *Extranet Objects Distributor*; it runs on port 18263.

Trust is established when you configure your extranet partners. You now understand the concept behind the secure import; but to truly understand the process, you must go through it. The next section explains the process of creating an extranet partner and how trust is established.

Creating a New Extranet Partner

To set up a partner, from your extranet community general properties, click New Partner or, from the menu, click Manage ➤ VPN Communities ➤ New ➤ Partner. Doing so will display a window similar to Figure 8.4. In the General page, specify the name and color for your extranet partner.

FIGURE 8.4 Extranet Partner Properties

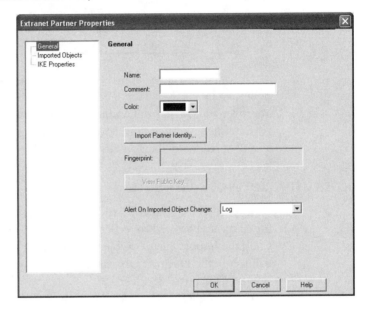

Click Import Partner Identity, and the Partner Identity window shown in Figure 8.5 will appear. Enter the IP address of the partner's extranet-enabled gateway as the Resolution Server. Click Get, and the SmartCenter Server will connect to the Extranet Public Key Distribution Server on port 18262 and get the public key. The fingerprint of the public key will be displayed. Compare this fingerprint to the one you previously received from your extranet partner. If the fingerprint matches, the extranet partner is confirmed to be who they claim to be, and you can click Approve to establish trust.

After you click Approve, the Partner Identity window will disappear and the fingerprint will be displayed in the Extranet Partner Properties window. You can see the Public Key by clicking the View Public Key button. The Alert On Imported Object Change option allows you to select an alert from the drop-down menu that will notify you when an imported object is changed and needs to be imported again.

FIGURE 8.5   Partner Identity window

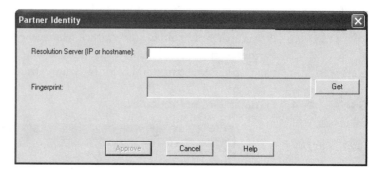

Now that you have defined your partner as an extranet partner, install the policy, and your changes will be compiled and saved. If your extranet partner approves your fingerprint and installs the policy, then secure communication is established; you and your partner can import each other's network objects. The next section will discuss the process of importing network objects.

Importing Network Objects

To import your extranet partner's objects, go to the Imported Objects tab of the Extranet Partner Properties window that you created in the last section. Click the Import Partner Objects button, and the SmartCenter Server will connect to the Extranet Objects Distributor with a certificate-based SSL session on TCP port 18263.

The ICA CRL is transferred during the SSL session to ensure that the SmartCenter Server is valid and trusted on your side and that the extranet-enabled gateway is valid and trusted on your extranet partner's side. In addition, using a unique DN syntax insures that only certificates issued for gateways or the SmartCenter Server will be trusted by the other side.

After the secure communication is established and verification occurs, the objects will be imported. Information about the objects that are imported will appear in the Import Partner Objects window. The information will vary slightly depending on whether the objects are new or have been updated. The Status column will list the object as one of the following:

- New

- Changed

- Not Changed

- Removed

The Display Name and Comment values can be edited so you can adjust the objects to your own naming convention. The Original Name is the name of the object on your extranet partner's network. The original name cannot be changed.

After your initial import, the Import Partner Objects button changes to an Update Partner Objects button; you can click it whenever you want to update your partner's imported network objects. By issuing the empstatus command from the SmartCenter Server command line, you'll be able to see a status of your network objects versus your partner's current objects. If any of the objects show up as Changed, you should update that partner's imported network objects. Install the Security Policy after importing the objects.

As always, whenever a change is made to your objects, the Security Policy must be installed for the change to take effect. Any time public keys or network objects are changed, imported, or updated, the policy must be reinstalled.

Now that you've imported your partner's objects and know how to keep them updated, you are ready to configure your partner's IKE properties. The next section discusses the final step in creating your extranet partner.

Defining IKE Properties

The extranet VPN that you create requires both sides of the VPN to have the same encryption properties. You and your extranet partner should evaluate the sensitivity of the data that will pass through your extranet VPN to determine how to configure your IKE properties. If your data is more sensitive, then you may want to use a stronger encryption and data integrity algorithm. If speed is your main concern for this VPN, then you may want to use a weaker but faster encryption and data integrity algorithm.

As shown in Figure 8.6, the IKE Properties are configured on the third tab of the Extranet Partner Properties window. The IKE properties on this page should be configured to represent the minimum IKE methods that will be accepted when working with this extranet partner.

Figure 8.6 shows the four options you can configure. These options should be set the same way on the partner's side of the extranet VPN:

Perform Key Exchange Encryption With   With this option, you specify the encryption algorithm. Obviously, AES-256 is the strongest algorithm supported by Check Point NG and will be most secure.

Perform Data Integrity With   This option allows you to specify the type of one-way hash algorithm you want to use. SHA-1 is the strongest algorithm supported by Check Point NG and the most secure option.

Use Diffie-Hellman Group   This option allows you to strengthen security by choosing a longer Diffie-Hellman group.

Renegotiate IKE Security Associations Every   This option allows you to choose the number of minutes between renegotiations of IKE security associations.

FIGURE 8.6   Extranet Partner IKE Properties

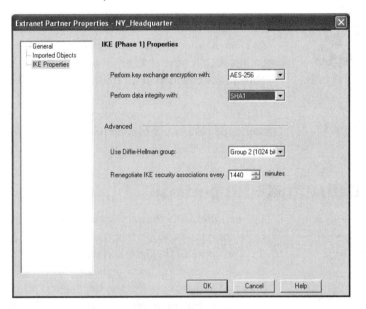

Configuring Extranet Management in the Rule Base

Now that you have set up your IKE properties and the objects have been imported on both sides of your extranet, you can create rules in your rule base to put the extranet VPN into effect. As you know from earlier chapters, everything you have done so far was just preliminary setup—nothing really happens until the rule base is configured. When using the EMI, your rule base can be configured only in Traditional VPN mode. Extranet Community rules cannot be created in Simplified mode. There are two types of extranet community rules:

Specific Rules   Contain specific objects imported from the extranet partner. These objects are always specified using the @ symbol. Specific rules can be used to encrypt between specifically defined objects from site to site, allowing you to be more granular in your extranet rules. You can use a specific rule to allow encrypted access from one client to one server, a group of clients to one server, and so on.

General Rules   Allow you to create rules with an object—displayed as *Any—that represents all of your exported objects or all of your extranet partner's imported objects. Doing so lets you create a general rule so you do not have to list each imported network object individually. The *Any object will include only the objects you have imported or the objects your partner has imported.

Figure 8.7 shows the menu that appears when you right-click on a Source or Destination of a rule. If you choose Add Extranet Groups from the menu, an Extranet dialog box opens in which you can choose your partner from a drop-down menu; all of their imported objects will then appear.

FIGURE 8.7   Add Extranet Groups

By choosing the objects you want to use in the rule, you can create a specific rule and limit access in the extranet VPN rule by rule. When you're adding imported objects to the Source and Destination, you specify the partner name after an @ symbol. For example, if the object name is Linux-net and the partner is Sybex, the object is listed in the extranet VPN rule as Linux-net@Sybex.

Figure 8.8 shows a sample rule that allows a VPN between e-mail servers, SAP servers, the Detroit-Net, and a RedWing server. The e-mail and SAP servers are imported objects; the other two are local. Sometimes, you may need to limit your VPN to just one server or just FTP access on one server. Whatever the case may be, you can create extranet VPN rules for one partner or multiple partners. So, you do not need as many extranet VPN rules as you would without the EMI.

FIGURE 8.8 Sample extranet rule

NO.	SOURCE	DESTINATION	SERVICE	ACTION
1	Detroit-Net SAP_Servers@UK_Subsidiary Email_Servers@UK_Subsidiary RedWing-server	Email_Servers@UK_Subsidiary SAP_Servers@UK_Subsidiary RedWing-server Detroit-Net	✱ Any	🔒 Encrypt

Extranet rules can also be limited with authentication rules, where the Source may be an internal user group and the Action can be User, Session, or Client Authentication. If you use an authentication rule, you must right-click the Authentication icon in the Action column and choose the Add Encryption option.

Summary

The Extranet Management Interface allows you to create an extranet VPN community and then securely import predefined network objects from your extranet partners. Creating the extranet VPN community includes the process of defining export network objects that your extranet partners can import from your extranet-enabled gateway. Once these network objects are imported into both sides of a VPN and IKE properties are agreed upon, the imported network objects can be added to rules in the rule base to configure the VPN.

For companies with many extranets, it is much easier and more accurate to import network objects that are already configured by the owners of that network. Any time a change is made, rather than coordinating a meeting or a conference call, an administrator can simply click an Update button. All partners, imported network objects, and IKE properties can be easily changed whenever necessary.

The EMI is a great add-on component for a company that plans to set up several extranet VPNs. For companies that already have extranets in place, it may be worth purchasing EMI licenses to help simplify the management of the current configuration. The convenience and reliability offered by the EMI may save hours of administrative and troubleshooting time.

Exam Essentials

Know how to establish an extranet community.   Understand the steps involved in establishing an extranet community. First you must set at least one gateway to be an extranet-enabled gateway. Then, define the properties of your extranet community. Finally, you must define at least one export object that is in an encryption domain of the extranet-enabled gateway.

Understand how to create extranet partners and import network objects.   You should know how to create extranet partners, establish trust, and import network objects. You should also understand how to update imported network objects and define IKE properties.

Know how to set up extranet rules in the rule base.   After properly establishing an extranet community and importing network objects, the final step in configuring your extranet VPN is creating the rules in the rule base. You should know how to effectively create VPN rules with import objects for extranet VPNs.

Key Terms

Before you take the exam, be certain you are familiar with the following terms:

export network objects	Extranet Resolution Servers
extranet community	extranet VPN
Extranet Objects Distributor	extranet-enabled gateway
extranet partners	PKI-based extranets
Extranet Resolution Protocol	Public Key Distributor

Review Questions

1. What must an export network object be part of in order to be valid?

   A. The network

   B. The firewall

   C. The SmartCenter Server

   D. The encryption domain

   E. The VPN community

2. What is required on the other end of the extranet VPN for the Extranet Management Interface to work?

   A. A firewall that can VPN

   B. Any encryption device that supports IKE

   C. A Check Point NG firewall with an EMI license

   D. A Check Point firewall

   E. None of the above

3. Which license increments are *not* available for the EMI product? (Choose all that apply.)

   A. One partner

   B. Ten partner

   C. Five partner

   D. Unlimited

   E. All of the above

4. Which of the following will *not* be displayed in the Status column of the imported objects list?

   A. Changed

   B. Not Changed

   C. New

   D. Updated

   E. Removed

5. After retrieving your extranet partner's public key, verifying the fingerprint, and clicking Approve, what must be done before your extranet partner can import your network objects?

   A. Your policy must be installed.

   B. You must provide your partner with a password.

   C. You must e-mail your partner a fingerprint.

   D. You must set your IKE properties.

   E. None of the above.

6. On which TCP port do the SmartCenter Server and the Public Key Distributor communicate?

   A. 18300

   B. 18262

   C. 32067

   D. 18263

   E. 259

7. How do you add imported objects to a rule in the rule base?

   A. Right-click in the Source or Destination field and choose Add.

   B. Right-click in the Source or Destination field and choose Extranets.

   C. Right-click in the Source or Destination field and choose Add Extranet Groups.

   D. Right-click in the Source or Destination field and choose Add Users Access.

   E. None of the above.

8. When creating an extranet partner, which of the following tabs do *not* exist in the Extranet Partner Properties window? (Choose all that apply.)

   A. General

   B. Exported Objects

   C. Imported Objects

   D. IKE Properties

   E. All of the above exist.

9. What is the name of the Extranet Resolution Server that uses a certificate-based SSL and runs on TCP port 18263?

   A. Public Key Distributor

   B. Extranet-Enabled Gateway

   C. Extranet certificate authority

   D. Extranet Objects Distributor

   E. None of the above

10. What needs to be established with an extranet partner to initiate the configuration?

    A. A gateway

    B. Trust

    C. Public keys

    D. Export objects

    E. All of the above

11. What encryption schemes does the Extranet Management Interface support? (Choose all that apply.)

    A. Blowfish

    B. IDEA

    C. IKE

    D. FWZ

    E. All of the above

12. Where do you enable an extranet-enabled gateway?

    A. In the VPN tab in Global Properties

    B. In the VPN tab

    C. In the Topology tab

    D. On the firewall or cluster object

    E. In the rule base

13. Without using a shortcut button, how do you set up an extranet?

    A. In the menu under Manage ➤ Network Objects

    B. In the menu under Manage ➤ VPN Communities

    C. In the menu under Manage ➤ Servers

    D. In the menu under Manage ➤ Resources

    E. None of the above

14. What type of network objects can your export network objects be? (Choose all that apply.)

A. Workstations

B. Networks

C. Address ranges

D. Groups including workstations, networks, and address ranges

E. All of the above

15. What is the first item that you compare to be sure your extranet partner is who they claim to be?

A. Public key

B. Private key

C. Fingerprint

D. IKE properties

E. None of the above

16. Which of these properties can you *not* edit on the imported objects?

A. Name

B. Original Name

C. Comment

D. Description

E. Color

17. Where is the extranet fingerprint calculated?

A. The ICA

B. The extranet-enabled gateway

C. The extranet partner's firewall

D. The SmartDashboard

E. The Extranet Resolution Server

18. What is the strongest encryption algorithm that is supported in Check Point NG's Extranet Management Interface?

A. DES

B. 3DES

C. CAST

D. FWZ-1

E. AES-256

19. What is the strongest data integrity algorithm supported by the Extranet Management Interface?

A. MD4

B. MD5

C. SHA-1

D. None of the above

20. What command can be issued to check the status of your extranet partners from the command line?

A. cpconfig

B. empstatus

C. fw stat

D. cphaprob

E. cplic print

Answers to Review Questions

1. D. An export network object must be part of the extranet-enabled gateway's encryption domain to be a valid export network object.

2. C. The EMI product will work only if both sides of the extranet are using a Check Point NG firewall with a valid EMI license.

3. B. The EMI license is not sold as a 10-partner license package. Ten licenses can be achieved by buying 2 five-partner licenses or 10 one-partner licenses. The unlimited choice is always an option for a growing company.

4. D. The Status column is meant to provide information about the status of an object since it was last imported or updated. Updated would not be a useful description of status. Changed, New, Removed, and Not Changed provide much more useful information.

5. A. After retrieving your public keys and establishing trust, your changes don't take effect on the firewall until you install the policy. After installing the policy, provided that everything else is properly configured, your extranet partner will be able to import your objects.

6. B. The SmartCenter Server communicates with the Public Key Distributor on TCP port 18262. This is not an important port to remember unless you want to block or allow the port on your firewall.

7. C. To add an extranet, you must right-click in the Source or Destination field and choose Add Extranet Groups. Doing so will allow you to choose a partner and see all the objects you have imported from the partner. Choosing Add lets you add your network objects but not imported network objects.

8. B. All the tabs exist except Exported Objects. Because you are only importing objects from your extranet partner, there is no need to keep track of objects that have been exported. You only know about your export objects, which are available to your extranet partners for import.

9. D. The Extranet Objects Distributor is the certificate-based SSL that enables the secure import of network objects from extranet partners. The Public Key Distributor exchanges public keys to accommodate the encryption process for the Extranet Objects Distributor.

10. B. Without having trust established, an extranet partner's gateway cannot communicate with your extranet-enabled gateway. Trust must be established before any type of communication can take place. After trust is established, public keys can be exchanged and the process of importing objects can be set up.

11. C. IKE is the only encryption scheme supported on the EMI. Although this sounds limiting, IKE is the most widely used encryption scheme and fits most standards. At the same time, EMI is only supported by other Check Point NG firewalls, which will also only use IKE.

12. D. The Extranet tab on the firewall object is where you enable the firewall to be an extranet-enabled gateway. If you run your firewalls in a cluster, you enable it in the Extranet tab of the cluster object.

13. B. Extranet partners are located on the VPN Communities menu. An extranet is a VPN, so it is appropriate to keep it there. The Setup Extranet button is so convenient to click that sometimes you may forget how to get there without the shortcut.

14. E. The export objects can only be workstations, networks, and address ranges, or a group of these types of objects. This is not really a limitation, because these types of objects and a group of these types of objects should cover more than the majority of the objects that you plan to use in your extranet.

15. C. The fingerprint is the first item that allows you to ensure that you can trust your partner's identity. You have the option to compare extranet fingerprints before choosing to approve the Extranet Resolution Public Key.

16. B. The Original Name is the name of the object on your partner's network. There is no real need to change this name. The other properties of the object can be changed to match your internal naming and color conventions.

17. A. The fingerprint is calculated on the ICA running on the Smart-Center Server. Having the certificate authority local makes extranet management more efficient.

18. E. AES is the only 256-bit encryption algorithm supported by Check Point NG; it's also the strongest algorithm supported by NG. In previous versions of Check Point, 3DES was the strongest algorithm supported. AES is the new strong encryption standard.

19. C. SHA-1 is a 160-bit data integrity algorithm. MD5 is 128 bits. Although both algorithms provide good data integrity, SHA-1 is considered to be stronger because it is longer, with more bits. More bits is not always the better choice, because more bits equals more math-intensive computation. More intensive math computation slows performance, but the difference may not be noticeable to the human eye.

20. B. By issuing the `empstatus` command, you can determine whether your extranet partners have changed their export network objects. If they have, you can go to that partner's extranet properties and update your imported network objects.

Chapter

9

SecuRemote

In Chapter 6, "Virtual Private Networks," you learned about Intranet and Extranet VPNs. SecuRemote is Check Point's client-to-site VPN technology. A *client-to-site* VPN frees a user to be mobile—to work from home, a remote office, or anywhere else—and maintain encrypted communication with the corporate network. As long as a user can access the Internet, they can use SecuRemote to VPN into the corporate network and access the network resources they are permitted to use.

SecuRemote is used worldwide as an effective mobile solution that increases convenience and productivity. In this chapter, you will learn about SecuRemote and client VPN technology. You will not only learn how it works and how to configure SecuRemote, you'll also learn how to successfully deploy SecuRemote and accommodate backward compatibility.

How SecuRemote Works

Because of the growing demand of people working from home or on the road in the past few years, many products have been released that provide client VPN technology. A client VPN provides secure mobility for a user by encrypting information from the client to a VPN device and from a VPN device to the client. The SecuRemote software installs on the client machine and creates a client-to-site VPN with the Check Point firewall. The majority of SecuRemote clients are installed on a Windows operating system, but Mac OS and Linux are also supported. With all three platforms supported, SecuRemote allows almost any type of information from any type of desktop or laptop to be securely passed across the Internet.

SecuRemote provides an encrypted VPN, SecureClient (discussed in Chapter 10, "SecureClient , The Policy Server, and Clientless VPNs") provides desktop security in addition to the encrypted VPN. SecuRemote and Secure-Client are virtually the same software, but SecureClient requires an additional license and provides some additional functionality.

For the firewall to support SecuRemote connections, it must have a VPN license and a SecuRemote license. The licensing for SecuRemote exists in the license string on the firewall. There is no additional license or charge per SecuRemote client.

Figure 9.1 demonstrates how SecuRemote works. SecuRemote encrypts data as it leaves the laptop and passes over the Internet to the firewall. Data is then decrypted at the firewall and passes as cleartext to the appropriate server. As the information comes back to the laptop, the process happens in reverse so information is encrypted at the firewall and then decrypted at the laptop. For example, if the laptop was retrieving an e-mail, the e-mail would leave the e-mail server as cleartext, be encrypted at the firewall, pass across the Internet as encrypted ciphertext, and then reach the laptop where it would be decrypted by the SecuRemote software.

FIGURE 9.1   How SecuRemote works

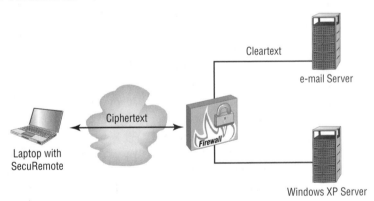

For the initial connection to occur, the SecuRemote software must be configured to know how to connect the laptop to the firewall and perform the VPN. This process is started when the user creates a *site* in the SecuRemote software. A SecuRemote site identifies the firewall with which the user will make the initial connection to gather encryption domain and network information. This information is called the *topology*. Multiple sites can be created to identify multiple VPN-1 firewalls for client-to-site VPNs. The topology will contain encryption domain and network information for each site created. The topology is available only to authorized SecuRemote users.

After creating the site and connecting to the firewall, the user is challenged for authentication to be sure they are an authorized SecuRemote user. The following Check Point authentication schemes are supported: SecurID, RADIUS, Lightweight Directory Access Protocol (LDAP), S/Key, and VPN-1/FireWall-1 password. The user logs in using the authentication scheme you choose.

When choosing authentication schemes, strong authentication is always preferred and considered the most secure. Certificates or SecurID tokens are the strongest.

If the user successfully authenticates and is an authorized SecuRemote user, the topology is downloaded to the client machine and stored locally in the userc.C file. The userc.C file is located on the client's machine; it stores topology information for all SecuRemote sites set up by the client. To save the end user from having to configure the SecuRemote client software, an administrator can use the SecuRemote Packaging Tool to issue a complete configuration to the end user without the user being able to make any changes.

SecuRemote supports dynamic IP addressing for dial-up connections, so users can connect from anywhere in the world where an Internet connection is available. You also have an option to limit the IP addresses from which connections originate, to make certain connections more restrictive and granular when needed.

The SecuRemote software connects using Internet Key Exchange (IKE) encryption and supports Data Encryption Standard (DES), Triple DES (3DES), AES-128 (Advanced Encryption Standard), and AES-256 encryption algorithms. The decision of which algorithm to choose is up to you, but most companies use strong encryption like AES-128 or 3DES. For dial-up connections speed is an issue, so DES might be faster—but it's less secure. For extremely confidential data, it's best to use the strongest algorithm: AES-256.

Real World Scenario

On the Road with SecuRemote

As a traveling consultant, I have spent many nights in hotels with a dial-up or high-speed connection and have been able to use SecuRemote to access my e-mail and shared folders on the local LAN. Whether I am in Dallas, New York, Detroit, Europe, or Asia, I can securely VPN from my laptop to the corporate firewall through an Internet connection.

Sometimes, however, I cannot use my VPN because my laptop is on a LAN that is protected behind a firewall. SecuRemote uses special protocols and ports that would normally be blocked by a firewall; so, when your SecuRemote connection tries to communicate with your VPN site and there is a firewall in between, the firewall blocks the communication. In this instance, if your laptop is on a LAN that is protected by a firewall, you need to configure that firewall to allow your SecuRemote connection through.

 Check Point offers a line of SecuRemote/SecureClient appliances called SofaWare. The SofaWare products provide SecuRemote connections through the appliance and eliminate the need to install the SecuRemote software on each client machine. The appliance acts as a small switch and provides Network Address Translation (NAT), so one IP address can be shared among many machines. With a SofaWare appliance, a small remote office would not need a full-blown firewall and would be able to VPN through the appliance to a corporate firewall at company headquarters. For more information, visit www.checkpoint.com.

SecuRemote Setup

You need to configure many components to set up SecuRemote. Both the firewall and the SecuRemote software must be configured to provide the client-to-site VPN. The procedure for configuring SecuRemote can be summarized in the following general steps:

1. Create SecuRemote users on the firewall.

2. Configure the firewall to accommodate SecuRemote connections.

3. Configure the Global Properties for SecuRemote connections.

4. Define SecuRemote rules in the rule base of the firewall.

5. Install the SecuRemote client software on the client computer(s).

6. Set up the SecuRemote software.

Now that you understand how client-to-site VPNs and SecuRemote work, it's time to learn how to configure SecuRemote. In this section, we will discuss how to set up SecuRemote users.

Setting Up SecuRemote Users

The first step in configuring the firewall is to identify the users who will be using SecuRemote to VPN into the firewall. These users are created in the SmartDashboard GUI and installed to the User database of the firewall. Creating these users is similar to creating users for authentication, as discussed in the CCSA courseware. SecuRemote users are typically created for the following reasons:

- To allow specific employees to access sensitive corporate data from a specific location

- To provide encrypted access to partners, customers, or suppliers so they can retrieve sensitive information or specific data from a specific server

- To let remote users securely communicate with the firewall from a remote office without having a firewall-to-firewall VPN in place

- To provide general network access for telecommuters working from home or on the road

- To let a group of workers dealing with sensitive information (financial or accounting) keep communication private by only allowing a specific SecuRemote group to access a specific server

When you're configuring SecuRemote rules, the Source column of the rule is defined as a group of users. You will first create users and then create groups to which you can assign your new users. These groups will then be used in the rule base.

Creating Users

To create a new user, follow these steps:

1. Click Manage ➢ Users and Administrators. The Users screen will appear.

2. Click New ➢ User by Template ➢ Default. The General tab will appear.

3. Enter your login name.

4. On the Personal tab, adjust the expiration date. If you leave it blank, the user will never expire.

5. Click on the Authentication tab, where you can define the authentication scheme this user will use. As shown in Figure 9.2, a drop-down menu lists all the authentication schemes available for a user. Choose the authentication scheme you want to use.

FIGURE 9.2 User Properties Authentication tab

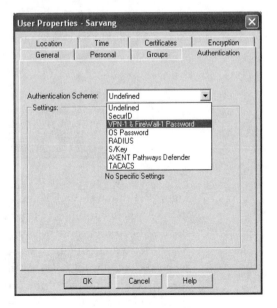

When you choose an authentication scheme, you must make sure that your firewall or cluster object has the same authentication scheme enabled. If the authentication is not enabled on your firewall or cluster object's authentication properties, the authentication will not work.

6. On the Encryption tab, shown in Figure 9.3, your only choice for the client encryption method is IKE. In versions prior to FP1, you could also use FWZ encryption, but this method is not supported in NG FP1 and beyond. Select IKE as your encryption scheme and click Edit, and you will see the IKE Phase 2 encryption properties for your user.

FIGURE 9.3 User Properties Encryption tab

7. Figure 9.4 shows the IKE Phase 2 Properties window. Choosing Public in the Authentication tab lets you configure your SecuRemote user to use certificates for authentication. Choosing Password (Pre-Shared Secret) lets you configure the user with a password that will be used when exchanging keys. Rather than the password scheme identified in the Authentication tab of the properties, the user's SecuRemote password is identified here.

FIGURE 9.4 IKE Phase 2 Properties Authentication tab

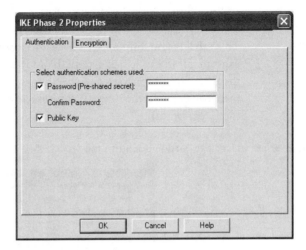

8. Move to the Encryption tab, shown in Figure 9.5. You can either configure the user to use the encryption settings from the Global Properties for SecuRemote or configure the encryption settings individually for this particular user. If you are dealing with many users, like most SecuRemote deployments, it's better to define the encryption properties globally for all users in the firewall's Global Properties.

FIGURE 9.5 IKE Phase 2 Properties Encryption tab

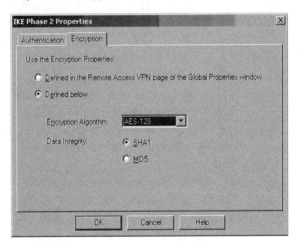

After clicking OK, you have set the name, expiration date, authentication scheme, and encryption for the user. If you want to limit the user by IP address, you can do so on the User Properties Location tab, shown in Figure 9.6. This tab lets you limit a user's access to a certain number of IP addresses. For example, if the user has a static IP address at home and you want to give them SecuRemote access to a specific server from home and only from home, then you can add the home IP address as an object to the Source window on the Location tab.

FIGURE 9.6 User Properties Location lab

If you want to limit the user by day or time, you can do so on the User Properties Time tab. For example, you can configure a user to have SecuRemote access only on weekends or only between 5 P.M. and 10 P.M. It's easier to limit the SecuRemote rule rather then limit access on a per-user basis. That way, you have to make changes in only one place instead of for the many users you have created.

The User Properties Certificates tab allows you to generate certificates and monitor their state for strong authentication. If you are using certificates, this is where you generate or revoke each user's certificates. After you generate the certificate, it will appear in the Certificate State section of this tab.

Now that you have understand how to create users, you can create the rest of the users for your SecuRemote connections. You can do so by clicking New ➤ User by Template ➤ Default and filling in each tab. Or, to simplify the process, you can create a template that has all the user settings you want to configure for the Personal, Authentication, Location, Time, and Encryption tabs. After you create the template, you can quickly create each user by clicking New ➤ User by Template ➤ (Your Template) and then entering a login name.

Creating Groups

Now that you've created your users, let's create groups that will be used in your rule base. To create a group, follow these steps:

1. Click Manage ➤ Users and Administrators ➤ New ➤ Group. Figure 9.7 provides an example of a new group called SybexRemoteAccess.

2. To add a user to the group, highlight the user in the Not in Group window and click Add. The user will appear in the In Group window as a member of the group. To remove a user from the group, highlight the user in the In Group window and click Remove. The user will disappear from the right window and be removed from the group.

FIGURE 9.7   Group Properties window

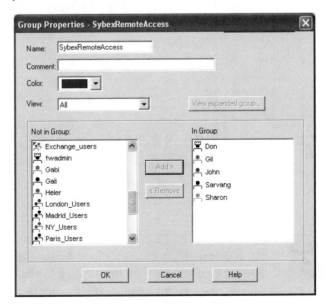

Now that you have created and configured your users and groups for SecuRemote, you'll configure the firewall to accommodate SecuRemote VPNs. The next section discusses how to configure the firewall for SecuRemote.

Configuring the Firewall for SecuRemote

Your Firewall objects require configuration of the VPN tab in order to accommodate SecuRemote. Figure 9.8 illustrates the Firewall object's VPN tab in NG FP3. On the VPN tab of the Firewall object, you can identify the VPN communities the firewall will participate in, define Traditional mode VPN properties, and configure certificates.

FIGURE 9.8 Firewall object VPN tab

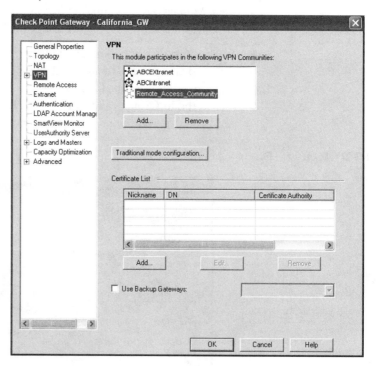

 For SecuRemote to work, the IP Address of the gateway's external interface must be reachable from the Internet. In addition, the authentication scheme for your users must be enabled on the Authentication tab of the Firewall object.

The VPN communities are listed for use with simplified VPN encryption. Click Add to add a VPN community to the list. When creating your SecuRemote rules, you can use Simplified mode or Traditional mode (these VPN modes were explained in previous chapters). Using Traditional mode VPNs will help you stay consistent if you are using backward compatibility with older versions of VPN-1/FireWall-1 in your environment.

If you plan to set up SecuRemote with Traditional mode VPN encryption rules, click the Traditional Mode Configuration button to open the IKE properties. The Firewall object's Traditional Mode IKE Properties window is displayed in Figure 9.9. The upper portion of the window lets you enable encryption and data integrity algorithms for this gateway.

FIGURE 9.9   Traditional Mode IKE Properties window

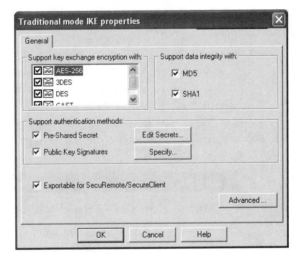

The lower portion of this window lets you specify the authentication methods that will be supported when this gateway participates in a VPN. Your options are:

Pre-Shared Secret   The SecuRemote client and FireWall-1 gateway authenticate each other by verifying that the other party knows the pre-shared secret.

Public Key Signatures   The SecuRemote client authenticates itself to the FireWall-1 gateway by using its certificate. The firewall verifies the certificate against a *certificate revocation list (CRL)*.

Prior to NG FP3, a third option appeared in this window: Hybrid Authentication for SecuRemote. Hybrid authentication extends IKE's authentication capabilities to support all the VPN-1/FireWall-1 authentication schemes for SecuRemote clients. It is now enabled on the VPN Basic tab under Remote Access in the Global Properties.

At the bottom of the window is a check box labeled Exportable for SecuRemote/SecureClient. Check this box to allow this gateway to export IKE properties to SecuRemote client machines. SecuRemote will not work in Traditional mode unless this box is checked.

Prior to NG FP3, the Exportable for SecuRemote/SecureClient option was located on the Topology tab of the Firewall object and could be enabled there.

Click Advanced to open the Advanced IKE Properties window, where you configure some SecureClient functionality; we will discuss this window in Chapter 10. The settings for the Advanced IKE properties were explained in Chapter 6. These settings can remain at their defaults when you're configuring SecuRemote; Note the settings that are selected by default.

EXERCISE 9.1

Configuring the Firewall Object for Traditional Mode

This exercise will show you how to prepare your Firewall object to accommodate SecuRemote connections using Traditional mode VPNs. This is an important part of configuring SecuRemote and helps you understand what needs to be enabled on the Firewall object. Follow these steps:

1. Go to the Firewall object and click on the VPN tab.

2. Click the Traditional Mode Configuration button.

3. Enable the Pre-Shared Secrets and Public Key Signatures options.

4. Check the Exportable for SecuRemote/SecureClient box.

5. Click Advanced to see the Advanced IKE Properties. Click OK.

6. Click OK on the Traditional Mode IKE Properties tab.

7. On the Authentication tab, make sure the authentication scheme used on your users is enabled.

8. Click OK on the Firewall object tab.

9. Install the security policy.

You've configured your Firewall object to accept SecuRemote connections. The next section discusses how to configure your Global Properties for SecuRemote.

Global Properties Configuration

Configuring the firewall for SecuRemote requires some Global Properties configuration. Under the Remote Access tab of the Global Properties, you can configure the firewall to accommodate SecuRemote connections. This tab has five more tabs related to remote access: VPN Basic, VPN Advanced, Certificates, Secure Configuration Verification, and Early Versions Compatibility. To configure SecuRemote, you'll be most concerned with using the Remote Access, VPN Basic, and VPN Advanced. If you plan to use certificates for authentication, you will also use the Certificates tab. Figure 9.10 shows the Remote Access tab.

Three of the five major sections on the Remote Access tab refer to SecuRemote and are explained in detail in the following sections.

Topology Update

The SecuRemote topology is updated either whenever SecuRemote is started or when the specified time has elapsed. This option doesn't need to be enabled and is disabled by default. The three topology update options are as follows:

Update Topology Every…Hours   If the specified time has elapsed since the last time SecuRemote was started, then the topology is updated the next time the SecuRemote session starts.

Automatic Update   If this option is enabled, the site will be updated after the key exchange without prompting the user to update.

Upon VPN-1 SecuRemote/SecureClient Start Up If this option is enabled, the user will be prompted to update the topology when the SecuRemote client starts.

FIGURE 9.10 Global Properties Remote Access tab

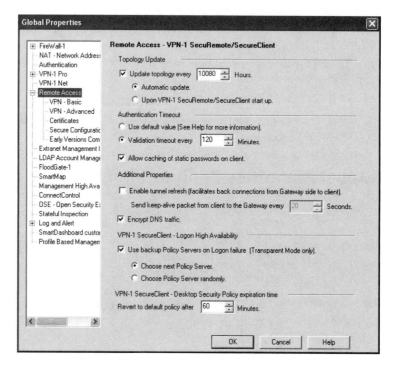

Authentication Timeout

This section of the Remote Access tab refers to the amount of time that passes before a SecuRemote user must re-authenticate. The options are as follows:

Use Default Value If this option is checked, certificate users will not need to re-authenticate. Static password and one-time password users will need to re-authenticate unless static passwords are allowed to be cached on the client (as discussed in a moment).

Validation Timeout Every…Minutes If this option is checked, users need to re-authenticate after the specified time. One-time password users will still need to re-authenticate with every gateway they encrypt with, regardless of this setting.

Allow Caching of Static Passwords on Client   If this option is checked, static passwords will be cached on the SecuRemote client machine and the user will not have to re-authenticate. Passwords will remain cached on the desktop until the user does one of the following:

- Selects Erase Passwords from the Passwords menu
- Selects Stop VPN-1 SecuRemote form the File menu
- Performs Disconnect in Connect mode
- Reboots the computer

Additional Properties

SecuRemote provides optional advanced features, including the following:

Enable Tunnel Refresh   If this option is enabled, SecuRemote will ping the firewall module with a keep-alive packet when the defined keep-alive period has expired (the default is 20 seconds). This process maintains session key information for the client and allows encrypted back connections so the client machine can remain idle for a longer period of time when connecting via SecuRemote or SecureClient.

Encrypt DNS Traffic   Enabling this feature will encrypt DNS traffic to secure internal DNS information. Most larger companies that have an elaborate DNS setup enable this feature.

The VPN-1 SecureClient Logon High Availability option and the VPN-1 Secure-Client Desktop Security Policy Expiration Time option will be discussed in Chapter 10 when we talk about SecureClient.

Remote Access VPN Basic and Advanced Options

Under the Remote Access tab are two VPN tabs: VPN Basic and VPN Advanced. The VPN Basic tab appears in Figure 9.11. The top portion of the tab relates to SecuRemote; you can enable the three types of authentication that are used with IKE encryption for Remote Access: Pre-Shared Secret, Public

Key Signatures, and Hybrid Mode. By checking the box next to an authentication method, you enable your firewalls to support that authentication method. (These authentication methods are discussed earlier in the chapter.)

FIGURE 9.11 Remote Access VPN Basic tab

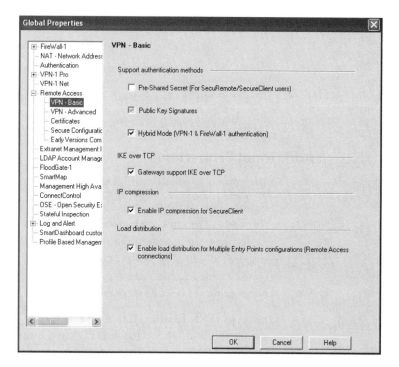

The Gateways Support IKE over TCP check box also relates to SecuRemote. Typical IKE negotiations occur using UDP packets. Using UDP can generate multiple IP fragments that can cause packet loss for SecuRemote clients using NAT. Certain NAT devices are not able to accommodate IP fragments, so packets will drop and SecuRemote communication will fail. If you enable gateways to use IKE over TCP, the phase 1 IKE negotiations will use TCP instead of UDP, so IP fragments will not be generated and communication loss will not occur.

The VPN Advanced tab, shown in Figure 9.12, allows you to configure the user encryption properties, the IKE security association properties, and the resolving mechanism. Setting the encryption and data integrity algorithms in the User Encryption Properties section lets you set encryption properties for all users. New users created in NG FP2 or newer will inherit the properties set in this window by default, whereas older versions will keep their original encryption settings. If the Enforce Encryption Algorithm and Data Integrity on All Users check box is selected, then the encryption set in each user's properties will not be used anymore and this will be the default setting for all users created in NG FP2 and beyond.

FIGURE 9.12 Remote Access VPN Advanced tab

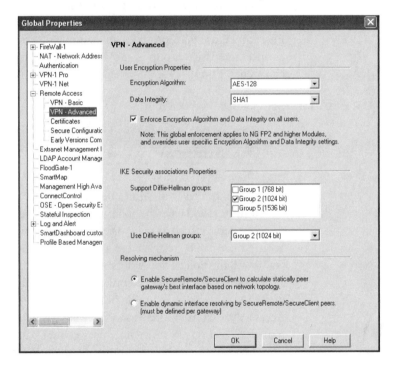

The IKE Security Association Properties section lets you choose which Diffie-Hellman group to use. As you learned in Chapter 6, the longer the key, the more secure you are—but more CPU-intensive computation is required.

You use the Resolving Mechanism section when you're dealing with multiple interfaces on multiple sites. This section allows you to enable SecuRemote to resolve an interface to communicate with either statically or dynamically. If you choose the dynamic option, you must enable this functionality on each gateway. This is a new NG FP3 feature and will not be used in this chapter.

Defining SecuRemote Rules

Now that you've configured the Firewall object and the Global Properties, you need to configure your rule base to accept SecuRemote connections. When you're creating a SecuRemote rule, the Source should be a group of SecuRemote users. The Destination is a network, a server, or a group of servers that is part of the encryption domain, behind the firewall.

For example, create a rule with the group of users you created earlier as the Source and a network or group of servers you want the client to connect to as the Destination. Use a Service value of Any and an Action value of Client Encrypt. Figure 9.13 provides an example of a SecuRemote rule where the SecuRemote Users group is allowed access to the Detroit-net network using client encryption.

FIGURE 9.13 Sample SecuRemote rule

NO.	SOURCE	DESTINATION	SERVICE	ACTION	TRACK
1	SecuRemoteUsers@Any	Detroit-net	✳ Any	Client Encrypt	Log

SecuRemote rules are quite flexible and can be very granular. As the administrator, you have the ability to restrict the SecuRemote group to a specific device or service such as mail, or to a specific network or group of servers. The Service value can be restricted to a specific service. After creating the rule, when you install the policy, you will be ready to accept SecuRemote connections.

SecuRemote can also be configured using the Simplified VPN mode. Figure 9.14 provides an example of the Participant User Groups in the Remote Access VPN Community Properties that can be used for SecuRemote in Simplified VPN mode. SecuRemote user groups can be added, removed, and edited within the VPN community. By default, the system creates a Remote-Access VPN icon, which can be configured for SecuRemote and added to the If Via column of a rule. Simplified VPNs are covered in more detail in Chapter 7, "Simplified VPNs."

The next section will show you how to install and configure the SecuRemote software. To follow along, either grab the Check Point NG FP3 CD or download the latest version of SecuRemote from the Check Point website.

FIGURE 9.14   Participant user groups using simplified VPNs

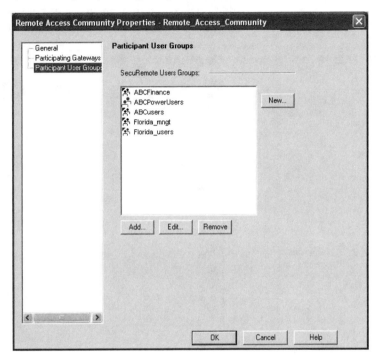

Installing SecuRemote

To be sure you have the latest version of SecuRemote, it's a good idea to download the package from the Check Point website. After that, the installation is quick and simple. Follow these steps:

1. After the welcome screen and the End User License Agreement (EULA), you are prompted with the location where you would like to install SecuRemote. Unless you have a major reason not to, choose the default location. The files are copied to your hard drive.

2. You are prompted with the important choice shown in Figure 9.15. Here you indicate which product you want to install. If you choose SecuRemote, your PC will act as a regular VPN client. If you choose to install SecureClient, your PC will have extra features that can download policies from a policy server and enforce a desktop security policy

on the machine. These additional features are useful, and there is an additional cost to implement them. For our purposes in this chapter, choose SecuRemote as shown in Figure 9.15.

FIGURE 9.15 Choosing SecuRemote or SecureClient

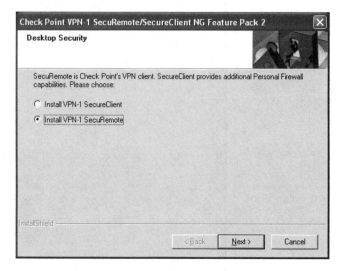

3. The next screen asks if you want to install SecuRemote on all the network adapters or just dial-up adapters. With the many uses of a laptop or desktop these days, Internet access is not limited to dial-up; so, it's a good idea to select all network adapters. The software will install and then prompt you to reboot.

After rebooting, SecuRemote is installed on your PC. The SecuRemote client is made up of a kernel module and a daemon. The kernel module is installed between the TCP/IP stack and the NIC driver; it filters all TCP/IP communication that passes through the PC. The daemon runs on the client machine as a graphical interface for the user to configure, to facilitate communication. SecureClient operates in the same fashion but can also stop or block packets through an enforced policy.

Now that you've successfully installed SecuRemote, you can play with it and learn about its features. The next section teaches you how to configure the SecuRemote software for client-to-firewall VPNs.

Setting Up the SecuRemote Site

Once you reboot your machine after installation, you will notice the SecuRemote software running in your system tray. (It looks like an envelope with a key in it.) If you click on it, a blank window will pop up. In this window, shown in Figure 9.16, you can create your SecuRemote sites. A SecuRemote site is a firewall running VPN software that is configured to accept SecuRemote traffic.

FIGURE 9.16 Blank SecuRemote client

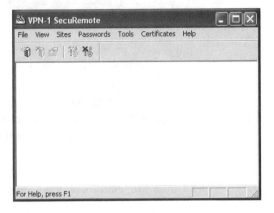

Click on the Sites menu, and you will have an option to create a new SecuRemote site. To create a site, add the IP address or host name into the Create New window and click OK.

When the client connects to the site or to a host within the encryption domain of the site, the SecuRemote daemon holds the first packet without transmitting it. This packet is examined to determine the relevant site and the VPN-1 Module in the site. The site will challenge you for authentication; upon successful authentication, the daemon will initiate a key exchange with the site. After the keys are exchanged, the first packet is encrypted and transmitted.

This process is transparent to the user. For the user, after successful authentication, the topology of the site is downloaded to the userc.C file and the VPN has begun. The user will only see the graphical representation of the site in the software.

You can create multiple sites in the SecuRemote software to let the user have a client VPN with multiple firewalls, but only one site can be enabled at a time. If you have more than one site, the others must be disabled when you are participating in a client-to-site VPN. These topologies are stored in the userc.C file on each client machine.

EXERCISE 9.2

Creating a SecuRemote Site

In this exercise, you will create a SecuRemote site. In addition to creating a site, this exercise will show you a couple of buttons that will teach you how to maneuver through the SecuRemote GUI. After creating a site, the best way to learn the ins and outs of the SecuRemote GUI is to play with it. This exercise requires a firewall that is configured to accept SecuRemote connections. Follow these steps:

1. Click Sites ➢ Create New.

2. Enter the IP address of your firewall in the Create New window.

3. As it connects, you will be challenged for authentication. Type in your username and password.

4. After successful authentication, your site will be created. Click the Update button to update your topology and see the time change in the Last Updated window. Click OK.

5. Your site's icon will appear in the SecuRemote window. Right-click on it to see the menu that appears. Choose Disable to disable the site; a red X appears on the site's icon.

It will be helpful to understand what the SecuRemote software does and what features are available to you as the administrator. The next section gives an orientation to the SecuRemote menus.

Understanding the SecuRemote Software Menus

This section lists the important menu options in the SecuRemote software and explains the important parts of each menu option. Under each menu option are multiple commands, which are defined here. In addition, for some options we provide instances where you might use the function.

Sites Menu

Under the Sites menu, shown in Figure 9.17, are options that let you create new sites, update your existing sites, disable a site, or delete a site. These features help you maintain multiple sites while using SecuRemote.

FIGURE 9.17   SecuRemote Sites menu

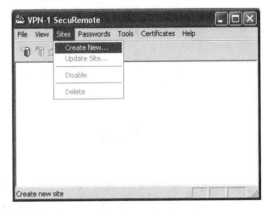

The menu options are as follows:

Create New   Creates a new site. In order to create a new site, the user must be able to connect to the site and authenticate. Otherwise, the topology cannot be downloaded and the site cannot be created.

Update Site   Updates a topology. You only need to update your topology when changes have occurred; otherwise, a user can go weeks without updating.

Disable   Stops the use of a site that has been created. You can disable a site if you have more than one site. When you are connected to one of your sites, the other sites must be disabled for the connection to occur. This can happen manually (using the menu option) or automatically.

Delete   Deletes a site that has been created. If you no longer need to connect to a site, you can delete it.

Passwords Menu

In the Passwords menu, shown in Figure 9.18, the options allow a user to maintain their password information:

FIGURE 9.18   SecuRemote Passwords menu

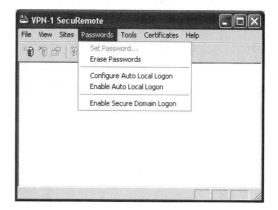

Set Password   Sets a new password to be used for the next authentication.

Erase Passwords   Removes all passwords from the SecuRemote software's memory.

Configure Auto Local Logon   Lets you configure single signon so that one username and password can log you into your Windows domain and the SecuRemote software. Figure 9.19 illustrates the screen that appears when you choose to configure auto logon.

FIGURE 9.19   Auto Logon configuration

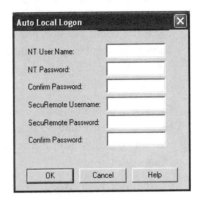

Enable Auto Local Logon   Enables or disables the single signon feature.

Enable Secure Domain Logon   Lets you remotely log in to your Windows domain and your SecuRemote software using auto logon.

Tools Menu

In the Tools menu, shown in Figure 9.20, you have options to configure IKE properties, rebind adapters, configure Client mode, or launch SecureClient diagnostics. A basic SecuRemote user will not use most of these features; an administrator or advanced SecuRemote user will generally use these tools:

FIGURE 9.20   SecuRemote Tools menu

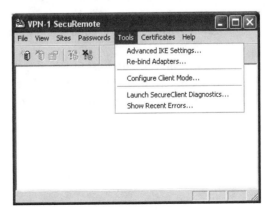

Advanced IKE Settings Lets you force UDP encapsulation and/or support IKE over TCP. UDP encapsulation is used to prevent encryption failure if the client is using NAT. If IKE passes over TCP, it provides better communication than passing over UDP by overcoming issues with IP fragments; it may also enhance the SecuRemote connection if it's passing through NAT.

Re-Bind Adapters Used if you have removed or added a network adapter because you installed SecuRemote. You will need to rebind the adapters when a change occurs so the SecuRemote kernel can work with a new or changed NIC.

Configure Client Mode Lets you use either Transparent Client mode or Connect Client mode. Transparent is the traditional mode in which SecuRemote authenticate a user against a VPN-1 gateway and provide client-to-firewall encryption. Connect mode can be set to either a disconnected or connected state. The disconnected state allows a user to run SecuRemote idle while not encrypting with a gateway. The connected state enables the user to run SecuRemote without encryption, but the ability to encrypt with a VPN-1 gateway is available.

Launch SecureClient Diagnostics Discussed in the next chapter.

Show Recent Errors Shows a log of errors that have occurred using SecuRemote.

The Certificates menu is used to configure Check Point or Entrust certificates. If the SecuRemote user will be using certificates to authenticate, the certificates can be created, recovered, or configured here.

Now that you understand the SecuRemote menu options, it's time to look at the practical nature of the product. There are many considerations with dealing with SecuRemote in a real-world deployment, and we'll discuss some of these issues in the next section.

Deploying SecuRemote

Some companies have hundreds or thousands of SecuRemote clients that are currently connecting to an older version of VPN-1/FireWall-1. Backward compatibility is needed for these existing SecuRemote configurations. SecuRemote and SecureClient version 4.1 will work with FireWall-1 4.1, Policy Server 4.1, or FireWall-1 NG. This compatibility is helpful because you can upgrade your firewall to NG without worrying about the SecuRemote clients running a 4.1 version.

SecuRemote and SecureClient NG will work with FireWall-1 4.1. SecureClient NG will only work with Policy Server NG. If you have a large number of SecuRemote clients already in existence, the availability of backward compatibility makes it easier to upgrade to Check Point NG. With backward compatibility, all clients don't have to be upgraded before you upgrade the firewalls.

 Real World Scenario

SecuRemote/SecureClient NG Packaging Tool

When you're dealing with a SecuRemote deployment, you must consider many factors. For example, if you have 500 users, you may wonder how you can install the SecuRemote software on every machine on your network. And, once you get all the clients installed, how can you configure the software or have each user configure it properly? The answer lies in using the SecuRemote/SecureClient NG packaging tool. This packaging tool is an application that allows administrators to create a SecuRemote or Secure-Client installation package with the proper site information and attributes pre-configured for each user.

Using the tool, the administrator creates a self-extracting package and distributes it to each user. The user runs the executable package, and after rebooting, SecuRemote will be installed. Without reconfiguring anything, the user just updates the topology—and the client machine is ready to encrypt with SecuRemote.

Summary

SecuRemote allows users to work from home or on the road in a secure manner by encrypting communication from a PC to a VPN-1 gateway over the Internet. The SecuRemote software runs on a client machine between the TCP/IP protocol and the NIC and allows a user to create multiple sites to VPN to. The SecuRemote license resides on the VPN-1 gateway; no additional license is required on the client PC.

Setting up SecuRemote on the firewall requires configuration on the Firewall object, in the Global Properties, and in the rule base. SecuRemote NG FP1 and later versions support IKE encryption, whereas earlier versions also supported FWZ encryption.

You configure the SecuRemote client software by creating a site that points to a specific VPN gateway. The gateway challenges the user for authentication, and then keys are exchanged to set up a client-to-firewall VPN. The software also allows you to set up automatic logon and secure domain logon; you can store your Windows password in the SecuRemote software and log in to your Windows domain securely from a remote location by using one username and password.

Deployment of SecuRemote is easier with the SecureClient NG packaging tool. You can create pre-configured, self-extracting packages and distribute them to many client machines to automate the software distribution. Backward compatibility exists between SecuRemote 4.1 and NG; so, in a company that has existing SecuRemote 4.1 clients, there is no urgent need to upgrade every client to SecuRemote NG.

Exam Essentials

Understand how SecuRemote works and its uses.   It's imperative to understand how SecuRemote works before you configure it. It's also a good idea to understand client VPN technology and its functional uses.

Know how to configure the firewall to accommodate SecuRemote. Know the different settings that you must configure on the Firewall object and in the Global Properties. Understand how to configure the rule base to accommodate SecuRemote connections.

Know how to configure the SecuRemote client software.   By understanding the SecuRemote software and being aware of its functionality, you will be able to use the product to its fullest potential. Know how to operate SecuRemote. Know the menu options and what they can do.

Understand the SecureClient NG packaging tool.   Understand what the SecureClient packaging tool does. This tool can simplify the deployment of many SecuRemote packages.

Key Terms

Before you take the exam, be certain you are familiar with the following terms:

certificate revocation list (CRL)	topology
client-to-site	userc.C
SecuRemote site	

Review Questions

1. What needs to be enabled on the Topology tab of the Firewall object?

   A. Authentication

   B. IKE VPNs

   C. Hybrid Mode

   D. Exportable for SecuRemote/SecureClient

   E. UDP Encapsulation

2. Which tab in the Global Properties is the primary place where SecuRemote settings can be configured?

   A. SecuRemote

   B. VPN

   C. Remote Access

   D. Remote VPN

   E. VPN-1 Net

3. Where does the SecuRemote software install on the client machine?

   A. In the Application layer

   B. Between the TCP/IP protocol and the NIC

   C. Between the modem and the NIC

   D. Between the OS and the RAM

   E. In RAM

4. When setting up rules in the rule base for SecuRemote, what should be in the Source column?

    A. Network object

    B. Service

    C. Firewall object

    D. Workstation object

    E. User group

5. If you are using FireWall-1 Password as a SecuRemote authentication scheme, where must you enable it to be sure it is supported?

    A. In Global Properties

    B. In the rule base

    C. On the Firewall or Cluster object

    D. In the VPN properties

    E. None of the above

6. Which file is stored on the SecuRemote machine and contains topology information?

    A. userc.C

    B. Groups

    C. GUI-clients

    D. objects.C

    E. rulebases.fws

7. Which encryption scheme do SecuRemote NG FP1 and later versions support?

   A. Skip

   B. Blowfish

   C. IKE

   D. FWZ

   E. IDEA

8. Which data integrity algorithms does VPN-1 support for SecuRemote encryption? (Choose all that apply.)

   A. MD4

   B. SHA-1

   C. MD5

   D. All of the above

   E. None of the above

9. Which of the following requires users to re-authenticate after the specified timeout?

   A. Validation Timeout

   B. SecuRemote Timeout

   C. Re-authentication Timeout

   D. Topology Timeout

   E. None of the above

10. Which of the following needs to be enabled on the VPN Basic tab in the GlobalProperties to allow you to use SecuRemote with all of the Check Point supported authentication schemes?

A. Pre-shared Secret

B. Hybrid Mode

C. Public Key Signatures

D. Gateways support IKE over TCP

E. All of the above

11. Which of the following does IKE over TCP overcome when running SecuRemote behind a NATed connection? (Choose all that apply.)

A. IP fragments

B. Phase I

C. Phase II

D. NAT

E. All of the above

12. If static passwords are cached, passwords will be cached until the user does which of the following? (Choose all that apply.)

A. Reboots the computer

B. Selects Stop VPN-1 SecuRemote from the File menu

C. Selects Erase Passwords from the Passwords menu

D. Performs Disconnect in Connect mode

E. All of the above

13. Where should the license be installed for SecuRemote to function properly?

    A. On each SecuRemote client

    B. On the VPN-1 gateway

    C. On both the client and the firewall

    D. On the SmartCenter Server, the client, and the firewall

    E. None of the above

14. How does Check Point NG make the deployment of SecuRemote easier? (Choose all that apply.)

    A. Provides multiple CDs with the software

    B. The SecureClient packaging tool

    C. The Secure Remote installation tool

    D. None of the above

    E. All of the above

15. Where are the IKE settings configured for SecuRemote? (Choose all that apply.)

    A. On the VPN Advanced tab under Remote Access in the Global Properties

    B. On the VPN-1 Pro tab in the Global Properties

    C. On the VPN-1 Net tab in the Global Properties

    D. On the Firewall object

    E. All of the above

16. When choosing Diffie-Hellman groups, what must be considered? (Choose all that apply.)

    A. Shorter length is more secure.

    B. Longer length is more secure.

    C. Longer length is less math intensive.

    D. Longer length is more math intensive.

    E. Shorter length is more math intensive.

17. When a site is first created, what happens on the SecuRemote client screen?

    A. The user has VPN access.

    B. The user has cleartext access.

    C. The user is challenged for authentication.

    D. The user is prompted to reboot the machine.

    E. None of the above.

18. When would you rebind adapters in your SecuRemote software? (Choose all that apply.)

    A. When you install a new modem

    B. When you add a wireless NIC to your laptop

    C. When you reboot your machine

    D. When you install new software

    E. None of the above

19. What does the Auto Local Logon option do for you?

    A. Enables you to automate SecuRemote

    B. Enables you to automatically create a VPN

    C. Enables you to automatically log on

    D. Enables you to store your Windows password and use it like a single-signon device

    E. None of the above

20. What does the Enable Secure Domain Logon feature do? (Choose all that apply.)

    A. Allows you to secure your domain

    B. Allows you to securely log in to your Windows domain

    C. Allows you to use single signon

    D. Allows your Windows domain to be used with SecuRemote

    E. All of the above

Answers to Review Questions

1. D.   The box at the bottom of the Topology tab of the VPN-1 firewall that enables Exportable SecuRemote and SecureClient connections must be checked. This same setting existed in previous versions of FireWall-1 but was not found on the topology tab of the Firewall object.

2. C.   The Remote Access tab is the primary tab; it has three tabs under it. Here, you configure most of the Global Properties for SecuRemote. If you're using certificates or MEP, the VPN-1 Pro tab has some CRL settings, but that choice was not offered.

3. B.   The SecuRemote software operates between the TCP/IP protocol stack and the NIC driver. It's important to understand this, to realize how the software works in Windows.

4. E.   A group of SecuRemote users should be in the Source column of your SecuRemote rule. The Destination column can contain a Network object or a Workstation object. The Service column can contain a service.

5. C.   The Firewall object must have the encryption scheme enabled for SecuRemote to work. In fact, you can have multiple users configured to use different authentication schemes, and the Firewall object must have each authentication scheme enabled for them all to work. If your firewalls are in a cluster, the authentication will be enabled on the Cluster object.

6. A.   The `userc.C` file holds the topology information for all the sites that are created in the SecuRemote client software. The topology includes network and encryption domain information.

7. C.   SecuRemote prior to NG FP1 supported both IKE and FWZ. In newer versions of SecuRemote, only IKE is supported because it is the most widely used encryption scheme.

8. B, C.   The firewall supports MD5 and SHA-1 data integrity algorithms for all encryption. MD4 is supported for S/Key authentication but not for encryption.

9. A.   The Validation Timeout setting on the Remote Access tab in the Global Properties allows you to specify a timeout in minutes after which SecuRemote users must re-authenticate. This timeout can help alleviate the possibility of a user walking away from their computer and allowing someone else to connect to a VPN.

10. B.   If you plan to use Check Point supported authentication schemes for SecuRemote, you need to enable Hybrid mode on the VPN Basic tab of the Global Properties.

11. A.   When running SecuRemote behind a NAT device, UDP's IP fragments cause packet loss. By running IKE over TCP, issues with IP fragments are solved.

12. E.   If static passwords are enabled to be cached in the Global Properties, they will remain cached unless the user does something to remove them from the cache. These answers are the four ways to remove passwords from the cache.

13. B.   The license resides on the VPN-1 gateway. No license is needed for each client, which makes SecuRemote much easier to manage.

14. B.   The SecureClient packaging tool allows you to customize a preconfigured, self-extracting package and distribute it to multiple users. Doing so can help you not only distribute the package quickly, but also avoid user errors during installation.

15. A, D.   User encryption properties are configured on the VPN Advanced tab under Remote Access in the Global Properties, and firewall encryption properties are configured on the VPN tab of the Firewall object. Together, they configure SecuRemote IKE settings.

16. B, D.   The longer the key length, the more secure—but also the more math intensive. It is not always beneficial to choose the greatest key length algorithm, because that key length will take more CPU-intensive math to compute.

17. C.   The user is challenged for authentication when a site is first created on the SecuRemote software. This step makes sure that anybody with the SecuRemote software cannot randomly VPN into a firewall and gain remote access.

18. A, B.   You should rebind adapters when you have added or removed a network adapter. If you add a new modem or a NIC, you should rebind adapters so that SecuRemote can run properly when you use those devices.

19. D.   Auto logon was called single signon in previous versions of SecuRemote. This feature lets you store your Windows password and use it as a single signon product in conjunction with the Secure Domain Logon feature.

20. B.   The Enable Secure Domain Logon option lets you use SecuRemote to securely log in to your Windows domain. This feature is used in conjunction with the Auto Logon feature and enables a user to log in to their Windows domain from a remote Internet location.

Chapter 10

SecureClient, the Policy Server, and Clientless VPNs

THE CCSE EXAM TOPICS COVERED IN THIS CHAPTER INCLUDE:

- ✓ The SecuRemote/SecureClient Packaging Tool.
- ✓ Client encryption within the LAN.
- ✓ Configuring workstation properties for Policy Server.
- ✓ Configuring a SecureClient and Policy Server rule base.
- ✓ Installing and utilizing SecureClient.

n Chapter 9, we discussed SecuRemote: what it does, how it works, and how to configure it. In addition, you briefly learned about SecureClient, another product that provides functionality beyond SecuRemote. SecureClient adds desktop security to the Client VPN by connecting to a *Policy Server,* which issues a Security Policy to a SecureClient machine. The Policy Server is a Check Point component that runs on the NG firewall; it issues a *Desktop policy*, which protects the user's machine from potential threats. For example, when a SecureClient machine logs into a Policy Server, a Desktop policy is downloaded to the machine that can be configured to not accept incoming connections or to only allow outgoing connections. This policy prevents potential incoming attacks from exploiting the client machine and accessing information, or infecting the client with a virus and spreading it through the VPN.

The use of SecureClient takes Client VPN technology to another level with its policy enforcement capability. In addition to remote uses outside the LAN, SecureClient can be used on the local LAN to enforce Desktop Security Policies on internal client machines. Not only can SecureClient machines be protected from incoming connections with a Desktop policy, but—depending on the rules you create—internal LAN traffic can be encrypted to protect it from internal traffic sniffing.

In this chapter, you will learn what a Policy Server is and how it works in conjunction with SecureClient. You will see how SecureClient is configured and how to create, install, and manage Desktop policies. You will learn about Clientless VPNs and the advantages and disadvantages of using them instead of IPSec-based Client VPNs. You will also gain an understanding of how to configure all this functionality in Check Point NG. The next section will begin your journey by explaining what a Policy Server is.

Before we begin, let's briefly summarize the different remote access technologies available in Check Point NG:

- SecuRemote provides an IPSec-based VPN from a desktop to a firewall to prevent information from being compromised.

- SecureClient does what SecuRemote does and also downloads a Desktop policy from a Policy Server while participating in a client-to-site VPN, to prevent the client machine from being compromised.

- Clientless VPNs provide SSL-based VPNs for remote access to web-based applications and do not require special software.

What Is the Policy Server?

A Policy Server is a Check Point NG component that runs on a VPN-1/FireWall-1 Module. It's called a Policy Server because it allows an administrator to centrally manage desktop security by issuing a Desktop policy to SecureClient machines. The Desktop policy can be enforced on machines inside and outside a LAN, to prevent authorized connections from being compromised. In addition to enforcing a Desktop policy, the Policy Server adds security by authenticating and authorizing users, verifying memberships to user groups, and verifying secure configuration of SecureClient machines.

Figure 10.1 provides an example of how machines with SecureClient are protected from unauthorized connections. Once the SecureClient machines connect to the Policy Server and download a Desktop policy, connections that are unauthorized or not allowed by the Desktop policy will be dropped. In Figure 10.1, as the unauthorized user tries to connect to the other machines on the network, the SecureClient machines can block the connection. Meanwhile, the machine without SecureClient is open to the unauthorized attack.

FIGURE 10.1   How SecureClient works

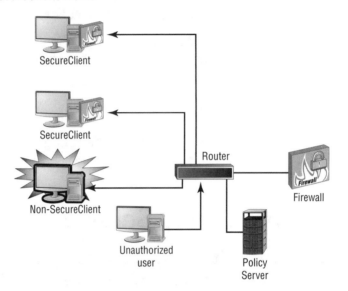

> ## ⊕ Real World Scenario
>
> ### Using SecureClient Internally
>
> More than 70% of computer attacks happen within the corporate LAN. These attacks are usually executed by malicious authorized users and are usually more successful than outside attacks because they are not expected. For this reason, some companies are deploying SecureClient within the corporate network to protect confidential data.
>
> A company may have confidential or top-secret data on servers that are protected behind a firewall and Policy Server. An administrator can set up the Policy Server so that only certain machines can access this information. If you use SecureClient with a Desktop policy enforced, you can secure your network and host machines. The information is secure when it passes across the network because it is encrypted, and the Desktop is secure because the SecureClient software enforces the Desktop policy. A curious coworker will not be able to sniff the data coming from the machine and also will not be able to access any information on the Desktop because of the Desktop policy. All information that passes between the firewall and the SecureClient machine is completely secure.

Now that you understand what the Check Point NG Policy Server is and what it does, let's look further into its technical nature. We'll discuss licensing and configuration as well as the Policy Server daemon and the files that make it work.

Licensing the Policy Server and SecureClient

It's important to understand the licensing process for the Policy Server and SecureClient. The SecureClient license is located on the SmartCenter Server and is based on the number of SecureClient users you have. The Policy Server license is located on each Policy Server and is independent of the number of users.

All SecureClient licenses contain one Policy Server license, so additional Policy Server licenses are necessary only when multiple Policy Servers are deployed. This arrangement is different from the way licensing worked in VPN-1 4.1. The NG method is more scalable for Policy Server High Availability implementations. NG includes another new feature: The Policy Server can run on gateway clusters.

The Policy Server can be installed on a Windows, Solaris, Linux, or IPSO platform. Just like the VPN-1/FireWall-1 package, the Policy Server must be installed or uninstalled in a certain order. The Policy Server must be installed on an existing FireWall Module. When you're uninstalling the Policy Server, it must be removed before the VPN-1/FireWall-1 package, which is removed before the SVN Foundation package.

Configuring the Firewall Object as a Policy Server

The Policy Server is installed on a firewall and configured in the SmartDashboard GUI on the Firewall or Cluster object. The first step in configuring the Policy Server is to enable it on the General Properties tab of the Firewall object. Figure 10.2 shows the General Properties tab of a Firewall object that has the SecureClient Policy Server component enabled on it.

FIGURE 10.2 Firewall object with Policy Server enabled

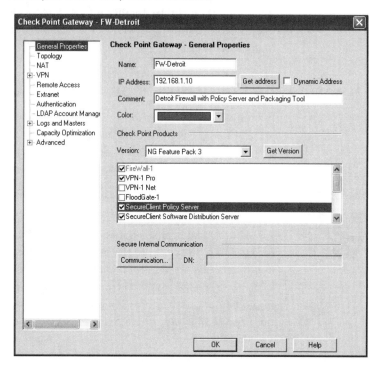

After selecting Policy Server on the Firewall object's General Properties tab, go to the Firewall object's Authentication tab and define a group of SecureClient users. This group must be created to identify users who will be logging in to the Policy Server from SecureClient. The group must include all users of SecureClient.

Figure 10.3 shows the Authentication tab with a SecureClient group selected. This group was created before enabling the Policy Server. Notice that you can click the New button and create a new group on the fly if a group is not already created. While you're on the Authentication tab, you can enable all the authentication schemes you plan to use with SecureClient.

FIGURE 10.3   Firewall object Authentication tab

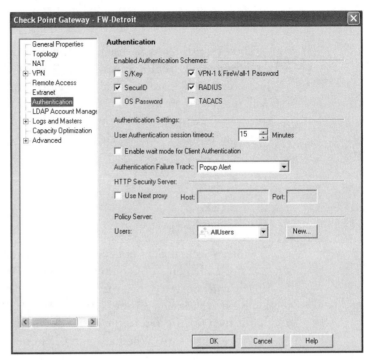

Now that you understand how to create the Policy Server in the Smart-Dashboard, let's explore how the Policy Server works.

How the Policy Server Works

The Policy Server daemon (process) is called *dtps*. It is active after the Policy Server is configured and the Security Policy is successfully installed. The dtps daemon (**dtps.exe** in Windows) will stop if the FireWall-1 service is stopped or killed. The dtps service consists of three threads:

Main Thread   The main thread is responsible for initialization and creation of the tftp and policy install threads. It creates the group files.

tftp Thread   The tftp thread is responsible for communication with the Desktop, sending files, and fetching logs. It notifies the main thread to prepare the group file when a user logs on.

Policy Install Thread The policy install thread communicates with the Check Point daemon (cpd) and notifies it when a new policy arrives or when the database is updated.

These three threads are used to create, communicate, and process the necessary resources to enforce Desktop policies on all the machines in the WAN. Just as certain files are involved when enforcing a Security Policy on the FireWall module, there are files needed that store the information necessary to enforce a Desktop policy on the SecureClient machine. Four major files are downloaded to the desktop client:

- `local.dt`
- `local.scv`
- `local.lp`
- `group_file`

When a SecureClient policy is configured and saved, the information is saved to a file named `Standard.S` in the `$FWDIR/conf` directory on the SmartCenter Server. When the policy is installed, the `Standard.S` file is compiled to a file called `local.dt`. The `local.dt` file is a pseudo-inspect file that is then transferred to the Policy Server in the `$FWDIR/state/local/Policies` directory. When a SecureClient machine logs in to the Policy Server, the client downloads the `local.dt` file, loads it into the SecureClient's kernel, and provides the Desktop policy and topology information to the SecureClient software. This information indicates what sites to connect to and the Policy Servers from which to download a policy. The Desktop policy is used to enforce the Security Policy on the SecureClient.

The `group_file` is downloaded from the Policy Server and also stored in the SecureClient's kernel to determine the rules that are applicable to the user who is logged on. The Desktop policy will only enforce the policy applicable to the logged-on user. Each time a SecureClient logs on to the Policy Server, the `group_file` is downloaded.

The `local.lp` file defines how the SecureClient will log events and upload them to the Policy Server.

The downloaded files are located in the `\SecuRemote\Policy` directory. (The full path is usually under the `c:\Program Files\CheckPoint\SecuRemote\Policy` directory in Windows.) When the SecureClient logs on, all the files that have changed are downloaded and updated on the SecureClient machine. If the files are deleted, logging in to the Policy Server fetches all the files.

The `local.scv` file will be discussed in the next section. The next section discusses how the Policy Server ensures that the SecureClient machine is secure.

Secure Configuration Verification (SCV)

Secure Configuration Verification (SCV) is a mechanism that determines whether the SecureClient machine is securely configured (clean) or not securely configured (dirty). SCV makes sure SecureClient machines that are attempting to VPN with the firewall are protected by the Policy Server's policy and their security is not being compromised.

The SCV process is done with an *SCV Manager* component running on the Policy Server. The SCV Manager is responsible for configuration and maintenance of the SCV state from all *SCV plug-ins*. SCV plug-ins are DLLs registered with SecureClient; they contain functions that can notify the SCV Manager of the DLL's state. When the SCV Manager wants SCV status, it queries all registered SCV plug-ins about the SCV state for which they are responsible. If all SCV plug-ins indicate that the machine is securely configured, the SCV Manager sets the general SCV state to "securely configured." Otherwise, it considers the SecureClient machine to be not secure. One of the files that carries the SCV information is `local.scv`; it is stored on the SecureClient machine with its other configuration files.

Future versions of SCV will support Check Point NG and third-party SCV plug-ins such as Open Platform for Security (OPSEC) products. Administrators will be able to configure both the SCV plug-ins and the SCV checks. Doing so will help the administrator customize the SCV operation and gain more control over the SecureClient machine.

The next section discusses SecureClient, its deployment, and the SecureClient Packaging Tool.

Understanding SecureClient

SecureClient is the same software as SecuRemote, with added functionality. Just as with SecuRemote, the client-to-site VPNs created with SecureClient use IPSec-based encryption. The major difference in using the SecureClient graphical interface (shown in Figure 10.4) is the Policy menu, which helps users interact with the Policy Server. Most of the other menu options are the same as in SecuRemote and are defined in Chapter 9.

The installation of SecureClient is similar to the SecuRemote installation, explained in Chapter 9. The only difference is the selection of the default SecureClient with desktop security, instead of SecuRemote. However, despite the similarity in the GUI interface and the installation, SecureClient provides greater functionality than SecuRemote with its desktop security.

FIGURE 10.4 SecureClient Policy menu

As you can see in Figure 10.4, an option in the Policy menu lets you log on to a Policy Server. When you choose the Logon to Policy Server option, a list of the installed Policy Servers is displayed as a submenu; you can then choose a Policy Server to log on to. When the SecureClient user logs on to the Policy Server, the Desktop policy is downloaded to the SecureClient machine.

The logon occurs as either an *implicit logon* or an *explicit logon*. During an implicit logon, a Desktop policy is automatically installed on the SecureClient machine when the client authenticates. During an explicit logon, you click the Update button to update the Desktop policy. The logon is considered explicit because you initiate the download and are prompted to specify whether you would like to download a Desktop policy. The policy is downloaded only when you add or update a site that contains a Policy Server.

The Policy menu lets you disable a Desktop policy. If a Desktop policy is required by a Policy Server and you disable the policy, you will not be able to VPN with the firewall until you log on again and a new policy is issued to the client. If you disable the policy while participating in a VPN, the VPN will continue, and the change will take effect after you restart SecureClient.

SecureClient does not support IP forwarding. IP forwarding may be enabled to forward packets to another NIC on a machine. When IP forwarding is detected, a warning message is shown to the user. If you are implementing SecureClient, be sure you off turn IP forwarding.

System Tray Icons

You'll recall the envelope and key icon in the Windows System Tray from the SecuRemote configuration in Chapter 9. In SecureClient, the icon in the System Tray has four variations. These icons in the bottom-right corner of the Windows machine can be a helpful status indicator to the user. When using SecureClient, the envelope and key icon indicates that a Desktop policy has not been enforced. SecureClient adds three additional system tray icons that are represented by different locks on the original envelope and key to illustrate the secure state of the SecureClient machine:

Blue Lock with Red Ribbon   A default or user-specific Desktop policy is being enforced and the security of the SecureClient machine has been verified by SCV.

Blue Lock   A default or user-specific Desktop policy is being enforced. If the blue lock is flashing, then the SecureClient is logging on to the Policy Server.

Red Lock   A packet has been dropped or rejected by the Desktop policy. The attack is tracked as a Log or Alert.

Using the System Tray Icons

When you're using SecureClient from home or on the road, you can look at the icon in the System Tray of your machine to see the status of your SecureClient connection. If the icon has a blue lock with a red ribbon, then you know the machine is logged in to the Policy Server, a Desktop policy is being enforced, and the SecureClient configuration has been verified by the SCV mechanism. If your SecureClient icon turns red, packets are being dropped by SecureClient, and you may be under attack. If the icon repeatedly turns red, you know something is trying to connect, and you can take action.

SecureClient Connect Mode

SecureClient *Connect Mode* allows an administrator to ease the user's interaction with SecureClient by configuring *connection profiles*. Connection profiles contain site, preferred gateway, and preferred Policy Server information. They are configured through the Connection Profile Properties window shown in Figure 10.5. You access this window by choosing Manage ➢ Remote Access ➢ Connection Profiles from the SmartDashboard menu. Then, click New and choose Connection Profile to create a new profile.

FIGURE 10.5 General Connection Profile Properties

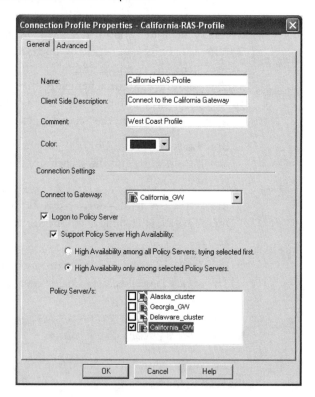

At the top of the General tab, you can fill in the name, comment(s), and color. The Client Side Description is a description the user will see, and the Comment is a note directed toward administrators. The Connection Settings portion of the window allows you to choose the gateway to connect to and enable Policy Server logon and Policy Server high availability.

NOTE Policy Server High Availability, also shown on the General tab, will not be discussed in this book.

The Advanced tab of the Connection Profile Properties is shown in Figure 10.6. This tab lets you enable different features of SecureClient: Support Office Mode, Support IKE over TCP, and UDP Encapsulation. These features are part of the SecuRemote and SecureClient configuration. We'll discuss Office Mode in the next section of this chapter; IKE over TCP and UDP Encapsulation were explained in Chapter 9.

FIGURE 10.6 Advanced Connection Profile Properties

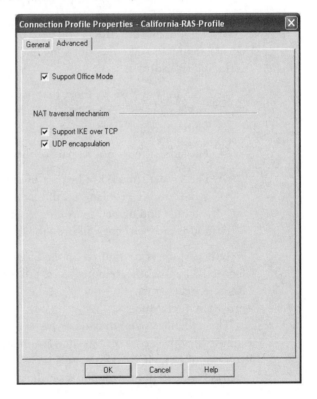

A remote user can use these connection profiles to connect to different Policy Servers for different needs. For example, if a remote user travels to California, the user can use the California connection profile. When the same user travels to New York, the user can use the New York profile. The user can choose the connection profile by right-clicking the icon, selecting which firewall and Policy Server to connect and authenticate to, and then clicking the Connect button.

SecureClient Office Mode

SecureClient Office Mode allows administrators to assign internal IP addresses to SecureClient users. It's called Office Mode because when the SecureClient machine is assigned an internal IP address, the machine can act as if it is on the internal LAN. The SecureClient user's remote access will not seem remote; it will seem as though the user is in the office, and the user will be able to browse the network using internal DNS and WINS services. This ability will benefit the user in accessing the resources on the corporate LAN.

To configure Office Mode, you need to assign internal IP addresses to the clients. You must take the following guidelines into consideration when assigning IP addresses:

- You must choose a subnet that is outside the internal network. All traffic from the internal network to addresses in the subnet must be routed through the firewall gateway.

- The subnet must not be part of the gateway's encryption domain.

- The subnet should not be part of the client's physical network. To avoid routing problems on the client side, assign IP addresses that are routable and owned by you or assign private, non-routable IP addresses the client will probably not use.

Office Mode is configured on the Firewall object's Remote Access tab. Figure 10.7 shows the Remote Access tab. After enabling Office Mode on the Remote Access tab, you can choose a group of users to which you want to provide Office Mode.

This tab allows you to choose the method you would like to use to distribute IP addresses. You can choose a manual approach, using IP pools, or you can offer DHCP and specify a DHCP server. If you choose the manual method with IP pools, you must set the duration of the IP lease.

FIGURE 10.7   Remote Access tab for Office Mode

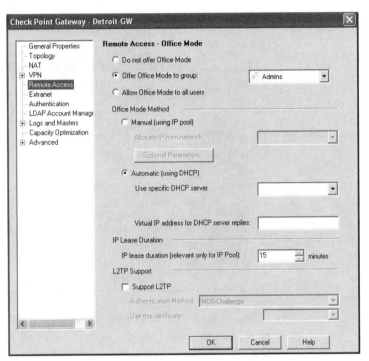

SecureClient Logging

It's beneficial to be able to monitor activity when using SecureClient. New additions to Check Point NG let you log SecureClient events two ways:

VPN-1/FireWall-1 Logs   The FireWall-1 log in the SmartView Tracker provides connection information. You can see when a user logged in, the IP address from which they logged in, and what they are accessing through the VPN.

SecureClient Log Viewer   This feature is new to Check Point NG and helps administrators and users monitor events on SecureClient machines for troubleshooting. SecureClient logs provide internal messages that are specific to each client machine. Logs are generated for rules that are marked for logging in the Desktop Security Policy. The Log Viewer will log Policy Server communication, connections that pass through the SecureClient kernel, and SCV state. Figure 10.8 shows the SecureClient Log Viewer.

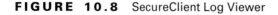

FIGURE 10.8 SecureClient Log Viewer

Figure 10.8 illustrates that you can see date, time, direction, and other pertinent information in the SecureClient Log Viewer. This information can help a user or administrator see what Desktop policy is being enforced and what connections are blocked and accepted. In a troubleshooting situation, an administrator can use this information to figure out the problem.

The next section talks about the SecureClient Packaging Tool and how it is used to ease deployment of SecureClient.

Using the SecureClient Packaging Tool

The SecureClient Packaging Tool, which we briefly discussed in Chapter 9, is an application that allows administrators to create a SecuRemote or SecureClient installation package with the proper site information and attributes preconfigured for SecureClient users. The Packaging Tool creates a self-extracting package and allows an administrator to distribute the pre-configured package to each user. The user just needs to run the executable package to install SecureClient and then reboot. Without reconfiguring any-thing, the user updates the topology, and the client machine is ready to encrypt and download a Desktop policy.

When you're using the Packaging Tool to create a package, you must create a profile. A profile holds configuration information that will be applied to a SecureClient package. The Packaging Tool provides a wizard that helps you through the creation of a profile. To create a profile, follow these steps:

1. Choose Profile ➤ New in the SecureClient Packaging Tool, as shown in Figure 10.9.

FIGURE 10.9   Create a new profile

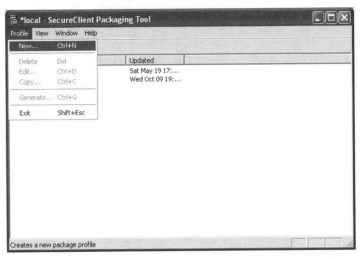

2. The wizard's welcome screen appears. Click Next to open the General window, where you can enter a profile name and comment.

3. Click Next to reach a screen that allows you to choose Connect Mode or *Transparent Mode*. Transparent Mode is the default client mode in SecureClient versions earlier than NG FP1. In this mode, encrypted connections are based on the first packet sent from the client to an IP address in the site's encryption domain. In versions NG FP1 and later, Connect Mode has been made available: In this mode, a user is required to connect to a site prior to accessing internal network resources that require encryption from outside the encryption domain. This process allows a user to define connect and disconnect events in SecureClient. If you enable mode transition, you can toggle between both client modes.

4. Click Next to move to the SecureClient window, shown in Figure 10.10. Here, you can configure SecureClient connection properties for the package you are creating. Each section of this window has been defined for you to clarify what can be configured:

FIGURE 10.10 SecureClient window

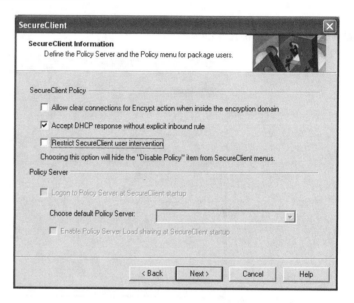

Allow Clear Connections for Encrypt Action When inside the Encryption Domain This option is used for portable SecureClient users. If a user is at work inside the encryption domain during the day, this option allows the laptop to connect to the LAN without encrypting. If the user moves outside the encryption domain, only encrypted connections will be accepted.

Accept DHCP Response without Explicit Inbound Rule This option allows SecureClient to accept DHCP connections for connectivity purposes even if they are not explicitly allowed in the defined Desktop policy.

Restrict SecureClient User Intervention Enabling this property removes the Disable Policy menu item from the Policy menu in the SecureClient GUI on the client machine.

Logon to Policy Server at SecureClient Startup Enable this option if you want SecureClient to attempt to log on to the default Policy Server automatically. This feature does not work with Connect Mode.

Choose Default Policy Server Select the Policy Server for SecureClient.

Enable Policy Server Load Sharing at SecureClient Startup If this option is enabled, SecureClient will automatically attempt to log on to any Policy Server available.

5. Click Next, and you'll see the Additional Options window shown in Figure 10.11. In this window, you can configure advanced encryption options and user control options. These options should seem familiar—they are functions of SecuRemote and SecureClient that we discussed in Chapter 9. You will be familiar with most of the options in the wizard because it walks you through a preconfiguration of the SecureClient software.

FIGURE 10.11   SecureClient Packaging Tool Additional Options window

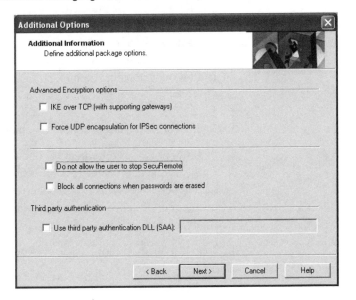

The SecureClient Packaging Tool lets you preconfigure every option SecureClient offers, and lets you define what the user is allowed to configure. The Packaging Tool is very useful because the administrator can create and

configure a package once and avoid potential user errors during SecureClient installation. The best way to understand how a package is created is to create one yourself. Exercise 10.1 guides you through the creation of a profile.

EXERCISE 10.1

Creating a SecureClient Packaging Profile

This exercise is designed to give you a hands-on understanding of how to create a SecureClient package and to introduce you to the options available when creating a package. As you perform this exercise, take the time to read through each screen in the wizard so you can see the different options. You will need to run the SecureClient Packaging Tool from a machine that can connect to the SmartCenter Server—the SecureClient Packaging Tool is a GUI that must be connected to the SmartCenter Server for verification that the user is authorized.

You'll notice that this exercise has you configure a package that does not reboot a user's machine when it is done installing SecureClient. This is one of the many options available to you when you design your self-extracting package. Keep in mind that although you can choose not to force a machine to reboot after installation, for the package to take effect after the install, the machine must be rebooted.

Follow these steps:

1. Create a site on a SecureClient machine.

2. Copy the SecureClient directory (including the userc.C file) from the SecureClient machine to the machine where you are running the SecureClient Packaging Tool. Open the SecureClient, go to the folder for the operating system you are going to use (winnt, WINDOWS, win98), and replace the userc.C file with the one you just created.

3. Open the SecureClient Packaging Tool. Click Profile ➢ New.

4. Click Next in the Welcome Screen. Type **Exercise** as the profile name. Click Next.

5. Keep the default of Transparent Mode; click Next.

6. Select the Restrict SecureClient User Intervention check box and click Next.

7. Select the IKE over TCP check box and click Next.

8. Enter topology information and click Next.

9. Review the default and click Next to not choose certificates.

10. Select the Choose Prompts That Will Be Shown to Users radio button.

11. Uncheck all Silent Installation options except the last one, Ask the User Whether to Restart the Machine. Click Next.

12. Keep all the defaults except the last one: Uncheck the Restart after Installation By Default box. Click Next.

13. Uncheck all the boxes in the Operating System Logon window. Click Next.

14. Choose the Yes, Create Profile and Generate Package radio button. Click Finish.

As you can see, the Packaging Tool allows you to preconfigure a Secure-Client installation and distribute it to many users. This type of software distribution is much easier than passing several CDs from user to user or manually installing SecureClient on each machine. The Packaging Tool also eliminates the many potential errors and security risks that may occur when each SecureClient package is manually installed.

 Real World Scenario

Educate SecureClient Users

The SecureClient Packaging Tool will ease the configuration of the Secure-Client package. Once the user installs the self-extracting package, what's next? If the next step is not clearly documented and demonstrated, then the time saved by using the Packaging Tool will be lost in taking calls and troubleshooting the software for new users.

By educating SecureClient users on how to properly use SecureClient, administrators can make deployment easier on users and themselves. The more comfortable the user is with using SecureClient, the fewer phone calls the administrator will get as a result of user errors.

Providing documentation or group training will be helpful to all remote users. Many companies start with a few SecureClient users; then, as time goes on, more people begin to use SecureClient. This growth should be planned for. An effective plan should be developed for the following:

- How to properly deploy SecureClient (using the Packaging Tool)

- How to add users and handle usernames and passwords

- How to educate users about SecureClient

- How to handle increasing numbers of SecureClient users

Having a strong plan will help make the deployment go smoothly.

The next section talks more about Desktop Policies and how to implement them. This discussion will help clarify how the Policy Server works in conjunction with SecureClient.

Implementing Desktop Policies

Desktop policies for SecureClient are defined on the Desktop Security tab of the SmartDashboard. The rule base has a similar concept to the Security Policy you would create on your firewall; it includes a source, destination, service, action, and track. For SecureClient, the policy is divided into Inbound rules and Outbound rules. Outbound rules apply to incoming connections, so the Source is the SecureClient desktop or laptop and the destination is specified in the Destination column. Inbound rules apply to connections going out to the desktop, so the Destination is the SecureClient desktop. The Service can be any service you would use in a firewall rule base.

The Action column is a little different from the firewall Action column. Your choices for Action are Accept, Block, and Encrypt. The Accept option accepts the connection, and Drop drops inbound connections and rejects outbound connections. Encrypt only accepts encrypted connections, so it will perform a check. If the connection is encrypted, it will be accepted; if not, it will be dropped.

The Track column is also different from the firewall Track column. Your choices for Track are None, Log, and Alert. Log generates a log entry; None protects the device but does not generate a log; and Alert generates a log and sends an alert to the SmartCenter Server.

Figure 10.12 shows an example of a Desktop policy. Notice the Inbound and Outbound sections.

FIGURE 10.12 Desktop policy rules

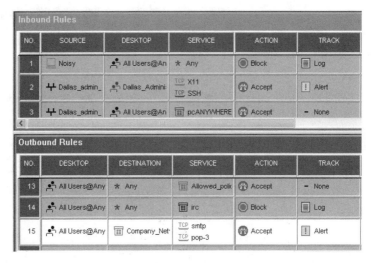

Desktop policy rules can be added and configured the same way a firewall rule is added or configured. Simply right-click on a number to add a rule; or add a rule from the Rules menu by clicking Rules ➢ Add Rule and choosing Bottom, Top, Below, or Above. Right-click on a column to add an object, user, action, or track. For Inbound desktop rules, you edit the Source column; the Destination column will be a SecureClient group. For Outbound desktop rules, you edit the Destination column; the Source column will be a Secure-Client group. Install the Security Policy, and the Desktop policy is in effect.

When the Desktop Security Policy is installed, the Policy Server receives the policy that will later be downloaded by SecureClient machines and installed as their Desktop policy. This Desktop policy is translated to the four files discussed earlier: `local.dt`, `local.scv`, `user_groups`, and `local.lp`.

Global Properties for SecureClient

Some of the Global Property settings must be set for SecureClient. Figure 10.13 shows the Global Properties Remote Access tab. At the bottom of the tab is the SecureClient portion. It allows you to choose SecureClient High Availability options and SecureClient Desktop Security Policy.

FIGURE 10.13 Global Properties Remote Access tab

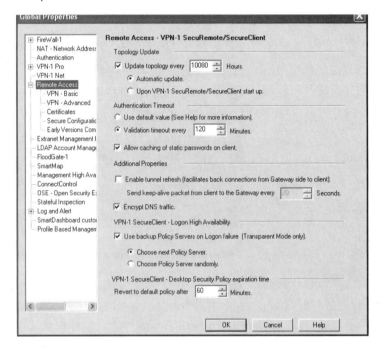

The choices for these settings are as follows:

Use Backup Policy Servers on Logon Failure   Checking this box enables the high availability of Policy Servers.

Choose Next Policy Server   If SecureClient fails to log on to a Policy Server, it will attempt to log on to the next Policy Server in the list of defined sites.

Choose Policy Server Randomly   If SecureClient fails to log on to a Policy Server, it will try to log on to a Policy Server randomly selected from the list of defined sites.

VPN-1 SecureClient - Desktop Security Policy Expiration Time   This section allows you to configure the Desktop policy expiration time for SecureClient users.

Revert to Default Policy After   This setting is the period of time during which the Desktop policy is valid. It is calculated since the last logon to the Policy Server; the default is 60 minutes.

Under the Remote Access tab is the VPN Basic tab, which allows the administrator to define authentication methods and choose IKE over TCP, Enable IP Compression for SecureClient, and Enable Load Distribution. We discussed the upper portion of this tab in Chapter 9. The settings that are SecureClient specific are Enable IP Compression and Enable Load Distribution. The IP compression uses the DEFLATE algorithm and compresses IP packets using SecureClient. Load distribution refers to *Multiple Entry Point (MEP)* configurations where the SecureClient has alternative (backup) gateways to achieve a remote access VPN. MEP is discussed in more detail in the advanced Check Point courseware, CCSE+.

Another branch under the Remote Access tab is the Secure Configuration Verification tab, where you can configure SCV settings. The SCV settings are self-explanatory and are shown in Figure 10.14. Notice that they allow you to set your own notifications in case SCV finds a machine that is not secure (a violation).

The final Global Property you need to configure is for backward compatibility. The Early Versions Compatibility tab is also located under the Remote Access tab; it's shown in Figure 10.15. The pull-down menu lists the SecureClient policies that were available in VPN-1 version 4.1:

- Allow All is just like SecuRemote: No Desktop policy will be enforced.

- Encrypt Only allows only encrypted communication to enter or leave the machine.

- Outgoing Only blocks incoming communication and only allows outgoing connections for communication.

- Encrypted and Outgoing allows only outgoing encrypted information to leave the machine and no incoming connections to communicate with the machine.

FIGURE 10.14 Secure Configuration Verification tab

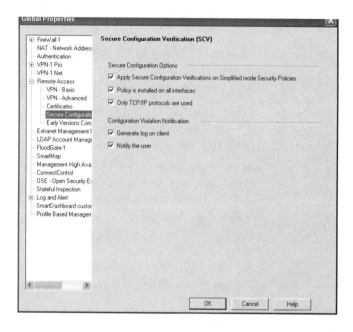

FIGURE 10.15 Early Versions Compatibility

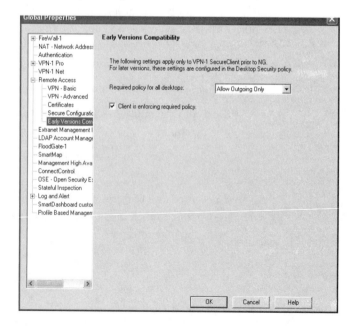

You now have an understanding of the Policy Server and the SecureClient software, and how they work with Check Point NG. The best way to learn more about these components is to install them, configure them, and play with them. It's a good idea to use the SecureClient software on your own before deploying it to a group of users. Doing so will give you, the administrator, a familiarity with the everyday functions your users will need to use.

Until now, you have learned about the IPSec-based remote access that Check Point provides. Both SecuRemote and SecureClient use Client VPN technology with IKE (an IPsec-based encryption) as their encryption scheme. The next section discusses Clientless VPNs and the uses of HTTPS-enabled remote access.

Clientless VPNs

SecuRemote and SecureClient use IPsec-based Client VPN technology. However, a new *Clientless VPN* technology has been added to Check Point NG FP3 that uses SSL (Secure Sockets Layer)-based VPN technology. A Clientless VPN is referred to as being clientless because most web browsers today offer HyperText Transfer Protocol using SSL (HTTPS) encryption support, so special client software is not required to participate in the VPN. With a Clientless VPN, a web browser or another HTTPS/SSL-enabled application can be used to VPN into the corporate LAN and access web-based information such as e-mail or other data.

More companies are moving toward web-based solutions for e-mail, calendars, and many other applications; in addition, more people are using mobile devices such as PDAs, cell phones, and laptops that have built-in Internet connectivity and web browser capabilities. With a Clientless VPN, a user can securely check web-based e-mail from a laptop, cell phone, or PDA web browser using HTTPS, which will perform SSL encryption over TCP port 443, as illustrated in Figure 10.16. Encryption will exist between the browser and the firewall, and then the packets will pass as cleartext or HTTP from the firewall to the web-based e-mail server.

Clientless VPNs are performed using the HTTP Security Server. After inbound HTTPS traffic is decrypted, the HTTP Security Server can provide authorization, full stateful inspection, and content screening of the decrypted data. The HTTP Security Server is covered in detail in Chapter 4, "Content Security."

FIGURE 10.16 Clientless VPN in action

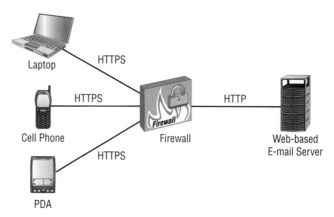

Using SSL-based encryption to deploy Clientless VPNs offers several advantages:

- The most significant advantage is that there is no additional software to install (making the technology truly clientless), because most web browsers support HTTPS.

- With a Clientless VPN, compatibility is relatively simple because remote access can exist from any HTTPS-enabled browser on a PC, PDA, or cell phone.

- Less user education is required, because there is no additional software for the user to operate. The user can use a web browser and securely access an application.

- SSL encryption operates transparently across proxy servers, firewalls, and NAT devices. Many remote users may be behind a firewall, proxy server, or NAT device that would require packet encapsulation, a rule that allows outbound IKE in the firewall, or additional configuration when using an IPsec VPN. With an HTTPS-based VPN, the connection passes across a device with no special rules—just outbound HTTPS, which is usually allowed.

- In the initial *SSL handshake*, or initial message exchange using SSL, session keys can be reused to minimize the performance hit on key exchanges.

Using Clientless VPNs is not without its disadvantages. These disadvantages are not related to Check Point software, but involve the use of SSL as a VPN solution:

- There are limitations in using an SSL-based VPN. The major limitation is that only TCP services are supported for Clientless VPNs—usually only HTTP or POP3/IMAP/SMTP over SSL, so the applications that can be accessed using Clientless VPNs must be web-based and support SSL.

- No Desktop security is available for Clientless VPNs. The data is secure in transit because it's encrypted, but the client is not secure like a SecureClient machine. There is no Policy Server or client software to enforce a Desktop policy on the remote access machine.

- Performance is another concern when using SSL. The more SSL connections traverse your firewall, the slower performance will be. There is a performance hit when computing the SSL key for each transaction that occurs in an SSL session. Multiple SSL handshakes may be required for each SSL session. Although it will take thousands of SSL connections before performance becomes too slow, performance should be a consideration.

- No failover is available for Clientless VPN sessions. In a situation where high availability is required for remote access, there is no way to make a Clientless VPN failover transparently. In the event of a failure, the user must reload the URL in the web browser to failover to the alternate firewall.

 Real World Scenario

Choosing a Remote Access Solution

The best choice for remote access is based on the goals and requirements for a given remote access project. If Desktop security or high availability is important to your remote access project, then SecureClient will be the right option for you. If you don't have access to user machines to install or configure software, or you want the user to have the flexibility of securely accessing information from a cell phone, a PDA, or any web browser without additional software, then a Clientless VPN is a better solution for your remote access project. Larger companies may be able to use a combination of all three technologies: SecuRemote, SecureClient, and Clientless VPNs.

Clientless VPNs are the best fit for a remote access solution when:

- All traffic is web-based or e-mail–based.

- Remote access needs to be universally available from cell phones, PDAs, home PCs, public PCs, and so on.

- The client machine is already secure, or the machine does not need to be secure because Desktop security is not available.

- The organization does not have control over the remote access user's computer configuration, so software cannot be installed or configured.

- Remote access is required from anywhere. Whether the client is behind a firewall, NAT device, or proxy server, HTTPS is usually allowed outbound, but IKE is not.

The next section discusses the Clientless VPN configuration.

Configuring Clientless VPNs

Configuring Clientless VPNs is not complicated. It's a matter of enabling the technology on the Firewall object and then creating objects and rules. To configure Clientless VPNs, you need to configure the following objects:

- The Firewall object

- A web server object that will be the destination of the SSL connection

- The HTTPS service

If you choose to use certificates in the web browser (Internet Explorer) for authentication, certificates can be generated by the Internal Certificate Authority (ICA).

Enabling Clientless VPNs on the Firewall Object

The first step in configuring Clientless VPNs is to enable them on the Firewall object. The VPN Advanced tab of the Firewall object, shown in Figure 10.17, has a Clientless VPN section. Select the Support Clientless VPN check box. Select a certificate from the drop-down list. If a certificate doesn't exist, create one by clicking Add.

FIGURE 10.17   VPN Advanced tab for the Firewall object

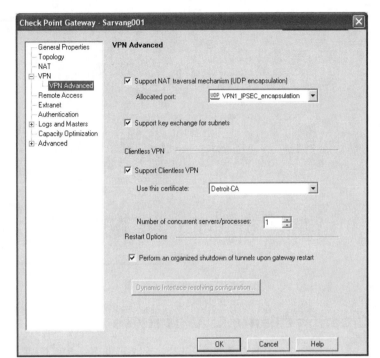

Create the Web Server Object

After enabling Clientless VPNs, create a Network object for the web server you will be using as the destination for your Clientless VPN. Create a Node object by selecting Manage ➢ Network Objects, click New, and select Node ➢ Host. Configure the web server with a name, IP address, and color.

Define HTTPS as HTTP

After creating the web server, you have to define the HTTPS service as HTTP. Select Manage ➢ Service and edit the HTTPS service. Click Advanced, and the Advanced TCP Service Properties screen shown in Figure 10.18 will appear. Select HTTP from the Protocol Type drop-down list. Click OK.

FIGURE 10.18 Advanced TCP Service Properties for HTTPS

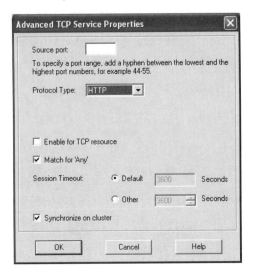

Creating Clientless VPN Rules

Now that the objects are configured and edited, you can create Clientless VPN rules in the rule base. If a user group is not already created, create a user group called ClientlessUsers. This group should include the users to whom you want to grant Clientless VPN access. Create a rule similar to the one shown in Figure 10.19 that has a Source of ClientlessUsers@Any, a Destination of the web server you created, a Service of HTTPS, and an Action of User Auth with a Track of Log. Install the Security Policy to save and compile the changes.

FIGURE 10.19 Clientless VPN user authentication rule

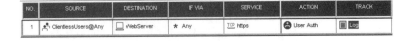

To configure the web client to use Clientless VPNs, open Internet Explorer and select Tools ➤ Internet Options. Choose the Content tab and click on Certificates to open the Certificates screen, where you can import certificates for authentication. You can use the Certificate Import Wizard to import a user's ICA certificate.

Clientless VPNs are a useful option for corporations to add to their remote access infrastructure. I am sure you will see more enhancements to the Clientless VPN portion of Check Point NG in future Feature Packs.

Summary

SecureClient is a great product for providing secure mobility to a corporation's employees. Policy Server NG has many enhancements that ensure an employee's computer will not be compromised while participating in a Client VPN. In addition, you can use SecureClient to provide secure access to selected parts of a company's network for suppliers, partners, and customers. The Desktop security features of SecureClient ensure the protection and confidentiality of data communication while protecting the client machine from potential threats during the VPN.

SecureClient NG has introduced many new Desktop security features and considerable flexibility. One of the features that increases protection is the Secure Configuration Verification (SCV) component, which checks the configuration of each SecureClient machine and verifies that it is securely configured. Although Desktop policies are much more advanced in SecureClient NG, the Policy Server is completely backward compatible so it can accommodate earlier versions of SecureClient with the earlier versions of Desktop policies.

Configuring a Desktop policy is similar to configuring a firewall policy. The Desktop policy can restrict inbound and outbound connections by service and by user. This provides the flexibility of having many groups of Client VPN users with many different levels of access and many different Desktop policies.

Clientless VPNs are a new feature in Check Point NG FP3 that enable users to securely access web-based information using SSL. Because most web browsers are HTTPS-enabled, there is no need to install additional software on a client computer. This technology is best suited for web-based or e-mail–based applications that do not require a secure client so a client can access the information from anywhere using a web browser or other SSL-enabled client software.

Exam Essentials

Understand the differences between SecuRemote and SecureClient. It's imperative to understand how SecuRemote works before configuring it. It's also a good idea to understand Client VPN technology and its functional uses.

Know what the Policy Server is and how it works. Know the different settings that you have to configure on the Firewall object and in the Global Properties. Understand how to configure the rule base to accommodate SecuRemote connections.

Know how to configure the SecuRemote client software. By understanding the SecuRemote software and being aware of its functionality, you will be able to use the product to its fullest potential. Know the menu options and what they can do.

Understand Clientless VPNs. By understanding Clientless VPNs and the pros and cons of using the technology, you will have a better understanding of how to use it. This technology is new to Check Point NG FP3 but will grow in future Feature Packs. SSL VPN technology will be used increasingly for remote access and other secure communication over the next few years.

Key Terms

Before you take the exam, be certain you are familiar with the following terms:

Clientless VPN	Multiple Entry Point (MEP)
Connect Mode	Policy Server
connection profiles	SCV Manager
Desktop policy	SCV plug-ins
dtps	Secure Configuration Verification (SCV)
explicit logon	Transparent Mode
implicit logon	

Review Questions

1. What is the name of the Policy Server process?

   A. daemon

   B. dtps

   C. ps

   D. SCV

   E. None of the above

2. Which of these threads is not a dtps thread?

   A. FTP thread

   B. tftp thread

   C. Main thread

   D. Policy install thread

   E. All of the above are dtps threads

3. Which file on the SecureClient machine is downloaded each time the SecureClient machine logs on to the Policy Server to determine what access users have?

   A. `local.dt`

   B. `group_file`

   C. `local.scv`

   D. `local.lp`

   E. None of the above

4. What does the `local.dt` file do?

   A. Checks user's authorization

   B. Deals with Secure Configuration Verification

   C. Communicates between the Policy Server and the Check Point daemon

   D. Represents the Desktop policy

   E. None of the above

5. Where is the Desktop policy loaded into the SecureClient machine?

   A. In the NIC

   B. Into memory

   C. In the kernel

   D. In the CPU

   E. All of the above

6. What is the name of the file that is compiled to be `local.dt`?

   A. `Standard.W`

   B. `Default.W`

   C. `Standard.pf`

   D. `Default.S`

   E. `Standard.S`

7. What operating systems does SecureClient run on? (Choose all that apply.)

   A. Solaris

   B. Windows

   C. Linux

   D. HP-UX

   E. DOS

8. What does SCV check for?

    A. Desktop policy

    B. A secure Policy Server

    C. A secure configuration

    D. A secure firewall

    E. None of the above

9. Which tab in the Global Properties will allow you to configure backward compatibility for SecureClient?

    A. Early Version Compatibility

    B. Backward Compatibility

    C. VPN-1 Net

    D. Early Version Configuration

    E. Desktop security

10. Which file on the SecureClient machine defines how SecureClient will log events and upload them to the Policy Server?

    A. `local.scv`

    B. `local.lp`

    C. `user_groups`

    D. `local.dt`

    E. None of the above

11. What protocol do Clientless VPNs use?

    A. HTTP

    B. HTTPS

    C. Telnet

    D. SSH

    E. FTP

12. What is the first thing that needs to be created when creating a package in the SecureClient Packaging Tool?

    A. An object

    B. A network

    C. A host

    D. A profile

    E. A gateway

13. What menu item is different between the SecuRemote GUI and the SecureClient GUI?

    A. File

    B. Desktop

    C. Policy

    D. Security

    E. Sites

14. When uninstalling the Policy Server, what order should it be removed in?

    A. Policy Server, FireWall-1, SVN Foundation

    B. FireWall-1, Policy Server, SVN Foundation

    C. SVN Foundation, Policy Server, FireWall-1

    D. FireWall-1, SVN Foundation, Policy Server

    E. None of the above

15. Do you need to buy an additional license for a Policy Server if you've already bought SecureClient?

   A. Yes, so you can use it immediately

   B. Only if you have more than one Policy Server

   C. Only if you have more than 25 SecureClient users

   D. Only if you have more than 100 SecureClient users

   E. No, you don't need to buy a Policy Server license

16. Where is the license for the Policy Server located?

   A. Firewall Module

   B. SmartCenter Module

   C. Separate server

   D. SecureClient machine

   E. None of the above

17. Which of the following are Early Version Compatibility options? (Choose all that apply.)

   A. Accept Outgoing Only

   B. Allow Outgoing and Encrypted

   C. No Policy

   D. Allow Encrypted Only

   E. All of the above

18. When creating a Desktop policy rule, where is the Desktop column on the Inbound rules and Outbound rules?

    A. It is the Source on Inbound and the Destination on Outbound.

    B. It is the Destination on both Inbound and Outbound.

    C. It is the Source on Outbound and the Destination on Inbound.

    D. It is the Source on both Inbound and Outbound.

    E. None of the above.

19. What are the Action options when creating a Desktop policy? (Choose all that apply.)

    A. Reject

    B. Accept

    C. Drop

    D. Block

    E. Encrypt

20. What are the Track options when creating a Desktop policy? (Choose all that apply.)

    A. Alert

    B. User Defined

    C. Log

    D. No Log

    E. None

Answers to Review Questions

1. B. Dtps is the process that is running when the Policy Server is running. The dtps process on Windows machines runs as `dtps.exe`.

2. A. There is no FTP thread. The other threads are part of the dtps process.

3. B. The `group_file` determines what the user can access. The file is downloaded each time the SecureClient logs in; it is stored with the rest of the policy files.

4. D. The `local.dt` file is the Desktop policy that is loaded on the SecureClient machine. The other descriptions tell what the other files do.

5. C. The Desktop policy is loaded into the SecureClient kernel. The files that are available on the Policy Server are downloaded to the client during logon if the files have changed.

6. E. The `Standard.S` file is compiled to be the `local.dt` file. The `Standard.W` file is the firewall policy file that is compiled to be `Standard.pf`. Using the same name makes it a bit confusing.

7. B, C. SecureClient mainly runs on Windows and has just recently been ported over to Linux. HP-UX and Solaris versions don't exist at this time and are probably not a major priority. A DOS version would be difficult to configure.

8. C. The SCV component checks for a secure configuration on the SecureClient machine. If the SecureClient machine is not securely configured, then it will not allow the connection.

9. A. The Early Version Compatibility tab allows you to configure the 4.1 SecureClient settings. A pull-down menu lists the four settings that existed in SecureClient 4.1. Without this feature, an existing 4.1 SecureClient deployment would be a difficult upgrade.

10. B. The `local.lp` file is responsible for log events and uploading them to the Policy Server. It resides in the same place as the other policy files on the SecureClient machine.

11. B.   Clientless VPNs use the HTTPS protocol. Using SSL-enabled applications with web browsers that support SSL as clients allows a user to securely access information from anywhere.

12. D.   The Packaging Tool is based on profiles that are created in the Packaging Tool GUI. The GUI also has a wizard that guides you through the creation of a profile.

13. C.   The SecureClient configuration GUI has an additional Policy menu. The Policy menu deals with Desktop policy security, which does not exist in the SecuRemote GUI.

14. A.   The Policy Server cannot run if it is not on a FireWall-1 gateway. For this reason, the Policy Server must be uninstalled first. The SVN Foundation must always be removed last.

15. B.   There is an additional license for a Policy Server. It's not needed if you have only one Policy Server because one Policy Server license comes with the purchase of SecureClient. When adding more than one, you need an additional license.

16. B.   The Policy Server license is located on the SmartCenter Module. The SecureClient licenses are located on each of the firewalls.

17. E.   All four options were available in Check Point FireWall-1 4.1. Check Point NG has greatly improved the Desktop security functionality.

18. C.   On all Outbound rules, the Desktop is the Source. The Inbound must be the opposite; so in the Inbound Rules, Desktop is the Destination.

19. B, D, E.   The Action options are a little different from the firewall policy. The only options are Accept, Block, and Encrypt. These three actions are all you need when enforcing Desktop policy.

20. A, C, E.   The three options are Alert, Log, and None. Usually a simple log is all that is needed. User Defined can be used on SecureClient rules if needed but not on Desktop policy rules.

Glossary

A

alertd   The Check Point daemon that executes alerts. The alertd process runs on the log server (usually the SmartCenter Server).

allowed routing modes   During Voice over IP (VoIP) configuration, this option identifies which connections will be rerouted endpoint-to-endpoint.

aSMTPd   An SMTP content security daemon that controls the SMTP commands the firewall will recognize.

asymmetric encryption   An encryption process in which a public/private key pair is utilized. The public key is used to encrypt the data, and the private key is used to decrypt the data.

Authentication Header   One of the headers of an IPSec packet that contains references to the Security Parameters Index (SPI) and message digest.

B

backlog queue   A TCP/IP stack table on a server that keeps track of open connections.

bandwidth   The amount of data that can be transmitted during a fixed period of time.

C

central gateway   The center point of a star Simplified VPN topology. Consists of one or more gateways.

certificate authority   A trusted third party that is responsible for holding other entities' public keys and issuing certificates.

certificate key   A 12-character alphanumeric code used for Check Point product licensing. The key is located on the product packaging, and identifies a Check Point product to the Check Point User Center website. The Check Point license will be generated based on this information.

Certificate Revocation List (CRL)   A list of expired or revoked certificates maintained as part of a public key infrastructure (PKI) or virtual private network (VPN) type solution.

ciphertext   Data after it has been encrypted.

cleartext   Data before it has been encrypted.

clientless VPN   HTTPS-based VPN used for remote access. It is considered clientless because most web browsers support SSL. This feature is new with Check Point NG FP3.

client-to-site VPN   A VPN from a remote user to a Check Point firewall that is established using SecuRemote or SecureClient software. A client-to-site VPN frees a user to be mobile: to work from home, a remote office, or anywhere else, and maintain encrypted communication with the corporate network.

ConnectControl   The license string feature that turns on load balancing. ConnectControl is also sometimes used as an alternate name for load balancing.

connection profile   A profile that contains Connect Mode configuration information for SecuRemote and SecureClient. Connection profiles contain site, preferred gateway, and preferred Policy Server information.

Connect Mode   A client mode that eases a user's interaction with Secure-Client by allowing the user to choose between different Policy Servers. Connect Mode has been available in SecuRemote and SecureClient since Check Point NG FP1.

Content Security   The ability of FireWall-1 to granularly check HTTP, SMTP, FTP, and TCP traffic.

Content Vectoring Protocol (CVP)   An Open Platform for Security (OPSEC) API that runs on port 18181 and allows the firewall to communicate with a virus/content server.

Cpconfig   A command that can be issued from the command line, which produces a menu you can use to configure or reconfigure Check Point NG installation components.

CPShared The Check Point operating system that facilitates ease of integration and management between Check Point products installed on the same machine. CPShared should always be installed first, before Check Point NG products are installed, and should always be removed last during an uninstall. CPShared is also referred to as the SVN Foundation.

CVP server An Open Platform for Security (OPSEC) application object representing the server that performs virus/content security.

D

default filter A security mechanism that turns off IP forwarding and thereby blocks all IP connectivity to the firewall, to protect the firewall during vulnerable times (such as reboot). This filter must be altered to allow for connectivity during installation so that remote connectivity is not blocked after reboot.

demilitarized zone (DMZ) Traditionally known as an insecure area between secure areas. A DMZ in reference to a Check Point firewall is a segment or subnet of the firewall that is on its own network interface, separate from internal traffic. The DMZ is a network that houses public servers such as web servers, FTP servers, DNS servers, and so on. The DMZ is used to allow public access to services without exposing internal data. To connect from the DMZ to internal data, a user must pass through the firewall.

Denial of Service (DoS) An attack that involves a computer sending a large number of requests to a server or another computer, such that the recipient computer or server is overloaded and denies service to legitimate requests.

Desktop policy Policy created to protect SecureClient machines from potential threats outside the client-to-site VPN in which it's participating.

Differential Quality of Service (DiffServ QoS) A standard that controls the packets that are tagged to facilitate bandwidth management using QoS. (Quality of Service [QoS] is a networking term that refers to a guaranteed throughput level.)

Diffie-Hellman A calculation in which public keys are exchanged between partners. Each partner combines their private key with their partner's public key to produce a shared secret/basic session key. Diffie-Hellman is used in Internet Key Exchange (IKE) to establish session keys. Diffie-Hellman is a component of Oakley Key Exchange.

digital signature A combination of a message digest and a private key, used to authenticate and verify the integrity of a data exchange.

Distinguished Name (DN) A string of information that uniquely identifies a user or group in a directory server. The distinguished name usually contains the username or ID, the organization name, and a country designation: for example, cn=Bob, ou=sales, c=US.

Distributed Denial of Service (DDoS) A coordinated attack that involves many computers attacking one computer or a group of computers with a large number of requests that overload the computer or group of computers and cause them to deny legitimate service. The best-known DDoS attacks took place in February, 2000; a number of major websites were brought down for hours.

distributed environment Check Point architecture where the Smart-Center Server is on a separate machine from the FireWall Module(s). A distributed environment is generally used when the SmartCenter Server is managing more than one enforcement point.

domain A load balancing algorithm in which reverse DNS is used to determine which server in the server farm gets the next connection.

dtps The Policy Server daemon (process) that is active after the Policy Server is configured and the Security Policy is successfully installed. The dtps daemon will stop if the FireWall-1 service is stopped or killed.

dynamic address translation When the Other load balancing method is used, automatic translation of inbound destination IP connections and outbound source IP addresses as the connections pass through the firewall.

E

echo   Signal reflection of your voice back to you during a Voice over IP (VoIP) call. Occurs when the round-trip delay is greater than 50 milliseconds.

Encapsulating Security Payload (ESP)   One of the headers in an IPSec packet that references the Security Parameters Index (SPI) and an Initialization Vector (IV).

encryption   The process by which cleartext is changed into ciphertext. Encryption is usually used to achieve confidentiality.

enforcement point   The Check Point component that enforces the rule base with the objects and users configured in the SmartDashboard and sends logs to the SmartCenter Server. Also known as a FireWall or Enforcement Module.

explicit logon   A logon that does not happen automatically. The client is asked to download a Desktop policy after authentication. The policy is downloaded only when the user adds or updates a site that contains a Policy Server.

export network objects   Network objects that are configured to be shared in an extranet VPN with extranet partners using the Extranet Management Interface (EMI).

extranet community   A group, similar to a VPN domain, that contains the extranet-enabled gateway and the export network objects that will be exported to an extranet partner.

extranet-enabled gateway   An existing gateway that is enabled to participate in an extranet VPN using the Extranet Management Interface (EMI).

Extranet Management Interface (EMI)   A Check Point component that eases the configuration of extranet VPNs by enabling the firewall to securely export and import network objects to and from extranet VPN partners.

Extranet Objects Distributor   An Extranet Resolution Protocol server that runs on TCP port 18262 and facilitates the secure export of network objects to extranet partners using the Extranet Management Interface (EMI).

extranet partners   Select partners with which a company creates VPN communication to share data in a secure manner for mutual benefit.

Extranet Resolution Protocol   A certificate-based, secured protocol that helps communicate the establishment of trust between extranet partners when using the Extranet Management Interface (EMI).

Extranet Resolution Servers   Two servers that are started when a gateway becomes an extranet-enabled gateway. These servers help secure the communication between extranet partners when using the Extranet Management Interface (EMI). The servers are the Public Key Distributor and the Extranet Objects Distributor.

extranet VPN   A private network that enables a company to have secure, one-on-one encrypted communications with its partners, suppliers, and customers.

F

Feature Packs (FPs)   Updated versions of the Check Point NG software that include hotfixes and patches and also offer significant feature enhancements and code improvements.

fingerprint   A unique set of words used to verify secure communication between modules. The fingerprint assures an administrator that communication between two parties is authentic.

FireWall Module   A Check Point component that enforces the rule base with the objects and users configured in the SmartDashboard and sends logs to the SmartCenter Server. Also known as an enforcement point.

FloodGate   A Check Point product used for QoS and bandwidth management.

folding   The process by which connections are moved from the FireWall-1 kernel to be handled by the Security Servers.

FTP GET   The option in an FTP resource that allows the resource to retrieve files via File Transfer Protocol (FTP).

FTP PUT   The option in an FTP resource that allows the resource to deposit files via File Transfer Protocol (FTP).

FTP resource   A Content Security resource that controls FTP GETs and PUTs as well as virus scanning.

FW1_cvp   A predefined TCP service that runs on TCP port 18181 and is defined as part of a resource object to facilitate virus/content scanning.

FW1_ufp   A predefined TCP service that runs on TCP port 18182 and is defined as part of a resource object to facilitate virus/content scanning.

fwalert   A built-in, prewritten script provided by Check Point that will pop up an alert on your screen and provide brief information about what caused the alert.

fwrl.conf   A file located in $FWDIR/conf that references a URI resource of URI Match Specification Type: File.

fwssd   The Security Server process that is spawned based on information contained in $FWDIR/conf/fwauthd.conf.

G

gatekeeper   The focal point for all calls within a H.323 Voice over IP (VoIP) network. It connects all IP phones and could connect to the VoIP H.323 Gateway as well.

Gateway   Part of an H.323 Voice over IP (VoIP) network setup that converts analog phone signals to digital signals the gatekeeper can understand.

GUI Clients   The graphical interface tools that are used to configure and monitor Check Point products. Also known as Management Clients in NG FP1 and FP2 or SmartClients in NG FP3.

H

H.323 The ITU standard for Voice over IP (VoIP) that defines how audio-visual data is transmitted across a network.

hardening the operating system A process of removing vulnerabilities and unnecessary services from an operating system to make the OS secure. An operating system is usually hardened prior to installing security software on it to make the server secure. Examples of security software that would require a hardened operating system include firewall software, IDS software, authentication software, and so on.

hash A one-way mathematical function used to create a message digest and to verify the integrity of the message.

HTML weeding A process used by SMTP and HTTP resource objects to filter HTTP traffic such as ActiveX, Java Script, and FTP port strings.

HTTP method One of the load balancing methods that uses the built-in ability of web browsers to redirect HTTP traffic.

HTTPS The secure Hypertext Transfer Protocol using SSL (Secure Socket Layer) protocol, which provides encryption over the Web.

I

If Via A new column in a Simplified VPN rule base. When populated, this column automatically encrypts the connections between the object(s) listed in the Source and Destination columns.

IKE (Internet Key Exchange) The IETF standard for encryption. It combines the Oakley Key Management Protocol and Internet Security Protocol (IPSec).

implicit logon A SecureClient logon that automatically installs a Desktop policy on the SecureClient machine when the user authenticates.

in.lhttpd A line entry in fwauthd.conf that controls the load balancing daemon parameters such as the port number on which the daemon listens.

in.pingd   A line entry in fwauthd.conf that corresponds to the processes in load balancing that ping the servers in the server farm to check the web server's availability.

internal certificate authority (ICA)   The certificate authority generated during the installation of a Check Point SmartCenter Server. Certificates generated by the ICA are used for encryption and authentication.

International Telecommunications Union (ITU)   An intergovernmental agency responsible for adopting international treaties, regulations, and standards governing telecommunications.

Internet Engineering Task Force (IETF)   The standards organization for the Internet.

Internet Security Association and Key Management Protocol (ISAKMP)   An IPSec protocol, described in RFC 2408, that negotiates, establishes, modifies, and deletes Security Associations (SAs). This protocol is also responsible for exchanging key generation and authentication data, key establishment protocols, encryption algorithms, or authentication mechanisms.

Internet telephony   Hardware/software that enables people to use the Internet for telephone calls as opposed to using traditional PBX.

interoperable device   An object created in the Network Objects Manager that represents a device that has no Check Point software installed on it but that participates in a VPN with Check Point objects.

IP phones   Telephones that required a digital instead of an analog signal and that can integrate with a Voice over IP (VoIP) solution.

IP Security (IPSec)   A set of protocols developed by the IETF to define secure exchange of packets at the IP layer. Used to create virtual private networks (VPNs).

L

lhttpd   A daemon defined in $FWDIR/conf/fwauthd.conf that redirects HTTP connections when the HTTP load balancing method is selected.

license key   An important piece of software that controls the components installed on your firewall. The architecture and features of your Check Point product depend on your license key to function. Without the proper license key, the Check Point product will not work properly.

load agents   Executables loaded on servers in the server farm to facilitate a server load algorithm in load balancing.

load balancing   A function of the firewall that allows the firewall to act as the decision maker and determine which servers in the server farm get the next connection.

logical server   The object created in the Network Objects Manager to facilitate load balancing.

M

Mail Queue Daemon (MQD)   A daemon that runs when an SMTP resource is defined. It is responsible for moving mail in and out of the mail spool on the firewall and for sending and retrieving mail from a Content Vectoring Protocol (CVP) server as well as forwarding the mail to the internal mail server.

mail relay   A process in which the firewall acts as a relay for mail when an SMTP content security server is defined. Mail is directed to the firewall, and the firewall passes it to the internal mail server.

Management GUI Client   The graphical interface tools used to configure and monitor Check Point products. Also known as a GUI Client in NG FP1 and FP2 or a SmartClient in NG FP3.

Management Module   The Check Point component that manages the enforcement points and stores all the configuration files, including the rule bases, objects database, user database, logs, and so on. The server that the Management Module is installed on is called the Management Server in NG FP1 and FP2. The Management Server is called the SmartCenter Server in FP3.

Management Server   The server that contains the Management Module. This server is called the SmartCenter Server in NG FP3. It stores all the configuration files, including the rule bases, objects database, user database, logs, and so on.

mesh   A Simplified VPN configuration in which every participant in the VPN community has a VPN tunnel between every other participant in the VPN community.

message digest (MD)   The result of a one-way hash function, which is used for message integrity.

Multiple Entry Point (MEP)   A high-availability method used for SecuRemote and SecureClient. It allows users to transparently log on to a backup enforcement point if the primary entry point is not available or fails.

O

Oakley Key Exchange Protocol   A key establishment protocol based on Diffie-Hellman and designed to be a compatible component of Internet Security Association and Key Management Protocol (ISAKMP).

OPSEC   Open Platform for Secure Enterprise Connectivity. This Check Point program encourages other vendors to use Check Point's APIs to integrate with the firewall. Detailed OPSEC information can be found at www.opsec.com.

Other method   One of the load balancing methods. It uses dynamic address translation to facilitate load-balanced connections.

P

participant   A gateway defined in a VPN community that takes part in a mesh Simplified VPN configuration.

participating gateway   A gateway defined in a VPN community that takes part in a mesh Simplified VPN configuration.

Passive SYN Gateway   A SYNDefender option that is similar to SYN Gateway, that waits for the client's acknowledgment (ACK) packet before completing the handshake to the server. Passive SYN Gateway is the least intrusive SYNDefender option.

Perfect Forward Secrecy   An option that can be selected when configuring Internet Key Exchange (IKE) encryption to add a Diffie-Hellman key exchange to Phase II negotiations, thereby reducing performance but increasing security.

Persistent Server Mode   A load balancing option that forces a connection to stay with the server to which it was load balanced, based either on service or server.

PKI-based extranet   An extranet that uses Public Key Infrastructure (PKI) for certificate authentication.

Policy Server   A Check Point component that runs on the NG firewall that houses a Desktop policy, which protects SecureClient machines from potential threats outside the VPN in which they're participating.

pre-shared secret   A password shared between two gateways to authenticate and initiate an Internet Key Exchange (IKE) VPN tunnel.

Public Key Distributor   An Extranet Resolution Protocol server that runs on TCP port 18262 and facilitates the secure export of public keys between extranet partners using the Extranet Management Interface (EMI).

Public Key Infrastructure (PKI)   An infrastructure that stores and provides X.509 certificates that authenticate the identity of computer systems and individuals. Certificates can be used for authentication, data confidentiality, data integrity, and non-repudiation features.

public switched telephone network (PSTN)   The international telephone system based on analog signals carried on copper wire. Telephone service on a PSTN is also referred to as plain old telephone service (POTS).

R

random   A load balancing algorithm in which the server in the server farm that gets the next connection is chosen arbitrarily.

Realtime Blackhole List   A way to identify hosts that have been associated with the sending of SPAM mail. More details can be found at `http://www.mail-abuse.org/rbl/`.

round robin   A load balancing algorithm in the server farm that gets the next connection and is chosen based on a list of servers. The first server in the list gets the first connection, the second server gets the next, and so on. Once the logical server reaches the end of the list, it starts over.

round trip   A load balancing algorithm in which each server in the server farm is pinged three times and the connection is sent to the server with the shortest average ping time.

S

satellite gateway   A gateway in a star Simplified VPN configuration that is not part of the central gateway(s). These gateways have VPN tunnels with the central gateway(s) but cannot have a VPN tunnel between each other.

SCV Manager   A Policy Server component that is responsible for configuration and maintenance of the SCV state from all SCV plug-ins. When the SCV Manager wants SCV status, it queries all registered SCV plug-ins about the SCV state they are responsible for.

SCV plug-ins   DLLs registered with SecureClient that contain functions that can notify the SCV Manager of their DLL's state.

Secure Configuration Verification (SCV)   A mechanism that determines whether the SecureClient machine is securely.

Secure Virtual Network (SVN)   The umbrella of Check Point products that, when combined, provide a true end-to-end security solution for any type of organization.

Secure Internal Communications (SIC)   A certificate-based SSL encryption method used to provide secure communication between Check Point modules. SIC is necessary for communication to take place between Check Point modules in a secure, trusted manner.

SecuRemote site   (*see* Site)

SecurePlatform   A product introduced with Check Point NG FP2 that provides a full Check Point installation with a custom pre-hardened operating system in a quick and easy way. SecurePlatform will boot from a CD and install the full OS and VPN-1/FireWall-1 package on any Intel-based machine.

Secure Sockets Layer (SSL)   A security protocol that provides reliable, private (encrypted), and authentic communications between parties.

Secure Virtual Network (SVN) Foundation   The Check Point operating system that facilitates ease of integration and management between Check Point products installed on the same machine. SVN Foundation should always be installed first, before Check Point NG products are installed, and should always be removed last during an uninstall. SVN Foundation is also referred to as CPShared.

Security Association (SA)   The methods negotiated between VPN gateways for encryption, data integrity, and authentication. Both Internet Key Exchange (IKE) and Internet Security Protocol (IPSec) use SAs, although SAs are independent of one another. IKE negotiates and establishes SAs on behalf of IPSec. SAs are identified uniquely by destination (IPSec endpoint) address, security protocol (AH or ESP), and Security Parameters Index (SPI).

Security Parameters Index (SPI)   A hexadecimal number (such as 0x134556) with a destination IP address and a security protocol, which uniquely identifies a particular security association.

Security Server A set of processes responsible for Content Security and authentication. When these processes are invoked, the INSPECT Engine diverts all the packets in the connection to the Security Server, which performs the required authentication and/or Content Security inspection. If the connection is allowed, then the Security Server opens a second connection to the final destination. In essence, it acts as a proxy. Both sets of connections are kept track of in the firewall's connections table.

server farm A group of Node-Host objects that will be load-balanced to use a Logical Server object.

server load A load balancing algorithm in which each server in the server farm has a load-measuring agent installed, which communicates its load to the Logical Server. The server in the server farm with the lightest load gets the connection.

Session Initiation Protocol (SIP) A protocol (RFC 2543) that equips platforms to signal the setup of voice and multimedia calls over IP networks.

signaling The process of sending a transmission signal over a physical medium for the purpose of communication in a Voice over IP (VoIP) network.

Simplified Mode Simplified Mode refers to using a simplified policy to configure Simplified VPNs.

Simplified Policy An alternative to the Traditional Policies in which the encryption options are removed from the Action column of the rule base. The additional If Via column facilitates automatic encryption rules to be configured based on Simplified VPN definitions.

Simplified VPN A VPN created with a single function by adding gateways (VPN sites) to a VPN community. All the gateways share the same VPN security parameters (encryption algorithms, data integrity methods, and so on). New gateways added to a VPN community are automatically included in the established VPN tunnels between community members based on their configuration (star, meshed, or star/meshed).

site Created in SecuRemote/SecureClient software to identify the firewall with which the user will make an initial connection to gather encryption domain and network information.

SMART Clients   The graphical user interfaces that help an administrator configure and monitor Check Point VPN-1/FireWall-1. In versions prior to Check Point NG FP3, they were called Management Clients.

SmartCenter Server   A server that contains the Management Module. This server was called the Management Server prior to NG FP3. It stores all the configuration files, including the rule bases, objects database, user database, logs, and so on.

SmartDashboard   The graphical interface that allows administrators to configure FireWall-1. In versions prior to Check Point NG FP3, it was known as the Policy Editor GUI.

SmartDefense   A Check Point component providing a unified security framework for various components that identify and prevent cyber attacks.

SmartView Status   The graphical interface that allows administrators to monitor FireWall-1. In versions prior to Check Point NG FP3, it was known as the Status Manager.

SmartView Tracker   The graphical interface that allows administrators to see traffic that is accepted, dropped, rejected, and encrypted by FireWall-1. In versions prior to Check Point NG FP3, it was known as the Log Viewer.

SMTP Resource   A Content Security resource that controls what SMTP commands the firewalls will respond to (re-writing mail headers, controlling mail size, virus scanning, and so on).

smtp.conf   A file located in $FWDIR/conf that contains the configuration parameters for SMTP resource objects and SMTP Content Security.

soft phones   Digital phones that have IP addresses to enable Voice over IP (VoIP) traffic without the use of a VoIP Gateway.

SSL handshake   The communication exchange when SSL is employed in communication.

star   A Simplified VPN configuration with a central gateway(s) and satellite gateways. All connections between the central gateway(s) and satellite gateways are encrypted, but connections between satellite gateways are not encrypted.

Suspicious Activity Monitor (SAM)   A protocol used by FireWall-1 to block connections using the Block Intruder feature. SAM is also used by third-party vendors to integrate suspicious activity monitoring and blocking functionality with Check Point FireWall-1.

SVN Foundation   The Check Point operating system that facilitates ease of integration and management among Check Point products installed on the same machine. SVN Foundation should always be installed first, before Check Point NG products are installed, and should always be removed last during an uninstall. SVN Foundation is also referred to as CPShared.

symmetric encryption   An encryption process in which the same key used to encrypt the data is also used to decrypt the data.

SYNDefender   A Check Point FireWall-1 feature that allows firewall administrators to protect themselves against a specific Denial of Service (DoS) attack called a SYN flood.

SYN flood   A Denial of Service (DoS) attack where a hacker spoofs the IP address of a legitimate client machine and sends a large number of SYNs to a server. For each SYN, the server opens crucial memory buffers to accommodate communication with the client and sends a SYN/ACK back to the legitimate client. Because the client IP is spoofed, the SYN/ACKs do not receive acknowledgment (ACK), and the server leaves the crucial memory buffers open, waiting for an ACK response. Eventually, the server's backlog queue becomes overloaded and the server denies service to legitimate requests.

SYN Gateway   A SYNDefender option that counters a SYN flood by having the firewall send an acknowledgment (ACK) packet to the server in response to the SYN/ACK packet sent to the client. This step completes the handshake between the server and the firewall, thereby removing the connection from the backlog queue and opening the connection to the server (as far as the server is concerned).

SYN Relay   A SYNDefender option that counters a SYN flood by making sure the TCP/IP handshake is valid before sending a SYN packet to the server. The advantage of using SYN Relay is that the server doesn't receive any invalid connection attempts.

T

talker overlap   A situation that occurs when there is a greater than 250 millisecond one-way delay in a Voice over IP (VoIP) call, causing talkers to step on each other's conversations because the delay makes it sound as if they're finished speaking when they're really not.

TCP/IP handshake   A three-step process that establishes TCP/IP communication. The initiator of the "conversation" (in this example, computer A) sends a SYN packet requesting a connection and specifying the port on which it wants to communicate. If computer B agrees to communicate with computer A, it replies with a SYN/ACK packet and a queue for the connection. To complete the transaction, computer A sends an ACK packet to computer B; the TCP/IP handshake is complete, and the connection is opened. After the connection is opened, data can flow between the computers.

TCP resource   A Content Security resource that can be used with TCP protocols other than HTTP, SMTP, and FTP for UFP or CVP scanning.

topology   Information downloaded to a SecuRemote/SecureClient machine that contains encryption domain and network information for each site created. The topology is available only to authorized SecuRemote/SecureClient users.

Track options   Predefined events that provide alerts of the administrator's choice. They can be used as monitoring or troubleshooting tools.

Traditional Mode   A rule base in which VPN rules are written manually. It does not contain the If Via column used in Simplified Mode.

Traditional Policy   A rule base in which VPN rules are written manually. It does not contain the If Via column used in the Simplified Policies.

Transparent Mode   A client mode that is the default in SecureClient versions earlier than NG FP1. In this mode, encrypted connections are based on the first packet sent from the client to an IP address in the site's encryption domain.

U

UFP server An Open Platform for Security (OPSEC) certified server that maintains a list of URLs that you wish to block. This server communicates with the firewall on port 18182 and utilizes a URI resource to filter web traffic through the UFP server.

URI Filtering Protocol (UFP) An Open Platform for Security (OPSEC) API that runs on TCP port 18182 and allows the firewall to communicate with a web-filtering server.

URI Match Specification Type A category in the General tab of a URI resource that determines where the resource obtains information about filtering HTTP traffic. There are three types: Wild Card (you define each site specifically), File (you define and maintain a list of URLs), and UFP (a third-party server is utilized for HTTP information).

URI resource A Content Security resource that controls HTTP traffic such as malicious code, redirecting to other websites, HTML weeding, virus scanning, and so on.

Userc.C A file that stores topology information on SecuRemote and SecureClient machines.

UserDefined Alerts that can be configured to perform the way the administrator wants them to in the Alert Commands tab in the Global Properties of the firewall.

V

Virtual Private Network (VPN) Utilizing the public Internet for private/confidential data transfer by encrypting the data.

Voice over IP (VoIP) A group of protocols and software that uses networks to transmit voice and multimedia communication instead of the public phone network.

VPN community   A group of VPN sites defined in star, meshed, or star/meshed configuration to facilitate the automatic writing of encryption rules in a Simplified VPN policy.

VPN routing   A new configuration option in FP3 that allows you to create a hub-and-spoke VPN configuration in which all VPN traffic is routed through a single VPN-1 module.

VPN site   A gateway that participates in a Simplified VPN by being added to a VPN community object.

W

worm   A script or program that replicates itself over a network and usually performs malicious activity. Malicious worms have been used to steal confidential information, format hard drives, corrupt data, and so on.

Index

Note to the Reader: Throughout this index **boldfaced** page numbers indicate primary discussions of a topic. *Italicized* page numbers indicate illustrations.

F

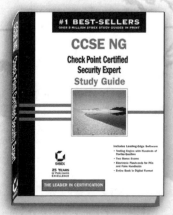

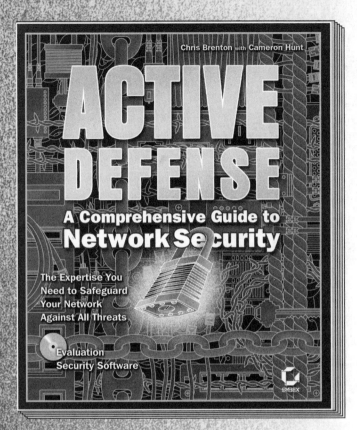

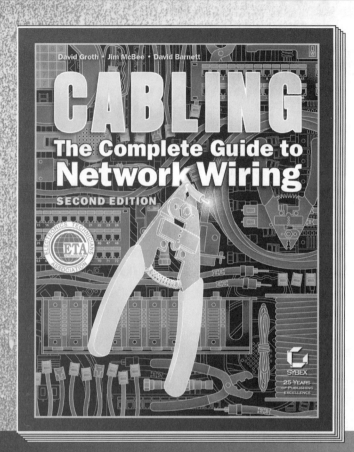